GRE Analytical Writing:

Answers to the Official Pool of Argument Topics

Chuanwei Li

Drew Chovanec

ISBN: 978-1-7370049-3-6

Acknowledgements

It has been twenty years since I supervised the project of China's first book of GRE test questions–*20 Simulated GRE Tests* as Head of R&D of New Oriental, the largest provider of English language training in the country. Over the years, I have been crafting test-prep books as well as teaching students who want to achieve high scores in standardized tests such as GRE and GMAT. Everyone involved in the process, including my collaborator Drew Chovanec, did their best to make *GRE Analytical Writing: Answers to the Official Pool of Argument Topics* an outstanding student study guide. For more than three years, we have analyzed and written what potential graduate students really need: The practical, specific, and efficacious GRE Analytical Writing strategies and sample essays.

I thank all the students that have provided feedback on my GRE teaching and their application of the strategies for GRE writing. A special thank you goes to the late Barbara Pan, my advisor at Harvard who commented on some of the GRE essays. Sincere thanks go to Drew Chovanec, co-author of this book, who wrote prolifically and made timely changes. Finally, I would make special mention of my family that has been supporting me, as always.

Chuanwei Li

Editor-in-Chief

Lead Author –GRE *Analytical Writing*

Contents

How to Use This Book

This book offers crucial information about the argument task of GRE Analytical Writing, including the types of prompts together with the knowledge and skills they require. The book will help you:

1. Acquaint yourself with the test format and prompt types
2. Acquire practical test-taking strategies for each prompt type
3. Achieve progress by studying responses to the pool of argument topics

The following five-step program has been created to help you make the most use of this book.

STEP 1 Learn About the Measure of the Argument Task of GRE Analytical Writing

Chapter 1 of this book offers an overview of the argument task of GRE Analytical Writing. Read this chapter to find information about the rubric, time limit, and types of instructions. You will also learn about proven test-taking strategies for how to craft a high-scoring GRE argument essay.

STEP 2 Study Organization of Essays with Different Instructions

Chapter 2 of this book presents sample essays for each type of writing instruction. You will also find what the prompts aim to test, and you will learn organizations and language that you can use in your own essay.

STEP 3 Keep in Mind Common Logical Fallacies of an Argument

Chapter 3 describes the logical fallacies, common errors in reasoning that will undermine an argument, that are tested most often. Some knowledge of them will help you spot loopholes of the argument more easily. In addition, general strategies for addressing each fallacy and an example will complete your toolkit for tackling it.

STEP 4 Practice Answering the Official Pool of Argument Topics

Chapter 4 contains sample essays for each argument topic of the official pool. The topics appear in the order they appear on the official website of ETS where you can find the most recent version before you take the test. Read the prompts, make outlines, and practice writing a few essays for each type of instruction until you feel comfortable crafting a good essay within the 30-minute time limit. Then, you may study the sample essays, either to determine whether yours is up to standard, or to glean some ideas and language from them. Caveat: do not use the sample essays verbatim in your future answer!

STEP 5 Learn About Most-tested Topics & Similar Topics

Chapter 5 shows you that some topics appear more than once in the official pool, each time with a different instruction. Such topics are more likely to appear in the test. While familiarizing yourself with the pool, you can review as a group these topics and their respective sample essays, some of which are almost the same. Chapter 6 groups topics according to logical fallacies or themes and offers you an opportunity to learn how to tackle a large number of topics each time with one strategy.

GRE Argument Cheat Sheet

1. Every topic is seeded with about three logical fallacies, common errors in reasoning that will undercut an argument.
2. An argument's conclusion having the word "should" is often a recommendation and this indicates that the author assumes that some action is necessary (and sufficient) for resolving a problem.
3. One place often cannot follow the example of another place: Two places could be too different from each other to justify a similar policy, plan, or course of action.
4. A prediction may turn out to be unreasonable; A promise and desire may not be fulfilled.
5. Prediction of profits often fails to weigh costs against revenue.
6. Every logical fallacy involves an assumption. When you spot a missing link in an argument's reasoning, but do not know how to address it, you can always say: The author assumes that A(evidence) means B (conclusion of the argument, or an intermediate claim).
7. An either-or assumption may be false because there is always a third option.
8. The cause-and-effect fallacy is tested most often: many topics are seeded with at least one.
9. The connection between two events is often a coincidence, because other factors could contribute to the effect.
10. A sample could be small and unrepresentative.
11. The trend last year, last month or recently could be an aberration and may not continue.
12. A nationwide trend may not hold true for a particular area and vice versa.
13. A number by itself means little and may be insignificant.
14. The original amount might be small, so an increase could be insignificant.
15. Self-reported data are often unreliable, because the participants report this way to make others see them positively.

CHAPTER 1

Overview of GRE Analytical Writing: The Argument Task

INTRODUCTION TO THE ARGUMENT TASK

In this section, we will look at the "Analyze an Argument" writing task. In this task, the examiners will evaluate your ability to assess an argument according to a set of guidelines provided and express your assessment clearly in your response. You must discuss the validity of the author's argument or solution by analyzing the logic and evidence it presents based on the instructions of the prompt. According to the official rubric, your essay will be scored in terms of how well you do the following:

1. Identifying and examining key aspects of the argument (i.e., spotting logical fallacies)
2. Organizing, connecting, and developing ideas (i.e., Ordering paragraphs logically and with proper signal words)
3. Providing support for main points (i.e., explaining why a line of reasoning is faulty and/or discussing counterevidence)
4. Commanding the aspects of standard written English (i.e., using effective vocabulary and varied sentences and following good grammar, usage, and mechanics)

During the test, you are to spend 30 minutes writing on the computer screen an Argument essay of about 400 or more words. You should familiarize yourself with the computer screen by writing the essay using the PowerPrep software that accompanies the GRE official guide. Normally, one screen will give you the essay prompt with instructions on what you should do and how you can do it. The other screen will provide space on which you will write, with icons like time count, word count, cut, paste, and cancel.

The prompt that you will be given is from the published official Pool of Argument Topics, which you can download from the official ETS website. The pool is sometimes updated, with a few additions or substitutions at the end of the pool each time in about one or two years. For the most recent pool of argument topics, please find them at **https://www.ets.org/gre/revised_general/prepare/analytical_writing/argument/pool**.

A caveat is in order here. Unlike the Issue task, the Argument task is **not** asking you to

1. discuss whether your position aligns with the position stated in the argument, or
2. state your own views on the subject under discussion, or
3. decide whether the facts and evidence in the argument are true.

INSTRUCTIONS OF THE ARGUMENT TASK

The task includes a passage where the author suggests a solution or makes an argument and supports it with reasons and evidence. The passage is often preceded by its source and followed by a set of instructions. For example,

> *The following appeared in a memorandum written by the vice president of Health Naturally, a small but expanding chain of stores selling health food and other health-related products.*
>
> *"Our previous experience has been that our stores are most profitable in areas where residents are highly concerned with leading healthy lives. We should therefore build one of our new stores in Plainsville, which clearly has many such residents. Plainsville merchants report that sales of running shoes and exercise equipment are at all-time highs. The local health club, which nearly closed five years ago due to lack of business, has more members than ever, and the weight-training and aerobics classes are always full. We can even anticipate a new generation of customers: Plainsville's schoolchildren are required to participate in a program called Fitness for Life, which emphasizes the benefits of regular exercise at an early age."*
>
> *Write a response in which you examine the stated and/or unstated assumptions of the argument. Be sure to explain how the argument depends on these assumptions and what the implications are for the argument if the assumptions prove unwarranted. (Topic 63)*

As the passage shows, it is preceded by its source: "The following appeared in a memorandum written by the vice president of …" and followed by a set of specific writing instruction: examine assumptions of the argument and explain how they underlie the argument and would make it fall apart in case of unwarranted assumptions.

It is vital that you evaluate the argument of the passage by following the specific instruction. Listed below are the types of instructions that appear on this task, each one asking you to address a specific issue with the author's argument or solution.

- Write an essay to identify the specific evidence necessary for evaluation of the argument and discuss how the evidence may support or undermine it.

In the official pool of argument topics, 50 have this instruction. For each topic having this instruction, you will see it simplified as "Specific Evidence".

- Write an essay to analyze the assumptions of the argument. Make certain to discuss how these assumptions underlie the argument, and how the argument may fall apart if the assumptions turn out to be groundless.

In the official pool of argument topics, 47 have this instruction. For each topic having this instruction, you will see it simplified as "Assumptions".

- Write an essay to analyze factors other than the proposed explanation and discuss how your factor(s) may convincingly explain the scenario(s) given in the argument.

In the official pool of argument topics, 18 have this instruction. For each topic having this instruction, you will see it simplified as "Alternative Explanations".

- Write an essay to analyze what questions the author needs to answer in order to
    - determine whether the recommendation is sound. Make certain to discuss how the answers to relevant questions would contribute to assessing the recommendation.
    - determine whether the advice is sound. Make certain to discuss how the answers to relevant questions would contribute to assessing the advice.
    - determine whether the recommendation may have the predicted result. Make certain to discuss how the answers to relevant questions would contribute to assessing the recommendation.
    - determine whether the prediction is sound. Make certain to discuss how the answers to relevant questions would contribute to assessing the prediction.
    - determine whether the conclusion is sound. Make certain to discuss how the answers to relevant questions would contribute to assessing the conclusion.

In the official pool of argument topics, 67 have this instruction. For each topic having this instruction, you will see it simplified as "Questions to Be Answered".

Remember that despite the different types of instruction, except the type "Alternative Explanations", the other three types, including "Specific Evidence", "Assumptions", and "Questions to Be Answered" are in large measure interchangeable. This means when you have written an essay that has one of the three instructions, you may, with minor changes (to the last sentence of the introduction, the first sentence of each paragraph, and other parts of the essay), get an essay that has one of the other two instructions. This is possible because the examiner makes practically the same requirement in the three types of instruction: discuss more evidence needed to evaluate an argument. No wonder the sample essays for the same topic having different types of instruction are similar to one another. However, it falls to you to follow the specific instruction for your assigned topic and craft an argument essay accordingly. To see how the three types of instruction are almost interchangeable, you may look at three sample essays for the same topic (e.g., Building a jazz club in Monroe) having three different instructions (Topic 3: Specific Evidence; Topic 73: Assumptions; Topic 75: Questions to Be Answered).

STEPS TO A TOP-NOTCH ARGUMENT ESSAY

A wise way to prepare for the argument task is to practice writing on some of the official argument topics, particularly those that have the same subject matter but different instructions. Previous experience has shown that your practice may become more productive if you follow some of the following steps.

Step 1 Read the argument and the specific instructions

In this step, you are advised to do the following:

1. Identify the argument's conclusion and claims
2. Identify assumptions underlying the conclusion and claims
3. Brainstorm specific extra evidence needed to undermine or strengthen the claims
4. Brainstorm questions to be answered to evaluate the argument
5. Brainstorm alternative explanations and counterevidence, particularly counterexamples
6. Brainstorm how the argument may improve

Aside from identifying the conclusion, claims and assumptions, you do not always need to do all the other evaluation noted above. Before you begin to tackle the passage, a glimpse of the instruction after the passage will give you an idea of what to identify and/or brainstorm: assumptions, specific evidence needed, questions to be answered or alternative explanations for the scenario. As you evaluate the argument, take notes of your ideas. When you have enough ideas, think about them and number them for putting them in a logical order.

To learn how to analyze an argument in a more systematic way, you may make use of the Toulmin method. As a style of argumentation developed by British philosopher Stephen E. Toulmin, the Toulmin method breaks an argument into six parts: claim, grounds, warrant, qualifier, rebuttal, and backing. According to the method, every argument starts with three essential parts: the claim, the grounds, and the warrant. With a little knowledge of them, you may feel more confident that you can analyze a GRE argument insightfully. A claim is an assertion that an author tries to establish. The grounds of an argument include the evidence and facts that support the claim. The warrant is the assumption that establishes a connection between the grounds and the claim and may be explicitly stated or simply implied. For example,

> *When Stanley Park first opened, it was the largest, most heavily used public park in town. It is still the largest park, but it is no longer heavily used. Video cameras mounted in the park's parking lots last month revealed the park's drop in popularity: the recordings showed an average of only 50 cars per day. In contrast, tiny Carlton Park in the heart of the business district is visited by more than 150 people on a typical weekday. An obvious difference is that Carlton Park, unlike Stanley Park, provides ample seating. Thus, if Stanley Park is ever to be as popular with our citizens as Carlton Park, the town will obviously need to provide more benches, thereby converting some of the unused open areas into spaces suitable for socializing. (Topic 41)*

We may break the argument down into the three fundamental parts:

Claims	Grounds	Warrants (=Assumptions)
When Stanley Park first opened, it was the largest, most heavily used public park in town. It is still the largest park, but it is no longer heavily used.	Video cameras mounted in the park's parking lots last month revealed the park's drop in popularity: the recordings showed an average of only 50 cars per day.	A significant decrease in Stanley Park's popularity has occurred.
Thus, if Stanley Park is ever to be as popular with our citizens as Carlton Park, the town will obviously need to provide more benches, thereby converting some of the unused open areas into spaces suitable for socializing.	In contrast, tiny Carlton Park in the heart of the business district is visited by more than 150 people on a typical weekday.	Carlton Park's popularity is the result of its ample seating.
	An obvious difference is that Carlton Park, unlike Stanley Park, provides ample seating.	Building more benches in Stanley Park will affect its popularity.
		……

Here is another example.

> *A recent study reported that pet owners have longer, healthier lives on average than do people who own no pets. Specifically, dog owners tend to have a lower incidence of heart disease. In light of these findings, Sherwood Hospital should form a partnership with Sherwood Animal Shelter to institute an adopt-a-dog program. The program would encourage dog ownership for patients recovering from heart disease, which should reduce these patients' chance of experiencing continuing heart problems and also reduce their need for ongoing treatment. As a further benefit, the publicity about the program would encourage more people to adopt pets from the shelter. And that will reduce the incidence of heart disease in the general population. (Topic 44)*

We may break the argument down into the three fundamental parts:

Claims	Grounds	Warrants (=Assumptions)

In light of these findings, Sherwood Hospital should form a partnership with Sherwood Animal Shelter to institute an adopt-a-dog program.	A recent study reported that pet owners have longer, healthier lives on average than do people who own no pets. Specifically, dog owners tend to have a lower incidence of heart disease.	The study participants are representative of dog owners in general.
which should reduce these patients' chance of experiencing continuing heart problems and also reduce their need for ongoing treatment.	The program would encourage dog ownership for patients recovering from heart disease,	Allowing shelter dogs into a hospital setting will benefit the patients recovering from heart disease.
And that will reduce the incidence of heart disease in the general population.	As a further benefit, the publicity about the program would encourage more people to adopt pets from the shelter.	Enough people would be willing to adopt dogs from the shelter to cause a significant reduction in heart disease in the general population.
		……

For more information about how to use the Toulmin method, you may consult the article "Using Toulmin's Model of Argumentation" by Joan Karbach.

Now you are ready for the next big step: writing itself.

Step 2 Craft the first paragraph

Writing the first paragraph can be difficult as well as easy. It can be difficult when you sweat over small stuff and want to have a perfect beginning. If you are one of this cohort, you may skip the first paragraph until you have finished the body of your essay. It can be easy if you follow the following guidelines that have proved effective.

The introductory paragraph usually consists of three parts: restatement of the claim of the prompt; summary of the premise, including evidence and reasons; responding to the specific writing instruction for the prompt. The summary of the premise does not have to be thorough, but it is detailed in this book for your reference in case you do not have the official pool of argument topics at hand. Also, whether you should preview the points to be discussed in the body paragraphs is optional. The following is one of the acceptable versions that have three parts:

The author concludes/claims/recommends/predicts that... To justify/substantiate the conclusion/claim/recommendation/prediction, the article/passage cites the fact that...and a study that found that.... It also bases the conclusion on the following line of reasoning:.... To fully assess the argument, we need answers to some key questions.

This structure gives you an idea of your wording for a "Questions to Be Answered" instruction. For other types of writing instruction, you may simply change the wording of the last sentence of the introduction as follows.

To fully assess the argument, we need additional evidence. (for the "Specific Evidence" instruction)

To determine the soundness of the argument, we need to scrutinize the assumptions that underlie it. (for the "Assumptions" instruction)

The explanation, while not invalid on its own, is not the only one that could account for the facts. (for the "Alternative Explanations" instruction)

For example,

The author recommends that the company Health Naturally construct a new health foods store in Plainsville (restatement of the claim). *To justify the recommendation, the memo claims that Plainsville's populace are highly health-conscious and cites three facts to support this: 1) sales of athletic paraphernalia in Plainsville are at an all-time high, 2) the local health club has succeeded in attracting and retaining customers, and 3) the mandatory "fitness-for-life" program through the local schools is indoctrinating a new generation of customers* (summary of the premise). *To determine the soundness of the argument, we need to scrutinize the assumptions that underlie it* (responding to the instruction). *(Topic 63)*

The following is another way to craft the introduction:

Relying on a study which... (and on...), the author concludes/claims/recommends that.... Yet we need further evidence in order to see if the argument is indeed valid.

The above structure first summarizes the evidence and reasons, then restates the claim or conclusion of the prompt, and finally responds to the writing instruction by paraphrasing it. This structure gives you an idea of your wording for a "Specific Evidence" instruction. For other types of writing instruction, you may simply change the wording of the last sentence of the introduction.

For example,

Relying on a study which reports that in an area called East Meria, people only visit the doctor for cold-related issues once or twice a year, while at the same time consuming large amounts of fish (summary of the premise), *the author recommends that people in West Meria take Ichthaid, a nutritional supplement derived from fish oil, to prevent colds and reduce absences from school and work* (restatement of the claim). *Yet we need further evidence in order to see if the argument is indeed valid* (responding to the instruction). *(Topic 14)*

Step 3 Develop the body paragraph

One way to develop a body paragraph is to follow the writing instruction specific to each of the four types of question.

For the "Specific Evidence" type, you must do at least two things: identify evidence needed to evaluate the argument; explain how the evidence may weaken or support it. For example,

> *The following appeared in a memorandum written by the vice president of Health Naturally, a small but expanding chain of stores selling health food and other health-related products.*
>
> *"Our previous experience has been that our stores are most profitable in areas where residents are highly concerned with leading healthy lives. We should therefore build one of our new stores in Plainsville, which clearly has many such residents. Plainsville merchants report that sales of running shoes and exercise equipment are at all-time highs. The local health club, which nearly closed five years ago due to lack of business, has more members than ever, and the weight-training and aerobics classes are always full. We can even anticipate a new generation of customers: Plainsville's schoolchildren are required to participate in a program called Fitness for Life, which emphasizes the benefits of regular exercise at an early age."*
>
> *Write a response in which you discuss what specific evidence is needed to evaluate the argument and explain how the evidence would weaken or strengthen the argument. (Topic 61)*

The following is one paragraph of the response to the above prompt:

> *In addition, there must be evidence for the assumption that the health club's membership and class attendance is a sign that the entire town follows a healthy lifestyle. However, the assumption could be an overestimation based on a small sample. Gyms and health centers usually cater to middle to higher-income earners, who may make up a smaller percentage of a population. Thus, without information about the sample size, it is entirely likely that the number of members in the health club represents only a small portion of Plainsville's total population, despite an increase in membership and some full classes. The market capacity could be negligible to begin with, so an all-time high in numbers could be an increase of a handful, hardly justifying the opening of a new store. The fact that the weight training and aerobics classes are full is not convincing, either, as it may simply be that the club is too small to accommodate many clients or does not have enough people to teach many classes. The fact that it almost closed for lack of business five years before could also be a cause for concern. Should this be true, the argument would be undermined.*

For the "Assumptions" type, you must do at least three things: identify assumptions of the argument; describe how they underlie it; discuss how unwarranted assumptions may contribute to its collapsing. For example,

Nature's Way, a chain of stores selling health food and other health-related products, is opening its next franchise in the town of Plainsville. The store should prove to be very successful: Nature's Way franchises tend to be most profitable in areas where residents lead healthy lives, and clearly Plainsville is such an area. Plainsville merchants report that sales of running shoes and exercise clothing are at all-time highs. The local health club has more members than ever, and the weight training and aerobics classes are always full. Finally, Plainsville's schoolchildren represent a new generation of potential customers: these schoolchildren are required to participate in a fitness-for-life program, which emphasizes the benefits of regular exercise at an early age.

Write a response in which you examine the stated and/or unstated assumptions of the argument. Be sure to explain how the argument depends on these assumptions and what the implications are for the argument if the assumptions prove unwarranted. (Topic 164)

The following is one paragraph of the response to the above prompt.

First, the author assumes that the reports by merchants on the sales of exercise clothing and running shoes represent an overall mindset of the populace that will continue into the long-term future. However, the reports are not accompanied by any statistics or time-frames. It is possible that this recent sales trend is nothing more than a short-lived fad, or, depending on the size of the town, a trend that will end once products reach market saturation. The fact that sales of running shoes and exercise clothing are at all-time highs means little by itself. The sales may be miniscule to begin with and still insignificant compared with sales in other comparable cities. Moreover, all-time highs in these sales do not necessarily mean Plainsville residents live healthy lives –perhaps people often buy such merchandise to show off rather than use it. Even assuming that they lead healthy lives, the author has yet to establish the connection between living healthy lives and buying enough products of Nature's Way to make the new store profitable. If this turns out to be the case, then there is a high chance that the new Nature's Way store in Plainsville will not be profitable. If the assumption is warranted that this trend is indicative of a mindset of the populace and will persist, the residents in Plainsville may live healthy lives, making the argument more persuasive.

For the "Alternative Explanations" type, you must do at least two things: identify other factors that may explain the facts in the argument; discuss how they account for the facts. For example,

Workers in the small town of Leeville take fewer sick days than workers in the large city of Masonton, 50 miles away. Moreover, relative to population size, the diagnosis of stress-related illness is proportionally much lower in Leeville than in Masonton. According to the Leeville Chamber of Commerce, these facts can be attributed to the health benefits of the relatively relaxed pace of life in Leeville.

Write a response in which you discuss one or more alternative explanations that could rival the proposed explanation and explain how your explanation(s) can plausibly account for the facts presented in the argument. (Topic 65)

The following is one paragraph of the response to the above prompt.

One possible explanation is that workers in Leeville are healthier as a result of factors other than its less stressful life. It may simply be that it has a smaller number of workers. If workers take the same number of sick days on average in both Leeville and Masonton, it is reasonable that those in Leeville would have fewer days of sick leave. Also, if both places have the same number of facilities for exercise and fitness, Leeville workers may have access to a higher number of them and exercise more. They may even have higher physician-resident ratios, more clement weather, and less air pollution. Perhaps they have healthier lifestyles in other respects. For example, they may eat more healthily. Or perhaps they are born healthier than those in Masonton. Any of the scenarios, if true, would rule out Leeville's relaxed pace of life as the sole reason for the fact that its workers take fewer sick days.

For the "Questions to Be Answered" type, you must do at least two things: identify questions to be answered; discuss how answers to such questions may help to evaluate the soundness of the conclusion, recommendation, advice, or prediction. For example,

According to a recent report, cheating among college and university students is on the rise. However, Groveton College has successfully reduced student cheating by adopting an honor code, which calls for students to agree not to cheat in their academic endeavors and to notify a faculty member if they suspect that others have cheated. Groveton's honor code replaced a system in which teachers closely monitored students; under that system, teachers reported an average of thirty cases of cheating per year. In the first year the honor code was in place, students reported twenty-one cases of cheating; five years later, this figure had dropped to fourteen. Moreover, in a recent survey, a majority of Groveton students said that they would be less likely to cheat with an honor code in place than without. Thus, all colleges and universities should adopt honor codes similar to Groveton's in order to decrease cheating among students.

Write a response in which you discuss what questions would need to be answered in order to decide whether the recommendation and the argument on which it is based are reasonable. Be sure to explain how the answers to these questions would help to evaluate the recommendation. (Topic 180)

The following is one paragraph of the response to the above prompt.

Lastly, there is of course the question of the cultural differences among all universities and colleges that may affect the success rate of an honor code system. For example, Groveton could be a small school where the honor code is easily implemented and naturally efficacious, whereas at larger universities it would be hard to implement the code and even if implemented, the code would be less effective. Groveton students could be more likely to report cheating, or less likely to cheat with an honor code in place, than students in other universities and colleges. Even if it has worked in Groveton, this does not necessarily mean that it will work in other colleges and universities. All this is incumbent on the willingness of students to follow the honor code, and currently there is no accurate measure of this variable. Even if the code will be effective in other colleges and universities, there is the possibility that some universities and colleges may have had in place an honor code comparable to Groveton's, thereby making a new one redundant. If Groveton is typical in respects relevant to the incidence of cheating, it will be plausible for other universities and colleges to enforce a similar honor code. Otherwise, the recommended action would be indefensible.

Another way to develop a body paragraph is to explain the line of reasoning involved in each of the common logical fallacies committed by the author and discuss how this leads to an invalid or unsound argument. For example, if the prompt is loaded with a cause-and-effect fallacy, here is the way in which you may develop a paragraph critiquing such a fallacy: providing a topic sentence naming the fallacy, explaining why the reasoning is a fallacy, discussing factors other than the one given that may be responsible for the result, and concluding the paragraph.

For example,

> *The data from a survey of high school math and science teachers show that in the district of Sanlee many of these teachers reported assigning daily homework, whereas in the district of Marlee, most science and math teachers reported assigning homework no more than two or three days per week. Despite receiving less frequent homework assignments, Marlee students earn better grades overall and are less likely to be required to repeat a year of school than are students in Sanlee. These results call into question the usefulness of frequent homework assignments. Most likely the Marlee students have more time to concentrate on individual assignments than do the Sanlee students who have homework every day. Therefore teachers in our high schools should assign homework no more than twice a week.*
>
> *Write a response in which you discuss what specific evidence is needed to evaluate the argument and explain how the evidence would weaken or strengthen the argument. (Topic 108)*

The following is one paragraph of the response to the above prompt that addresses a cause-and-effect fallacy.

> *Even if we grant that there is a huge gap in academic performance between Sanlee and Marlee students, there needs to be evidence regarding whether this disparity is the result of the difference in how often teachers in each district assign homework. It is possible that students in Sanlee schools are academically inferior to begin with. It is also possible that they seldom do their homework, that they experience stricter grading than Marlee students, or that their teachers are less efficacious than those of Marlee schools. Even if they do their homework, it may be easy and only take a few minutes to finish each time, whereas Marlee students may be assigned challenging homework and spend much more time on it every time. It is even possible that Marlee students are assigned more homework each time or do homework even on days when they have no assignments, ending up doing more homework each week. Similarly, the two districts may have different policies for deciding whether a student should repeat a year of school. Any of the scenarios, if true, would weaken the connection between less frequent homework and better grades. Without ruling out other feasible explanations, the author cannot justifiably claim that the gap in students' academic performance is attributable to the difference in frequency with which teachers assign homework.*

For how to develop a paragraph featuring logical fallacies, please read the third chapter of the book "Common Logical Fallacies and Strategies for Addressing them."

Step 4 Conclude the passage

The concluding paragraph generally recapitulates the author's opinion of the soundness and validity of the argument, what issues the argument leaves out and how to improve or strengthen it. The following are some of the acceptable forms of a concluding paragraph.

> *In summary, the argument is not compelling as it stands now. To better ascertain the soundness/validity of the argument, we need answers to the following questions: whether..., whether..., and whether....*
>
> *In summary, the argument is not compelling as it stands now. To better assess the argument, we need evidence regarding the following assumptions: that..., that..., and that....*
>
> *In conclusion, the author founds the argument on.... To bolster it, the author must provide evidence.... Specifically, the author must offer data demonstrating.... (To better evaluate the argument, we need information about....)*

For example,

> *In conclusion, the author founds the argument on doubtful assumptions, undermining its validity* (author's evaluation of the argument). *To bolster it, the author must provide experimental evidence by way of a survey of Plainsville residents to show that Plainsville has a health-conscious population that would purchase Health Naturally products* (what the author leaves out). *Specifically, the author must offer data demonstrating the reasons for the increased purchase of exercise clothing, the dedication and motivation of club members, and the effectiveness of the school's physical education program* (specific data needed to improve the argument). *(Topic 63)*

PUTTING EVERYTHING TOGETHER

Sample response to Topic 63:

> *The author recommends that the company Health Naturally construct a new health foods store in Plainsville. To justify the recommendation, the memo claims that Plainsville's populace are highly health-conscious and cites three facts to support this: 1) sales of athletic paraphernalia in Plainsville are at an all-time high, 2) the local health club has succeeded in attracting and retaining customers, and 3) the mandatory "fitness-for-life" program through the local schools is indoctrinating a new generation of customers. To determine the soundness of the argument, we need to scrutinize the assumptions that underlie it.*
>
> *First, the author relies on the assumption that those who work out are generally health-conscious people. However, several lurking variables exist to undermine the strength of such a correlative argument. For example, an upsurge in crime may encourage people to desire a more intimidating physique. In this case, they would value exercise, not necessarily healthy living. Without evidence to demonstrate a definitive link between exercise and overall health-consciousness, the author fails to prove satisfactorily that Plainsville residents are concerned with healthy living.*

Next, the author implies that a connection exists between athletic clothing and health food sales. However, the author fails to substantiate this. Several variables other than a health-conscious population could positively affect the sale of athletic apparel while not impacting the sales of Health Naturally products. For example, athletic apparel may be fashionable or less expensive, driving up demand for this good without affecting markets for other health products. Alternatively, the population of Plainsville may be so obese that their only recourse for comfortable clothes lies in the elastic waists of sweatpants and the arch support of running shoes. In any case, however, the author fails to establish a clear link between sales of athletic clothing and health food products.

The author continues by suggesting that the turnaround of a local health club demonstrates the populace's recently discovered dedication to healthy living. However, of more importance than this club's recent reemergence as a viable business is why it was at the brink of bankruptcy in the first place. Five years is simply not long enough to demonstrate an enduring trend; indeed, the erratic nature of such a turnaround indicates volatility rather than stability in the Plainsville market. Thus, while the success of the fitness club may demonstrate a present interest in healthy living, it does not indicate that this interest will last into the future.

Finally, the author assumes that compulsory physical education will secure Plainsville's health-products market into the distant future. However, this takes it for granted that the "fitness-for-life" program impacts lifestyles and that the specific program utilized in Plainsville is effective. Regarding the latter, the author has yet to demonstrate whether Plainsville's program itself is any good. As for the former, the program may be ineffective. Specifically, its compulsory nature may provoke a reaction against health-conscious living, especially among teenagers. In that event, Plainsville's "fitness-for-life" program may not generate a new wave of loyal customers for Health Naturally.

In conclusion, the author founds the argument on doubtful assumptions, undermining its validity. To bolster it, the author must provide experimental evidence by way of a survey of Plainsville residents to show that Plainsville has a health-conscious population that would purchase Health Naturally products. Specifically, the author must offer data demonstrating the reasons for the increased purchase of exercise clothing, the dedication and motivation of club members, and the effectiveness of the school's physical education program.

CHAPTER 2

Organization of Essays with Different Instructions

ETS readers of your essays will often skim the first sentence of each body paragraph to verify whether you have written according to the instruction specific to each prompt. This may help examiners decide whether your writing is just a response to a general statement such as "how well-reasoned you find this argument" that can be memorized in advance. The argument tasks are often seeded with a few logical fallacies so that they read like hasty generalizations. This means deciphering the argument by sorting out its conclusion, claim, recommendation, advice, or prediction and the evidence, assumptions, and reasoning in support of the conclusion. Thereafter, you are supposed to examine the evidence given to see whether it supports the argument and what evidence you need to fully assess it. To this end, you need to marshal your points, for example, by paraphrasing the writing instruction in the first sentence of each paragraph. The following are examples of organization of essays having different instructions. After examples of each instruction, you will find scaffolding language that you may incorporate in your own writing.

ORGANIZATION FOR "SPECIFIC EVIDENCE"

Prompt (Topic 172)

> *Fifteen years ago, Omega University implemented a new procedure that encouraged students to evaluate the teaching effectiveness of all their professors. Since that time, Omega professors have begun to assign higher grades in their classes, and overall student grade averages at Omega have risen by 30 percent. Potential employers, looking at this dramatic rise in grades, believe that grades at Omega are inflated and do not accurately reflect student achievement; as a result, Omega graduates have not been as successful at getting jobs as have graduates from nearby Alpha University. To enable its graduates to secure better jobs, Omega University should terminate student evaluation of professors.*
>
> *Write a response in which you discuss what specific evidence is needed to evaluate the argument and explain how the evidence would weaken or strengthen the argument.*

Sample Response and Organization

The author recommends that student evaluation of professors, a survey program, at Omega University be terminated to improve its students' employment opportunities. To justify the recommendation, the article claims that higher grades assigned by professors, occurring after the implementation of the evaluation procedure, have been suspected of being fraudulent by employers, allegedly hurting post-graduation employment rates of the students at Omega University in comparison to those from Alpha University. To fully assess the argument, we need additional evidence regarding why Omega professors have assigned higher grades, why Omega students are less employable than Alpha students, and why the evaluation procedure has to be discontinued.	Introduction
There must be evidence regarding the connection between the professor-evaluation procedure at Omega and the increase in grade averages of its students. However, the author does not inform us how many students at Omega participated in its professor-evaluation procedure. The fewer the participants, the more unreliable the conclusion about the connection between student evaluation and professors' grade inflation. If the increase in grades has resulted from students who are more intelligent and more diligent, or from better instruction, there would be less justification for the proposal to end the survey program. If it is attributable to grade inflation by the professors, there would be more justification for the proposal. However, even in this case, termination of the survey program could be unwarranted, because it may have no connection to Omega students' post-graduation employment rates. In addition, the article does not provide any concrete evidence that the increase in grade averages is fraudulent; it merely says that potential employers believe this to be true. No employers in particular have been named, and those who refuse to employ Omega graduates based on this belief would be at risk of a defamation lawsuit without evidence, pending an investigation into any allegations of discrimination on account of baseless presumptions of inflated grades. In fact, given a span of fifteen years, a 30% increase in grade averages may not be grade inflation, because a few excellent grades could boost the averages by a great margin if the original averages were very low. In that event, the recommendation of ending student evaluation of professors at Omega would be unreasonable, undermining the argument.	2nd paragraph: 1st piece of evidence needed

There should also be evidence that Omega can emulate Alpha to boost its students' employment opportunities. However, there is no evidence that Alpha students' success at landing jobs results from its lack of grade inflation. Several factors other than lack of grade inflation could lead to their success at finding employment. For instance, Alpha could simply have better internship opportunities, or corporate recruitment programs. Even assuming that Alpha's students are more successful at securing employment because of no grade inflation, this does not necessarily mean that Omega's students will automatically do well for the same reason. If Omega's comparison to Alpha is to be a useful one, the two institutions should be sufficiently alike in ways that might affect the impact of grade inflation on graduates' job prospects. However, Omega may have inferior teaching quality or career services. It is also likely that Omega offers less marketable academic programs. It is even likely that Omega admits less academically competent students. Any of the scenarios, if true, would cast serious doubt on the assumption that Omega can boost its graduates' employment opportunities by emulating Alpha. Even if Omega can succeed in helping its students find jobs by taking the same course of action, there is no guarantee that the jobs found will be better. If this should be the case, then the author's recommendation would be severely weakened, as Omega would be implementing measures based on a false precedent.

3rd paragraph: 2nd piece of evidence needed

Finally, there needs to be evidence that ending the survey program is viable and the only way to help Omega students find better jobs. Even if terminating the professor-evaluation procedure is able to eliminate grade inflation and in turn help Omega graduates find jobs, there is no guarantee that it is viable. There must be a cost-benefit analysis to reveal advantages to terminating the survey program relative to the disadvantages. Ending the program may help Omega students find jobs momentarily, but keeping the program may offer far greater benefits. For example, it could provide a key third-party metric to see how well their professors teach. If there is no such metric, the university could hardly know whether it has excellent professors, a primary factor that attracts potential students. Even if the procedure is viable, it need not be the only way. For example, raising its admission standards, hiring better teachers, and improving its career services, could all be viable alternatives. The program could even improve if the university implements it in a way that does not give rise to grade inflation.

4th paragraph: 3rd piece of evidence needed

For example, students can evaluate their professors first, but the professors are not allowed to see the evaluation until they have submitted their students' grades. Without ruling out these and other possibilities, the author cannot justifiably claim that terminating the survey program would be the only viable option for boosting Omega graduates' job opportunities.

In conclusion, ending the professor-evaluation procedure without establishing it as the cause of declining employment success rates of its graduates would ultimately harm Omega rather than help it. If the blame is to be placed squarely upon the procedure, there would need to be proof showing that the professors did indeed inflate the grades because of the procedure, that the superior rates of employment of Alpha students are not the result of other factors, and that ending the procedure is the only viable option. — Conclusion

For the "Specific Evidence" prompt, you may use the following organization:

2nd paragraph: There must be evidence....

3rd paragraph: There should also be evidence....

4th paragraph: Finally, there needs to be evidence....

You may also use the following organization.

2nd paragraph: Firstly, we need evidence....

3rd paragraph: Furthermore, we must have evidence....

4th paragraph: Finally, we lack evidence....

ORGANIZATION FOR "ASSUMPTIONS"

Prompt (Topic 71)

The following is a recommendation from the business manager of Monarch Books.

"Since its opening in Collegeville twenty years ago, Monarch Books has developed a large customer base due to its reader-friendly atmosphere and wide selection of books on all subjects. Last month, Book and Bean, a combination bookstore and coffee shop, announced its intention to open a Collegeville store. Monarch Books should open its own in-store café in the space currently devoted to children's books. Given recent national census data indicating a significant decline in the percentage of

the population under age ten, sales of children's books are likely to decline. By replacing its children's books section with a café, Monarch Books can increase profits and ward off competition from Book and Bean."

Write a response in which you examine the stated and/or unstated assumptions of the argument. Be sure to explain how the argument depends on these assumptions and what the implications are for the argument if the assumptions prove unwarranted.

Sample Response and Organization

The author recommends that Monarch Books open a café in its store in order to boost profits and compete with Book and Bean, a bookstore and café combined. To justify the recommendation, the article claims that it could remove the children's book section to make space for the café, citing census data showing a considerable decline in the percentage of the people under the age of ten. However, before we determine whether Monarch should undertake such a renovation, we must consider some issues surrounding the argument and its underlying assumptions.	Introduction
The author assumes that using the space for children's books to open a café in its own store is necessary for Monarch. The article mentions that Monarch has a large customer base and is well-known for its book selection. Yet by recommending major changes, the manager implies that having a wide customer base is meaningless. The article makes no mention of declining profits or a loss of customers, nor does it indicate whether Monarch's readers are interested in having a café in its store, so we must wonder whether spending the money to renovate its location would even be necessary. Should this plan fail, not only would the store lose money from the initial renovation and its damaged reputation of being a bookstore stocking a wide range of books, but it would then need to spend even more money to renovate once again to remove the café and repair its reputation, rendering its business unprofitable. In that event, the assumption about the need for a café in Monarch's store would prove unwarranted and the argument in support of Monarch opening a café in its own store would be gratuitous.	2nd paragraph: 1st assumption that underlies the argument
The author also implies that Book and Bean, which already planned to open a combination bookstore and coffee shop in the same city, will benefit from the new store. However, the article gives no evidence that opening such a store would help Book and Bean at all. For all we know, the café in the store could hurt its business by adding a huge maintenance cost to its budget. After all, a bookstore	3rd paragraph: 2nd assumption that underlies the argument

by itself is fairly easy to maintain and all one needs to do is to keep the building at a certain temperature and humidity, but a café has to be constantly cleaned, repaired, and resupplied. As a result, Book and Bean may have been adversely affected by its coffee shop in its store. If this is true, there is no guarantee that Monarch will benefit from a café, not to mention that launching a café will help it to compete with Book and Bean's planned store in the city. In this way, the implication is unsubstantiated. A detailed analysis of the effects of Book and Bean's café on its business is needed before Monarch passes judgement on the benefits of opening one. If there is evidence that Book and Bean has not profited from its café, the author cannot confidently claim that Monarch should open one in its own store. The worst scenario could be that Book and Bean does not open a Collegeville store at all, rendering the assumption unsubstantiated and undermining the argument.

Finally, the author suggests that a trend will continue. The article recommends making room for the café by getting rid of the children's book section, using national census data that shows a decline in the percentage of the population under the age of ten. This assumes that the trend will remain unchanged into the future. However, as we know, census data accounts for past trends and cannot always be trusted to predict future scenarios. Monarch has been in business for over twenty years and is known for its wide selection of books, after all; therefore, if it hopes to stay in business for another twenty years, or even longer, it needs to plan for the real trend. If there is no decrease in the number of children younger than ten in the future, the store may lose much business by replacing its children's book section with a café because doing so may hurt its reputation as a store with a variety of books on every subject and with one section devoted to children's books. Even if there is a drop in the portion of the people below ten, there may not be a drop in the number of children below ten, because the total population could rise. Even assuming that there is an eventual decrease in the number of children under ten, there may be an increase in the number of children above ten. Granted that there is a decline in the number of all the children, there may be no decline in sales of children's books, because children may buy more books on average as a result of factors such as parents' desire to nurture their children's literacy skills through reading or programs that they participate in. Even if the national trend continues, there is no guarantee that it will be true for Monarch where the percentage of the population under age ten may not decrease locally and will

4th paragraph: 3rd assumption that underlies the argument

remain so in the future. Should this be true, the assumption and the argument that it underlies would be unfounded.

In conclusion, the evidence in the argument needs further scrutiny before Monarch decides to spend a considerable amount of money to add a café to its store. It must consider whether its customer base or profits are under threat and whether the example of Book and Bean is indeed a valid one. It must also take into account the long-term effects of removing its children's section if it is to maintain in the future its reputation for being reader-friendly and having a large selection of books.

Conclusion

For the "Assumptions" prompt, you may use the following organization.

2nd paragraph: The author assumes that...

3rd paragraph: The author also implies that...

4th paragraph: Finally, the author suggests that...

You may also use the following organization.

2nd paragraph: The author implies that...

3rd paragraph: Building on the implication that..., the author suggests that....

4th paragraph: Even if the suggestion is valid, the author also assumes that...

ORGANIZATION FOR "ALTERNATIVE EXPLANATIONS"

Prompt (Topic 76)

> *There is now evidence that the relaxed pace of life in small towns promotes better health and greater longevity than does the hectic pace of life in big cities. Businesses in the small town of Leeville report fewer days of sick leave taken by individual workers than do businesses in the nearby large city of Masonton. Furthermore, Leeville has only one physician for its one thousand residents, but in Masonton the proportion of physicians to residents is five times as high. Finally, the average age of Leeville residents is significantly higher than that of Masonton residents. These findings suggest that the relaxed pace of life in Leeville allows residents to live longer, healthier lives.*
>
> *Write a response in which you discuss one or more alternative explanations that could rival the proposed explanation and explain how your explanation(s) can plausibly account for the facts presented in the argument.*

Sample Response and Organization

Relying on the fact that businesses in the town of Leeville report fewer sick days for individual workers than those in Masonton, that it has a lower proportion of physicians to residents, and that its residents are considerably older on average, the author posits that the disparity in three respects is due to Leeville's relaxed pace of life. While this may be the case, other possible explanations are worth exploring, including a desire to keep a job or earn more money, physicians' concerns and the residents' needs, and the residents' genes and lifestyles, among other things.

Introduction

Regarding the days taken off work by individual workers, there are two explanations for the disparity. One possible explanation is that Leeville has a smaller number of workers. If workers take the same number of sick days on average in both Leeville and Masonton, it is reasonable that those in Leeville would have fewer days of sick leave. Another likely explanation is that the days taken off work by individual workers may not be health-related at all, but instead is the result of other job-related pressures. Specifically, it may be the case that for whatever reason, workers in Leeville do not feel secure in their jobs, and fear that taking time off work may cause their bosses to fire them. Alternatively, it may also be the case that a slowing economy, combined with a system of hourly wages, has made it necessary for people to work as often as possible to make ends meet at home. Perhaps since Leeville is rather small, the businesses in the town report fewer days of sick leave for individual workers because of a cultural sensibility that taking sick leave would make one seem weak. This indicates that factors other than the health benefits of the relatively relaxed pace of life could be responsible for reporting fewer days of sick leave in Leeville.

2nd paragraph: 1st explanation that could account for the observed facts

When it comes to the physician-resident ratios, a myriad of other factors might explain the disparity. It is possible that Leeville could only afford one physician for its one thousand residents. It is also possible that few physicians would like to work there because of its low salaries and living standards. Perhaps the residents there eat a more nutritious diet and exercise more; therefore, they are healthier and do not need more than one physician. Or perhaps they go to the nearby Masonton for physical examination and treatments because of its lower charges and better doctors. All such scenarios would obviate the need for more than one physician. On the

3rd paragraph: 2nd explanation that could account for the observed facts

contrary, it is likely that Masonton is much richer and has the money to hire as many physicians as it wants for its citizens. It is also likely that physicians enjoy working there for its hefty jobs and good life quality. The citizens there could care little about their eating and do little exercise; therefore, they are less healthy and need more physicians. They could also be more inclined to see a doctor. All such factors, rather than the relaxed lifestyle of Leeville, could contribute to the difference in the number of physicians each city has.

With respect to average ages, many factors besides Leeville's less stressful lifestyle might be the reasons for the disparity. It could be that Leeville, with agreeable weather and few crimes, is a popular town for people to retire in. It could also be that since the town is small, a few very old citizens that have recently relocated there raise the average age of the town considerably. At the same time, many young residents may be moving outside of Leeville. It could even be that Leeville has fewer incidences of disease as a result of less air pollution in the town. Above everything else, the residents may be genetically programmed to live longer, healthier lives. All such scenarios would rule out the relaxed pace of life in Leeville as the sole factor in contributing to its residents' better health and greater longevity. Conversely, Masonton may be a popular town for young people who choose to work there for its plentiful good jobs. It may also have higher rates of disease because of its severe air pollution. Most importantly, many of its citizens may be less fortunate in genetics, having genes that promise shorter lifespans, or they tend to have less reasonable regimens, leading to many young deaths. Should this be true, the difference in residents' ages of both places is attributable to factors other than the less stressful pace of life in Leeville.

4th paragraph: 3rd explanation that could account for the observed facts

While it may very well be the case that Leeville does have a relatively relaxed pace of life which contributes to longer, healthier lives, we should not rule out other possible explanations. Once we have explored all the possibilities, we will be able to decide whether the author should recommend small towns to people seeking health and longevity.

Conclusion

For the "Alternative Explanations" prompt, you may use the following organization.

2nd paragraph: One possible explanation is that….

3rd paragraph: Another likely explanation is that….

4th paragraph: Still another explanation could be that….

You may also use the following organization.

2nd paragraph: Firstly, it could simply be the case that….

3rd paragraph: It may also be the case that ….

4th paragraph: Finally, there is a possibility that …

ORGANIZATION FOR "QUESTIONS TO BE ANSWERED"

Prompt (Topic 180)

According to a recent report, cheating among college and university students is on the rise. However, Groveton College has successfully reduced student cheating by adopting an honor code, which calls for students to agree not to cheat in their academic endeavors and to notify a faculty member if they suspect that others have cheated. Groveton's honor code replaced a system in which teachers closely monitored students; under that system, teachers reported an average of thirty cases of cheating per year. In the first year the honor code was in place, students reported twenty-one cases of cheating; five years later, this figure had dropped to fourteen. Moreover, in a recent survey, a majority of Groveton students said that they would be less likely to cheat with an honor code in place than without. Thus, all colleges and universities should adopt honor codes similar to Groveton's in order to decrease cheating among students.

Write a response in which you discuss what questions would need to be answered in order to decide whether the recommendation and the argument on which it is based are reasonable. Be sure to explain how the answers to these questions would help to evaluate the recommendation.

Sample Response and Organization

Relying on the fact that Groveton has experienced a decrease in the reported cases of cheating over a period of five years, as well as a recent survey which found that most students would be less inclined to cheat with an honor code in place, the author recommends that all colleges and universities adopt an honor code similar to that of Groveton college. However, before we determine whether any other college or university should take action, we need answers to certain questions.	Introduction
First, the argument raises the question of whether the honor code has been successful. The system in which teachers monitored students found thirty cases of cheating, whereas in the newer student-reporting system, only twenty-one cases were reported in the first year, and then only fourteen five years later. This begs the question of whether there has been a	2nd paragraph: 1st question to be answered

reduction in the number of cases of cheating because the honor code was in place, or whether cheating has decreased for other reasons. For example, students often hesitate to report their classmates' cheating. They may simply have become more and more reluctant to report cheating each year since adoption of the honor code. They may also have been less adept at detecting their classmates' cheating than teachers and former students who had been more experienced. Potential cheaters may even have chosen not to cheat during the period regardless of the honor code. If one of the scenarios turns out to be true, we will need to reinvestigate Groveton's "success" before other universities adopt a similar honor code.

Secondly, the question arises of whether the survey is reliable, valid, and representative. The recent survey of Groveton's students found that most reported that they would not cheat with an honor code in place. However, since these answers were self-reported by the students, it is safe to assume that they would give answers on the survey that would benefit them the most. This raises the question of whether the honor code is reliable at all since it obviously works in favor of dishonest students. Perhaps most students answered that the honor code would make them less likely to cheat because it made cheating easier, and therefore they hoped to keep it by falsely claiming that it would make them less inclined to cheat. This indicates that the participants of the survey may be an anomaly consisting mostly of people who hope to benefit from the honor code. Even if the respondents are representative of Groveton students, there is no guarantee that they will do as they have claimed in the survey. Besides, the researchers could have asked the irrelevant question of whether an honor code is better than none, instead of how it compares to the old system of teacher monitoring. In all such scenarios, the survey is neither valid nor representative, rendering the recommendation and its argument unreasonable.

3rd paragraph: 2nd question to be answered

Lastly, there is of course the question of the cultural differences among all universities and colleges that may affect the success rate of an honor code system. For example, Groveton could be a small school where the honor code is easily implemented and naturally efficacious, whereas at larger universities it would be hard to implement the code and even if implemented, the code would be less effective. Groveton students could be more likely to report cheating, or less likely to cheat with an honor code in place, than students in other universities and colleges. Even if it has worked in Groveton, this does not necessarily mean that it will work in other colleges and universities. All this is incumbent on the willingness of students to follow the honor code, and currently there is no accurate measure of this variable. Even if the code will be effective in other colleges and universities, there is the possibility that some universities and colleges may have had in place an honor code comparable to Groveton's, thereby making a new one redundant. If Groveton is typical in respects relevant to the incidence of cheating, it will be plausible for other universities and colleges to enforce a similar honor code. Otherwise, the recommended action would be indefensible.

4th paragraph: 3rd question to be answered

In conclusion, the adoption of an honor code across all universities and colleges requires further analysis in the areas of its actual success rate, not only at Groveton, but at other

Conclusion

institutions as well. Furthermore, surveys of student opinions of the system change should be disregarded as those who wish to cheat will skew the results, since they stand to benefit from an honor code system. Finally, there should be further testing of the honor code system nationally and internationally to see if institutional differences will affect the willingness of students to report on one another.

For the "Questions to Be Answered" prompt, you may use the following organization.

2nd paragraph: First, the argument raises the question of whether....

3rd paragraph: Secondly, the question arises of whether....

4th paragraph: Lastly, there is of course the question of....

You may also use the following organization.

2nd paragraph: To begin with, we must know....

3rd paragraph: Secondly, we should know....

4th paragraph: Finally, we need to know....

CHAPTER 3

Common Logical Fallacies and Strategies for Addressing Them

You may find your task easier if you can readily detect all the logical fallacies of an argument, because each fallacy has its own tackling strategies. The most common fallacies on the test involve the following: unestablished cause and effect relationships, weak analogies, unreliable statistics, unrepresentative surveys, assuming that a trend never changes, and assuming that a condition is necessary and/or sufficient, among other things.

Also, remember that you do not have to name the logical fallacy in your writing, and you do not even have to know formal logic to do a good job. What matters is your ability to recognize the faulty line of reasoning involved in the argument that you will explain in your essay. For example, no argument in the official pool offers sufficient evidence that the conclusion is valid. Therefore, you just need to examine the relationship between each piece of evidence or reasoning identified and the conclusion of the argument to see how it falls short of supporting or substantiating the conclusion. In this way, you may figure out what specific evidence is needed or what questions need to be answered to bolster or assess the argument. This way of identifying all logical loopholes in terms of evidence needed is intuitively effective, in that it is a procrustean, or one-size-fits-all, strategy that works to an examinee's advantage. An equally efficacious way to address logical fallacies of a prompt is to treat all of them as assumptions that must be warranted to support the argument. For each piece of evidence or reasoning, the author assumes that a connection is established between the piece of evidence or reasoning and the conclusion, but this is not necessarily the case. Once you have identified as many assumptions as possible, you may begin to evaluate the argument in your writing: present the assumption, state which claim it underlies, and demonstrate how the argument becomes implausible when it is based on an unwarranted assumption. As follows are common logical fallacies tested and strategies for discussing them.

UNESTABLISHED CAUSE-AND-EFFECT RELATIONSHIPS

This fallacy occurs when someone claims that just because two events happen together, one has caused the other. For example, suppose you are in a new city and come across a café with many customers waiting in line to get inside. An initial assumption would be that the café must be a popular spot for the locals. However, this may not be the case. It could have opened recently and is offering a promotional discount, or perhaps there is some special event occurring inside today only. Thus, it is unjustifiable to assume that the line of people waiting is indicative of the café's popularity. A good way to remember this fallacy is to keep in mind that *correlation does not necessarily imply causation.* The cause-and-effect fallacy is the one tested most often: almost every argument prompt features such a fallacy. For the "Alternative Explanations" prompts, all of them ask you to discuss factors other than the one presented in the argument that may be responsible for the facts given. <u>One way to address a cause-and-effect fallacy is to discuss relevant factors real or hypothetical one by one and explain how they may contribute to the given situation</u>.

Below is an example in which the author confuses a concurrence of decline in business and increased skateboarding with a cause-and-effect relationship between them.

The following appeared as a letter to the editor from a Central Plaza store owner.

"Over the past two years, the number of shoppers in Central Plaza has been steadily decreasing while the popularity of skateboarding has increased dramatically. Many Central Plaza store owners believe that the decrease in their business is due to the number of skateboard users in the plaza. There has also been a dramatic increase in the amount of litter and vandalism throughout the plaza. Thus, we recommend that the city prohibit skateboarding in Central Plaza. If skateboarding is prohibited here, we predict that business in Central Plaza will return to its previously high levels."

Write a response in which you discuss what questions would need to be answered in order to decide whether the recommendation is likely to have the predicted result. Be sure to explain how the answers to these questions would help to evaluate the recommendation. (Topic 158)

Sample paragraph of the response to the above prompt featuring the fallacy of cause and effect:

The first question that the author must answer is whether the decline of business in Central Plaza is a result of increased skateboarding. The author mentions that the number of shoppers has been dropping while skateboarding has been rising significantly, but no other details are provided in this regard. It is possible that because Central Plaza is located in a small suburb where most people rely on a few companies to provide most of the jobs, a recent mass layoff and in turn reduced purchasing power could be to blame. It is also possible that online shopping and delivery has become cheaper and more convenient. It is even possible that some popular shops or eateries have left, or that factors other than the skateboarders' presence in Central Plaza have contributed to a considerable increase in crime rates in surrounding areas. Any of the scenarios, if true, would undermine the claim that the current drop in business in Central Plaza is attributable to skateboarders' behavior. Thus, the recommendation of prohibiting the skateboarders could be unfounded and would only leave Central Plaza with even fewer visitors.

When it comes to a cause-and-effect fallacy, you may tackle it in the following way.

1. Identify: look for signal words in the argument (due to, contribute to; precede, follow, since, years ago; while, during the same year).
2. How to critique: you need to provide alternative explanations that can rival the one given in the argument. This means that you try to account for the phenomenon in the argument with factors other than the one provided in the topic. You may list the factors and explain how they may be responsible for the effect.
3. How to develop a cause-and-effect paragraph:

    1) Provide a topic sentence: The author assumes that a cause-and-effect relationship exists between Event A and Event B; // The author must answer whether a cause-and-effect relationship exists between Event A and Event B; //The author must provide evidence that a cause-and-effect relationship exists between Event A and Event B.
    2) Explain why this line of reasoning is a fallacy: A sequence/concurrence of events does not necessarily mean a causal relationship between them; A correlation between events does not necessarily mean a causal relationship between them.
    3) Analyze by identifying the factors given: Event A, Event B, and how they are related.
    4) List factors other than A that may be responsible for Event B and explain how.
    5) Conclude the paragraph: Without ruling out other possibilities, the author cannot justifiably claim/assume that merely Event A contributes to Event B.

WEAK ANALOGIES

Analogies can be powerful rhetorical devices, but a weak analogy in logic can completely undermine an argument. Such an analogy occurs when the situations, ideas, or objects that you are comparing are not similar in a relevant fashion, and therefore are not useful to support your argument. The analogies on the test often involve whether one place should emulate another place by adopting the latter's strategy, plan, or policy, or whether the strategy, plan, or policy of one place should be implemented in other places. One way to address a weak analogy is to discuss differences between two places to demonstrate that because of their huge dissimilarities, one place cannot emulate another place.

Below is an example in which the author draws a weak analogy between Belleville and Amburg.

> *The following appeared in a recommendation from the President of the Amburg Chamber of Commerce.*
>
> *"Last October, the city of Belleville installed high-intensity lighting in its central business district, and vandalism there declined almost immediately. The city of Amburg, on the other hand, recently*

instituted police patrols on bicycles in its business district. However, the rate of vandalism here remains constant. Since high-intensity lighting is clearly the most effective way to combat crime, we recommend using the money that is currently being spent on bicycle patrols to install such lighting throughout Amburg. If we install this high-intensity lighting, we will significantly reduce crime rates in Amburg."

Write a response in which you discuss what questions would need to be answered in order to decide whether the recommendation is likely to have the predicted result. Be sure to explain how the answers to these questions would help to evaluate the recommendation. (Topic 132)

Sample paragraph of the response to the above prompt featuring the weak analogy:

We should also have the answer to whether high-intensity lighting will be effective in Amburg. High-intensity lighting may have been efficacious in curbing vandalism in Belleville, but this does not necessarily mean it would carry the intended result in Amburg. It is likely that the people behind vandalism in Belleville were deterred by police patrols on bicycles rather than by high-intensity lighting. If Amburg's citizens are not deterred by a police presence in the area, it is possible that the addition of this lighting will not deter them. It is also possible that the bicycle patrols were instituted too recently in Amburg for their effects to be observed. It is even possible that the bicycle patrols have been effective in Amburg, but the incidence of vandalism remains unchanged because at the same time, other factors have been contributing to an increase in the rate of vandalism. Should this be the case, the assumption that Belleville and Amburg are similar enough to justify the same course of action would be groundless, rendering the recommendation invalid. Even if high-intensity lighting is good at controlling vandalism in Amburg, this does not necessarily mean that it is the ideal way to tackle other crimes. Similarly, other crimes may be best deterred by a police presence. If this should be true, the assumption that just because high-intensity lighting is effective at combating vandalism, it is effective at tackling other crimes, would be gratuitous and the prediction of its effect on considerably reducing crime rates in Amburg would be unreasonable.

When it comes to a weak analogy, you may tackle it in the following way.

1. Identify: look for signal words in the argument (nearby, neighboring, similar).
2. How to critique: You need to discuss differences between two places or companies to demonstrate that because of their huge dissimilarities, one cannot emulate the other.
3. How to develop an analogy paragraph:

    1) Provide a topic sentence: The author assumes that just because one place/company has succeeded by…, the other place/company can achieve the same results by taking the same course of action.
    2) Explain why this line of reasoning is a fallacy: The two places/companies could be too different from each other to warrant the same course of action.
    3) Analyze by identifying the two places/companies and their similarity given in the topic.

4) List differences between the two places/companies and explain how the differences may make it difficult for one place/company to follow the example of the other place/company.
5) Conclude the paragraph: Unless there is evidence that the two places/companies are essentially comparable in what may affect the desired outcome, the author cannot reliably conclude that one can succeed by emulating the other.

UNRELIABLE STATISTICS

This occurs when the author uses statistics or data that are far too vague to be useful in supporting the claim, recommendation, advice, prediction, or conclusion the author is presenting. There may be aggravating circumstances surrounding the data which the author neglects to address, a lack of evidence needed to confirm the statistics, or other issues with the data presented. It is your job to consider how the statistics may be unjustifiably used to support the claims being made by the author. One way to address unreliable statistics is to discuss how they may be interpreted in different ways. For example, they may be significant or not significant, depending on the whole population or the original number.

Below is an example in which the author relies on unreliable statistics like 2% and "many servers" to draw the conclusion of the argument.

> *The following memorandum is from the business manager of Happy Pancake House restaurants.*
>
> *"Butter has now been replaced by margarine in Happy Pancake House restaurants throughout the southwestern United States. Only about 2 percent of customers have complained, indicating that 98 people out of 100 are happy with the change. Furthermore, many servers have reported that a number of customers who ask for butter do not complain when they are given margarine instead. Clearly, either these customers cannot distinguish butter from margarine or they use the term 'butter' to refer to either butter or margarine. Thus, to avoid the expense of purchasing butter and to increase profitability, the Happy Pancake House should extend this cost-saving change to its restaurants in the southeast and northeast as well."*
>
> *Write a response in which you discuss what questions would need to be answered in order to decide whether the recommendation is likely to have the predicted result. Be sure to explain how the answers to these questions would help to evaluate the recommendation. (Topic 28)*

Sample paragraph of the response to the above prompt featuring unreliable statistics:

> *The company must ask whether the fact that only two percent of customers have complained truly represents a ninety-eight percent satisfaction rate. If two percent of customers involve a large number of people, it is unfair to claim that customers have been hardly impacted. It is likely that customers who have complained account for a much larger portion of those who have asked for butter. This could be a nightmare for the company, since this indicates a great percentage of customers unsatisfied with the*

replacement. Also, refraining from expressing one's dissatisfaction might not equate to an expression of contentedness. It may be the case that a large number of customers simply do not wish to voice their concerns at the moment, or that many customers who have heard about the replacement have chosen to buy butter elsewhere. It may also be the case that the replacement has happened too recently to yield significant feedback, alerting Happy Pancake House to a potentially much higher rate of negative response to the replacement later. If this should be true, the assumption of a ninety-eight percent satisfaction rate would be unfounded and the recommendation of replacing butter with margarine in other parts of the United States would be unlikely to have the predicted result of saving money on butter and boosting profits. To better evaluate the argument, we need a customer survey to see if people are truly happy with the change.

When it comes to unreliable statistics, you may tackle it in the following way.

1. Identify: look for signal words (increase, data, percent).
2. How to critique: You need to discuss how the data set or percentages may be interpreted in different ways.
3. How to develop a statistics paragraph:

   1) Provide a topic sentence: The data/percentages/increase could be insignificant; The data/percentages/increase could imply....

   2) Explain why this line of reasoning is a fallacy: How the data set or percentages given may be unreliable, or why there may be interpretations of the low/high numbers presented other than the assertion made by the author.

   3) Analyze by identifying the data set or percentages given in the topic.

   4) Discuss the ways in which the data set or percentages could be interpreted, their reliability, and implications.

   5) Conclude the paragraph: Unless there is evidence that the statistics are reliable, the author cannot fairly conclude that....

UNREPRESENTATIVE SURVEYS

An unrepresentative survey is very similar to unreliable statistics, the difference being that the passage will usually focus on a single survey, and make assumptions based upon its findings, whereas unreliable statistics will be used as a single piece of evidence to support a claim. When presented with an unrepresentative survey, you must carefully consider the validity of the survey, whether the assertions the author makes based on the survey's results are valid, and whether the recommendation or advice given by the author based on the survey is warranted. <u>One way to address an unrepresentative survey is to discuss how small the sample may be and why it may not be typical of the target population</u>.

Below is an example in which the author unfairly assumes that two districts represent all places, and two subjects represent all subjects.

> *The data from a survey of high school math and science teachers show that in the district of Sanlee many of these teachers reported assigning daily homework, whereas in the district of Marlee, most science and math teachers reported assigning homework no more than two or three days per week. Despite receiving less frequent homework assignments, Marlee students earn better grades overall and are less likely to be required to repeat a year of school than are students in Sanlee. These results call into question the usefulness of frequent homework assignments. Most likely the Marlee students have more time to concentrate on individual assignments than do the Sanlee students who have homework every day. Therefore teachers in our high schools should assign homework no more than twice a week.*
>
> *Write a response in which you discuss what specific evidence is needed to evaluate the argument and explain how the evidence would weaken or strengthen the argument. (Topic 108)*

Sample paragraph of the response to the above prompt featuring unrepresentative surveys:

> *There must be evidence that high schools in Marlee and Sanlee represent those in the author's area. However, there is a dearth of data to suggest that this is the case. The survey could be invalid and unreliable. Perhaps many Sanlee teachers have reported assigning homework more frequently to show that they have a better understanding of how students learn. Should this be true, the survey would be invalid. While the comparison between Marlee and Sanlee seems compelling at first glance, these are only two districts, and their high schools may not be an accurate representation of other high schools. Furthermore, the only classes covered by the survey were math and science, which are only a fraction of the subjects that students must take in school. The author's area and other subjects may assign homework more often and report higher grades. Should this be the case, the assumption about the representativeness of Marlee and Sanlee districts would be unjustified and the argument that the teachers in the author's area should follow Marlee's homework schedule would be undermined. An in-depth study across more school districts and more subjects with actual figures would be a far better metric by which to evaluate the proposed change.*

When it comes to an unrepresentative survey, you may tackle it in the following way.

1. Identify: look for signal words (survey, poll, census, study, research).
2. How to critique: You need to discuss what (for example, a sample that exhibits characteristics different from those of the target population) could have led to an unrepresentative survey.
3. How to develop a survey paragraph:

    1) Provide a topic sentence: The author assumes that the survey respondents typify the target population in general; //The author must answer whether the survey respondents are representative of the target population in general; //The author

must provide evidence that the survey respondents are representative of the target population in general.

2) Explain why this line of reasoning is a fallacy: The sample could be too tiny to represent the whole population;// The sample could be an aberration;// Research methodology could cause researchers to collect certain types of data while overlooking other kinds.
3) Analyze by identifying the sample given in the topic.
4) Discuss how the sample could be unrepresentative because of a potentially large target population or nonrandom selection.
5) Conclude the paragraph: Unless there is evidence that the survey is valid, reliable, and representative, the author cannot fairly conclude that....

ASSUMING THAT A TREND NEVER CHANGES

This fallacy consists of the author basing an argument on a past or present trend, with the expectation that the trend will continue. The issue with this is, of course, that there is not enough evidence provided to guarantee that the given trend will in fact continue, and therefore the argument being made is weakened. One way to address the fallacy is to discuss how things may have changed since the past or will change in the future.

Below is an example in which the author gratuitously assumes that the current trend of rising enrollment will continue.

> *The following appeared in a memo from the director of student housing at Buckingham College.*
>
> *"To serve the housing needs of our students, Buckingham College should build a number of new dormitories. Buckingham's enrollment is growing and, based on current trends, will double over the next 50 years, thus making existing dormitory space inadequate. Moreover, the average rent for an apartment in our town has risen in recent years. Consequently, students will find it increasingly difficult to afford off-campus housing. Finally, attractive new dormitories would make prospective students more likely to enroll at Buckingham."*
>
> *Write a response in which you discuss what specific evidence is needed to evaluate the argument and explain how the evidence would weaken or strengthen the argument. (Topic 163)*

Sample paragraph of the response to the above prompt featuring the assumption that a trend never changes:

> *To begin with, the author must provide evidence that Buckingham's enrollment will double over the next 50 years to make current dormitory space inadequate. The memo states that according to existing trends, the author expects the enrollment to increase one hundred percent over the next 50 years, but this projection is taken for granted. A myriad of factors may contribute to a decline in future student enrollment in Buckingham. For example, it is possible that college is considered worth the money now, because it is essential for a reasonable job, but many may question the utility of a*

college education over the next 50 years because it is too expensive. Even if people do not question the benefits of college education in general, they may doubt those of an education in Buckingham. It is also possible that many attend college now because federal loans are easily available, but fewer people may do so because it is harder to get federal loans. Even if the enrollment will increase over the next 50 years, there is no guarantee that it will double. Even assuming that it will increase to twofold the original size, this does not necessarily mean that existing dormitory space will fall short of the demand, because future students may choose not to live in the dormitory. Any of the scenarios, if true, would invalidate the claim that the enrollment will double in the future to make the dormitory space inadequate. If the college relies on the enrollment trend alone to make the decision to expand its on-campus housing, it risks making projections on the basis of a very limited amount of data.

When it comes to a "trend never changes" fallacy, you may tackle it in the following way.

1. Identify: look for signal words (years ago, last, past, will). The premise may involve a period of time in the past, whereas the conclusion may be about a period related to the present or the future.
2. How to critique: You need to discuss what may have changed since the past or will change in the future.
3. How to develop a "trend never changes" paragraph:
   1) Provide a topic sentence: The author assumes that a trend may remain unchanged over time.
   2) Explain why this line of reasoning is a fallacy: What was valid in the past may not be valid in the future; what is valid today may not be valid in the future.
   3) Analyze by discussing the situation given.
   4) Point out how things may be different at present or in the future.
   5) Conclude the paragraph: Unless there is evidence that things will remain the same over time, the author cannot claim with certainty that....

ASSUMING THAT A CONDITION IS NECESSARY/SUFFICIENT

When concluding that to achieve a result, an organization or an individual should take a certain course of action, the author assumes that this measure is a condition necessary for the result to occur, suggesting that the measure is the *only* way to get the desired result. However, this is not necessarily true, since there may be other better ways to achieve the desired outcome. Similarly, when concluding that by taking a certain course of action, an organization or an individual will be able to achieve a result, the author implies that the measure is a condition sufficient for the result to occur. However, the author may fail to take into account other measures needed to attain the goal. The arguments that have the word "should" in the conclusion often assume that a course of action is necessary, whereas those that have the word "will" in the conclusion tend to assume that a course of action is sufficient. Of such arguments, those that draw conclusions about profit or productivity often feature this fallacy that assumes that a strategy, plan, or policy is sufficient for increasing profits. <u>One way to address this fallacy is to discuss</u>

other strategies, plans, or policies that may be no less effective, or analyze other measures needed to achieve the outcome.

Below is an example in which the author assumes that a change to a news talk format is a condition necessary for reversing a drop in the number of listeners.

> *The following appeared in a memorandum from the manager of WWAC radio station.*
>
> *"WWAC must change from its current rock-music format because the number of listeners has been declining, even though the population in our listening area has been growing. The population growth has resulted mainly from people moving to our area after their retirement, and we must make listeners of these new residents. But they seem to have limited interest in music: several local stores selling recorded music have recently closed. Therefore, just changing to another kind of music is not going to increase our audience. Instead, we should adopt a news-and-talk format, a form of radio that is increasingly popular in our area."*
>
> *Write a response in which you discuss what questions would need to be answered in order to decide whether the recommendation and the argument on which it is based are reasonable. Be sure to explain how the answers to these questions would help to evaluate the recommendation. (Topic 66)*

Sample paragraph of the response to the above prompt featuring the assumption that a condition is necessary/sufficient:

> *Next, we should know whether a change to a news talk format is the condition necessary for reversing a drop in the number of WWAC's listeners. Yet, the memorandum offers no details in this regard. Just because there is a drop in listener numbers does not necessarily mean there should be a change of the form of radio. The drop could be negligible and normal fluctuations. Also, just because the news talk form of radio has become more and more popular in the area does not necessarily mean it is the only viable option. It could be that while a news and talk format has become increasingly popular, listeners prefer the format of an existing competitor only. Perhaps there is a strategy better than changing to a news and talk format, for example, changing to a music format to the retirees' tastes. Or perhaps listeners have dropped in number because they dislike the time the music is broadcast or because they dislike the music anchor; simply changing the broadcast time or the anchor would accomplish the goal. Or perhaps WWAC has transmission problems; simply repairing the transmission would achieve the outcome. In such scenarios, the claim that a change to the new format may benefit WWAC radio station would be weakened. It would be far more convincing if there were some actual survey data to back up this claim. Without identifying what is responsible for the decline in listener numbers, the author cannot fairly assume that the news talk format is the only strategy for increasing the number of WWAC's listeners.*

When it comes to a "necessary and/or sufficient condition" fallacy, you may tackle it in the following way.

1. Identify: look for signal words in the conclusion (should, will).

2. How to critique: You need to discuss other options that may be as good as or even better than the one recommended; you need to discuss other strategies required to achieve the goal.
3. How to develop a "necessary and/or sufficient condition" paragraph:

    1) Provide a topic sentence: The author assumes that … is a necessary/sufficient condition for attaining the goal.
    2) Explain why this line of reasoning is a fallacy: The assumption may not be substantiated, because other options may be as efficacious as or more efficacious than the one given or because other measures are needed at the same time to achieve the desired outcome.
    3) Analyze by discussing how this strategy may fail to deliver the goal or may deliver the goal less effectively than other strategies.
    4) Note other strategies and discuss how they may contribute to accomplishment of the goal.
    5) Conclude the paragraph: Unless there is evidence that this strategy is required or adequate for the intended result, the author cannot justifiably make such an assumption.

CHAPTER 4

Answers to the Official Pool of Argument Topics

1. Child-rearing practices on the island of Tertia (Assumptions)

The author claims that Dr. Field was completely wrong in his observation-based conclusion that Tertian children were raised by their entire village and that Dr. Karp's interview-centered method is more valid than the observation-centered approach for studying child-rearing in the future. To justify the claim, the article notes that in later interviews with the children conducted by Dr. Karp, he found that the children spent more time talking about their biological parents than about other village adults. The argument relies on some assumptions that we must scrutinize before we ascertain its soundness.

The threshold assumption that the author makes is that no significant changes have taken place since Dr. Field's research. However, the author does not provide any evidence to substantiate this. Dr. Field's observations took place twenty years ago, enough time for an entire generation of young people to mature into adulthood. It is entirely possible that over the past twenty years, the island of Tertia has seen significant socio-economic changes. Perhaps children on Tertia were raised by a whole village twenty years ago, but they were raised by their biological parents because of outside influences when Dr. Karp conducted the interviews. Researchers should look into the recent history of Tertia to see if such influences have existed that may account for the apparent change in child-rearing practices. If yes, the claim that Dr. Field drew a wrong conclusion about child-rearing practices on Tertia would be weakened. Otherwise, there would be a stronger case for the claim. Without relevant information, the author cannot convince me of Dr. Karp's claims regarding Dr. Field's conclusion and the comparative merit of interviewing versus observation.

The next assumption that the author relies on is that Dr. Karp used the proper methodology to measure the Tertians. However, there is the possibility that Dr. Karp's method was not an accurate metric by which to measure the child-rearing habits of the Tertian people. After all, he merely interviewed the children, who he claims talked mostly about their biological parents. He did not observe the children in their daily lives as Dr.

Field's had done, so his conclusion is based only on what the children said. These interviews should be met with scrutiny, as we do not know what questions could have been asked. If the questions were mostly about who gave birth to them and whom they lived with, the majority of the children's answers would focus on their biological parents. In that case, Dr. Karp's claims regarding Dr. Field's conclusion and observational research and his own interviewing methodology would be rendered invalid. Even if Dr. Karp's use of interviews was superior to Dr. Field's use of observations, a single case does not necessarily mean that the interview-centered approach is generally better than the observation-centered approach at obtaining accurate information about child-rearing practices. Before the claims are established, the author needs to provide many similar studies comparing the merits of interviewing methodology with those of observational methodology.

A final assumption that underlies the argument is that the people in the group of islands that Dr. Karp studied are comparable to those on Tertia. Dr. Field's observational research was conducted only on the island of Tertia, whereas Dr. Karp's research took place throughout the group of islands which included the island of Tertia. This implies that all the people of these islands share the same culture, and Dr. Karp's study results also dilute the data that specifically relates to Tertia. One could assume, for example, that all the children from the island of Tertia talked about most of the adults in their village. However, these responses may not be typical when all the children throughout the island chain are considered. This would mean that Dr. Field's conclusion that children on Tertia were reared by an entire village may have been sound, undermining Dr. Karp's claim to the contrary.

In sum, if we were to accept Dr. Karp's assertion that Dr. Field was wrong, and that future child-rearing studies should follow an interview-centered method, there must be a timeline of recent historical events on Tertia that may have contributed to a shift in child-rearing methods. There should also be careful attention to the specific questions asked during the interviews to avoid guided answers and to the demographic information of the island chain to see if the cultures are distinct from one another. Finally, there need to be many studies of benefits of interviewing relative to observation in terms of yielding accurate information before a claim can be made about superiority of each methodology.

2. Reducing headaches using salicylates (Questions to Be Answered)

Relying on a decision by many companies to use salicylates as flavor additives, the author predicts that the citizens of Mentia will have fewer headaches in the future as a direct result. To support the prediction, the author also cites a study that found a reduction of headaches reported by participants on average over a period of 20 years in the city of Mentia as salicylates became more commonly used commercially. Before we accept the results of this study alone as the basis for the prediction and its argument, we need to consider issues surrounding the link between consumption of salicylates and decrease in headaches, use of salicylates as flavor additives, and other causes of headaches.

To begin with, the author must answer whether a concrete link has been established between consumption of salicylates and the reduction of headaches. According to the given information, the study found only a correlation between the reduction of headaches per capita and the rise in use of salicylates. Since the article does mention that many foods already contain large quantities of salicylates, there is no way of knowing if the reduction is a result of these naturally occurring salicylates in the foods or their increased use in manufactured food. There is also the possibility that the lower numbers of headaches are due to false reporting or healthier lifestyles, or even environmental changes. For example, the residents may have felt less and less inclined to report headaches as this makes them seem healthier. If this should be true, the prediction that Mentia residents will suffer fewer headaches as a result of consuming more salicylates would be unfounded. Moreover, just because salicylates are the members of the same chemical family as aspirin does not necessarily mean they can be used like aspirin to treat headaches. Even if they can cure headaches, there is no guarantee that they can prevent headaches, viz. lowering the average number of headaches. If this is the case, it is even likely that the effect can be attributed to aspirin or similar medicine that has become increasingly common. Regardless, without relevant evidence, the author cannot fairly assert a direct connection between more use of salicylates and fewer incidences of headaches.

Next, the author should answer whether companies will use salicylates as flavor additives. However, before companies finalize the plan to use salicylates as flavor additives, there needs to be testing to see if this is the case. After all, the article itself states that salicylates are chemically similar to aspirin, which can be quite harmful if overconsumed. This is even more of an issue if the research is on salicylates' effects on headaches. If they do indeed help reduce headaches, then that would mean they somehow influence a person's circulatory or nervous system. Given this, the use of salicylates would need strict regulation so as not to cause a pharmacological issue and may not obtain the government's approval of this use. Even if salicylates can be used safely as flavor additives, there is no guarantee that the residents will consume enough food with salicylates to reduce their headaches, because they may not like the flavor of the additives. Also, there is no guarantee that companies will be able to increase consumption of salicylates this way because they may find it difficult to add salicylates without destroying the original flavor of the food. It could even be that companies will give up salicylates as flavor additives altogether in favor of other cheaper alternatives. If this is the case, using salicylates as flavor additives may not be viable, rendering the prediction of fewer headaches among Mentia residents unreasonable.

Finally, the author needs to answer whether all other conditions that might affect the incidence of headaches will remain unchanged when companies use salicylates as flavor additives. However, the author offers no data in this regard. It is possible that disease outbreaks will cause a dramatic increase in the number of headaches. It is also possible that the residents of Mentia will overwork and experience more stress and fatigue. It is even possible that the weather there will change in the future– for example, it may become more humid and hotter. Perhaps the residents will have a different lifestyle –for example, they may drink more alcohol. Or perhaps companies will add fewer salicylates as preservatives to foods because the residents do not enjoy them. In such scenarios, the citizens will probably suffer a greater number of headaches. This means even if more consumption of salicylates reduces incidence of headaches, the reduction is likely to be offset by the increase that other factors may lead to, thereby causing the number of headaches to remain unchanged or even rise. In this case, the prediction of fewer headaches for the residents of Mentia and the argument for the therapeutic effect of consuming salicylates would be unjustified. Absent such scenarios, the prediction and its argument would be more credible.

In conclusion, it would be potentially disastrous for a company to add any new ingredient to its food products, much less one that has the possibility of affecting a person's health. To bolster the argument, the author must assure us that no changes serving to increase the average number of headaches will occur in the future. To better assess the argument, we should have more case studies of more diverse populations, with narrower parameters to see if salicylates do indeed have a positive effect on headaches, or conversely, if they have any harmful side effects.

3. Building a jazz club in <u>Monroe</u> (Specific Evidence)

The author concludes that a jazz club would be a lucrative venture in the city of Monroe. To support the conclusion, the article cites the popularity of jazz music in the area by presenting examples such as a highly-rated jazz radio program, a recent jazz festival, and the famous jazz musicians that reside there. However, before the loan for the proposed jazz club is approved, we need extra evidence regarding the examples to decide whether the argument is valid.

First, we must have evidence that attendees at the annual jazz music festival are representative of the local people that enjoy jazz music. The application states that the recent jazz music festival attracted 100,000 people. However, there is no mention of the exact number of people from Monroe; therefore, we do not know the portion, if any at all, of the attendees from Monroe. Census information that showed the population of Monroe and a survey that showed whether locals or tourists comprised a significant percentage of the jazz festival attendees would be evidence needed to evaluate the business-loan applicant's argument. If a large portion of the attendees were from Monroe, it could be proof of popularity of jazz there, making the case for a jazz music club in Monroe more convincing. It is also likely that Monroe is a town of only 100 and few attendees were locals. However, even if the people from Monroe accounted for a considerable portion of the attendees, it is likely that the trend last summer was an aberration and may not continue. Should this be true, the argument would be weakened.

To further assess the argument, we should have evidence that the local musicians can play at the proposed club at a reasonable rate. The article points out that a few famous jazz musicians make their homes in Monroe, but there is no guarantee that they would like to perform at the local jazz club C-Note or that locals would be willing to hear them perform. They may perform elsewhere and even at the nearest jazz club but reside in Monroe simply to take advantage of peaceful small-town life. If this is true, their proximity to the club may have no bearing on its success. As a result, the argument for a new jazz club in Monroe will be weakened. If the jazz musicians are willing to play at the club, are appreciated in the area, and do not demand unreasonable compensation for performing at the club, the argument will be strengthened. Lacking relevant evidence, we cannot fully evaluate the potential success of a new jazz club in Monroe.

To better assess the argument, we also need evidence that the fact that the jazz radio station is the highest rated station in Monroe indicates that jazz is popular in the city. It is possible, especially in the current age of MP3 players and the internet, that it is simply the only radio station that is listened to at all, and that the number of listeners is relatively small. As with the previous contention, population data and music preference surveys could help us appraise this counterargument. It would also help if the author could provide the ratings for all radio stations in Monroe, so that we could have a clearer picture of how much more popular the jazz station is than the other radio stations. If the difference in ratings is small, then it would weaken the case for starting a club that plays jazz music exclusively. Even if the jazz station is popular, there is no guarantee that its listeners would be interested in listening to jazz at the new club. It could even compete with the proposed club for listeners. Either scenario would undermine the case for a new club in Monroe.

Finally, we lack evidence that a jazz music club in Monroe would be extremely profitable. Assuming that jazz is popular in Monroe, we need information about whether the proposed jazz music club would dominate the local market just because the nearest jazz club is 65 miles away. It is likely that people are willing to drive such a distance because the club is competitive in terms of admission prices, atmosphere, and services, hurting the new club's potential revenues. Also, the nationwide study finds that an average jazz fan spends about $1,000 every year on jazz entertainment. However, it could be that the typical fan spends little in jazz music clubs. It could also be that a jazz fan in Monroe spends little on jazz entertainment and even less in jazz music clubs. When the new club is unlikely to receive the revenue, the prediction of an extremely profitable business would be groundless, because profit is a function of revenue and costs. It will become even more groundless if the applicant fails to consider all kinds of costs associated with launching a business. Before touting the profitability of the new club, the author must estimate all the costs as well as the revenues.

In conclusion, before receiving approval of this loan, the potential owner must first provide solid data on the population of Monroe, and the portion of people in the city who both like jazz music and are willing to spend money on going to a jazz club. It would also be in the owner's best interest to contact the local musicians, if they are appreciated in the area, to see if they are willing to play at the club at an affordable rate. Above everything else, the owner must weigh the potential revenue against the costs to make sure that the business would be lucrative.

4. Reducing headaches using salicylates (Specific Evidence)

Relying on the fact that many companies have found the new use of salicylates as flavor additives, the author argues that the citizens of Mentia will have fewer headaches in the future as a direct result. To support the argument, the author also cites a study that found a reduction of headaches reported by participants on average over a period of 20 years in the city of Mentia as salicylates became more commonly used commercially. However, we need additional evidence to better ascertain the soundness of the argument.

We must have evidence regarding the concrete link between consumption of salicylates and the reduction of headaches. According to the given information, the study found only a correlation between the reduction of headaches per capita and the rise in use of salicylates. Since the article does mention that many foods already contain large quantities of salicylates, there is no way of knowing if the reduction is a result of these naturally occurring salicylates in the foods or their increased use in manufactured food. There is also the possibility that the lower numbers of headaches are due to false reporting or healthier lifestyles, or even environmental changes. For example, the residents may have felt less and less inclined to report headaches as this makes them seem healthier. If this should be true, the argument that the average Mentia resident will suffer fewer headaches as a result of consuming more salicylates would be undermined. Moreover, just because salicylates are the members of the same chemical family as aspirin does not necessarily mean they can be used like aspirin to treat headaches. Even if they can cure headaches, there is no guarantee that they can prevent headaches, viz. lowering the average number of headaches. If this is the case, it is even likely that the effect can be attributed to aspirin or similar medicine that has become increasingly common. Regardless, without relevant evidence, the author cannot fairly assert a direct connection between more use of salicylates and fewer incidences of headaches.

In addition, we need evidence that companies will use salicylates as flavor additives. However, before companies finalize the plan to use salicylates as flavor additives, there needs to be testing to see if this is the case. After all, the article itself states that salicylates are chemically similar to aspirin, which can be quite harmful if overconsumed. This is even more of an issue if the research is on salicylates' effects on headaches. If they do indeed help reduce headaches, then that would mean they somehow influence a person's circulatory or nervous system. Given this, the use of salicylates would need strict regulation so as not to cause a pharmacological issue and may not obtain the government's approval of this use. Even if salicylates can be used safely as flavor additives, there is no guarantee that the residents will consume enough food with salicylates to reduce their headaches, because they may not like the flavor of the additives. Also, there is no guarantee that companies will be able to increase consumption of salicylates this way because they may find it difficult to add salicylates without destroying the original flavor of the food. It could even be that companies will give up salicylates as flavor additives altogether in favor of other cheaper alternatives. Should this be true, using salicylates as flavor additives may not be viable, rendering the prediction of further drop in headache numbers among the average Mentia resident unreasonable.

Finally, we lack evidence concerning whether all other conditions that might affect the incidence of headaches will remain unchanged when companies use salicylates as flavor additives. It is possible that disease outbreaks will cause a dramatic increase in the number of headaches. It is also possible that the residents of Mentia will overwork and experience more stress and fatigue. It is even possible that the weather there will change in the future– for example, it may become more humid and hotter. Perhaps the residents will have a different lifestyle –for example, they may drink more alcohol. Or perhaps companies will add fewer salicylates as preservatives to foods because the residents do not enjoy them. In such scenarios, the citizens will probably suffer a greater number of headaches. This means even if more consumption of salicylates reduces incidence of headaches, the reduction is likely to be offset by the increase that other factors may lead to, thereby causing the number of headaches to remain unchanged or even rise. In that event, the assumption would prove unwarranted, and the prediction of further drop in headache numbers for the average resident of Mentia would be unjustified. Absent such scenarios, the prediction and its argument would be more credible.

In conclusion, it would be potentially disastrous for a company to add any new ingredient to its food products, much less one that has the possibility of affecting a person's health. To bolster the argument, the author must assure us that no changes serving to increase the average number of headaches will occur in the future. To better assess the argument, we should have more case studies of more diverse populations, with narrower parameters to see if salicylates do indeed have a positive effect on headaches, or conversely, if they have any harmful side effects.

5. Building a new bicycle lane on Blue Highway (Specific Evidence)

To address the issue of rush-hour traffic and an increasing commuting time on Blue Highway, the motorists' lobby has already made a proposal to widen the highway, but the author suggests that a bicycle lane would be a better alternative, citing Green Highway, which added its own new lane but experienced worse traffic jams. To justify the suggestion, the letter points out that many residents like cycling very much, and therefore the bike lane would motivate them to ride bikes instead of driving. However, we need additional evidence to fully assess the argument before any final decisions are made.

To begin with, the author must provide evidence that the surveyed commuters on Blue Highway are representative of general commuters on the highway. However, there is no data in this regard. The sample may be small and biased. It could be that only a few commuters have complained and that only those who have experienced increased commuting time have complained. Should this be the case, the respondents do not typify Blue Highway commuters in general. Perhaps despite increased rush-hour traffic, most commuters have experienced no increase in commuting time. Even if their commuting time has doubled, it may still be reasonable and does not warrant any important changes. Even assuming that there should be any important changes, the author should identify the true causes of the dramatic rise in traffic jams and in turn of commuting time and propose tailored measures. Unless the survey is valid, reliable, and representative, the author cannot justifiably claim that increased rush-hour traffic on Blue Highway has contributed to the residents' doubling of commuting time.

Next, the example of Green Highway does not offer any evidence that the new lane led to its worsening traffic. However, we need such evidence to ascertain what the root cause of the traffic jams was. Before we accept the addition of a lane as the factor that has contributed to worse traffic, there needs to be more information on the area, such as how many people commute and the number of exit and entrance ramps, along with their locations. It may well be the case that Green Highway's traffic issues increased because of poor road design, loosened traffic rules, or other contributing factors. It may also be the case that the trend last year was an aberration and will not last into the future. If this should be true, the assumption that the new lane was responsible for worsening traffic would be unwarranted, and the case for a bicycle lane would be weakened. Even if a new lane on Green Highway was not effective, one on Blue Highway could be effective, given their differences. For example, it is possible that Green Highway had already had enough traffic lanes whereas Blue Highway has too few lanes. In that event, addition of a lane to Blue Highway may be a viable strategy, rendering the argument invalid. To rule out an additional lane of traffic as a feasible measure for Blue Highway in decreasing traffic jams, the author must provide evidence that the worsening traffic on Green Highway was a direct result of its new lane.

In addition, simply stating that many area residents like to ride bikes is not proof that they will commute by bike. We want to know how many of the residents commute and whether they ride their bicycles when they commute. If few of the "keen bicyclists" commute, the recommendation of addition of a bicycle lane to Blue Highway is unreasonable. If the distance between the suburbs and the city center is very far, it would make cycling very inconvenient, even dangerous, considering adverse weather conditions. Or if many residents need to use their cars at work, commuting by bike would be undesirable. Furthermore, there is no guarantee that traffic would be reduced if more people used bicycles. After all, it is possible that with more people riding bikes, there would be a proportional increase in road congestion due to cyclists. In this case, the argument for addition of a bicycle lane would be undermined. More research into the number of people willing to commute by riding their bicycles instead of driving and into traffic jam resulting from too many bike-riders on the road would provide better insight into whether rush hour traffic would be affected by the addition of a bike lane.

Finally, the author should offer evidence that adding a bicycle lane is the only alternative. The letter seems to suggest that addition of a bicycle lane is the only option better than a new traffic lane. There is no clear evidence that the additional lane of traffic has been ineffective. Even if it has not achieved the desired outcome, this does not necessarily mean a bicycle lane is the sole alternative. It could be that neither the new lane of traffic alone nor the bicycle lane alone will be able to reduce rush-hour traffic and commuting time. If this is the case, another strategy needs to be adopted. By adding a traffic lane and a bicycle lane at the same time, or by improving the road design, the commuters may anticipate less rush-hour traffic and commuting time. In that event, the assumption that merely a new bicycle lane is a more desirable alternative is not valid. Unless there is evidence that either a new lane of traffic or a bicycle lane must be efficacious, the author cannot fairly claim that the mere fact that a new lane of traffic has not accomplished its goal indicates that constructing a new bicycle lane will be the only more effective measure in reducing rush-hour traffic and commuting time on Blue Highway, rendering the argument unconvincing.

To summarize, the addition of a bike lane would not necessarily decrease the rush hour traffic on Blue Highway. To determine the soundness of the argument, we must evaluate the representativeness of the commuters surveyed. We should also investigate the case of Green Highway to find out why its added lane has failed and conduct a survey of the area around Blue Highway to gauge if a significant number of people would use a bike lane instead of driving. Finally, we need to assess the effectiveness of strategies other than adding a new traffic lane alone or a bike lane alone.

6. Reducing headaches using salicylates (Assumptions)

Relying on the fact that many companies have found the new use of salicylates as flavor additives, the author argues that the citizens of Mentia will suffer fewer headaches in the future as a direct result. To support the argument, the author cites a study that found a reduction of headaches reported by participants on average over a period of 20 years in the city of Mentia as salicylates became more commonly used commercially. However, this argument is based on a number of assumptions that render it unconvincing on its face and require further examination before we determine its validity.

The author assumes that a correlation means a causation. According to the given information, the study found only a correlation between the reduction of headaches per capita and the rise in use of salicylates. Since the article does mention that many foods already contain large quantities of salicylates, there is no way of knowing if the reduction is a result of these naturally occurring salicylates in the foods or their increased use in manufactured food. There is also the possibility that the lower numbers of headaches are due to false reporting or healthier lifestyles, or even environmental changes. For example, the residents may have felt less and less inclined to report headaches as this makes them seem healthier. If this should be true, the argument that the average Mentia resident will suffer fewer headaches as a result of consuming more salicylates would be undermined. Moreover, just because salicylates are the members of the same chemical family as aspirin does not necessarily mean they can be used like aspirin to treat headaches. Even if they can cure headaches, there is no guarantee that they can prevent headaches, viz. lowering the average number of headaches. If this is the case, it is even likely that the effect can be attributed to aspirin or similar medicine that has become increasingly common. Regardless, without relevant evidence, the author cannot fairly assert a direct connection between more use of salicylates and fewer incidences of headaches.

In addition, the author implies that companies will use salicylates as flavor additives. However, before companies finalize the plan to use salicylates as flavor additives, there needs to be testing to see if this is the case. After all, the article itself states that salicylates are chemically similar to aspirin, which can be quite harmful if overconsumed. This is even more of an issue if the research is on salicylates' effects on headaches. If they do indeed help reduce headaches, then that would mean they somehow influence a person's circulatory or nervous system. Given this, the use of salicylates would need strict regulation so as not to cause a pharmacological issue and may not obtain the government's approval of this use. Even if salicylates can be used safely as flavor additives, there is no guarantee that the residents will consume enough food with salicylates to reduce their headaches, because they may not like the flavor of the additives. Also, there is no guarantee that companies will be able to increase consumption of salicylates this way because they may find it difficult to add salicylates without destroying the original flavor of the food. It could even be that companies will give up salicylates as flavor additives altogether in favor of other cheaper alternatives. Should this be true, using salicylates as flavor additives may not be viable, rendering the prediction of further drop in headache numbers among the average Mentia resident unreasonable.

Finally, the author suggests that all other conditions that might affect the incidence of headaches will remain unchanged when companies use salicylates as flavor additives. However, the author offers no evidence that this is the case. It is possible that disease outbreaks will cause a dramatic increase in the number of headaches. It is also possible that the residents of Mentia will overwork and experience more stress and fatigue. It is even possible that the weather there will change in the future– for example, it may become more humid and hotter. Perhaps the residents will have a different lifestyle –for example, they may drink more alcohol. Or perhaps companies will add fewer salicylates as preservatives to foods because the residents do not enjoy them. In such scenarios, the citizens will probably suffer a greater number of headaches. This means even if more consumption of salicylates reduces incidence of headaches, the reduction is likely to be offset by the increase that other factors may lead to, thereby causing the number of headaches to remain unchanged or even rise. In that event, the assumption would prove unwarranted, and the prediction of further drop in headache numbers for the average resident of Mentia would be unjustified. Absent such scenarios, the prediction and its argument would be more credible.

In conclusion, it would be potentially disastrous for a company to add any new ingredient to its food products, much less one that has the possibility of affecting a person's health. To bolster the argument, the author must assure us that no changes serving to increase the average number of headaches will occur in the future. To better assess the argument, we should have more case studies of more diverse populations, with narrower parameters to see if salicylates do indeed have a positive effect on headaches, or conversely, if they have any harmful side effects.

7. Building a new bicycle lane on Blue Highway (Questions to Be Answered)

To address the issue of rush-hour traffic and an increasing commuting time on Blue Highway, the motorists' lobby has already made a proposal to widen the highway, but opponents recommend that a bicycle lane be a better alternative, citing Green Highway, which added its own new lane but experienced worse traffic jams. To justify the recommendation, the letter points out that many residents like cycling very much, and therefore the bike lane would motivate them to ride their bikes instead of driving. However, to determine whether opponents' recommendation should be adopted, we need answers to questions surrounding the representativeness of Blue Highway commuters surveyed, the connection between Green Highway's new lane and its worsening traffic jams, and the number of people willing to commute by bike.

To begin with, we must find out whether the surveyed commuters on Blue Highway are representative of general commuters on the highway. However, there is no data in this regard. The sample may be small and biased. It could be that only a few commuters have complained and that only those who have experienced increased commuting time have complained. Should this be the case, the respondents do not typify Blue Highway commuters in general. Perhaps despite increased rush-hour traffic, most commuters have experienced no increase in commuting time. Even if their commuting time has doubled, it may still be reasonable and does not warrant any important changes. Even assuming that there should be any important changes, the author should identify the true causes of the dramatic rise in traffic jams and in turn of commuting time and propose tailored measures. Unless the survey is valid, reliable, and representative, the author cannot justifiably claim that increased rush-hour traffic on Blue Highway has contributed to the residents' doubling of commuting time.

Next, we should consider whether the new lane on Green Highway led to its worsening traffic jams. Without relevant information, we can hardly ascertain what the root cause of the traffic jams was. Neither is there any indication as to the duration of those traffic jams. They could have been isolated incidents; but if they are a continuous issue since the new lane was constructed, then the argument may have a case. Before we accept the addition of a lane as the factor that has contributed to worse traffic, there needs to be more information on the area, such as how many people commute and the number of exit and entrance ramps, along with their locations. It may well be the case that Green Highway's traffic issues increased because of poor road design, loosened traffic rules or other contributing factors. It may also be the case that the trend last year was an aberration and will not last into the future. If this should be true, the assumption that the new lane was responsible for worsening traffic would be unwarranted, and the recommendation of a new bicycle lane would be weakened. Even if a new lane on Green Highway was not effective, one on Blue Highway could be effective, given their differences. For example, it is possible that Green Highway had already had enough traffic lanes whereas Blue Highway has too few lanes. In that event, addition of a lane to Blue Highway may be a viable strategy, rendering the argument invalid. To rule out an additional lane of traffic as a feasible measure for Blue Highway in decreasing traffic jams, the author must provide evidence that the worsening traffic on Green Highway was a direct result of its new lane.

In addition, we need to ask if the fact that many area residents like to ride bikes means that they will commute by bike. We want to know how many of the residents commute and whether they ride their bicycles when they commute. If few of the "keen bicyclists" commute, the recommendation of addition of a bicycle lane to Blue Highway is unreasonable. If the distance between the suburbs and the city center is very far, it would make cycling very inconvenient, even dangerous, considering adverse weather conditions. Or if many residents need to use their cars at work, commuting by bike would be undesirable. Furthermore, there is no guarantee that traffic would be reduced if more people used bicycles. After all, there is the possibility that having more cyclists on the road will cause comparable traffic congestion, even with the addition of a bike lane. In this case, the argument for a new bicycle lane would be undermined. More research into the number of people willing to ride their bicycles to work instead of driving and into traffic jam resulting from too many bike-riders on the road would provide better insight into whether rush hour traffic would be affected by the addition of a bike lane.

Finally, we wonder whether adding a bicycle lane is the only alternative. The letter seems to suggest that addition of a bicycle lane is the only option better than a new traffic lane. There is no clear evidence that the additional lane of traffic has been ineffective. Even if it has not achieved the desired outcome, this does not necessarily mean a bicycle lane is the sole alternative. It could be that neither the new lane of traffic alone nor the bicycle lane alone will be able to reduce rush-hour traffic and commuting time. If this is the case, another strategy needs to be adopted. By adding a new traffic lane and a bicycle lane at the same time, or by improving the road design, the commuters may anticipate less rush-hour traffic and commuting time. In that event, the assumption that merely a bicycle lane is a more desirable alternative is not valid. Unless there is evidence that either a new lane of traffic or a bicycle lane must be efficacious, the author cannot fairly claim that the mere fact that a new lane of traffic has not accomplished its goal indicates that constructing a new bicycle lane will be the only more effective measure in reducing rush-hour traffic and commuting time on Blue Highway, rendering the argument unconvincing.

To summarize, the addition of a bike lane would not necessarily decrease the rush hour traffic on Blue Highway. To determine the soundness of the recommendation and its argument, we must evaluate the representativeness of the commuters surveyed. We should also investigate the case of Green Highway to find out why its added lane has failed and conduct a survey of the area around Blue Highway to gauge if a significant number of people would use a bike lane instead of driving. Finally, we need to assess the effectiveness of strategies other than adding a new traffic lane alone or a bike lane alone.

8. Cutting Calatrava's funds budgeted for education and sports facilities (Specific Evidence)

In this article, a committee recommends that the city of Calatrava reduce its allocation of funds for public schools, athletic playing fields and other recreational facilities and increase funds for facilities and programs used by adults. To support the recommendation, the committee cites the previous year's birthrate, which was one-half that of five years before, as well as the expectation of an increase in adult population. To fully assess the argument, we need additional evidence.

We must have evidence that last year's birthrate is indicative of what will happen in the next decade. However, perhaps last year's birthrate was an aberration. Thus, the fact that the previous year's birth rate was half that of five years before is not itself proof that the birth rate is decreasing or will continue to decrease in the future. It could also be that the birthrate of five years ago was very high for some reason, but it began to decline four years ago and has remained unchanged or even slowly risen over the next four years. In these scenarios, it is unjustifiable to claim that the birthrate in the city is dropping and will continue to drop in the future, undermining the prediction of a significant drop in student enrollments in public schools. Since this budget plan spans a decade, there should be a better data set provided that can show the actual birthrate trend. If such a trend shows a real decline over the past five years, along with a credible reason that shows signs of continuing, then the suggested budgetary changes might be warranted. Conversely, if it cannot be proven that the decline will continue, then the foundation of the author's argument will be severely undermined.

Next, we should have evidence that the adult population of Calatrava will increase. However, the author offers no information on the number of people who will choose to stay in or leave the city. There is the chance that some adults will leave the city because of its reduced funding for education of their children. There is also the chance that changes in the economy or desirability of the area may result in an influx of younger residents, further lowering the rate of adults in the city. Should this be the case, the prediction that the number of adults in the city will rise may be unfounded, rendering the argument for increasing funding for facilities and programs used by adults unpersuasive. The argument would be better supported if census and immigration data showed that middle-aged and senior citizens are choosing to live in the city more and more in recent years. It would also be bolstered by survey data showing that people were growing less interested in having children.

Finally, we need evidence regarding the issue of the specific redirection of funds from athletic fields and other recreational facilities to more adult-oriented facilities. The author does not say exactly what these adult-oriented facilities are. It could be that they are not much different from the ones that are currently funded. If this should be the case, redirection of funds to facilities for adults would be unjustified. If the committee had survey data showing that the older population of the city desired different facilities, the argument would be strengthened. Moreover, it would be hard to justify defunding schools simply on the basis of potential but uncertain decreased enrollment in public schools, as we are not given any information on whether the current funds allocated to Calatrava's schools are sufficient for their needs. Even if the number of students enrolled in the public schools will drop considerably, this does not necessarily mean these schools' needs have been met, because they still need much funding for maintaining their facilities and hiring competent teachers each year, among other things. Even assuming their needs have been satisfied, there is no guarantee that the need of the city's education for funding for other uses has been gratified. Thus, we must have data on the city's facilities for adults and current funding of education to determine the soundness of the budget adjustment for the next ten years.

In conclusion, Calatrava's budget committee needs further research into the demographics of the city's population, specifically the birthrate trend, into the people's demand regarding facilities, and into the need of the city's education for funding. Without relevant evidence, we cannot properly evaluate the argument.

9. Does Parson City care more about good education than Blue City? (Specific Evidence)

The author concludes that Parson City citizens care more about a good public education than do Blue City residents, citing the fact that Parson has recently budgeted almost twice as much money each year as Blue for its public schools, despite having almost the same number of residents. However, this piece of evidence alone is not sufficient to support the conclusion. To fully assess the argument, we need additional evidence regarding reasons for both cities' disparity in spending on their respective public schools, representativeness of each city's recent spending behavior, and the actual needs for funding of each city's education.

There must be evidence that spending more tax money on public schools means placing a greater value on providing a good public education. However, the author offers no data in this regard. It is possible that Parson simply has more tax money to spend than Blue. The latter certainly wishes it had better-funded public education, but it may simply be unable to fund it. This does not necessarily mean it places less value on offering a good education in its public schools. It is also possible that Blue has spent a greater percentage of its overall budget on the public school system than Parson. Besides, the budgetary decisions of the local government do not necessarily reflect the desires of the citizens, but simply a trend of government behavior. It is likely that Blue's public schools rely more on donations from their citizens than those of Parson, and its residents have contributed much more on average to education in public schools than Parson residents. Any of the scenarios, if true, would undermine the conclusion that Parson residents care more about public education than the people of Blue, rendering the argument unconvincing. In the absence of relevant information, we find it hard to assess the argument.

In addition, there should be evidence that the recent spending behaviors of both cities presented by the letter are typical. However, the author furnishes no information in this respect. Even assuming that the budgetary differences represent residents' difference in value on public education, it is possible that the latest practices of both cities amount to just an aberration. It could very well be the case that with the exception of the most recent two years, Parson has budgeted less money in absolute terms and as a percentage of its total taxes for its public schools than has Blue. It could also be that Parson has invested large sums in construction of some new public schools recently. Either of the scenarios would weaken the claim that Parson residents value public education more highly than Blue residents do. Unless there is evidence that their recent practices are typical of their behaviors, the author cannot fairly assume that the former rank public education higher in importance than the latter do.

Finally, there needs to be evidence that Parson's public schools do not have greater needs than Blue's. If Parson's public school system has more needs, it must have a greater budget. For example, it may have a greater number of students. In this case, it requires a bigger budget. However, this does not necessarily mean its citizens care more about educating the students in its public schools. Also, there is an issue with the exact timeframe in which the spending disparity between Parson and Blue has occurred. The letter states that the difference in spending has happened recently, but gives no further information than that, making it possible that Blue's public schools have already been well-staffed and well-equipped with technology and other resources and no longer need to spend as much and that Parson is spending money that has been saved up for some time. Perhaps while Blue citizens are very concerned about quality of its public school education, the city encounters an urgent problem that calls for extra funding. All such scenarios would invalidate the claim that Parson citizens give higher priority to its public education than Blue residents do.

In sum, without further evidence, such as opinion surveys of the populace and budgetary plans from previous years with which to compare to predicted budgets, we cannot fully assess the claim that the people of Parson care more about a good public education than those of Blue.

10. Shortening work shifts to reduce the number of on-the-job accidents at Quiot (Assumptions)

The author recommends that Quiot Manufacturing make each of its work shifts shorter by one hour in order to reduce the number of on-the-job accidents, which the author claims has been a result of sleep deprivation, and boost productivity. To justify the recommendation, the article cites a statement by experts that fatigue and sleep deprivation are major factors responsible for the aforementioned issues, as well as a separate factory which already has work shifts shorter by one hour with an alleged successful result. The argument is full of assumptions and loopholes that we must scrutinize before we determine its soundness.

The author assumes that Quiot's longer work shifts are the reason for its higher number of on-the-job accidents and that the converse is true for Panoply. However, no evidence is provided to substantiate this. Poorly skilled employees could have contributed to more on-the-job accidents at Quiot. Equipment failure due to lack of maintenance could also have been responsible for them. In this case, it is likely that Quiot's greater number of on-the-job accidents is attributable to factors other than its longer work shifts. On the contrary, Panoply may have begun to hire more skilled workers or keep its machines in good repair. Perhaps it allowed its workers to take more breaks within a shift than Quiot. In that event, emulating Panoply by shortening work shifts at Quiot may not affect its number of on-the-job accidents. Also, the statement by "experts" regarding lack of sleep and exhaustion is itself quite vague. There is no study cited with relevant statistics to back it up. It is likely that fatigue or sleep deprivation has little to do with on-the-job accidents. Should this be true, Quiot risks wasting much time and losing productivity by implementing a scheme, which, while good-intentioned, may nonetheless have little effect on the number of its on-the-job accidents, rendering the argument in support of shortening its work shifts invalid.

Even if it is conceded that fatigue is to blame for the higher number of on-the-job accidents at Quiot, the author also implies that with the scheme in place, the workers will have enough sleep and an increase in productivity will certainly follow. However, this is not necessarily the case. It is possible that the employees will not use the extra hour to sleep or need more hours' sleep. For example, they may engage in after-work drinking with the extra hour and get very exhausted. If so, the assumption would prove unwarranted. Also, depending on the work ethic of the employees or simply the physical limitations they and the machines have, there is the chance that there will not be any significant increase in productivity at the plant. While there may be a connection between productivity and the number of accidents, the author has yet to establish that fewer accidents would boost productivity. In fact, if this proposal backfires, it may cause a decrease in productivity due to the fewer number of hours worked by the employees. Thus, if fatigue proves to be the root cause of Quiot's accidents, there will likely need to be additional measures put in place to ensure that productivity does not suffer from the reduced work times.

Finally, the author suggests that the past year's trend is typical of both plants. However, there is no evidence that this is true. It is possible that the trend during the past year was an aberration and may not continue: Quiot had more on-the-job accidents than Panoply because it had more new employees, but this year Quiot has the same number of on-the-job accidents and in the future, it may have fewer accidents than Panoply. Should this be the case, it would not be necessary for Quiot to reduce its accidents by following Panoply's example. Also, the phrase "30 percent more" is vague. It may indicate a significant number if the original number was great. If in the previous year Panoply had 100 on-the-job accidents whereas Quiot had 30 percent more, it means a great disparity. If Panoply had just 2 or 3 accidents whereas Quiot had 30 percent more, the difference is not significant. The assumption underlies the claim that if Quiot's employees work one hour less each shift, they will have adequate sleep and reduce the number of on-the-job accidents and increase productivity. However, if the trend last year is not typical of both plants, the assumption would be unwarranted, rendering the argument unfounded.

In sum, in order to determine whether Quiot will succeed by shortening each of its work shifts by one hour, we need more information about why the accidents at the plant occurred and in the case of the Panoply plant, whether its work-shift policy was the direct cause of the reduced number of accidents there. Also, we should have more evidence by way of research into whether fewer work hours would contribute to higher rates of production.

11. Is construction of <u>new generating plants</u> unnecessary? (Assumptions)

Citing surveys that indicate the increasing homeowner interest in energy conservation, newer and more energy efficient appliances, and new home heating technologies, the author concludes that there will be no need for new power plants in the future because the overall demand for electricity will not rise. The argument is replete with assumptions and loopholes that we must scrutinize before we determine its validity.

The author assumes that people will buy energy efficient appliances in quantities large enough to impact consumption of electricity. However, just because more energy efficient appliances will contribute to a lower demand for electricity does not necessarily mean that this is the case. After all, new technologies are often prohibitively expensive, such that only a marginal percentage of the population purchases them. It can often take decades for these high-tech appliances to be affordable to the masses, during which the need for electricity is unlikely to decrease. Besides, much in the same way that people overconsume "diet" food products because of their perceived healthiness, people may consume the same amount of electricity by increasing their usage of the more efficient appliances, due to their belief that they are using less electricity overall. If this should be true, the prediction that the demand for electricity may drop rather than rise would be unreasonable, and the argument that there will be no need for more generating plants would be undermined.

In addition, the author implies that many homeowners will buy new technologies for better home insulation and passive solar heating to reduce the need for electricity. However, no data is offered in this regard. It is likely that few homeowners will buy the new technologies. Even if some homeowners buy them, the quantities may not be large enough to cause less need for energy. Even if there is less need for energy, there will still be the same or more need for electricity, because better home insulation and passive solar heating may be applicable to new homes rather than old homes. Even though residential electricity usage levels off or drops because of use of efficient appliances and home heating technologies, there is no guarantee that commercial demand for electricity will not rise. Should this be the case, the assumption would prove unjustified, and the claim would be invalid that total electric usage in the area will not rise and that there will be no need for new generating plants.

Finally, while the memorandum states that the three current plants have met the area's power needs over the past two decades, it suggests that they will be adequate for future needs. However, no evidence is provided to substantiate this. A myriad of factors could cause an increase in the demand for electricity, such as some new power-hungry device that becomes widely popular, or a mass migration of people or businesses to the city for some reason. There is also the possibility of natural disaster or simple equipment failure that may cause a shortage of power that could be avoided by having new plants built. There is even the possibility that even though they will be adequate for the area's electric needs, the old plants are less energy efficient than new plants using new technology. Any of the scenarios, if true, would undermine the assumption and in turn the argument. Thus, it would be unjustifiable to assume that simply because the plants have always fulfilled the area's needs in the past, they will automatically do so in the future.

In sum, the memorandum's prediction that no new power producing plants will be needed in the future is not grounded in facts. The exorbitant cost of new energy-efficient technologies, along with unpredictable events in the future, could be reason enough to construct new power plants.

12. Monitoring employees' internet use (Assumptions)

The letter to the company president of Climpson Industries recommends that the firm install software on company computers to detect the internet use of employees in order to prevent them from wasting time, nurture a better work ethic, and boost the company's profits overall. The argument is rife with assumptions and loopholes that need close examination before we determine its soundness.

The author suggests that workers are wasting time on the internet on personal or recreational activities. However, there is no concrete proof given that they are doing so. It is likely that few workers participate in such activities. It is also likely that even if some do, they are simply taking a short break before beginning the next task. It is even likely that the employees' productivity is already optimal. If this should be true, the assumption that workers are engaging in something unproductive would be unfounded, invalidating the argument that installing software will help to deter workers from wasting time and boost productivity and profits. Before the company takes such an extreme measure as monitoring its workers' computer activity, there should first be some investigation into whether the workers are wasting time, and whether that is affecting their productivity. Otherwise, the company will be spending a large sum of money on installing what may turn out to be a piece of useless surveillance software.

Building on the suggestion that employees spend time doing something unrelated to work on the internet, the author implies that installing the monitoring software will be successful at preventing employees from wasting their time. However, this need not be the case. It is possible that if employees are engaging in the aforementioned activities and are determined enough to keep on doing so, they may find ways around the software, rendering it moot. Similarly, they may simply use their own personal devices as distractions, such as their smartphones or mobile gaming consoles. In either scenario, the monitoring software on the company's computers would be completely useless, rendering the argument gratuitous. Even if the monitoring software can succeed in deterring employees from unproductive internet activities, there is no guarantee that it can prevent them from using other ways to waste time, for example, talking much without doing anything in the workplace. If so, the assumption about the impact of installing the monitoring software is unwarranted. Before the company takes action, it must investigate whether the recommendation will carry the intended results.

Even if the implication is valid, the author also assumes that the monitoring software and punishments will do anything to spur productivity by enhancing work ethic and boosting overall profits. However, there is no evidence provided to support this. It is likely that workers will decide to become less productive in retaliation for what they may view as unfair treatment. Alternatively, they may quit altogether, and the company may have a hard time hiring new workers, thanks in large part to the ability of employees to complain publicly about policies that are perceived to be oppressive. In that event, the argument for the monitoring and punishments will be weak. Before identifying the cause of the present work ethic, the author cannot justifiably claim that the monitoring software and punishments will help enhance the company's work ethic. Other factors, such as salary and vacation, may be responsible for the current work ethic of the employees. Also, profit is a function of revenue and costs. Installing the software may cost large sums of money, rendering the policy undesirable. To substantiate the assumption about the benefits of installing the monitoring software and administering punishments, the author must account for other factors that may result in improved work ethic and weigh the costs of taking the course of action against the revenue.

In conclusion, the recommendation is not supported by enough evidence to justify its implementation. The worst-case scenario is that the company wastes much time and money on a piece of software that is either useless or demoralizing. Before the recommendation is adopted, there should be a close examination of the assumptions that underlie the argument to see whether they are warranted.

13. Restricting showerhead water flow in Sunnyside Towers (Questions to Be Answered)

Relying on the recent change to low-flow showerheads in three of the buildings in an apartment complex by the name of Sunnyside Towers, the author predicts that modifying the rest of the twelve towers will help to increase the Sunnyside Corporation's profits significantly due to saving costs on water. Before we determine the validity of the prediction and its argument, we need answers to some key questions.

We must know whether after modification of showerheads, water will be saved in the first three of the buildings. The letter starts by mentioning that the showerheads only allow one-third the normal flow of water, and that there has not yet been any data on water usage before and after the change. Even if there has been data for the first month since the installation, we are not sure that it will be representative of the water use of the three buildings in the future. It is possible that if less water flows through the showerheads, and, as the letter mentions, the pressure is lower, the tenants may use the shower for a longer period. It is also possible that future tenants will use more water per capita, or that other uses of water will rise. In such scenarios, there may be no net change in their water use or there may be even an increase; thus, there would be no financial savings. Even if there will be financial savings, there is no guarantee that the savings will be significant. In that event, the prediction of profits as a result of modifying showerheads in the first three buildings would be gratuitous. To determine whether there will be a drop in water use, we need information about actual water usage before and after the adjustment.

Conceding that the showerheads will lower the cost of water, we should know whether the complaints about low water pressure involve serious issues. It is possible that there have been only a few residents since the adjustment, so there are only a few complaints. This may mean a high percentage of complaints. It is also possible that many have complaints, but they do not bother to report them. The worst scenario would be that many who have heard about the showerhead problem have chosen not to live in the buildings. Even if there have been only a few complaints about low water pressure and no problems with showers during the first month since the adjustment, there is the possibility that in the future many more complaints will be made, that many more problems with showers will be reported, and that many more tenants will vacate because they are displeased. In this case, the argument for financial savings and the prediction of increasing profits for the company will be tenuous. If the complaints do not involve serious issues, and there are no issues other than the complaints, the argument for saving money and the prediction of the profits would be strengthened.

Even accepting that there is no issue other than the few complaints that do not involve serious problems, we also need to know whether change to low-flow showerheads to restrict water flow throughout the rest of the buildings will boost the profits of the company more remarkably. Profit is a function of revenues minus costs. The potential costs as well as financial savings should be considered. It is likely that the cost to modify all the showerheads in the entire twelve-building complex will not be offset by the savings on water, not to mention any problems that may require fixing down the line; while there have not been any major issues with showers yet, there may be unforeseen difficulties in the future. It is also likely that the adjustment will cost much more on average in the rest of the buildings than in the first three buildings. It is even likely that the rates charged by water companies will rise. Any of the scenarios, if true, would undermine the prediction of further considerable increase in profits. Otherwise, there would be a better case for the prediction. However, without information about the costs of adjusting the showerheads and future rates, we cannot ascertain the soundness of the prediction and its argument.

In conclusion, the owner of Sunnyside Towers should rethink the decision to modify all the apartments' showerheads with the new low-flow model, as there is not enough data to support the claim that it will save on water and increase profits significantly. To better evaluate the argument, we need a clear cost-benefit analysis that incorporates room for future maintenance expenditures and higher rates.

14. Using fish oil supplements to prevent colds and reduce absenteeism by emulating East Meria (Specific Evidence)

Relying on a study which reports that in an area called East Meria, people only visit the doctor for cold-related issues once or twice a year, while at the same time consuming large amounts of fish, the author recommends that people in West Meria take Ichthaid, a nutritional supplement derived from fish oil, to prevent colds and reduce absences from school and work. Yet we need further evidence in order to see if the argument is indeed valid.

The author must provide evidence for the connection between the consumption of fish and the low number of cold-related doctor visits in East Meria. However, no data is given in this regard. There is the possibility that the study involves a small sample and is not statistically reliable and the people surveyed are not representative of the general population of East Meria. There is also the possibility that people in East Meria simply do not see as much of a need to go to the hospital if they have a cold, save for the most serious situations. In these scenarios, the connection is groundless. If the connection is to be established, there needs to be more data on the actual number of colds contracted by the people in the area on a yearly basis, which can then be compared to the number of cold-related hospital visits. Assuming that the people in East Meria do get colds less often, there is still no real proof provided to show that their consumption of fish is the cause. There could be a myriad of other factors that contribute to such a phenomenon, like naturally strong immune systems, hygienic practices, or even other foods. It could even be that the people in East Meria cannot afford to see a doctor for more than once or twice a year for the treatment of colds and choose to buy some medicine from OTC. Unless there is evidence that some chemical in fish, specifically fish oil, can help the human body resist the colds, the author cannot justifiably assert that consuming fish will do anything to help prevent colds.

Even if there is a connection between fish consumption and fewer colds, the author should offer evidence that taking Ichthaid works as well as eating fish. Even if the connection between fish consumption and the small number of cold-related doctor visits in East Meria is established, this does not necessarily mean that it will hold true in West Meria. The people in West Meria may be allergic to fish, already consume too much fish, find fish too expensive, or have other more effective ways to prevent colds. Even if consuming fish will contribute to fewer colds in West Meria, there is no guarantee that taking Ichthaid will be equally effective. Since Ichthaid is simply a nutritional supplement derived from fish oil, it is likely that taking Ichthaid will not be able to prevent colds, as the author alleges for fish consumption, rendering the recommendation of taking Ichthaid unreasonable. Even assuming that taking Ichthaid is as effective at reducing colds as eating fish, the author needs to provide clear evidence that the daily use of Ichthaid is necessary. There is the possibility of negative health effects resulting from an overdose of the supplement. It stands to reason, then, that without detailed analysis of the contents of Ichthaid, the suggestion that students and employees take it every day carries a high chance of causing unforeseen health problems even worse than colds, making the recommendation unfounded.

Even if the daily consumption of Ichthaid is able to prevent colds, the author also needs to furnish evidence that preventing colds can reduce absenteeism. However, the author only states that colds are offered most often as the reason for absenting oneself from school and work. Just because colds are the reason given most frequently does not necessarily mean they are the real reason. It is possible that students or employees give colds as the reason because colds are the most acceptable reason. It is also possible that using colds as the reason requires no medical proof whereas other excuses often require some form of proof. It is even possible that students or employees are absent because they are not motivated to study or work. In such scenarios, no connection between colds and absences has been established. Even if such a connection is substantiated, there is no guarantee that there exists the link of absenteeism to colds. Perhaps colds cause absences, but they may not cause absenteeism, chronic absence that could result from economic factors or chronic health problems. Therefore, preventing colds does not necessarily lower absenteeism. Without relevant evidence, we cannot fully evaluate the recommendation of taking Ichthaid daily to prevent colds and decrease absenteeism.

In conclusion, the author should provide more evidence before we determine the soundness of the argument. We must know if there are truly fewer cases of the cold in East Meria, and if this lower number of incidences is the result of fish consumption. Also, we should have detailed lab research into the chemical contents of the supplement Ichthaid to ensure that there is no component that may cause undue harm. Finally, we need proof of the connection between colds and absenteeism.

15. Revitalizing Transopolis through industrialization of a residential area (Specific Evidence)

The planning department of the city of Transopolis recommends the implementation of a revitalization initiative in which substandard housing areas are redeveloped into industrial zones for factories. To support the recommendation, the article cites a previous plan in another area of the city near the freeway that saw a decrease in crime rates in the area, and an overall property tax increase in the city. It also posits that since some of the houses near the proposed area are vacant, the tenants displaced by the plan will be able to find new accommodation easily. Yet we need some extra evidence before we determine whether the city should approve of such a plan.

To begin with, we must have evidence that there exists a link between the adaptation of the freeway area for industrial use and its later success. However, the author does not cite any concrete statistics pointing to a link between the industrialization of the area and the decline in crime and property tax increase. A ten-year span could witness numerous other factors that may have played a role, such as a general economic improvement in the city, or new actions by local law enforcement that deterred criminal activity. There is the possibility that since the people were displaced by the factories, the criminal elements simply migrated to different areas and are now wreaking havoc elsewhere in the city. There is also the possibility that despite the increase in the city's overall property tax revenues, tax revenue from properties in the freeway area after conversion did not increase while the properties in other areas of the city contributed to the city's overall property-tax revenue rise. There is even the possibility that the city increased its property tax rates soon after the redevelopment of the freeway area. Any of the scenarios, if true, would undermine the link between the conversion of the area and its later success.

As to the potential for the industrial development to revitalize the city, we should have evidence that because the plan worked in one part of the city, it will work in another. There is the risk that the area of the city the department plans to alter may not be suitable for industrial development. Demographics play a very important role in the implementation of economic programs. For example, there could be a dearth of skilled workers who are able to work in factories or other facilities, or perhaps the property owners will be hesitant to lease their land for fear of drastic price fluctuations caused by the rezoning of the area. There is also the possibility that the land will be too expensive for industrialization. Even if the new area is suitable for conversion, its crime rates may not drop, and its property tax revenues may not rise. For example, the probably non-residential nature of the freeway area could have witnessed a decrease in rates of crimes such as burglary while the houses and apartments in the neighborhoods of the new area may be targets for burglary, making it more difficult to reduce crime rates. Besides, the city may be lowering its property tax rates in response to decreasing property sales. If the area to be converted differs in so many ways from the part industrialized, it is likely that similar action in it may fail, rendering the argument unconvincing. Unless the author can offer evidence that the freeway area and the area to be converted are sufficiently alike in ways that might affect the impact of conversion, we are not convinced that the new area will have the same success.

Finally, we need evidence that because there are vacancies in nearby neighborhoods, displaced residents will be willing or able to relocate. However, the author provides no data in this regard. The fact that houses and apartments are currently unoccupied does not necessarily mean the people to be displaced want to live there. It is likely that they are in disrepair, unfit for living. Even if the people want to relocate to the houses or apartments available, they may be usually priced far outside the range of the people who come from lower income areas such as the one targeted for redevelopment. It is also likely that the number of houses or apartments is too small to accommodate the residents to be displaced, causing a homelessness issue that the city may find hard to address. Thus, this plan could have a very high chance of creating an even worse economic situation for the people it may displace. Should this be the case, the recommendation of revitalizing the city by industrial development of another area would be weakened.

In conclusion, if this plan is to be seriously considered, the author must first provide solid evidence that it was a direct contributor to the decline in local crime rates and the increase in property taxes. Furthermore, the author should analyze the previous example and the new area in question to see if they are comparable in order to ensure that the plan will have a similar effect. Lastly, the city should take measures to guarantee that the citizens who will be forced to relocate will have the opportunity to afford homes in the nearby area so as not to negatively affect their lives.

16. Will Sartorian's new <u>alpaca overcoat</u> sell well? (Specific Evidence)

The author argues that Sartorian, a men's clothing company, should recontinue its line of alpaca overcoats. To support the argument, the memo assumes that the coats will sell well because of "pent up customer demand" for the product since the last time they were sold five years ago and because of the fact that its main competitor has discontinued producing such coats. It also assumes that because prices for clothing have increased in the preceding five years, consumers will be willing to pay higher prices for the overcoats and the company will garner more profits. However, to determine the soundness of the argument, we need some crucial evidence.

To begin with, we must have evidence that a new fabric supplier is a sufficient condition for resuming production of Sartorian's popular alpaca overcoats. However, the author provides no data in this regard. The overcoats were popular five years ago, but there is no guarantee that they will still be popular. Given the rapid change of fashion, it is highly likely that they represent something outmoded. If this is true, the company risks wasting money by restarting its manufacturing of this line of products. Also, the company discontinued the business because it was unable to secure reliable supplies of excellent wool fabric. The article simply mentions that it has a new fabric supplier. It is likely that the new supplier will be an unreliable one of alpaca. It is also likely that one supplier will be too small in number to be reliable in providing the required fabric, or that factors other than the supplier were responsible for the unreliability at the time and could still make the alpaca supply unreliable nowadays. Any of these scenarios, if true, would cast serious doubt on Sartorian's plan to resume production of its alpaca overcoats.

In addition, we need evidence regarding demand of customers and their willingness to pay high prices for alpaca coats. The author claims that there will be a strong demand for the coats akin to pressure that builds up over time. If there were some relevant statistics, such as consumer demand surveys to back up this claim, it could be more plausible. However, as it stands, the idea sounds a bit incredible in the face of a market that tends to change rather quickly. Even if there is still a strong demand for the coats, it may have been satisfied by new companies. Also, the disappearance of pressure from the company's major competitor in alpaca overcoats does nothing to help the situation; if anything, it may suggest a decrease in demand for alpaca overcoats. There is even the chance that the plan could backfire completely, as people may perceive the company as backwards or lacking vision due to its backing of a dated style. If this should be true, the assumption about pent-up customer demand would be unwarranted and the argument for resuming production of the alpaca overcoats gratuitous. Moreover, there needs to be evidence that customers will be willing to pay high prices for alpaca coats. The author assumes that people still want the product very much and that their perception of alpaca overcoats will be comparable to that of the clothing whose price has increased. However, there is the possibility that people will not want to pay for the overcoats at all, much less at higher prices than before, even though the overall prices of clothing have increased. In fact, those who remember the lower cost of the alpaca overcoats in the past may refuse to buy the newer, higher priced ones, sparking a backlash against the product. Should this be the case, the assumption about customers' willingness to pay higher prices for the same product would be unfounded.

Finally, we lack evidence regarding company profits. The author claims that because of potential high demand for and higher prices of the product, the company profits will rise. We have poked holes in the assumptions about the high demand and higher prices, but even if the assumptions prove warranted, there is the likelihood that the company profits will remain the same or even decrease. Profit is a function of revenue and costs. If the revenues that come from selling large quantities of alpaca overcoats at prices higher than in the past exceed the costs of purchasing fabric, manufacturing and selling the overcoats, and employing people, among other things, the company may anticipate an increase in profit. Otherwise, the company can only hope for no change or a negative change in profit. A span of five years could have witnessed a dramatic rise in fabric prices and employee salaries. The new supplier may not be able to supply the company with enough fabric. Such scenarios could dramatically raise the costs and make the business unprofitable, rendering the argument implausible. Even if the company can be profitable in its sale of alpaca overcoats, there is no guarantee that it can turn a profit in the sale of other clothing. Should this be true, the claim that resuming production of the company's alpaca overcoats would boost its overall profitability is warrantless.

To conclude, the key evidence that we should have before the company moves forward with this plan involves whether pent-up customer demand for its alpaca overcoats exists. The author could obtain it through customer surveys and other market research strategies to see if people are buying comparable items. Included in such surveys could be questions as to whether consumers would be willing to pay higher prices for the new coats. Without relevant information, we cannot fully assess the argument and without a sound argument, the company could incur a huge risk by restarting to sell alpaca overcoats at increased prices.

17. Will a new seafood restaurant in Bay City be successful? (Specific Evidence)

The author recommends building a new Captain Seafood restaurant in Bay City because it will be both popular and profitable. To justify the recommendation, the article cites a thirty-percent increase in seafood dish consumption in restaurants in the city, along with the fact that there are no seafood-focused restaurants in the city and that most Bay City families are double-income homes, which, according to a nationwide study, eat out more than ten years ago, and are more health-food oriented. Unfortunately, these bits of information are not sufficient evidence to bolster the argument.

We must have evidence that a 30 percent increase in seafood consumption in Bay City restaurants justifies the opening of a Captain Seafood restaurant that specializes in seafood. While the increase is worth looking at, it does not indicate with any certainty that people will be willing to eat at the new seafood-focused restaurant. A 30 percent increase may not be significant if the consumption five years before was very small or even negligible. Also, there is no guarantee that the trend of increase will continue. Even if seafood consumption continues to increase, the rise may not be significant enough to sustain a new restaurant that concentrates on seafood. It is equally likely that people will prefer to eat at the restaurants they are familiar with or will simply prefer the specific seafood dishes that those locations offer to those of the new restaurant. This could be especially true in the case of families, as one or more members may not wish to eat seafood and would feel alienated at a restaurant that specializes in seafood. If this is true, the new seafood restaurant will be unnecessary, rendering the recommendation unreasonable.

We should also have evidence that just because a family eats out more often, it will for some reason want to eat at the new restaurant. A national survey has found that double-come families eat fewer home-cooked meals recently, but such a trend may not continue, nor may it be true for the people in Bay City. It is likely that the residents in Bay City eat as many home-cooked meals as before or even more home-cooked meals than before. In this case, the recommendation would be unjustified. Even assuming that the residents there have fewer home-cooked meals than before, this does not necessarily mean that they eat out more often; perhaps they rely on catering services and delivered meals more. Even if they eat out more, it is possible that they do not consume seafood. Even if they consume seafood, it is possible that they will not do it at the new restaurant. These families, though benefiting from having a little extra money, may have no room in their budgets for new restaurants; they may, instead, prefer to stick with what they know they like to avoid wasting money. In that event, the finding that two-income families dine out more than before may not benefit a sit-down restaurant that only serves seafood dishes, invalidating the suggestion of operating a profitable restaurant that features seafood. Also, the article mentions that these families are more health food oriented, which seems to imply that seafood is healthy, or is at least perceived as such. However, there is no evidence for this in the article; seafood may be more often contaminated with pollutants such as mercury and other harmful chemicals. Therefore, the idea is unfounded that the new restaurant will succeed based on the implication that seafood is healthy.

Finally, we need evidence that the new seafood-focused restaurant will be quite profitable. It is likely that the new restaurant will be unprofitable. This likelihood could account for the fact that no current restaurant in the city serves only seafood dishes. Profit is a function of revenue and costs. The new restaurant can anticipate some revenues from double-income families if they dine in it, but its revenues may not be able to cover its costs, rendering it unprofitable. We do not know the costs of launching and promoting the restaurant and obtaining healthy seafood. Nor do we know how many families will eat at the new restaurant, how often they will, and how much they are willing to pay. In this case, the prediction of a profitable seafood restaurant in Bay City is unreasonable. Moreover, it is possible that there were some city restaurants whose specialty was seafood, but they closed because of unprofitable business. It is also possible that the demand for seafood in the city has been fulfilled by the currently operating restaurants that do not specialize in seafood. If this is true, a restaurant dedicated to seafood alone is unlikely to be profitable, obviating the need for the new Captain Seafood restaurant in Bay City.

In sum, the argument is in dire need of further research into the profitability of starting a new restaurant that specializes in seafood in terms of the willingness of Bay City residents to eat at such a restaurant instead of the current restaurants that serve seafood as well as other dishes. It would also help if evidence could be provided showing that the incomes of the families in Bay City are sufficient to fit in another restaurant option. Lastly, the connection between healthy eating and seafood needs considerable explanation by way of current scientific data and a survey showing consumer perceptions regarding seafood's healthiness.

18. Consuming dairy products to prevent osteoporosis (Specific Evidence)

The author concludes that consuming a large quantity of dairy products as a part of one's diet can increase the risk of osteoporosis, even though such foods are rich in substances that are necessary for building and maintaining bones. To support the conclusion, the author cites a study that found a correlation between high dairy product consumption and high rates of bone fractures. However, this study alone is not sufficient to justify the author's claim, and thus we need further evidence to better assess the argument.

We must have evidence regarding the sample of the study. The author provides no information about the number of participants other than saying that the study observed "a large number of people". Without more specific details on the sample size, it is possible that while the number of people may have indeed been significant, they could have been from a single area or genetic group, an anomaly which would distort the results. In this case, the increase in breakages could have come from those people who were already prone to the condition. Since osteoporosis can be influenced by genetic factors, it would be necessary to study not only a large number of people, but a large number of people with diverse genetic histories, divided into groups where researchers could see if consuming large quantities of dairy products results in higher rates of bone fractures regardless of genetic predispositions. If the answer is affirmative, the argument would be strengthened. Unless the sample is valid, reliable, and representative, it is unfair to claim that a diet rich in dairy products may raise the risk of osteoporosis instead of reducing it.

Even assuming that genes do not play a role in osteoporosis, we need evidence that some participants of the study had a diet rich in dairy products. In order for the results to be correct, we should have surveys of the study group in order to find out how many people already had osteoporosis, and then factor that into the statistical findings accordingly. It is likely that those who consistently ingested dairy products throughout the study had consumed few such products before whereas the other participants had consumed large quantities of such products, leading to the scenario where the former group had had a higher rate of bone fractures to begin with. In that event, the author ignores the possibility that consumption of dairy products could have been responsible for a lower rate of bone breakages, rendering the argument incredible. Moreover, there is no guarantee that the subjects with a higher rate of bone fractures had a diet rich in dairy products. Just because the participants consumed the dairy products consistently does not necessarily mean they had a diet rich in dairy products. It is likely that this group consumed the products in smaller quantities, which means it was a diet less rich in dairy products. Even if the participants consumed more dairy products, there is the possibility that the products had less vitamin D and calcium per gram and that their bodies absorbed less. If this should be true, the argument that diets rich in dairy products will increase rather than decrease the likelihood of osteoporosis would be undermined.

Genetic factors and dairy consumption aside, we lack evidence for the role that other factors play in bone fractures. The article mentions that osteoporosis causes the bones to weaken considerably with age. Perhaps the participants observed to have a higher rate of bone fractures were much older than the other participants. In this case, they could have had more bone fractures despite consumption of more dairy products. The author also overlooks the possibility that many of the bone fractures that were reported in the study are attributable to sports injuries, car crashes, or other accidents. Perhaps the people that consumed a proportionally large number of dairy products did so to supplement an active lifestyle that could have led to bone fractures. Or perhaps they had a higher incidence of bone fractures because they took less vitamin D and calcium as supplements. Or perhaps they had no access to special safeguards against accidental injuries which were available for all the other participants who lived in the nursing homes. Any of the scenarios, if true, would weaken the argument. Without knowing the precise cause of each case, the author cannot confidently assert that consuming large amounts of dairy products was responsible for higher rates of osteoporosis.

In conclusion, if the argument is to be taken seriously, there must be more specific information about the study cited. The information includes but is not limited to the following: genetic histories of the subjects indicating their chances of naturally developing osteoporosis, lifestyle surveys to see if the subjects regularly consumed dairy products and participated in sports or dangerous activities that could cause broken bones, and of course, more diverse study groups that could provide more solid evidence that the consumption of dairy products has similar effects across various groups.

19. Wearing helmets may not actually be good for bicycle safety (Assumptions)

Reasoning that the increase in helmet usage over a ten-year period by bicyclists has led to a two-hundred percent increase in bicycle-related accidents because bicyclists ride less safely as a result of an increased sense of security from wearing helmets, the author recommends that the government shift its focus from telling people to wear helmets to educating them on bicycle safety. To ascertain the soundness of the argument, we need to scrutinize its multiple assumptions.

The author assumes that the respondents of the two studies are representative of bicyclists nationwide. However, with reference to the studies, no clear details are given by the newsletter. One study only mentions the increase in the number of cyclists who wear helmets, which was self-reported, and the other study the 200 percent increase in bike accidents. The self-reported data may not have been reliable, because the respondents may have reported wearing helmets simply to appear that they are responsible and safety conscious. In this case, there could be no increase or even decrease in the number of people who wear helmets, invalidating the claim that more helmet usage by bicyclists over a decade has resulted in a dramatic rise in bike-related accidents. The respondents may also be an aberration, consisting mostly of youths who take more risks, distorting the results. Either of the scenarios would make the respondents unrepresentative of all bicyclists nationwide. Besides, the increase in accidents is not combined with any other data, such as the actual number of bike related accidents before and now. It is possible that there were only a small number of accidents ten years prior, and thus a two-hundred percent increase would still be a relatively insignificant number of accidents overall. If this should be true, then the recommendation of educating people about bike safety instead of telling them to wear helmets would be unfounded.

Next, the author implies that the accidents are a result of the feeling of safety bestowed by the helmets. Yet, no information about the real cause of the accidents is given. Perhaps the increase in the number of accidents is the result of an aging population of drivers that cannot see as well or react as quickly as their younger selves. Or perhaps the increase is attributable to roads in bad condition or the weather conditions. Or perhaps increasing numbers of people riding bikes now are responsible for the rise in accidents. If the number of bicyclists wearing helmets had been misrepresented, not wearing helmets could also have been the culprit in bike accidents. Any of the scenarios, if true, would render the assumption about the reasons for the rise in accident numbers unwarranted and invalidate the argument that the government should focus more on education about bicycle safety than on encouraging or requiring helmet use. Without more information about exactly what has happened in each case from post-accident interviews or traffic camera footage, it would be very illogical to simply link the cause to a feeling of safety that may not exist.

Finally, the author suggests that all the bike-related accidents have involved serious injuries and the proposed course of action of government will be adequate to prevent them. However, the author offers no evidence to substantiate this. The newsletter mentions that the goal of the government's new focus will be to reduce the number of serious injuries from bike accidents but does not differentiate between the seriousness of the accidents.

Even if there has been an increase in bike-related accidents, and the number may even be significant, it is possible that most of them are minor, or even involve no injury at all. In this case, the assumption about the severity of injuries would prove unwarranted, and the argument for the government to concentrate on education about safety rather than on more helmet usage would collapse. More importantly, the number of severe accidents may have decreased thanks to the increase in the wearing of helmets. If this is the case, then it is possible that the helmets are to thank and should not be ignored by the government. Also, just because wearing helmets fails to prevent bike-related accidents does not necessarily mean education about bike safety will help to reduce the number of severe bicycle-related accidents. For example, it is unlikely to be effective when the cause is road conditions. Perhaps education about bike safety often helps riders decrease the number of minor accidents. In that event, the argument would be undermined. Without more information about the severity of the bike accidents over the past decade, the author cannot justifiably recommend more focus on education about bicycle safety.

In conclusion, if the argument is to be taken seriously, it must first provide more specific study data to show that the two-hundred percent increase in accidents represents a significant number of accidents, and that an increased feeling of safety from wearing a helmet was the direct cause of the accidents. Furthermore, there should be an investigation into the severity of injuries to see if it is necessary for the government to shift its focus on the issue.

20. Beach sand erosion on the island of Tria (Specific Evidence)

Relying on the fact that replenishing the sand on the nearby island of Batia successfully protected buildings near the beach and on the assumption that such preservation on Tria Island will result in future improvements of the tourism industry there, the author concludes that the tourism bureau of Tria Island should start charging tourists for using the beaches in order to raise money for sand replenishment. However, we do not find the argument convincing, and believe its assessment requires extra evidence.

We must have evidence regarding whether charging tourists for beach use on Tria will raise enough money to cover all the costs of replenishing the sand on the beaches. Yet, the letter makes no mention of how much sand replenishment would cost, nor exactly how the money would be collected. It is very likely, for instance, that people would forgo visiting the area due to the charge, and instead choose to visit a free beach. Even if tourists agree to pay for using the beaches, there is no guarantee that the charge will be sufficient for replenishing the sand. It is also likely that both tourists and residents are willing to pay for beach access and make the beaches remain as crowded as it is now, rendering the plan a self-defeating endeavor. If this is the case, the assumption about securing enough funding for sand replenishment may prove unwarranted. Without a price quote or a budgetary plan, the author cannot decide whether the plan will raise adequate money, or whether after enough money has been raised, it will be wasted or misused.

Granted that the tourism bureau on Tria is able to successfully raise the necessary funds and manage them properly, we should have evidence regarding the chances of the sand replenishment plan's success. True, there is the given example of the island of Batia, but little information is given to prove that replenishing Batia's sand protected its buildings. Even if it did, that does not necessarily mean it will work on Tria. Perhaps Batia did not need to charge its tourists for using the beaches whereas Tria needs to, making it more difficult for Tria to succeed. Or perhaps Batia had fewer beaches that required sand replenishment. Or perhaps Batia's beaches had much less erosion of sand. Any of the scenarios, if true, would make Tria too different from Batia to justify the same course of action. Unless the author provides more specific information to show exactly how the plan succeeded on Batia and how this example relates to Tria Island, we cannot fully evaluate the argument.

Finally, we need evidence that the tourist industry will be positively affected. However, the letter gives no indication of how the tourism industry of Tria has been or could be affected. It says only that erosion of beach sand is a threat and overlooks other threats to beach preservation. It is possible that people have used the beaches so often for picnics that they are no longer attractive to tourists. It is also possible that they are littered with too much garbage to be a place of interest. In such scenarios, the beaches may not be preserved even after sand replenishment. Even if beaches on Tria are preserved, there is no guarantee that its tourist industry will become better in the long run. Factors such as geopolitical conflicts, all forms of pollution, or simply a shift in what is popular among tourists could render this initiative entirely moot. If this should be true, the conclusion that preservation of beaches and buildings is sufficient for long term improvement of Tria's tourist industry would be baseless.

In brief, before deciding to go ahead with this plan to prevent erosion of beach sand, Tria's tourism bureau should make a very clear financial plan both to collect and to spend funds for the project, as well as a more detailed analysis of the Batia example to clarify any parallels or differences between its situation and that of Tria. It would also be prudent to survey tourists to determine whether tourism trends still favor Tria's beaches, and whether charging for beach access will not negatively affect the tourism market.

21. The available space in West Egg's landfill may last much longer than expected (Specific Evidence)

The author relies on a range of evidence, including recycling statistics and a survey, to conclude that West Egg Town's landfill will last significantly longer than previously expected. However, the argument is not well supported and requires additional evidence for full assessment.

The first piece of evidence needed involves the past and future increase in recycling. The author assumes that the doubling of recycling is significant and will continue. However, the one-hundred percent increase in the past two years may be insignificant because the amount of recycling may have been negligible to begin with. Even if the increase is considerable, there is no guarantee that the trend will persist. The author also assumes that if the cost of normal trash pick-up doubles, it will act as an incentive to recycle. However, this is an unfair assumption, since we do not know how much the cost is, nor how inclined the residents will be to choose convenience over costs, nor whether West Egg citizens have a choice between recycling or disposing of the refuse that often feeds the landfill. Additionally, there is nothing mentioned about a method of enforcing recycling, leaving the plan vulnerable to the whims of the population. It is possible that the cost of normal trash pickup is so low that people will not care about its doubling or will still prefer the convenience of not separating their recyclables. It is also possible that even if they are inclined to recycle more, they have to contribute some refuse to the landfill. If this is true, a future rise in recycling may be gratuitous, rendering the author's projection that the landfill will not reach full capacity until much later than originally expected unfounded.

The second piece of evidence required has to do with the assumption that just because the amount of recycled plastic, metal, and paper will increase, there will be any significant effect on the lifespan of the landfill. However, the author provides no data in this regard. It may be the case that a different material, for example, glass, is the primary piece of waste in the landfill, which would make any increase in the recycling of the aforementioned materials ineffective at increasing the landfill's span of usefulness. Alternatively, other factors, such as an increase in the population over time and the habits of people other than West Egg residents who also send their trash to the landfill, may increase the need for the landfill regardless of the increase in recycling, as some waste simply cannot be recycled. Should this be the case, an increase in recycling of plastic, metal, and paper may contribute little to lowering the landfill's garbage depositing and to keeping it from being filled to capacity for longer than expected, rendering the argument unconvincing.

The final piece of evidence necessary is concerned with the representativeness of the survey. While it is encouraging to see the positive results of the survey, without more information of the sample size and respondents, the 90 percent statistic is meaningless. Depending on the number of people who were surveyed and responded, along with their specific demographics and honesty, their alleged commitment to recycle more in the future could be a misrepresentation of the town residents' beliefs that amounts to an empty promise, or a reflection of the residents' beliefs that represents a genuine commitment. The number of participants could have been small, and they could have been a self-selecting group that tends to recycle more. Or most participants would like to appear that they are environmentally conscious, but perhaps few are willing to make the commitment to sorting their trash every single day. In this case, the prediction of a longer-than-expected lifespan for the landfill would be unreasonable. Even if the respondents are representative of West Egg's residents who will honor their commitment to recycling, we must ask how much more recycling they will contribute and whether the increase will reduce the trash that feeds the landfill so significantly as to make it last substantially longer than previously predicted. If they do not contribute considerably to recycling in the future and in turn contribute sufficiently less trash to the landfill, the argument will be undermined.

In sum, if the West Egg Town Council is to seriously consider the memorandum's prediction that the landfill will last longer as a result of increased recycling, there should be further research to find out if town residents' recycling habits will be affected by the increase in costs of normal trash pick-up. Also, an investigation into what specific materials account for the majority of waste in the landfill will help to determine if recycling even has a chance of extending the landfill's period of usefulness. Finally, when the town council considers the survey, more specific information on the sample size and demographics of the town would go a long way toward assessing the argument.

22. Mining copper in West Fredonia (Assumptions)

Citing the fact that a mining company by the name of Crust Copper Company (CCC) has recently purchased over 10,000 square miles of land in a tropical area and reasoning that any mining done will pose an imminent threat to the environment and endangered species that live there, the author concludes that such a disaster can be prevented if consumers boycott CCC's products until the company ceases mining activity in the area. However, the argument is full of assumptions and loopholes that require close examination for its assessment.

The threshold assumption that the author makes, upon which the rest of the argument relies, is that the mining company will mine the land which it has bought. Yet there is no mention of any plan to mine the land, despite it being a mining company. It is possible that the land was bought to be turned into a nature preserve as part of a public relations marketing plan, or as a tax write-off. It is also possible that the land was purchased for relocation of some residents or in exchange for another piece of land in the country. Such activities are common among heavy industry companies that have a reputation for destroying the environment. If this should be the case, the assumption about the company's mining activity would be unwarranted and boycotting the company would only give it more of an incentive to develop the land to make up for lost profits, invalidating the claim that the boycotting will help to prevent the threat to the environment and endangered species.

Even if the company does plan to mine the land they have bought, the author assumes that CCC's mining activity will threaten any endangered animal species and cause pollution. However, the author provides no evidence to substantiate this. It is possible that

CCC's purchased land is not the home of any endangered animal species. Even if it is inhabited by some endangered animal species, the mining activity may not cause the extinction of animal species or severe pollution, not to mention environmental disaster. If the company follows the usual international and local laws regarding the disposal of hazardous material, then it will be obligated to take great care to avoid harming any wildlife in the area. In many cases, if there are indeed endangered species present, then it is usually forbidden for any potentially harmful activities to take place, or the company may risk massive financial penalties. Similarly, pollution caused by its mining activity could be minimized with preventive measures and technologies. If this should be true, CCC's mining activity would not pose a major threat to the endangered animal species or give rise to much pollution, rendering the assumption and argument unsubstantiated. Unless there is relevant evidence, the author cannot justifiably assume that the company's plans will cause serious pollution and do a great deal of harm to the endangered animals.

Finally, the author implies that a boycott is necessary and sufficient. The letter suggests that a boycott is the only way to influence the company's decision. It is hard to take such a limited view seriously. Laws, regulations, and technologies could help prevent and dramatically reduce the risks. A petition to the government could also force the company to abandon its plan or alter its plan to make it environmentally sound. Moreover, the letter suggests that a boycott will have a significant effect on its decision. However, most people may be unaware of where the copper in most of their daily products comes from, and it is doubtful that they will do exhaustive amounts of research to find out, making attempts at a boycott implausible. To attain their goal, consumers may also need to boycott other companies that pose a threat to the country's animal species and environment. Thus, it is unreasonable to claim that consumers must boycott the company and that the boycotting can force the company to give up its mining activity in the area and help to eliminate the environmental disasters.

In conclusion, this letter fails to provide enough evidence to substantiate the assumptions and the argument that they underlie. If it wishes to be taken seriously, it should provide more details about CCC's plans for the land and explain how these plans will affect pollution and the endangered animals that live there. It would also help if the letter provided other possibilities for swaying the company's inclinations, aside from just boycotts, perhaps a petition to the government, or public protests.

23. Humana University wants to expand online degree programs (Questions to Be Answered)

To address Humana University's current issue with nonincreasing enrollment, increased costs of maintaining buildings, and growing budget deficit, the author concludes that the university should follow the example of nearby Omni University by creating and promoting more online classes. However, we need answers to some key questions before we determine the soundness of the argument.

To begin with, the author must answer whether the decrease in spending on classroom and dormitory space by Omni has resulted from its increase in online student enrollment. However, the author provides no data in this regard. It is possible that the school simply chose not to allocate as much money to those particular sectors as before. This means no connection has been established between funding for classroom and dormitory space and online student enrollment. If the author wishes to connect the two events, she must provide information to show that the decrease in spending in those areas was the result of a reduced need, such as Omni's enrollment figures for both online and on-campus classes, as well as the number of on-campus students choosing to live in the dorms. Also, a 50 percent increase may be insignificant if the enrollment was negligible to begin with. At the same time, the situation last year could be an aberration and may not continue. In these scenarios, Omni would not be a good example to emulate.

Even granting that Omni's lower spending on classroom and dormitory space was the result of its increased online enrollment, another question arises as to whether this fact alone warrants the assumption that a similar result will occur at Humana. However, Humana may be too different from Omni to guarantee a comparable outcome. Omni may be a more reputable university than Humana and its students may be more willing to enroll in its online degree programs. Even if both universities are equally reputable, Omni may have the resources, including faculty and technology, to offer many online classes, whereas Humana may be weak in this regard. In this case, there is no guarantee that Omni's strategy would be as successful at Humana. If Humana is an institution that specializes in some programs that are easily taught online, then the scheme would have a higher possibility of success. To answer the question, we need a business plan that includes the following details: the specific appeal of attending the university itself and programs that students can and are willing to take online.

Finally, the author should answer whether introducing online degree programs like those at Omni will boost Humana's enrollment and resolve its problem of budget deficits. However, this need not be the case. The fact that its enrollment has not been increasing during the past three years may be attributable to its temporary policy to stop admitting more students, the greatest number of students that it could serve, or an aberration. In this case, starting to offer online degree programs at Humana may have little impact on its enrollment. Also, the author assumes that the building maintenance costs are to blame for the deficit, a connection that has not been established by the author. The word "increase" is too vague to give us any idea of the amount of and reason for the maintenance costs. The costs could have been very small to begin with and be insignificant in amount despite the increase. It is likely that teacher salaries have accounted for the majority of Humana's expenses, a factor that is unlikely to be mitigated by online classes. If this is true, Humana's maintenance costs are not to blame. Therefore, launching online programs like those of Omni may not address Humana's enrollment and budget deficits. It is even likely that this plan will increase Humana's budget deficits, since launching and maintaining the online system may cost huge amounts of money, let alone extra costs for marketing online programs. Should this be the case, the plan would be gratuitous. If the author could provide a record of Humana's expenditures, one showing that maintenance costs have constituted a sizeable portion of its overall spending, then the case for reducing them to address its budget deficits would be far stronger.

To conclude, we need answers to some questions before we determine whether Humana should shift its focus from on-campus classes to online programs. To make a stronger case for this initiative, the author should show clearly how Omni University's increase in online students has contributed to its lower costs that year. To better assess the argument, we need proof that Humana and Omni are similar in ways that would allow the same results to take place at Humana and evidence that Humana's deficit is the result of its building maintenance costs.

24. Reducing operating hours at Movies Galore to cut expenses (Specific Evidence)

The author concludes that in the face of declining profits, the movie-rental chain, Movies Galore, should reduce operating expenses by closing earlier and cutting down its overall inventory. To support the conclusion, the memorandum presents an example of one of the store locations in Marston having received very few customer complaints about the new policies. However, the argument is not very convincing and requires evaluation with additional evidence.

There must be evidence that reducing operating costs is sufficient and necessary for stemming the company's decline in profits. Before attempting to fix the problem, the author should determine whether operating expenses comprise the largest percentage of costs for the company. Without specific financial data, there is no guarantee that the proposed policies will have any effect on the company's performance. Alternative costs, such as licensing fees and losses due to unreturned movies, should be investigated. If they constitute the greatest expense, reducing operating hours would be far less effective than decreasing the alternative costs. While a shortening of operating hours and reduction of inventory do have the potential to save on the company's costs, they may not necessarily be the only way of increasing profits. The author gratuitously assumes that raising rental rates to boost profits is not feasible. However, raising prices may be a good option if customers could accept a reasonable rise in price because they rent the movies of the chain for their wide selection as well as for their low prices. A slight increase in rental prices is unlikely to damage its reputation for offering bargains. While it may not be a good strategy for the downtown store to raise its prices, because there are many competitors around, the other stores could raise their rental rates, because the demand there for rented movies may be very strong and there may be few competitors around. Even if raising rental prices is not viable, this does not necessarily mean that there are no other ways to boost profits than decreasing operating costs by cutting the company's hours and stock. Other initiatives, such as customer loyalty programs, which could offer discounts after a certain number of rentals, may also work to attract more business to the stores. Should this be true, it would be unjustifiable to assume that the only method to save the company's profits is to implement the operating expense reduction plan.

There should also be evidence that just because there have not been a significant number of customer complaints about the new policies of the downtown store, the policies have been successful and there will not be any consequences in the future. The new policies were only implemented at the Marston location one month ago, which is hardly enough time to yield any significant data. It is possible that many customers have simply chosen not to voice their complaints, or that they have avoided that location in favor of another. Even if there have been few complaints about the changes, this does not necessarily mean that the downtown store has decreased its operating costs. Even if it has, there is no guarantee that its profits have increased. It could even be that its profits have decreased because of reducing operating costs and stock. In addition, the consequences of cutting stock will become most apparent as society's tastes in movies change over time. For example, so-called "classic" movies often experience revivals in popularity, and thus the store could lose out if it reduced its stock of older movies. Therefore, it is entirely possible that the lost revenue from closing earlier and only stocking newer movies would outweigh the savings in decreased operating expenses, invalidating the claim that reducing operating costs would boost profits. All these scenarios would undermine the assumption about the success of the policies and the recommendation of implementing them at all other stores.

Even granting that the policies have been successful at the downtown Marston store, there needs to be evidence that the same level of success, if any at all, will be experienced at all other locations. The specific traits of this downtown store need to be analyzed and compared to each of the other nine locations in order to see if there are certain qualities of the nearby areas, such as population density and average income, that may affect customers' ability to rent from the stores. If these factors are found to be consistent across all locations, then the plan stands a better chance of working. However, there is no information given by the author about the specific circumstances of this particular location and considering that it is located in a downtown area, the new policies may have drastically different levels of success in less populated areas. It is possible that the people in downtown Marston do not rent movies very often, regardless of what the store has in stock. For this reason, the company might have received few complaints about the changes at the downtown store. However, if other areas have a different customer demographic, complaints may begin to roll in. It is also possible that in other locations most people rent movies between 6:00 p.m. and 9:00 p.m. and prefer DVDs released more than five years ago. If this is true, it is unfair to assume that just because the policies have succeeded in the downtown location, they will automatically succeed in all other locations, rendering the argument unconvincing.

In conclusion, before implementing the new policies, the owner of Movies Galore must first figure out what the specific causes of the recent decline in profits are and whether the situation of the downtown Marston location is unique. Furthermore, the owner should have evidence that the downtown store has received few complaints because customers do not take issue with the reduced inventory and operating hours.

25. Retiring in Clearview as a top choice (Specific Evidence)

The author concludes that retirees should move to Clearview, citing its scenic beauty and climate, recent decline in housing costs, lower taxes, and promises to improve streets, schools, and public services. The article also mentions that healthcare for senior citizens is great, due to there being a higher number of physicians in the area. However, these reasons, though numerous, are too vague to be convincing on their own. To better assess the argument, we need extra evidence.

The author must provide evidence regarding Clearview's housing costs and tax rates. Despite the dip in housing costs and lower taxes, since the article fails to mention exactly how much houses usually cost in Clearview, nor the cost of taxes, it is possible that Clearview is located in a wealthy region, and thus its reduced housing costs and lower taxes relative to neighboring towns' may be exorbitantly high compared to those of most parts of the country. It is also possible that the housing prices before last year had been extremely high, so a considerable decrease last year may have still left it at a very high price. Furthermore, a recent decline in housing costs and current tax rates say nothing about their potential to change in the future. Perhaps the housing prices in the past year were aberrations and may not continue. Similarly, taxes may rise considerably, making Clearview a place unsuitable for living. Any of the scenarios, if true, would weaken the argument for convincing retirees to move to Clearview. To fully assess the argument, we need evidence regarding whether Clearview's costs of housing and taxes are indeed acceptable to retirees.

Also, the author should offer evidence about the mayor's promise. The argument assumes that just because the mayor of Clearview promises to improve public services, such improvements will be completed. However, the article provides no evidence to substantiate this. It is likely that the mayor, like many public officials, campaigns on platforms filled with empty promises. Even if the programs are completed, there is no indication given that they will be of any benefit to retirees. As to the school and road improvements mentioned by the article, it seems that the improvements would be more attractive to families instead of retirees. Even if the public services are beneficial and available, they may not be affordable to many retirees. In these scenarios, the argument for moving to Clearview to retire would be undermined. To better evaluate the argument, we must have clear evidence that the mayor will fulfil the promise to improve public services and that such services will benefit retirees.

Finally, the author needs to furnish data concerning the number of physicians. The argument implies that simply because there are a large number of physicians, senior citizens can expect to have excellent healthcare. However, the article does not provide any information about whether these doctors specialize in elderly care, and thus, it may very well be the case that their specialties have no relation to older people. They could be pediatricians, or members of other medical practices. Moreover, even if Clearview has many doctors, there is no guarantee that its number of doctors per resident is greater than the national average, not to mention the per capita number of other towns ideal for retirement. Even assuming that it has a relatively high number of doctors per capita, this does not necessarily mean that the number will remain high as retirees get older. In these scenarios, people may be hesitant about retiring to Clearview. While retirees are often concerned about the number of physicians, natural beauty and a consistent climate may be much less important, and some may even prefer distinct four seasons. Should this be true, the argument for retiring to Clearview would be gratuitous.

In sum, if the article wishes to persuade retirees to move to Clearview, it must provide more specific numbers proving that the housing costs and taxes are low compared to the national average. It should also offer evidence that the mayor intends to implement public service improvements that are directly related to seniors, such as senior activity centers. Finally, it needs to support its healthcare claim with the number of available doctors per capita whose specialty is elderly healthcare.

26. Humana University wants to expand online degree programs (Assumptions)

To address Humana University's current issue with nonincreasing enrollment, increased costs of maintaining buildings, and growing budget deficit, the author concludes that the university should follow the example of nearby Omni University by creating and promoting more online classes. However, the argument relies on a number of assumptions that need scrutiny for its assessment.

The author assumes that the decrease in spending on classroom and dormitory space by Omni has resulted from its increase in online student enrollment. However, the author provides no evidence to substantiate this. It is possible that the school simply chose not to allocate as much money to those particular sectors as before. This means no connection has been established between funding for classroom and dormitory space and online student enrollment. If the author wishes to connect the two events, she must provide information to show that the decrease in spending in those areas was the result of a reduced need, such as Omni's enrollment figures for both online and on-campus classes, as well as the number of on-campus students choosing to live in the dorms. Also, a 50 percent increase may be insignificant if the enrollment was negligible to begin with. At the same time, the situation last year could be an aberration and may not continue. If this should be true, Omni would not be a good example to emulate.

Even granting that Omni's lower spending on classroom and dormitory space was the result of its increased online enrollment, the author implies that a similar result will occur at Humana. However, Humana may be too different from Omni to guarantee a comparable outcome. Omni may be a more reputable university than Humana and its students may be more willing to enroll in its online degree programs. Even if both universities are equally reputable, Omni may have the resources, including faculty and technology, to offer many online classes, whereas Humana may be weak in this regard. In this case, there is no guarantee that Omni's strategy would be as successful at Humana. If Humana is an institution that specializes in some programs that are easily taught online, then the scheme would have a higher possibility of success. To answer the question, we need a business plan that includes the following details: the specific appeal of attending the university itself and programs that students can and are willing to take online.

Finally, the author suggests that introducing online degree programs like those at Omni will boost Humana's enrollment and resolve its problem of budget deficits. However, this need not be the case. The fact that its enrollment has not been increasing during the past three years may be attributable to its temporary policy to stop admitting more students, to the greatest number of students that it could serve, or to an aberration. In this case, starting to offer online degree programs at Humana may have little impact on its enrollment. Also, the author assumes that the building maintenance costs are to blame for the deficit, a connection that has not been established by the author. The word "increase" is too vague to give us any idea of the amount of and reason for the maintenance costs. The costs could have been very small to begin with and be insignificant in amount despite the increase. It is likely that teacher salaries have accounted for the majority of Humana's expenses, a factor that is unlikely to be mitigated by online classes. If this is true, Humana's maintenance costs are not to blame. Therefore, launching online programs like those of Omni may not address Humana's enrollment and budget deficits. It is even likely that this plan will increase Humana's budget deficits, since launching and maintaining the online system may cost huge amounts of money, let alone extra costs for marketing online programs. Should this be true, the plan would be gratuitous. If the author could provide a record of Humana's expenditures, one showing that maintenance costs have constituted a sizeable portion of its overall spending, then the case for reducing them to address its budget deficits would be far stronger.

To conclude, the memorandum lacks sufficient evidence to support the plan for Humana to shift its focus from on-campus classes to online programs. To make a stronger case for this initiative, the author must show clearly how Omni's increase in online students has contributed to its lower costs that year. To better assess the argument, we need proof that Humana and Omni are similar in ways that would allow the same results to take place at Humana and evidence that Humana's deficit is the result of its building maintenance costs.

27. Using lavender to help with chronic insomnia (Specific Evidence)

Relying on a study in which a group of thirty volunteers with chronic insomnia were made to sleep on lavender-scented pillows for three weeks, the author asserts that lavender has been proven to be an efficacious remedy for insomnia. However, the study findings are vaguely described in the article, and thus we need more evidence to determine the soundness of the argument.

We must have evidence regarding the representativeness of the sample and the rigorousness of the study. The article mentions that there were thirty volunteers with chronic insomnia in the study, yet this sample size is hardly representative of all people with chronic insomnia, to say nothing of all insomniacs. The group of participants might be an aberration and more susceptible to the influence of lavender than other insomniacs. This indicates that the remedy of lavender-scented pillows may have been effective for some people with chronic insomnia. Even assuming that it is effective for all people with insomnia, there is no guarantee that it will work for other types of insomnia. Therefore, it is unfair to generalize about the effect of lavender for all insomniacs from a study of chronic insomniacs only. Moreover, since this study attempts to measure the viability of a substance in treating a medical condition, it should be subjected to the same scrutiny as pharmaceutical studies, which require large sample sizes throughout numerous repeat trials in order to replicate the results. There is also no mention of a control group in the study, a factor that is vital in determining whether a treatment has any effect compared to receiving no treatment. Similarly, there is no information about how the participants had slept without the pillows prior to the study; therefore, the author cannot conclude with any certainty that the lavender-scented pillows contributed to their better sleep quality. In this case, the claim that lavender can cure insomnia in a short term is unfounded.

We also need evidence regarding other factors that may have been responsible for the effect. The subjects slept each night for three weeks on lavender-scented pillows, and the author assumes that it is lavender that has cured their chronic insomnia. However, the author offers no evidence to substantiate this. It is likely that pillows have done the work. Also, the article states that all thirty subjects were given the lavender-scented pillows along with their medication during the first week, and then just the pillows in the second and third weeks, citing decreased sleep quality in the second week but greatly increased sleep quality in the third week compared to the previous two weeks. The lack of any control group could make these results meaningless, as there is no way of determining if the improved sleep in the third week was the result of lavender. Perhaps a recovery from withdrawal symptoms they may have experienced in the second week accounted for the scenario. Or perhaps the remaining effects of the sleeping medication of the volunteers were responsible for the result during the third week, because the sleeping medicine had been taken just two weeks before. Without ruling out such factors, the author cannot reliably conclude that lavender alone has contributed to the outcome.

Finally, we lack evidence that the study findings are relevant to insomnia. The article notes how long and how soundly the participants slept and how tired they felt after sleep. However, such findings may not indicate improvement in insomnia, the inability to go to sleep. It is likely that in the third week the participants still found it difficult to fall asleep each night but because they had worked very hard in the daytime and after a long time of insomnia, they went to sleep and slept better and longer than in the previous two weeks. Should this be true, their insomnia did not improve, invalidating the claim that lavender is effective at curing insomnia in a short term. The researchers may have asked "How long and how soundly did you sleep last night?" and "Did you feel tired when you woke up?" The questions may have led to the researchers' findings relevant to time and quality of sleep instead of the ability to go to sleep. Had they asked, "Did you find it difficult to fall asleep last night?" they could have obtained answers to the question of the effect of lavender on insomnia. To better assess the argument, we need a clear definition of insomnia distinguishable from sleep time and sleep quality.

In conclusion, if this article wishes to assert that the study proves the effectiveness of lavender at treating insomnia, it must first provide multiple trials that produce the same results, as well as peer review concurrent with other pharmaceutical studies. Also, a larger sample size must be used so that circumstantial factors may be ruled out, along with a control group to show that lavender is directly responsible for the improved sleep quality among the test subjects. It would also help the author's argument if the studies were extended over a longer period than three weeks in order to rule out any residual effects of sleep medication of the volunteers.

28. Should Happy Pancake House replace butter with margarine? (Questions to Be Answered)

Relying on the fact that after the replacement of butter with margarine in Happy Pancake House restaurants in the southwestern United States, only about 2 percent of customers have made complaints and on reports that some customers asking for butter but receiving margarine instead have not complained, the author recommends that Happy Pancake House take similar action in its restaurants in the southeast and northeast to eliminate the costs of buying butter and to become more profitable. However, before we determine whether the company should implement this plan, we need answers to some key questions.

The company must ask whether the fact that only two percent of customers have complained truly represents a ninety-eight percent satisfaction rate. If two percent of customers involve a large number of people, it is unfair to claim that customers have been hardly impacted. It is likely that customers who have complained account for a much larger portion of those who have asked for butter. This could be a nightmare for the company, since this indicates a great percentage of customers unsatisfied with the replacement. Also, refraining from expressing one's dissatisfaction might not equate to an expression of contentedness. It may be the case that a large number of customers simply do not wish to voice their concerns at the moment, or that many customers who have heard about the replacement have chosen to buy butter elsewhere. It may also be the case that the replacement has happened too recently to yield significant feedback, alerting Happy Pancake House to a potentially much higher rate of negative response to the replacement later. If this should be true, the assumption of a ninety-eight percent satisfaction rate would be unfounded and the recommendation of replacing butter with margarine in other parts of the United States would be unlikely to have the predicted result of saving money on butter and boosting profits. To better evaluate the argument, we need a customer survey to see if people are genuinely happy with the change.

The company should also ask if the absence of complaints among customers when given margarine instead of butter results from their inability to distinguish between the two, from the fact that they do not want to say anything, or from the fact that they use the word "butter" to refer to both butter and margarine. If the last scenario is true, then the company has little to worry about; but if the first two scenarios turn out to be true, this could lead to a backlash once the company replaces all butter with margarine and more customers become dissatisfied. Also, the phrase "a number of customers" is vague. We just do not know the percentage of such customers. If a number of customers account for a small percentage of all the customers, this may indicate little impact of the change on customers. Otherwise, this may mean a significant impact on the customers. Even if the number indicates a tiny portion, it could be that the servers report such a small figure to the management simply to seem competent at providing service and avoid punishment. In that event, the recommendation is unfounded. To fully assess the argument, we need to know the portion of servers who have received customer complaints about the replacement.

Finally, the company needs to ask if the cost of butter is a significant expense to affect the company's profitability. While butter accounts for a portion of the costs, other factors such as operating expenses may constitute a much greater percentage of the total costs. Should this be the case, replacement of butter with margarine may not be the ideal option for improving profitability. We should, therefore, inquire what specific factors comprise the greatest expenses of the restaurant chain to see where butter fits in that list. Also, just because the new strategy is effective in one part of the country does not necessarily mean it will be effective in other parts as well. It may be that the cost of butter is not the same in all regions of the country, depending on factors such as availability and customer demand. Perhaps it is cost-saving in the southwestern United States but will not save any cost in the restaurants in the southeast and northeast, not to mention the possibility that margarine will be more expensive than butter. Or perhaps people in the southwestern United States do not care so much whether it is butter or margarine as people in other regions, or they simply do not have many choices regarding breakfast restaurants. In these scenarios, the recommendation is unreasonable. To better assess the recommendation, we need information about the correlation between the cost of butter and the company's profitability and about the applicability of the strategy to other parts of the country.

In sum, the company has to ask many questions before it implements the plan to replace butter with margarine at all of its locations throughout the country. It must determine whether customers are truly satisfied with the change that has already taken place in the southwestern locations and whether customers can distinguish between butter and margarine. It should also investigate whether any regional differences would affect the cost of butter and the company's profits in its absence.

29. Restricting showerhead water flow in Sunnyside Towers (Questions to Be Answered)

Relying on the recent change to low-flow showerheads on the first five floors of an apartment complex by the name of Sunnyside Towers, the author recommends that the company modify the rest of the twenty floors to increase Sunnyside Corporation's profits due to saving costs on water. Before we determine the soundness of the recommendation, we need answers to some key questions.

We must know whether after modification of showerheads, water will be saved on the first five floors. The letter starts by mentioning that the showerheads only allow one-third the normal flow of water, and that there has not yet been any data on water usage before and after the change. Even if there has been data for the first month since the installation, we are not sure that it will be representative of the water use of the five floors in the future. It is possible that if less water flows through the showerheads, and, as the letter mentions, the pressure is lower, the tenants may use the shower for a longer period of time. It is also possible that future tenants will use more water per capita, or that other uses of water will rise. In such scenarios, there may be no net change in their water use or there may be even an increase; thus, there would be no financial savings. Even if there will be financial savings, there is no guarantee that the savings will be significant. In that event, the prediction of profits as a result of modifying showerheads on the first five floors would be gratuitous. To determine whether there will be a drop in water use, we need information about actual water usage before and after the adjustment.

Conceding that the showerheads will lower the cost of water, we should know whether the complaints about low water pressure involve serious issues. It is possible that there have been only a few residents since the adjustment, so there are only a few complaints. This may mean a high percentage of complaints. It is also possible that many have complaints, but they do not bother to report them. The worst scenario would be that many who have heard about the showerhead problem have chosen not to live in the buildings. Even if there have been only a few complaints about low water pressure and no problems with showers during the first month since the adjustment, there is the possibility that in the future many more complaints will be made, that many more problems with showers will be reported, and that many more tenants will vacate because they are displeased. If this should be the case, the prediction of a considerable savings and profits would be unfounded and the recommendation of adjusting the showerheads would be unjustified.

Otherwise, the recommendation may have the predicted result.

Even accepting that there is no issue other than the few complaints that do not involve serious problems, we also need to know whether change to low-flow showerheads to restrict water flow on the rest of the floors will further boost the profits of the company. Profit is a function of revenues minus costs. The potential costs as well as financial savings should be considered. It is likely that the cost to modify all the showerheads on all the floors will not be offset by the savings on water, not to mention any problems that may require fixing down the line; while there have not been any major issues with showers yet, there may be unforeseen difficulties in the future. It is also likely that the adjustment will cost much more on average on the rest of the floors than on the first five floors of the building. It is even likely that the rates charged by water companies will rise. Any of the scenarios, if true, would undermine the prediction of further increase in profits. Otherwise, there would be a better case for the prediction. However, without information about the costs of adjusting the showerheads and future rates, we cannot ascertain the soundness of the recommendation.

In conclusion, the owner of Sunnyside Towers should rethink the decision to modify all the floors' showerheads with the new low-flow model, as there is not enough data to support the claim that it will save on water and increase profits. To better evaluate the argument, we need a clear cost-benefit analysis that incorporates room for future maintenance expenditures and higher rates.

30. More healthful lifestyles in Forsythe (Specific Evidence)

The author concludes that the new lifestyles adopted by the citizens of Forsythe are more healthful than before. To support the conclusion, the article presents survey results in which the citizens' eating habits align more closely with government nutritional recommendations than ten years before. It also cites a fourfold increase in the sale of foods that contain kiran, which has been shown by a study to reduce cholesterol, and a decrease in the sales of sulia, a food which the healthiest citizens tend to avoid. However, to better assess the argument, we need extra evidence.

First, we must have evidence that the respondents are representative of the entire population of the town. Yet no data is provided in this regard. If the survey finding is to be accepted as evidence, the author needs to provide more information about the sample, such as the number of people and demographics of the citizens surveyed, the specific questions asked, and how they have been asked. Without relevant information, it is possible that the only people questioned were those that already fell into the healthiest portion of the populace. The sample could be very small and an anomaly, whereas the town residents in general still keep the lifestyle ten years before. It is also possible that the respondents misrepresented their lifestyles simply to seem health conscious, further skewing the results. In this case, the assumption about the representativeness of the respondents would prove unwarranted and the claim that the citizens of Forsythe have become more health-oriented would be invalid. Unless the survey is valid, reliable, and representative, the author cannot substantiate the claim.

Even granting that the survey was properly administered, we should also have evidence that following the government recommendations more closely is the same as living a healthier lifestyle. However, the author offers no information in this respect. After all, government recommendations usually only cover the bare minimum requirements; therefore, there is the possibility that these health recommendations are for people living at the poverty level. If this is true, the recommendations as a metric may be inadequate for measuring the relative healthiness of an entire populace. Perhaps the citizens' dietary habits are less wholesome today than ten years ago. Thus, the author has yet to establish the connection between aligning more with the government recommendations and adopting a more healthful lifestyle. Unless these recommendations are better explained, how closely the citizens of Forsythe follow them is irrelevant to this argument.

Finally, we need evidence that increased consumption of kiran and decreased consumption of sulia are proof of a healthier lifestyle. However, the article lacks data in this regard. It could be the case that the residents of Forsythe do not have high cholesterol levels and therefore do not need to consume kiran. Even if consumption of kiran may make them healthier, there is no guarantee that a fourfold increase will be adequate, since the amount could have been very small to begin with. Also, the fact that the healthiest citizens tend to avoid sulia does not necessarily mean that it is unhealthy; it could be that it simply is not palatable. In that event, the assumption about kiran and sulia would be gratuitous. Even if more consumption of kiran and less consumption of sulia indicate a more healthful lifestyle, kiran and sulia are only two foods and by no means the only sources of nutrition the citizens eat. It could even be the case that the citizens now have a less healthy lifestyle overall because they eat much more unhealthy food and exercise much less than before. Any of the scenarios, if true, would invalidate the claim that the people of Forsythe have followed more wholesome lifestyles. Without further information about the two particular foods, their consumption would be irrelevant.

In conclusion, if the assumptions that underlie the argument are to be considered valid, there must first be more specific details about the survey of dietary habits, particularly regarding the sample. Furthermore, there should be more information about the government guidelines for nutritional eating, such as whom the guidelines are meant for and what standard of health they are designed to meet. Lastly, there needs to be evidence that kiran and sulia have been significant staples in the diets of Forsythe citizens and that they have the stated effects on the consumers' nutritional health.

31. Disappearance of large mammal species on the Kaliko Islands (Assumptions)

Citing the fact that there is no evidence of humans having any significant contact with the mammals and reasoning that since there have not been any of the mammals' bones among the waste sites, they were not hunted, the author concludes that climate change or other environmental factors, not humans, were the cause of mass extinctions of large mammals on the Kaliko Islands. However, the author makes a number of assumptions that we must scrutinize to better assess the argument.

The author assumes that simply because no evidence of significant human contact with other mammals currently exists, humans could not have contributed to the extinction of large mammals on the Kaliko Islands. However, the author provides no evidence to substantiate this. There may have been significant human contact with the mammals, but no evidence has been found. Humans may also have caused the extinction of the mammals without any significant human contact. For example, they could have killed off the mammals indirectly by devastating the forests where the mammals had lived, by killing all the animals that the large mammals fed on, or by poisoning their water source. Any of the scenarios, if true, would indicate that humans could have been a factor in the mammals' extinction, rendering the assumption unwarranted and the argument unpersuasive that humans did not cause mass extinctions of large mammals on the Kaliko Islands.

The author also implies that simply because no large mammal bones were found in sites similar to those where fish bones were discarded, such animals were never hunted by humans. However, this is not necessarily true. It may simply be the case that humans had exported the mammal bones. It may also be the case that the bones were repurposed or discarded in an area that has yet to be discovered. It may even be the case that the bones had disappeared in the sites because of environmental factors after humans had discarded them there. If humans were able to hunt fish, they may have been able to hunt large mammals with the same tools. If this should be true, the assumption would be unfounded, and the argument would be severely undermined. Thus, the author has to establish the connection between the fact that large mammal bones were not found in similar sites and the claim that humans had not hunted the mammals.

Finally, the author suggests that the mammals' extinctions must have resulted from some climate change or other environmental factor if they were not caused by humans. However, there is no evidence that this is the case. Humans could have been responsible for the extinctions. Even if they did not contribute to the extinctions, there could have been factors other than climate change or some other environmental factor. It is likely that the large mammals' birthrates were lower than their deathrates, making it impossible to sustain the species. It is also likely that the mammals of the Kaliko Islands did not all die, but simply migrated to other islands or to the mainland, making the species extinct on the Kaliko Islands. Should this be true, the assumption would be gratuitous, and the argument undermined.

In conclusion, the assumptions made regarding the disappearance of the large mammals of the Kaliko Islands are not substantiated. It is possible that humans were the actual cause of the animals' extinction if the animals did not migrate to another area.

32. Sales of Whirlwind video games to increase dramatically (Assumptions)

The author concludes that sales of Whirlwind video games will likely rise significantly in the following months. To support the conclusion, the author cites results from a survey which asked what features videogame players thought were most important in a game and the fact that the new game's advertising targets people aged ten to twenty-five, which the editorial asserts is the age-group most likely to play video games. However, we need to examine the assumptions that underlie the argument to determine its validity.

A threshold assumption made by the author is that the sample of video game players surveyed is indicative of video gamers generally. According to the results of the survey, life-like graphics which require the most modern computers were what most gamers looked for. This alone indicates that most people questioned may have been those belonging to higher-income groups, since the most up-to-date computers could be very expensive. The people surveyed may be an aberration and did not represent other game players. In this case, while the games which Whirlwind is releasing cater to this group, they may in fact miss a majority of the market by selling games which most people cannot play, and thus will not be bought. There is also the possibility that a significant portion of the respondents were not ten- to twenty-five-year-olds, the group with the greatest number of potential gamers. In such scenarios, the assumption is warrantless. Unless the survey is reliable, valid, and representative, the author cannot justify the prediction of a significant rise in the sales of Whirlwind video games in the coming months.

Even if the survey's respondents are representative of the general population of video-game enthusiasts, the author also implies that simply because life-like graphics were the most preferred feature in a video game, this feature alone will be sufficient to attract gamers to the new titles. However, this need not be the case. Video games require a combination of features to be successful, such as an interesting storyline, fun gameplay mechanics, and an affordable price. It could be that while game players prefer life-like graphics, they take for granted that games have other features, without which they would not purchase them. In that event, it could be a very risky gamble to market the company's new games around only one of the points. If the games receive negative reviews because of its lack of features, sales may drop a few days after release. Also, the author assumes that video games with realistic graphics will reverse the decline in sales. However, without identifying the reasons for the decline, the author cannot substantiate the assumption. Perhaps the decline is the result of factors other than lack of realistic graphics, such as unreasonable pricing or poor management. In such scenarios, the assumption about life-like graphics as a feature sufficient to entice gamers would prove unwarranted, rendering the argument unfounded.

Even if a preference for games with realistic graphics will suffice to draw video-game enthusiasts to Whirlwind's new titles, the author also suggests that focusing the new games' advertising on attracting people aged ten to twenty-five will be successful. However, the author furnishes no evidence that this is true. The people involve a very wide age group, and depending on the games' content, there is no guarantee that many people from this demographic will purchase the new titles. For example, certain game rating systems prohibit people under a certain age from buying games with graphic violence or suggestive themes. Since the author does not mention the specific content of these games, it would be unfair to assume that they would be appropriate for all players aged ten to twenty-five. Even if they are good for the players, many players may not purchase them because they have played similar games and are fed up with them. They may also rent the games from shops instead of purchasing them. They may even buy Whirlwind's competitors' similar games at lower prices or with extra features. Any of the scenarios, if true, would invalidate the assumption about the effect of the advertising and the soundness of the argument.

To conclude, the assumptions of the argument lack necessary evidence to support them. Without relevant data, it is unfair to assume that the survey respondents represent a significant part of the population, let alone the group which the new games' advertising is targeting. The notion that life-like graphics alone will be enough to persuade players to buy the new games also has no clear evidence. Finally, there should be more consideration of the actual content of the games regarding the age demographic, as it could have significant effects on who would be allowed to purchase them.

33. Dura-Sock, Inc. to discontinue its Endure manufacturing process (Assumptions)

This memo from the vice-president of marketing at Dura-Sock, Inc. concludes that the company can become more profitable by ending use of the Endure manufacturing process. To support the conclusion, it mentions a study in which customers buy the company's socks every three months, despite the advertising which claims the socks can last two years. It also cites a survey in the northeastern United States that finds most customers value Dura-Socks' stylish appearance and numerous color options. However, the argument is rife with assumptions and loopholes that we must examine closely before we ascertain its soundness.

The author assumes that the respondents of the recent study represent Dura-Socks' customers in general. However, this need not be the case. The number of respondents could be tiny and may not be representative of all customers who buy Dura-Socks. It may be the case that the majority of study participants who buy the socks do so because they work in professions that quickly wear out their foot apparel, but they prefer Dura-Socks products to other brands that would wear out even faster. On the contrary, Dura-Socks' customers generally work in other professions and wear the socks for at least two years. It may also be the case that even if the respondents buy new Dura-Socks every three months, they will still wear the original ones for two years. In that event, if the Endure process were discontinued, the customers would be less satisfied. Even assuming that the customers did not wear their socks after three months, the Endure process advertised may still motivate them psychologically to purchase the socks. Consumers tend to buy products with extra features, even if they have little use for the features. If the process were terminated, regardless of its actual use, sales could decrease. If this should be the case, the assumption about the representativeness of the customers who have responded to the recent study would prove unwarranted, invalidating the claim regarding the utility of the Endure process and in turn the argument for ending use of the process to increase the company's profits.

The author also implies that the customers surveyed in the northeastern United States cities are representative of those in other regions. However, the sample could be small and therefore may not typify Dura-Socks' customers in general. The surveyed cities may be the largest single market, but regional preferences may not all be alike, and the other markets combined may outweigh the market of the northeastern region. Perhaps unlike the northeastern United States, other parts of the U.S. are less urbanized, and their people enjoy participating in outdoor sports such as camping and hiking, activities that put the durability of socks to the test. Or perhaps people in other regions are less wealthy and value durability of the socks over their appearance and colors. In addition, the fact that style and color options are the most valued feature does not itself imply that durability is unimportant to consumers. It could be that consumers take it for granted, and that were they denied it, they would buy socks of other brands. Should this be true, the assumption about the representativeness of the survey respondents is unsubstantiated and the argument would be weakened. If a survey could be conducted to find out what customers prefer across the country, it would allow Dura-Socks to determine whether the Endure process deserves discontinuation or whether people prefer socks manufactured with the Endure process.

Even granting that the recent study and consumer survey are valid and reliable, the author also suggests that ceasing use of the Endure process will result in higher profits. Discontinuing the process may mean that the company will need to spend money on reconfiguring its factories and changing its advertising campaigns, which can cost a considerable sum, not to mention the fact that the company will be giving up the feature around which the brand is built, causing it to lose dedicated customers. Ending the process may also mean that it will give up a cost-effective process, because the patented process may incur much lower manufacturing costs. Profit is a function of revenue and costs. If such a strategy helps the company to enhance revenues and decrease costs, the claim that discontinuing the process will make the company's business more profitable will be strengthened. Otherwise, it would be invalidated. To decide whether the argument is sound, we need data regarding the revenue and costs before and after the discontinuation of the Endure process.

In conclusion, the evidence given to support the discontinuation of the Endure process is insufficient. To convince me that the argument is valid, the author would need to provide evidence that customers really do not care about the Endure process and that the cost of rebranding the company and changing processes would be reasonable and not negatively affect its profits.

34. Dura-Sock, Inc. to discontinue its Endure manufacturing process (Specific Evidence)

This memo from the vice-president of marketing at Dura-Sock, Inc. concludes that the company can become more profitable by ending use of the Endure manufacturing process. To support the conclusion, it mentions a study in which customers buy the company's socks every three months, despite the advertising which claims the socks can last two years. It also cites a survey in the northeastern United States that finds most customers value Dura-Socks' stylish appearance and numerous color options. However, to determine the validity of the argument, we need more evidence.

We must have evidence that the respondents of the recent study represent Dura-Socks' customers in general. However, this need not be the case. The number of respondents could be tiny and may not be representative of all customers who buy Dura-Socks. It may be the case that the majority of study participants who buy the socks do so because they work in professions that quickly wear out their foot apparel, but they prefer Dura-Socks products to other brands that would wear out even faster. On the contrary, Dura-Socks' customers generally work in other professions and wear the socks for at least two years. It may also be the case that even if the respondents buy new Dura-Socks every three months, they will still wear the original ones for two years. In that event, if the Endure process were discontinued, the customers would be less satisfied. Even assuming that the customers did not wear their socks after three months, the Endure process advertised may still motivate them psychologically to purchase the socks. Consumers tend to buy products with extra features, even if they have little use for the features. If the process were terminated, regardless of its actual use, sales could decrease. If this should be the case, the assumption about the representativeness of the customers who have responded to the recent study would prove unwarranted, invalidating the claim regarding the utility of the Endure process and in turn the argument for ending use of the process to increase the company's profits.

We should also have evidence that the customers surveyed in the northeastern United States cities are representative of those in other regions. However, the sample could be small and therefore may not typify Dura-Socks' customers in general. The surveyed cities may be the largest single market, but regional preferences may not all be alike, and the other markets combined may outweigh the market of the northeastern region. Perhaps unlike the northeastern United States, other parts of the U.S. are less urbanized, and their people enjoy participating in outdoor sports such as camping and hiking, activities that put the durability of socks to the test. Or perhaps people in other regions are less wealthy and value durability of the socks over their appearance and colors. In addition, the fact that style and color options are the most valued feature does not itself imply that durability is unimportant to consumers. It could be that consumers take it for granted, and that were they denied it, they would buy socks of other brands. Should this be true, the assumption about the representativeness of the survey is unsubstantiated and the argument would be weakened. If a survey could be conducted to find out what customers prefer across the country, it would allow Dura-Socks to determine whether the Endure process deserves discontinuation or whether people prefer socks manufactured with the Endure process.

Even granting that the recent study and consumer survey are valid and reliable, we need evidence that ceasing use of the Endure process will result in higher profits. Discontinuing the process may mean that the company will need to spend money on reconfiguring its factories and changing its advertising campaigns, which can cost a considerable sum, not to mention the fact that the company will be giving up the feature around which the brand is built, causing it to lose dedicated customers. Ending the process may also mean that it will give up a cost-effective process, because the patented process may incur much lower manufacturing costs. Profit is a function of revenue and costs. If such a strategy helps the company to enhance revenues and decrease costs, the claim that discontinuing the process will make the company's business more profitable will be strengthened. Otherwise, it would be invalidated. To decide whether the argument is sound, we need data regarding the revenues and costs before and after the discontinuation of the Endure process.

In conclusion, the evidence given to support the discontinuation of the Dura-Socks' Endure process is insufficient. To convince me that the argument is valid, the author would need to provide evidence that customers really do not care about the Endure process and that the cost of rebranding the company and changing processes would be reasonable and not negatively affect its profits.

35. Monitoring employees' internet use (Specific Evidence)

The author recommends that Climpson Industries install software on company computers to detect the internet use of employees in order to prevent them from wasting time, nurture a better work ethic, and boost the company's profits overall. To better assess the recommendation and its argument, we need more evidence as outlined below.

First, we must have clear evidence that workers are wasting time on the internet on personal or recreational activities. It is likely that few workers participate in such activities. It is also likely that even if some do, they are simply taking a short break before beginning the next task. It is even likely that the employees' productivity is already optimal. If this should be true, the assumption that workers are engaging in something unproductive would be unfounded, invalidating the argument that installing software will help to deter workers from wasting time and boost productivity and profits. Before taking such an extreme measure as monitoring their computer activity, the company should first provide evidence that the workers have been using the internet for inappropriate purposes. Without such evidence, any measures to counteract the alleged employee behavior would be a wild guess, with indeterminate likelihood of success.

Secondly, we should have evidence that installing monitoring software will be the best way to prevent employees from wasting their time. However, the author provides no data in this respect. There is the possibility that employees, if they are indeed wasting time as the author claims, will simply find a way around the software, rendering it moot. Similarly, they may use their own devices as distractions, such as their smartphones or mobile gaming consoles. In either scenario, monitoring software on the company's computers would be completely useless, rendering the argument gratuitous. The company should thoroughly research the software it plans to use in order to see if it has had a high rate of success at tracking the activity of workers and is resistant to tampering to avoid misrepresentation of its usefulness. Instead of installing the software, the company may monitor workers' internet use by analyzing the search history of the workstation internet browsers. It could accomplish this simply by having someone from its IT department log the activity of workers on the computers to check if such activity involves a significant amount of time on shopping or entertainment websites. If it is found that workers spend little time using the Internet improperly, installing the monitoring software as the most effective way to stop employees from wasting time on the job would be unfounded.

Granted that the employees are wasting time on the internet, we still lack evidence to support the assertion that the monitoring software and punishments will do anything to spur productivity by enhancing work ethic and boosting overall profits. It is likely that workers may decide to become less productive in retaliation for what they may view as unfair treatment. Alternatively, they may quit altogether, and the company may have a hard time hiring new workers, thanks in large part to the ability of employees to complain publicly about policies that are perceived to be oppressive. In that event, the argument for the monitoring and punishments will be weak. Before identifying the cause of the present work ethic, the author cannot justifiably claim that the monitoring software and punishments will help enhance the company's work ethic. Other factors, such as salary and vacation, may be responsible for the current work ethic of the employees. Also, profit is a function of revenue and costs. Installing the software may cost large sums of money, rendering the policy undesirable. The claim would be more persuasive if the company provided a previous instance in which its workers were responsive to punitive measures and thus had better work ethic. Or at the very least, the company could implement the software on a trial basis to see how its employees will respond. In this way, the company can see if the proposed method is effective in enhancing work ethic and increasing the overall profits before implementing it permanently.

In conclusion, the recommendation is not supported by enough evidence to justify its implementation. To be convinced that this plan would work, we need solid proof that employees have been abusing computer and internet privileges, along with detailed information about the tracking software's effectiveness. It would also help if there were an established precedent in which the company's workers' behavior was positively influenced by punitive action.

36. Increasing the size of the family rooms and kitchens in new homes built by Bower (Examine Assumptions)

The author recommends that Bower Builders, a home construction company, increase the size of family rooms and kitchens and make state-of-the-art kitchens a standard feature in a bid to increase sales and profits. To justify the recommendation, the memo states that because its competitor Domus Construction's houses built with large family rooms and large kitchens have sold faster and at higher-than-average prices, Bower will have success as well. It also cites a national survey and testimonies from recent buyers: the survey finds that the most desirable home features are a large family room and modern kitchen, whereas the testimonies say that many recent buyers do not need a separate dining room for family meals. However, the argument is replete with assumptions and loopholes that require scrutiny before we determine its soundness.

The threshold assumption made by the author is that the nationwide survey is reliable. However, the author provides no evidence that this is the case. Despite it being a nationwide survey, it is possible that only a particular group was involved, which could make the results biased towards a particular house design that does not match the desires or purchasing power of the entire country. The surveyed people may prefer large family rooms and large, well-appointed kitchens, but they may have accounted for a small portion of the potential home buyers and were an anomaly. There is the possibility that the survey participants are not representative of Bower's customers in general and therefore building homes based on the survey results could be disastrous. Even if they are, there is no guarantee that the most desired home features will be the decisive factors when customers purchase homes; factors such as affordability and practical use of houses could have the most significant impact on customers' decision to buy, rendering it unwarranted to build houses merely on the basis of the two features. In addition, increasing the size of the family rooms and kitchens in all the homes may not be justified, since current family rooms and kitchens may be large enough for most families. Making state-of-the-art kitchens a standard feature may be even less justified because they could be much more expensive than large, well-appointed kitchens and too costly for most families and Bower. In these scenarios, Bower would not do well to build homes based on the findings of the nationwide survey, because such a strategy may decrease its sales and profits instead of increasing them.

Another assumption upon which the argument rests is that the competitor Domus' recent success was a direct result of the features being discussed and will be experienced by Bower. However, the author offers no evidence to substantiate this. It is likely that Domus' quick sales and high prices were the result of competent marketing and sales, effective advertising, or temporarily favorable market conditions. It is equally likely that they were the result of other features of its homes, such as furnished houses. Even if Domus has succeeded because of the two features, it is possible that the homes are not representative of its homes in general, since they are confined to one area and may be small in number. Even assuming they are, Bower may be too different from Domus to warrant a similar strategy. The former may serve lower middle-class or poorer customers whereas the latter middle-class or richer customers. Should this prove to be true, then Bower would be wasting much money on houses that do not sell at all, much less at higher-than-average prices. Unless there is evidence that Domus' quick sales and high prices were the result of the two features and that Bower is essentially comparable to Domus in ways that might affect sales and prices of housing, the author cannot confidently claim that Bower should emulate Domus.

Finally, the author makes the assumption that the opinions of recent buyers regarding dining rooms are representative of those of Bower's customers in general. However, this is not supported by any concrete evidence. The group of recent buyers could be very small and an anomaly. Just because those buyers say they do not need separate dining rooms does not necessarily mean that a large portion of buyers feel the same way, nor that if such a portion existed, they would be willing to pay more than the national average for the new homes. Also, it is unfair to assume that simply because the two features are the most desired, those surveyed would be willing to sacrifice dining room space in order to make room for larger kitchens and family rooms. Bower's employees could have asked the question in a way that led the buyers to choose large family rooms and large kitchens over a separate dining room. Even if the buyers do not need a separate dining room for family meals, they may need one to banquet guests. Should this be the case, the assumption about the representativeness of the buyers' opinions would prove unjustified and building homes without separate dining rooms risks sparking a backlash against Bower's houses with only large family rooms and kitchens.

In conclusion, the recommendation has a high chance of backfiring and costing the company more rather than boosting its profits if the assumptions are not warranted. To better evaluate the recommendation, we need information about the costs of implementing the new plan and about whether the current and future housing market can support the prediction that Bower will be able to sell enough homes fast enough to increase its profits.

37. Increased demand for heating oil and investment in Consolidated (Assumptions)

Predicting a rise in demand for heating oil, the author recommends that a client invest in a home heating oil seller called Consolidated Industries. To justify the recommendation, the letter states that most homes in the northeastern United States have always used oil as their primary fuel for heating, and that climate forecasters have predicted a cold weather trend that, based on 90 days of below-normal temperatures last heating season, will continue for years into the future. It also notes that the population in this region has grown recently, with a large number of new homes being constructed to address the issue. However, the argument is rife with assumptions and loopholes that we should scrutinize before we determine its soundness.

The author assumes that because oil has been the traditional choice of fuel for heating, it will remain so in the future. However, various other options may become more popular in the future for various reasons. For example, the push for green energy alternatives could make oil fall out of popularity, or a newer and cheaper source of energy may be discovered that would render oil obsolete. If this is the case, oil is unlikely to remain the main heating fuel. The letter also points out that new homes are being built in the region for the growing population. However, there is no information about the number of new homes being built and how many of them will use oil as their major fuel for heating. If few of them are sold and occupied, few of them rely on oil for heating, or they are better insulated, the prediction of a growing demand for heating oil would be unjustified. Unless there is relevant evidence, the author cannot confidently claim that oil will remain the main heating fuel in the future, rendering the prediction of an increasing demand for heating oil unreasonable and the argument for investment in Consolidated implausible.

Next, the author implies that the climate trends will continue. However, the author provides no evidence to substantiate this. The trend in the last heating season might have been an aberration and may not last into the future. Even if the trend persists, this does not necessarily mean there will be an increased demand for heating oil, since the letter does not indicate whether in the 90 days when the region underwent below-normal temperatures, residents used more heating oil. It is possible that the region experienced no more demand for heating oil during this period. Also, there is no guarantee that the prediction of forecasters will be accurate. With the onset of climate change, there may be a chance that the cold weather periods will shorten significantly in the near future. Even assuming that the climate prediction will hold true for as long as the forecasters have claimed, there may not be an increasing demand for heating oil because it may have become so expensive at some point that people will switch to other means of heating. There is even the possibility that some people, especially old people, will leave this part of the country for the south during winters, decreasing the need for heating oil. Even if there is a rising demand for heating oil in this region, the demand for heating oil in other parts of the country may decrease. Any of the scenarios, if true, would make the recommendation of investment in Consolidated unconvincing.

Even granting that the foregoing assumptions can be substantiated, the author also seems to suggest, without any evidence, that Consolidated is the only major retailer in this market worth investing in. It is likely that Consolidated does not have a track record of success in its business operations. It is also likely that even if the retail sale of home heating oil is one of its major business operations, it is not profitable, since its business scale is too small, its operating costs are enormous, and its stores are few and have inconvenient locations. Besides, there may be some other companies that do as well as or even better than Consolidated in the same industry, but the author makes no mention of them, or at least does not give reasons for them not being worthy investments. Even if Consolidated has been successful in its retail sale of home heating oil, there may be better investment opportunities in other industries. Should this be the case, the argument for investment in Consolidated would fall apart.

To conclude, the assumptions on which this letter's argument is based are not warranted. In this case, there is a chance that investors would be placing their money in a dying industry, or at the very least in a single company when other options are available but unmentioned. To bolster the argument, the author must provide evidence that substantiates the assumptions.

38. Cutting funding for the Grandview Symphony (Questions to Be Answered)

The author recommends that the Grandview Symphony's funding be completely removed from the following year's budget in light of what the author views as a newfound self-sufficiency. To justify the recommendation, the article cites a two-hundred percent increase in private donations and a doubling in attendance at the symphony's park concert series last year. It also mentions the plan by the symphony to increase ticket prices in the following year. Yet before we determine whether the city of Grandview should withdraw its financial support to the symphony, we should have answers to some questions.

One important question to consider is whether the increase in private donations is significant or even remotely close to covering the operating costs of the Grandview Symphony. It may certainly be possible for private donations to fully support the symphony, but without accurate data showing how much was previously donated versus the costs of running the symphony, a two-hundred percent increase is a meaningless statistic. The private contributions before last year may have been very small and therefore an increase of two-hundred percent may not be significant. Even if the contributions were significant, they may not be adequate for operating the symphony. Also, the trend last year could have been an aberration and may not continue. For example, the contributions could decrease dramatically this year and even more dramatically next year. Perhaps the city has provided the greatest amount of funding for the symphony last year, boosting private contributions for it. Therefore, if the city ceases funding for the symphony, private contributions may diminish as well. If the increase in donations has not been significant and is unlikely to sustain, the argument that the symphony can fully support itself and has no need for city funding next year would be gratuitous.

Another question to answer is whether the increase in attendance at the concerts-in-the-park series is grounds for elimination of funding for the symphony. As with the increase in private donations, the article does not cite any specific numbers regarding previous attendance, nor do we know how important this particular series of concerts is compared to other performances put on each year by the symphony. If the attendance had been negligible before last year, a double attendance may not be significant. If the series accounts for a small portion of all of the symphony's events annually, it may contribute a small amount to the funding for the symphony. We also want to know whether the attendance requires paying for tickets. If the attendance is free of charge, the series may increase the costs instead of increasing the revenue. If the city's funding helps promote the series and offset most of its costs, the argument for eliminating its funding for the symphony would be weakened. Even if the doubling of attendance means a significant rise in the number of attendees, the trend last year could have been an anomaly and may not hold true next year. Any of the scenarios, if true, would invalidate the claim that the symphony has no need for city funding next year.

Still another question to address is whether the plan by the symphony to increase ticket prices for next year, coupled with a double increase in its private contributions and one hundred percent increase in attendance at its park concert series, would guarantee that it will be self-sufficient and warrant elimination of funding for it. We would like to know whether raising ticket prices is a good option. As with private contributions and concert attendance, no concrete data is provided regarding current ticket revenues and potential increase for next year. If the amount of rise is too small, it will be meaningless for the symphony's operation. If the audience and the benefactors refuse to accept the rise, the symphony could not rely on this new source of funding. Even if the symphony can rely on the increase in ticket prices for next year, there is no guarantee that this increase, together with that in private contributions and concert attendance, will be enough to make up for the eliminated budget. Should this be the case, the argument for not including funding for the symphony in next year's city budget would be unjustified.

In sum, before the city of Grandview decides to cancel its financial support of the symphony, there should be a more in-depth investigation of the figures regarding the change in private contributions and attendance, along with how these and other factors may have influenced the symphony's decision to increase ticket prices.

39. Using UltraClean in our hospital system (Assumptions)

The author recommends that a group of hospitals offer UltraClean, an antibacterial hand soap, at all hand-washing stations throughout its hospital system in order to eliminate severe patient infections. To justify the recommendation, the memo cites a laboratory study that found UltraClean reduced bacteria populations 40 percent more than the hand soaps currently used. It goes on to say that a following test of the soap at one hospital resulted in fewer cases of patient infection than at any other hospitals in the group. However, the argument is based on assumptions that are shaky at best and require close scrutiny before we determine its soundness.

First, the author assumes that the laboratory test of the hand soap is a valid and reliable study. However, the author provides no evidence to substantiate this. It is likely that the concentrated solution of UltraClean used in the study was responsible for the better effect and UltraClean by itself may not be better at killing bacteria than the liquid hand soaps being used in the hospitals. In this case, the test is not a reliable measure by which to determine UltraClean's effectiveness in a real-world setting in which larger numbers of and more kinds of bacteria, in addition to viruses, are present. Also, the author makes no mention of exactly what kind of bacteria UltraClean was 40 percent better at killing, a point that should be seriously considered before people rely on the soap in a hospital. It may be more effective at killing some kinds of bacteria but may not be better at killing the bacteria that often lead to infections in hospitals. In this case, the laboratory test is invalid and unreliable. Without information about what bacteria UltraClean can kill and what other source of infection it can prevent, we cannot fully evaluate its efficacy at reducing infections, especially serious infections.

Secondly, the author implies that the reduction in patient infections at the Workby hospital was the direct result of using UltraClean. However, a myriad of other factors might explain the lower number of infections, such as physical contact protocol, or air filtration systems. It is likely that much fewer patients were present in the hospital when the test was conducted. It is also likely that the hospital in Workby reported fewer cases to help to promote UltraClean or to seem outstanding in preventing patient infections, distorting the results. While the hospital reported fewer cases of patient infection, it might have reported more cases of serious patient infection. If the test at Workby was not valid or reliable, then the results would not be representative of the effectiveness of UltraClean. Even if the test was reliable and valid, it is just one case and requires many similar studies to ascertain the efficacy of UltraClean at reducing patient infections. In such scenarios, the assumption would be unfounded and the argument for more extensive use of UltraClean undermined. Unless there is evidence that UltraClean was responsible for the decrease in patient infections, especially serious infections and that other hospitals throughout the system are comparable to the hospital in Workby, the author cannot justifiably claim that UltraClean should be offered at hand-washing stations throughout the hospital system.

Even granting that the laboratory test and the subsequent Workby test are valid, the author also suggests that having UltraClean at all hand soap stations will do anything to prevent serious infections. However, even if offering UltraClean can reduce infections caused by bacteria, it may not reduce infections caused by other factors such as viruses. Even assuming that UltraClean can decrease ordinary infections, there is no guarantee that it will be able to prevent any serious infections. Since serious patient infections are usually related to numerous causes, such as a patient's weakened immune system or extremely traumatic injuries, there is little evidence that the hand soap alone will do anything to prevent such infections. Even assuming that UltraClean is effective at reducing serious infections, this does not necessarily mean that it should be offered at all hand soap stations because some hospitals may have no severe infections. There may also be some equally efficacious but cheaper alternatives, for example, the liquid hand soaps being used in the hospitals. In that event, the assumption about the extensive use of Ultraclean would prove unwarranted and the argument would collapse.

In conclusion, the author should reconsider the assumptions about UltraClean; otherwise, the hospital group may waste a substantial amount of time and money replacing all hand soaps for no reason. The plan may also lead to an over-reliance on the hand soap at the expense of more effective solutions, such as sterile gloves, air-filtration systems, and face masks.

40. Parkville to discontinue organized children's athletics (Assumptions)

While the author may recommend out of a noble concern that Parkville end organized athletic sports for children under nine, the letter must furnish evidence that the disadvantages of youth-league sports outweigh the advantages. The argument is full of assumptions and loopholes that require careful consideration before we ascertain its validity.

Mentioning that, nationally, over 40,000 youth league participants under the age of nine experienced injuries while playing sports, the author assumes that these injuries were serious enough to warrant the discontinuation of youth sports altogether. Yet the author offers no specific details as to the severity of the injuries experienced, or if the number of participants affected was significant at all. It is possible that the number 40, 000 was not statistically significant if the participants totaled 4, 000, 000. It could have been important if the participants totaled no more than 400, 000. Also, the majority of cases could have been minor cuts and bruises, which are a common enough occurrence among young children playing outside. Without relevant data, we have no way of knowing. Moreover, the trend last year could have been an aberration and may not continue. If this should be true, there would be no need for being concerned about the students' severe injuries in the future. At the same time, the national trend may not hold true for Parkville. It is possible that last year the youth league participants under nine in Parkville experienced no injuries at all while playing sports, not to mention serious ones. Any of the scenarios, if true, would cast serious doubt on the assumption about the severity of the injuries and the argument for stopping youth-league sports for children younger than nine.

The author also implies that there is something wrong with the psychological pressure on the children to win games. While it can certainly be a problem for coaches and parents to castigate young players for losing, the author does not directly state that such events have occurred. Even if they have taken place, the respondents may not be representative of young children participating in sports in general. The study could have been unreliable and invalid: the players interviewed may have been small in number and constituted a self-selecting group who was most vulnerable to psychological pressure and reported it to avoid further participation in sports. In this case, it is likely that only the youth soccer players in several major cities had the psychological pressure whereas players of other sports or players in other places, including Parkville, did not have the pressure. Even if the psychological pressure did exist, it could not have been a problem if it were not damaging to the children's physical and mental health. Unless there is evidence that the pressure exerted by coaches and parents was harmful, it is unfair to claim that it was a disadvantage. Otherwise, the author seems to be implying that there is something wrong with instilling a motivation for success in the youth, a quality that youth sports have long been known to nurture. Since no proof of psychological damage has been proffered by the letter, psychological pressure is a non-issue. Since there is no evidence that the study was reliable, valid, and representative, it is unfair to conclude that Parkville should cease its organized athletic competition altogether for children under nine.

Finally, the author suggests that long practice sessions for sports like soccer have negative effects on education. While it should be ensured that sports are not taking time away from students' academic studies, no such thing is mentioned in the letter as having happened. We do not have any data pertaining to the length of all the practice sessions for these youth-league sports, so it is unfair to assume that they are negatively affecting young children's school performance. If such sessions are so long that the students are too exhausted to study, they may have an adverse effect on their academic performance. Also, as with pressure exerted by coaches and parents to win games, the letter seems to ignore the advantages to practicing sports. Just as a certain measure of pressure may nurture a motivation for success, so practicing sports for some time may make children energetic enough to study. Even if children playing youth league sports may experience injuries, some soccer players may report pressure to win, and long practicing sessions for such sports may take time from academic study, this does not necessarily mean that the disadvantages outweigh the advantages, since the author fails to mention the advantages. Even if youth-league sports are more detrimental than beneficial, this does not necessarily mean that other organized athletic competition has more disadvantages than advantages. In these cases, the assumption about the effect of practicing sessions for sports on academic performance would prove unwarranted, and the argument for discontinuing organized athletic competition altogether for children under nine in Parkville would be too sweeping to be plausible.

The letter does not provide any clear evidence to support the notion that organized athletics are negatively affecting children under nine in any way, and as a result, offers no valid argument for cancelling them. Academic performance should, of course, be a top priority for young people, but unless there is relevant evidence, the author cannot justifiably claim that organized athletics for children younger than nine should be discontinued completely.

41. Drop in popularity of Stanley Park (Assumptions)

Stanley Park's predicament, if true, is certainly worthy of serious consideration. However, in light of the evidence provided by the author, it is difficult to evaluate the argument in favor of boosting its popularity by providing more benches and socialization space. The argument is rife with assumptions and loopholes that we must scrutinize to determine its soundness.

The author's primary assumption is that a significant decrease in Stanley Park's popularity has occurred at all. Sure, there is the video camera footage showing only fifty cars on average visiting the park per day, compared to Carlton Park's one-hundred and fifty people on a weekday, but it is not reasonable to assume that this means fewer people have visited the park. It may be the case that depending on Stanley Park's relative location, people preferred to go to the park on foot or by bicycle. It may also be the case that people went there but parked their cars elsewhere that had not been recorded. Perhaps the fifty cars carried more than one hundred and fifty people to the park every day. Or perhaps on a typical weekday far more than one hundred and fifty people visit the park. Or perhaps the video camera did not work properly and failed to record anything in many days last month. Any of the scenarios, if true, would call into question the assumption about Stanley Park's popularity and the argument for increasing it by providing more benches and socialization space.

Another assumption made by the author is that Carlton Park's popularity is the result of its ample seating. However, there is no evidence provided by the article to support this assumption. Just because Carlton Park offers plenty seating does not mean it is popular because of the seating. A more likely explanation is that it is located in the heart of a busy city area and people take advantage of the parking spaces instead of having to pay for city parking spots, which in a business district can be prohibitively expensive. Also, while Carlton Park is visited by over one hundred and fifty people on a weekday, it may be visited by few people on weekends, reducing the average number of visitors per day dramatically. Just because more than one hundred and fifty people visit the park each weekday does not necessarily mean the park is popular. Such scenarios would cast doubt on the assumption that Carlton Park's abundant seating is responsible for its popularity and on the assumption that it is more popular than Stanley Park.

Still another assumption made by the article is that building more benches in Stanley Park will do anything to affect its popularity. Even granting that the number of cars is valid evidence of its popularity or the lack thereof, this does not necessarily mean so, since no cause of decrease in its popularity has been identified. People may have stopped coming to the park for various unrelated reasons, such as economic shifts that require people to work longer hours, thus limiting their ability to go to the park, or simply the seasonal climate that has made going to the park less enjoyable in the past month. The trend last month may even be an anomaly and may not continue. In such scenarios, the assumption about the effect of building more benches would prove unwarranted, undermining the recommendation of the measure to Stanley Park, especially when people may go to Stanley Park for its open areas and do not need ample seating for socialization. To better evaluate the argument, we need more information about if Carlton Park visitors spend much time on socialization when they sit on the benches and about whether ample seating would boost Stanley Park's popularity.

While it is important to ensure that public spaces like parks are fully enjoyed by citizens, there is little evidence to support the suggested measure. Unless the author can substantiate the assumption that Stanley Park and Carlton Park are sufficiently alike in ways that may affect the impact of ample seating on their respective popularity, implementing the measure could lead the town to waste money on benches and construction without due diligence.

42. Reducing in-store imported cheese inventory (Questions to Be Answered)

The author recommends that a chain of cheese stores improve profits by ceasing to stock many of its imported cheeses and instead focus on domestic ones. However, to fully assess the recommendation, we need answers to many questions surrounding the evidence provided.

To begin with, we wonder whether the newest store is representative of the entirety of locations the chain has across the United States. However, no relevant information is provided. The author states that the best-selling cheeses at one location last year were all domestic. This fact by itself does sound convincing. However, they may only account for a smaller portion of the total sales volume of the store. Even if they make up a great portion of the total sales, a myriad of factors might explain this phenomenon. It could be the case that the new location had some sort of sale on those particular cheeses, that customers in that region simply preferred those cheeses, or that the store was new and did not yet begin to stock many imported cheeses. In such scenarios, sales and customers' preferences of the newest store may not typify those of the chain's other stores. It could also be the case that the trend last year was an aberration and may not continue. In contrast, it could be that many customers in other parts of the country do not like cheddar cheeses but prefer imported cheeses. If this should be true, the recommendation of stopping stocking many imported cheeses and concentrating on domestic cheeses to increase profits would be unjustified. Customer surveys and more recent sales figures would go a long way toward evaluating the argument.

Next, the question arises as to whether the subscribers to the magazine Cheeses of the World are comparable to this chain's potential customers. However, no information is offered in this respect. The memo mentions that the survey found a popularity trend among the subscribers that favors domestic cheeses. But there is no survey data comparing the magazine readers to all the cheese-eaters in the entire nation. The survey results could be a gross misrepresentation. Then, the question arises as to whether the subscribers to this magazine constitute a considerable portion of this chain's customers or are at least similar to them. If yes, then the survey would be something worthy of consideration regarding the stocking recommendation. Also, we would like to know whether the survey is reliable and valid. The sample could have been a small group of self-selecting subscribers who tended to prefer domestic cheeses to imported ones. The researchers could have asked questions such as "Which do you prefer in terms of prices, domestic cheeses or imported cheeses?" In either scenario, the survey results would not be valid. Unless the survey is reliable, valid, and representative, the surveyed subscribers could not represent potential cheese buyers of this chain, the recommendation would be unreasonable, and the argument would be undermined.

Finally, there remains the question of whether discontinuing the chain's inventory of many varieties of imported cheese will improve its profits. However, the author provides no data in this regard. Even assuming that there is a nation-wide preference for domestic cheeses to imported cheeses, there could be price hikes by suppliers in the face of increasing demand, which may offset any expenses saved by removing imported stock. The chain should look into whether this could occur, and to what extent its stores would be affected. Also, stopping stocking imported cheeses may hurt the chain's reputation as a seller of imported cheeses as well as domestic cheeses. Customers may value the variety and choice of its stocked cheeses. Even if they prefer domestic cheeses, they may buy some imported cheeses at the same time. In this case, by discontinuing stock of imported cheeses, the chain may lose profits instead. In addition, the author needs to find out the profit margins of imported cheeses versus domestic cheeses. If imported cheeses have higher profit margins than those of domestic cheeses, the proposed course of action would be undesirable, because the expenses saved from reducing inventory of imported cheeses may be much less than loss of revenue that may result from stocking them. Furthermore, the author even fails to consider better options for improving profits. Perhaps expenses for stocking imported cheeses only account for a small portion of the total costs whereas those for renting the business space a significant part of the costs. In this case, it would be much more profitable to move to cheaper locations instead. Any of the scenarios, if true, would invalidate the assumption about increased profitability of and the argument for focusing on domestic cheeses.

While it may benefit the company to stock primarily domestic cheeses, as it stands, the argument in favor of the measure lacks the necessary scrutiny to assuage all concerns about it. The possibility exists that the measure will backfire, and unless the aforementioned issues are addressed, it would not be prudent to go forward with the author's recommendation.

43. Making big changes to save the Rialto Movie Theater (Questions to Be Answered)

While the situation of the Rialto Movie Theater seems to call for drastic changes to save its business, simply copying the Apex Theater's interior design and amenities will not necessarily help it maintain its share of moviegoers. We must have answers to certain questions about this plan before we determine its soundness.

The author must answer whether Apex's décor has contributed to its success. We wonder whether Apex has succeeded at all. The article simply mentions its location, the time when it opened, and its décor, but provides no information about how it has fared. If it has been doing badly or has closed, it should not be an example for Rialto to emulate. If it has prospered, we would like to know why. It may be that Apex simply has better management, or that its mall location allows it to attract customers who are already primed to make purchases. It may also be that Apex's success lies with its choice of films shown in the theater. Any of the scenarios, if true, would invalidate the claim that Rialto should offer the same features as Apex to maintain its business. Regardless, without customer survey data to show what it is that attracts more people to Apex and what seems to deter others from going to Rialto, the author cannot fairly assume that Apex has thrived because of its décor.

The next thing that warrants consideration is whether Rialto should emulate Apex. Even if Apex has prospered as a result of the features, this does not necessarily mean Rialto will succeed by offering the same features. It is likely that Rialto is vastly different from Apex to justify the same course of action. Even if the pool of moviegoers is declining, this does not necessarily mean Rialto is experiencing a decline of patrons. Even assuming that it is, the decline may be caused by factors other than those that may have been responsible for Apex's success. There may be many video arcades near the downtown location of Rialto and therefore one more video arcade offers little attraction. Rialto may be losing customers because it has been showing unpopular movies, or because the downtown economy is deteriorating, and many residents have moved out. Also, while Apex customers may prefer a new theater, the customers of downtown Rialto may want more parking space and reasonable ticket prices. Given the differences between Rialto and Apex, it is unfair to assume that Rialto can attract customers by providing the same features as Apex, rendering the recommendation unreasonable.

Even if Rialto is comparable to Apex and decides to remodel its theater, there is still the question of whether offering the new features is viable and the only way to keep its share of moviegoers. The features, including the video arcade, may be so costly that Rialto cannot afford them. There is the possibility that if it makes such big changes, it will run out of money for its operating expenses and have to close permanently. In this case, the recommendation that Rialto should make renovations by following Apex's example would be unreasonable. Even if Rialto is able to secure the money to finance the new features, the survey mentioned by the business plan states that eighty-five percent of people are dissuaded from going to cinemas because of the high price of tickets for newer movies. This seems to imply that lowering its ticket prices for newer movies may be another viable strategy to hold on to its share of viewers. This depends on whether the surveyed population is representative of Rialto's customers. If the sample constitutes a significant portion of its customers, it must figure out how it will manage the issue of attracting them. For example, it could lower the price of tickets for new movies if many respondents find its movies too expensive or risks losing some moviegoers. If the sample consists of a small group of people who tend to see new movies, the survey may not be reliable or valid, and the respondents would not be representative of Rialto's customers. In that event, a less expensive remodeling plan may be in order. To better assess the plan to offer the same features as Apex, we need to examine the costs of the renovations and alternative strategies, such as lowering ticket prices of new movies or implementing a more affordable remodeling plan.

Before we decide whether Rialto should adopt the recommendation of adding new features, we must have answers to many questions. The situation seems grim for Rialto, as there is no guarantee that any of its options will work very well. It runs the risk of spending much money to add new features, without much assurance that it will be able to recoup the costs. Perhaps the best route would be simply to lower prices and hope that customers would come for that reason alone.

44. Partnership between Sherwood Hospital and Sherwood Animal Shelter (Assumptions)

Citing a study reporting that dog owners have lower rates of heart disease, the author recommends that Sherwood Hospital form a partnership with Sherwood Animal Shelter as part of a plan to reduce the occurrences of heart disease in the area's population. Yet the argument is based on many assumptions that require scrutiny before we ascertain its soundness.

The threshold assumption that underlies the argument is that the study participants are representative of dog owners in general. However, there is nothing given in the article to support this idea. Without any data, such as sample size, control groups, and specific factors observed and recorded, the author cannot justifiably claim that any conclusive evidence of a link between owning a dog and incidence of heart disease exists at all. A small sample could be unrepresentative. Without a control group, it is hard to know whether owning a pet alone would be responsible for longer, healthier lives. It is likely that the sample happened to consist mostly of people with longer, healthier lives, or that a few participants had extremely long lives, skewing the results. Specifically, people who had no heart disease might own a dog, whereas those with heart disease might not own a dog. It is also likely that most of the participants simply had more free time, better healthcare, healthier lifestyles, and more opportunities for keeping a dog. In either scenario, the study is hardly valid, reliable, or representative, ruling out dog ownership as the main reason for a lower incidence of heart disease. To better evaluate the argument, we need evidence regarding whether there is a causal link between owning a pet and longer lives, in particular, owning a dog and a lower incidence of heart disease.

Even granting that a link exists between owning a dog and a lower incidence of heart disease, the author also implies that allowing shelter dogs into a hospital setting will benefit the patients recovering from heart disease. The author assumes that doing so will present no serious problems. However, the author provides no evidence that this is the case. Dogs may pose serious health risks and even be a breach of medical sanitation protocols. The article assumes that these dogs will all be amicable enough and free from disease, which may not be the case with dogs that have to go to a shelter. We do not know how many patients may be allergic to or afraid of dogs. If a great number of them are allergic to dogs or fear them, the program could be much less effective than initially thought. Nor do we know who will be responsible for taking care of these dogs and whether owning a dog will interfere with the patient's treatment. There is the possibility that none will be available to attend to them and they may detract from the resources that should be used for treatment of patients. There is also the possibility that patients recovering from heart disease are different from dog owners who have a lower incidence of heart disease, because the former may need more rest and have no time for taking care of the dogs. There is even the possibility that the program will increase rather than decrease need for ongoing treatment. Any of the scenarios, if true, would call into question the assumption about the benefits of the program and render the argument invalid.

Finally, the author suggests that simply because a number of patients are able to avoid further heart problems, enough people would be willing to adopt dogs from the shelter to cause a significant reduction in heart disease in the general population. However, the author offers no evidence to substantiate this. Taking in a dog may incur enormous costs and responsibilities to the new owner, such that many people may be unwilling to take on those obligations for what might be viewed as a marginal health benefit. The author notes that keeping a dog prevents incidence of heart disease rather than cures it. For this reason, people may be reluctant to participate in the adopt-a-dog program, avoiding huge responsibilities of an action despite its potential benefits. It may even be the case that the publicity about the program would be negative if the patients were critical of it because owning a dog has been detrimental rather than beneficial to them. Even if the publicity is positive and a great number of people are willing to own dogs from the shelter, there is no guarantee that this will help decrease heart disease in the common populace, since the connection between dog ownership and reduction of heart disease has yet to be established. Moreover, as with patients in hospitals, dog ownership may interfere with people's lives in other ways. In these scenarios, the argument in favor of adopting dogs from the shelter by the general population to prevent heart disease would be weakened.

After looking at these assumptions closely, we find that the author may be far too optimistic about the recommendation of forming a possible partnership between Sherwood Hospital and Sherwood Animal Shelter. The plan certainly has the best intentions, but it fails to consider the very real possibilities that could cause it to fail.

45. Is Zeta a superior construction company? (Questions to Be Answered)

The recommendation that a company use the construction company Zeta in lieu of Alpha does seem compelling at first, considering Zeta's stable workforce as well as the lower maintenance costs and lower energy consumption of its building. However, some concerns should be addressed before the company makes such a large and no doubt expensive decision.

The first question to consider is whether Zeta's higher building cost can be offset by its lower maintenance costs and lower energy use. The memo mentions that the building constructed by Zeta cost thirty percent more than Alpha's but tries to offset this fact by describing the cheaper maintenance costs and lower energy use. However, it does not provide information about how long it would take those savings to balance out the higher cost of the building. Nor does it consider the possibility that the lower maintenance costs were only for the last year, which may have been an aberration and the trend may not continue; the costs may even increase over time with wear and tear. It is even possible that since the building cost more to construct, there would be more maintenance costs once repairs become necessary. Similarly, the trend of lower energy consumption since erection of the building could have been an aberration and may change in the opposite direction in the future. If this is true, Zeta's higher building cost may not be balanced out by its lower maintenance costs and lower energy consumption and using Zeta instead of Alpha for the new building project would be unfounded.

Next, we wonder whether Zeta can justify, in other ways, its thirty percent higher construction cost and its possibly higher building cost of the new project. The previously mentioned savings seem to have been discovered after the fact and thus were not factored into the original cost. Therefore, it stands to reason that there must be some justification for the higher construction cost. The author's decision would be better supported if she could provide any other preexisting justification for Zeta's higher price in the face of identical floor plans. If Zeta has used high-end building materials that would make its building last longer, its building has been erected in a region that requires much higher labor costs, or it has had to follow stricter codes of construction in the region of the building, it could justify its thirty percent higher construction cost in the past and its higher building cost of the new project if the scenarios hold true in the future. Similarly, if it can finish the work ahead of schedule, follow the latest fashion in décor and adopt the latest technology, the company may not mind a little higher construction cost of the new project. In that event, the argument for preferring Zeta to Alpha would be strengthened. Otherwise, the argument would be undermined.

Finally, there is the question of what Zeta's workforce has to do with the matter at hand: whether it is one of the features that may tip the balance in favor of Zeta. There is no mention of Alpha's workforce. Therefore, it would seem that mentioning this piece of information is unfair, unless it has a significant effect on which company should be chosen, in which case it would help the author's argument to state specifically what benefits there are to be gained from the companies' respective workforces. Also, a competent workforce may be more important than a stable workforce, as long as it does not adversely affect the new building project. If Zeta has a workforce that is competent as well as stable, it would be an advantage in its bid for the project. However, the memo offers no details in this respect; therefore, the author cannot justifiably recommend that the company use Zeta rather than Alpha in its new building project. Additionally, we do not know whether there are other benefits that Alpha may offer but have not been described here. Perhaps aside from a lower building cost, which in most construction biddings would almost guarantee it the contract, Alpha is able to finish construction much earlier, or can guarantee that its structure will last longer. Or perhaps it requires no payment in advance whereas Zeta requires a large payment before the project starts. Or perhaps it even has more up-to-date, aesthetically pleasing designs whereas Zeta has mostly outmoded, monotonous ones. Any of the scenarios, if true, would make using Zeta rather than Alpha for the new project implausible. However, without more information about each company, there would be no way to know for certain. Alpha's bid for the new building in the memo.

While the initial information given could make Zeta a tempting choice in the bid for the company's new construction project, it would be unprofessional not to do more research into what both companies can offer in their buildings and an analysis of long-term costs and savings that might affect the total price of the structure.

46. Is Zeta a superior construction company? (Specific Evidence)

The recommendation that a company use the construction company Zeta in lieu of Alpha does seem compelling at first, considering the lower maintenance costs and less energy consumption of the Zeta building. However, to better assess the argument, we need extra evidence.

We must have evidence regarding whether Zeta's higher building cost can be offset by its lower maintenance costs and lower energy use. The memo mentions that the building constructed by Zeta cost thirty percent more than Alpha's but tries to offset this fact by describing the cheaper maintenance costs and lower energy use. However, it does not provide information about how long it would take those savings to balance out the higher cost of the building. Nor does it consider the possibility that the lower maintenance costs were only for the last year, which may have been an aberration and the trend may not continue; the costs may even increase over time with wear and tear. It is even possible that since the building cost more to construct, there would be more expensive maintenance costs once repairs become necessary. Similarly, the trend of lower energy consumption since erection of the building could also have been an aberration and may change in the opposite direction in the future. If this is true, Zeta's higher building cost is unlikely to be balanced out by its lower maintenance costs and lower energy consumption and using Zeta instead of Alpha for the building project would be unfounded. If the author could provide a detailed cost-versus-savings analysis to find out exactly how much money the Zeta building has saved in its maintenance and energy consumption and show that the money saved would be greater than or close to the gap between its construction cost and that of the Alpha building, the author's argument would be strengthened.

Additionally, we should have evidence given by Zeta to justify, in other ways, its thirty percent higher construction cost and its possibly higher building cost of the new project. The previously mentioned savings seem to have been discovered after the fact and thus were not factored into the original cost. Therefore, it stands to reason that there must be some justification for the higher construction cost. The author's decision would be better supported if she could provide any other preexisting justification for Zeta's higher price in the face of identical floor plans. If Zeta has used high-end building materials that would make its building last longer, its building has been erected in a region that requires much higher labor costs, or it has had to follow stricter codes of construction in the region of the building, it could justify its thirty percent higher construction cost in the past and its higher building cost of the new project if the scenarios hold true in the future. Similarly, if it can finish the work ahead of schedule, follow the latest fashion in décor and adopt the latest technology, the company may not mind a little higher construction cost of the new project. In that event, the argument for preferring Zeta to Alpha would be strengthened. Otherwise, the argument would be undermined.

Finally, we need evidence against Alpha's bid for the new building in the memo. All that is known for sure is that it may cost less than Zeta's, which in most construction biddings would almost guarantee it the contract. Therefore, it falls to the author to provide some reasons other than the weak evidence of uncertain lower maintenance costs and lower energy use for not choosing Alpha for the new building project. For example, Alpha may use building materials of inferior quality and erect buildings that will not last long. Its time-frames may be too long and it may finish construction much more slowly. Perhaps it requires an enormous payment in advance whereas Zeta asks for none. Or perhaps it has mostly outmoded, monotonous designs whereas Zeta has more aesthetically pleasing ones. Any of the scenarios, if true, would support the decision to use Zeta instead of Alpha for the new project. Otherwise, there would be little justification for choosing Zeta over

Alpha for the new building project. However, without more information about Alpha, there would be no way to know for certain.

While the initial information given could make Zeta a tempting choice in the bid for the company's new construction project, the author needs to provide clear evidence that its building will be superior to Alpha's, based not just on the previous projects, but on the new plan as well.

47. Reducing traffic in Waymarsh by learning from Garville (Specific Evidence)

The author's assertion that Waymarsh can resolve its traffic problem by imitating a policy of the nearby city of Garville is not supported by enough evidence, nor is the existence of a traffic problem certain. Thus, it seems that to determine the soundness of the argument, we need more evidence.

To begin with, the survey cited in the letter does not offer any details about the problems with Waymarsh's traffic aside from the increase in the time spent in transit. If it wishes to convince anyone that the problem exists, there needs to be further data supplied, such as the change in population of the area, as well as the average speed of cars travelling on the road. If the city could show that cars have been forced to drive significantly more slowly, it is able to make a clearer plan to implement solutions. The respondents of the recent survey that shows that the commute takes nearly 40 minutes may be unrepresentative of driving commuters in general. The author provides no information about the sample size and demographics. It is likely that the surveyed population is an aberration, a group of people who have the longest commuting time. In this case, the claim that Waymarsh is experiencing a traffic problem would be unfounded and the argument in support of following Garville's example by implementing a ride-sharing policy would be undermined. Without more information about the survey, we cannot properly assess the argument.

In addition, no evidence is provided to substantiate the statement about the disadvantages to building more roads. If the aforementioned research does show that congestion is to blame, then building a road would be the natural solution. However, the letter strongly implies that this would be far too expensive and disruptive to the residential neighborhoods. Yet no information is given to clarify this statement. The inclusion of projected expenses and quotes from construction companies about how loud their work would be could help us to assess the persuasiveness of this statement. The argument would also benefit from a survey to show that people in the area would be opposed to the noise and other disturbances that would result from constructing new roads in the area. If building a road is shown to be too expensive and the noise and other disturbances are intolerable to the neighborhood residents, it would make sense to reject this option in favor of the ride-sharing policy. Otherwise, the argument would be tenuous. To better evaluate the argument, we need concrete evidence of the disadvantages to building more roads.

As for the proposed measure of following Garville's example, there is nothing presented in the letter to explain the similarities between the two cities and whether reduction in commuting times in Garville is a result of its ride-sharing policy; therefore, the notion that a similar policy would work in Waymarsh could be a false analogy. It is possible that Waymarsh could not afford rewards like coupons for free gas, or that its residents do not accept the ride-sharing policy, rendering it undesirable. On the other hand, if the letter could provide a clear plan of implementation as well as some data showing that people in the city would be willing to follow the ride-sharing initiative, then the argument would be more convincing. Even if Waymarsh is comparable to Garville to justify a similar initiative, the author must furnish evidence of the link between Garville's policy last year and its significant improvement in commuting times, if there is such an improvement at all. It is entirely possible that good weather has lessened pollution levels in Garville. It is also possible that the people there who report significantly shortened commuting times happen to be a group of people who have the least commuting times, who have unreliable memories, or who want to make Garville seem like a city with no traffic problems. In that event, the assumption about Garville's success in its ride-sharing policy would be gratuitous. Unless there is evidence that Garville's initiative alone is responsible for less commuting time there and can be as successful in Waymarsh because of the two cities' comparability, the author cannot reasonably claim that Waymarsh should follow Garville's example.

While the ride-sharing program may be successful in Garville, it is not necessarily the only solution to the traffic problem in Waymarsh if a problem exists at all. Should the author offer clear evidence that a traffic problem does exist in Waymarsh, and that the people will not object to construction near their neighborhoods, then well-laid plans for a similar policy from Garville could be considered.

48. Is downsizing in Elthyria not as bad as a recent report claims? (Specific Evidence)

To discredit claims surrounding the hardship experienced by Elthyrian workers after losing their jobs due to company downsizing, the author asserts that such claims of hardship are refuted by an economic report showing that more jobs have been created than eliminated since 1999, and that most of the newly created jobs are high-paying full-time positions. Yet to fully assess the argument, we need extra evidence.

The author must provide evidence that the newly created jobs since 1999 are suitable for job-seekers downsized by corporations. The major issue with the argument is the recent report which the letter attempts to provide as evidence against the claim about the workers' economic suffering. If the jobs that have been created, according to the report, are comparable to the ones lost by most of the qualified workers, this could be evidence disproving prevalence of the competent workers' hardship. However, the letter does not show this. It is possible that there is a mismatch between the skills, experience, and interests required by the newly created jobs and those of the downsized employees. For example, the new jobs may require only low-level skills whereas many downsized employees have managerial skills. Alternatively, they may require experience and new skills that the unemployed competent workers do not have; therefore, the newly created jobs may have been taken by other workers. Therefore, it could be that the people mentioned in the article which this letter is refuting are among the allegedly smaller percentage of the populace unemployed for years, even though jobs created far outnumber jobs eliminated. If this should be true, the author's assumption that the downsized workers have not undergone serious economic difficulties would be groundless. Without more detailed data on those who were downsized and those who are currently unemployed, it is impossible to say for certain.

Next, although the report covers such a long period of time, it offers no specific details about how the economy has changed year to year, only relating the net change at the end of the period. In all likelihood, this does nothing to disprove the notion that victims of downsizing face serious long-term economic hardship. If it wants to undermine that argument, the letter should provide, instead of a net change overall, reliable statistics showing that people have regained lost employment in a relatively short time throughout this period. Just because Elthyria's unemployment rate is at its lowest level at the end of decades since 1999 does not mean few laid-off competent workers have experienced serious economic difficulties within the period of time. It is possible that during the decades, many competent workers have lost jobs because of corporate downsizing but could not secure proper employment for a long time. It is also possible that in the long period, some workers have even experienced this type of hardship for more than one time. Therefore, low unemployment rates at the end of decades do not necessarily mean that over the years, no downsized corporate employees have had to wait long before finding another suitable job and face severe economic difficulties, invalidating the argument that the recent report rejects the claims made by the newspaper's article on corporate downsizing. To better evaluate the argument, we need information about how long it has taken each of the laid-off workers to get proper new employment.

Finally, the author should furnish evidence regarding the pay and status of the new jobs that the laid-off workers have had. However, there is no information in this regard. Perhaps many of the laid-off workers end up with the part-time jobs newly created. Or perhaps they take one-third of the new jobs that do not pay above-average wages. Or perhaps they have wanted to take some of the two-thirds of the new jobs in industries that often pay above-average wages, but the jobs relate to positions outside the fields in which the downsizing took place. Even if the jobs are suitable for the workers, there is no guarantee that they are all high-paying. Above-average wages could still be very low and may not sustain the workers and their families, subjecting them to economic difficulties and multiple low-paying jobs for years. Any of the scenarios, if true, would cast serious doubt on the assumption that the laid-off workers can secure the full-time jobs that pay above-average wages. Should this be true, the argument would be undermined. If the letter wishes to use the pay and status of the created jobs as a relevant point, it must provide extra details about the actual jobs and pay the unemployed competent workers have.

In sum, the letter makes points without any clear connection to the argument which the author is attempting to refute. A more convincing argument would include specific jobs that were lost and subsequently created from 1999 to the present and evidence that the downsized corporate employees did not suffer any long-term hardship as a result of losing their jobs.

49. Milk prices in Batavia to be regulated by the government (Questions to Be Answered)

The author recommends that the Batavia government implement regulatory policies on retail milk prices in order to ensure fair prices for consumers. To justify the recommendation, the letter cites the growth of the dairy farm market, combined with rising milk prices at the Excello Food Market, as damning evidence. A corollary claim is that the farmers have been making excessive profits from the growth in the market. Whether this measure will have the intended result is questionable, especially in light of the poorly supported argument in the letter.

While a twenty-five percent increase in the number of dairy farms seems compelling, it is uncertain whether this has led to more production of milk and excessive profits for dairy farmers. It is likely that a twenty five percent increase is not significant. If the country had five dairy farms to begin with ten years ago, a twenty-five increase would mean one additional dairy farm. Even if there is a considerable rise in the number of dairy farms, this does not necessarily mean a rise in milk production. There is the possibility that some dairy farms produce increasingly less milk because they are not properly run, or that they have begun to produce dairy products other than milk. Even if the twenty five percent increase in dairy farms has led to more production of milk, this may not have led to profits, not to mention excessive profits, for dairy farmers. It could be that the costs, such as production costs, exceed the revenue. One would need to figure out if each farm is owned by a single farmer or business entity, or if there are conglomerates or other joint ventures among the owners. It would be reasonable to assume that if each farm is privately owned by one farmer, the profit margins would not be very high compared to those of dairy farms operated by large corporations. Moreover, without information about how much other goods are charged during the same period and what profit margins are from the sale of them, the author cannot fairly claim that farmers charge unreasonably high prices for milk and their milk-sale profits are unreasonably high. Unless there is relevant evidence, it is unfair to assume that more dairy farms mean more milk production and unreasonably high profits.

Also, we wonder whether the increase in milk prices at the local Excello Food Market is an exception and the result of famers' desire to make excessive profits from milk production. Since no information is given about dairy prices at other markets throughout the country, the increase from $1.5 to more than $3 per gallon, on its face, has almost no bearing on the argument. While the increase is impressive, its milk prices may still be lower than the national averages. Even if its milk prices are above the national averages, Excello may be an anomaly, rendering the recommendation of government regulation unjustified. Conversely, if it is found that this price hike is a part of a nationwide trend, then that would at least be a cause for consumers' concern. Yet farmers may still not be receiving excessive profits and the milk prices may still be fair for consumers. The rise in milk prices may be attributable to aggravating circumstances other than farmers' desire to profit excessively from milk production, such as inflation, increasing costs of renting store space, and rising delivery costs, among other things. Since many costs need to be covered, even if milk prices have risen dramatically, it does not necessarily mean milk business will be profitable, not to mention the likelihood of excessive profits either now or in the future. Should this be true, the assumption about farmers' receiving excessive profits on more milk production would be unwarranted, rendering the recommendation unfounded.

Even granting the two pieces of evidence provided by the letter, we still would like to know whether government regulation will have any effect on the creation of fair prices. The author must consider the particular economic conditions and predilections of the country as a whole in order to determine this. If, for example, Batavia's economy and society favors a free-market system, then regulatory action could devastate the market entirely, whereas a planned-economy system may respond favorably to regulation. Also, prices are normally determined by supply relative to demand. If there is a strong demand for milk but it is in short supply, the seller may have to increase the price. Imposing prices by government regulation rather than allowing demand and supply to determine prices could be unfair to farmers and lead to unlawful practices. They could even respond to the regulation by producing less milk, given that their milk is less profitable as a result of the regulation, raising prices instead of lowering them. In this case, the argument for government regulation would be gratuitous. Before taking such a drastic action, the government needs to investigate its potential consequences.

In conclusion, before enacting any laws regarding milk prices, the government of Batavia should first figure out the current pricing trend in all retail establishments in the country as well as the connection between more dairy farms and high profits. Furthermore, it should consider whether regulatory measures will be conducive to the economic and social system currently in place. Otherwise, there would be no reasonable way to ascertain the potential effects of price-control measures.

50. Should investors own stock in Old Dairy? (Questions to Be Answered)

The author advises investors of Old Dairy Industries (OD), including its stockholders, not to own its stock. To justify the advice, the newsletter cites the fat-rich and cholesterol-rich foods it sells as being unpopular found by a survey in which respondents seemed to want to lower their consumption of such foods. However, to determine the soundness of the advice and the argument, we need answers to many questions surrounding the evidence and the claim that the company's sales and profits will decrease.

The obvious question is whether the people surveyed are representative of a majority of potential OD consumers. The statistic of over eighty percent of respondents sounds very convincing. However, it is possible that the surveyed people are small in number and even fewer people have responded to the survey. The respondents could be an aberration and do not represent would-be OD customers. They could have indicated their desire to decrease their consumption of high-fat and high-cholesterol foods to seem health conscious. Even if the participants represent a significant portion of the potential consumers, we do not know whether their desire to eat healthier foods will translate into any subsequent behavior. It is entirely possible that they will continue to consume as many fat-rich and cholesterol-rich foods. If this should be true, the claims surrounding OD's sales and profits would be invalid and the advice on selling its shares and avoiding its stock would be gratuitous. To decide whether the advice is reasonable, we need information about the representativeness of the survey respondents.

This ties into another important question regarding the chances that OD's sales will decline significantly. With respect to the survey and the population it covers, should the data turn out to show that only lifestyles of specific areas align with the new healthy eating trend, then the company would be able to refocus its marketing in different areas to prevent decline in sales. Perhaps consumers are buying large quantities of high-fat and high-cholesterol dairy foods of OD because they have unique flavors while buying few foods of other companies that contain no fat or cholesterol because they are much more expensive and not palatable or purchasing low-fat non-dairy foods from other companies. Or perhaps consumers are turning to the company's foods that contain low fat and cholesterol. Or perhaps the company is introducing newer products to fit the new market. Should this be the case, the company's sales may not decrease, not to mention the likelihood that they will not decrease significantly. In fact, its newer products consistent with the new trend may even improve its sales. In such scenarios, the advice of not owning OD stock would be implausible.

Even granting that a decline in the company's sales is imminent, there is still the question of whether there will be a drop in profits and of whether this is grounds for dropping and avoiding its shares. Profit is a function of revenue and costs. Even assuming that the sales decrease, the revenue may not decrease if the company raises prices of its products. Even if the revenue drops, the profit may not drop if the company reduces its costs. Also, if the survey is not reliable or valid, investors need not sell off or stay away from the company's stock. Even if the surveyed population is representative of OD's would-be customers, how this would affect its sales and profits is not known. Even if its sales decline significantly and its profits drop, the trend may reverse some time later. Every company may experience market shifts with new consumption trends, but this company may adapt to the new changes and pivot. If investors sold off all their stocks at every hint of sales difficulties, there would hardly be any companies left to invest in. If current investors hold on to their stock and potential investors buy its stock, they may profit from an increase in the company's sales and profits in the future. If this should be the case, the advice to sell off and avoid the company's stock would be unjustified and the argument weakened. To better evaluate the argument, we need to know whether the stock will experience a decrease in profits.

In sum, investors should give due consideration to the reliability of the cited survey and its implications for the sales and profits of OD. Should it prove unreliable, they would run the risk of exacerbating the company's problems for no discernable reason and of marring the reputation of whoever has authored this newsletter. If, on the other hand, the survey respondents do represent a significant portion of the company's consumers, investors should still take care not to read too much into the claims by individuals about their dietary plans, as people rarely follow through.

51. Building a new golf course and resort hotel in Hopewell (Assumptions)

While it is understandable that Hopewell wishes to improve its economy, this is no grounds for entertaining the unwarranted assumptions made by the author of this memo. The example of Ocean View may be enticing, with its increased tourism, businesses, and tax revenues, but I do not see how a new golf course and resort hotel will help Hopewell. The argument is replete with assumptions and loopholes that we must scrutinize to determine its soundness.

First, the author implies that tourists are attracted by Ocean View's new golf course and hotel. However, this is not backed up by any evidence. Tourism has increased over the past two years, but numerous factors could be responsible for the trend. Other features, such as a growing national economy, or a shift in the location preferences of travelers may have had significant effects on this development. If this should be true, the assumption that Ocean View's new golf course and resort hotel alone have contributed to increased tourism would prove unjustified and the recommendation of following Ocean View's example would be groundless. Without more details about the tourists themselves and the reasons for their choices, we have no way of knowing why Ocean View has experienced the influx of visitors. Even if the new golf course and hotel have contributed to its increase in tourism, the increase could be insignificant since the number might have been very small to begin with and the trend of increase may not continue, undermining the argument for emulating Ocean View.

Another assumption made by the author is that Ocean View's new businesses and increase in tax revenue over the past two years have no other root causes than the new golf course and resort hotel. However, opening businesses usually takes much planning and time for other activities; thus, these businesses could have been started before the new hotel and golf course were built. Even if the businesses have opened during the two years since construction of the golf course and hotel, they could be tiny in number. Also, it is unfair to claim that a significant portion of the new tax revenues have been contributed by the allegedly higher numbers of tourists alone. Ocean View could have implemented a stricter policy of tax collecting, raised its tax rates, or created a new type of tax. Or it could simply have had an improved economy. At the same time, while a 30-percent increase in tax revenues is impressive, the revenues may be insignificant if they were small to begin with and the trend of dramatic increase may not persist. Any of the scenarios, if true, would undermine the assumption and argument. Without accounting for alternative possibilities, the author cannot justifiably conclude that the new golf course and hotel in Ocean View have led to opening of new businesses and more tax revenues there.

Even if all of Ocean View's recent benefits indicate significant progress and have common ties to the new resort hotel and golf course, the author also suggests that Hopewell and Ocean View are similar enough for the plan to be worth the considerable expense of Hopewell. However, this need not be the case. Just because they are situated near each other does not imply that the towns are sufficiently comparable. It is likely that Hopewell's natural environment would make it difficult for it to draw more tourists and new businesses to the area, the new golf course and hotel notwithstanding. It is also likely that in the surrounding areas, the need for a golf course and resort hotel has been fulfilled by Ocean View. It is even likely that Hopewell already has golf courses and resort hotels to be used to their capacity and therefore has no need for another golf course and hotel. Even if Hopewell can follow Ocean View's example, there is no guarantee that the plan will be the most effective way to better its economy since the true cause of its present economic situation has not been identified. Perhaps more advertising of its unique but possibly little-known scenery would be a better option. Without relevant information, we simply cannot decide whether Hopewell should take the same course of action as Ocean View.

To conclude, the assumptions made by the author are groundless and would pose significant financial risks to the town of Hopewell, should the city choose to follow the memo's recommendation despite the current lack of information. The costs of building new facilities as large as a golf course and resort hotel may even lead to reduced tax revenues, as the town would likely need to increase taxes temporarily to pay for them, which could deter citizens from starting any businesses in the area.

52. Does Buzzoff provide better pest control services than Fly-Away? (Specific Evidence)

The loss of products at the company's Palm City fast-food warehouse is regrettable and definitely warrants investigation, yet based on the information provided by the memo, there does not appear to be enough evidence to support the suggested plan to cease hiring Fly-Away Pest Control Company for pest control services in favor of the costlier Buzzoff Pest Control Company, despite the lower loss of products at the Wintervale warehouse the latter serviced.

To begin with, no concrete evidence is provided to suggest that the higher amount of pest damage at the Palm City warehouse is the fault of Fly-Away. In fact, other than the value of the lost product, there are no other details about the cause of damage at all. We do not know what pests caused the damage, nor the methods that Fly-Away had been using to prevent pests. Perhaps the warehouse was the victim of a unique species of insect that was resistant to insecticide or other standard pest prevention methods. Or perhaps the loss was the fault of the previous service provider Buzzoff but the amount of loss was not discovered until last month. Or perhaps the greater amount of loss at the Palm City warehouse was the result of the mistake of the warehouse operators, such as an accidental damaging of passive pest control equipment like rat traps. While the value of the lost product at the Palm City warehouse was greater than that at the Wintervale warehouse, the percentage of loss relative to the total value of the warehouse storage at the former may be much lower than that at the latter. Any of the scenarios, if true, would cast serious doubt on the assumption that Fly-Away's inferior performance has contributed to the greater amount of pest damage at the Palm City warehouse and on the argument that Buzzoff should replace Fly-Away for more of the company's pest control services.

Also, the memo does not offer evidence that Fly-Away and Buzzoff are sufficiently similar in ways that might affect the effect of their service on pest control. Both provide pest control services, but, other than that, they could differ vastly. The Palm City warehouse may be significantly larger than the Wintervale warehouse. If this were true, that could mean that the losses that allegedly occurred because of Fly-Away's incompetence would not seem so high as to warrant the cancellation of future business using its service. The Palm City warehouse may also have more species of pests unique to it that Fly-Away must tackle. It may even be that the food stored at the Palm City warehouse is more vulnerable to pests than that in Wintervale, or that the climate near the Palm City warehouse makes it more difficult to kill the pests. Should this be true, the assumption about comparability of both pest control service companies proves unsubstantiated and the argument against continuing to use Fly-Away's service would collapse.

Finally, the author should furnish evidence regarding whether the relatively lower damage at the Wintervale warehouse indicates that Buzzoff will save more money. However, there is no data in this respect. We do not know how much the two pest control companies are being paid as compared to the amount of damage done each month. The memo does mention that Fly-Away's charge for service is significantly lower; thus, there is the possibility that continuing to use its service would be the best cost-saving measure, especially if the Palm City warehouse was an isolated incident. The assumption about

Buzzoff's ability to save more money could be further undermined if Buzzoff's service at the Wintervale warehouse last month was also an aberration and its service in future months will be worse than Fly-Away's. Also, if Buzzoff cannot tackle certain species of pests peculiar to the warehouse in Palm City whereas Fly-Away can, using Buzzoff's service is likely to waste rather than save money. Moreover, if the contract with Fly-Away is terminated before expiry, the author's company may need to pay compensation. In such scenarios, returning to Buzzoff for all the company's pest control services to save money would be unjustified. Unless there is evidence that the difference in the prices charged by both companies is smaller than the money possibly saved from use of Buzzoff for pest control services, the author cannot confidently claim that Buzzoff rather than Fly-Away should be used for all pest control services to save money.

In conclusion, to determine the soundness of the argument, we need evidence that the higher amount of damage at the Palm City warehouse was a direct result of negligence and incompetence of Fly-Away, and that the Palm City warehouse is similar to its Wintervale counterpart in ways that might affect the effect of their service on pest control. We also need information by way of detailed comparisons of the losses and environment between both pest control services. Lastly, without relevant evidence, the author's company cannot terminate the contract with Fly-Away in good faith.

53. Newsbeat magazine considers changing focus to economics and personal finance (Questions to Be Answered)

The publisher of Newsbeat magazine recommends changing the magazine's focus from political news to economics and personal finance. To justify the recommendation, the article notes the trend of poorly selling magazine issues with political covers over the previous three years, as well as a survey of general interest magazine readers which found greater reader interest in economic issues than in political ones. While this does seem persuasive at first glance, we need answers to certain questions and a response to the editor's complaint about the move before we determine whether the magazine should make any significant changes.

The publisher needs to figure out why exactly the issues of the magazine which displayed political news on their front covers sold so poorly over the past three years. Circumstances such as political climate as compared to the political stance those particular issues seemed to take could have had serious effects on people's desire to buy them. For example, the nation at the time favored progressivism whereas the magazine covers implied that the content of the magazines supported extreme right-wing views. If this is the case, the magazine could have been the victim of a boycott during that period. However, the trend during the past three years could be an aberration and political climate may shift in the future to be more consistent with the magazine's political stance. It could also be that the worst-selling issues' articles covering politics have been generally poorly written, making readers lose interest. Perhaps the issues' designs have been aesthetically displeasing. Or perhaps over the past three years political events were not as intriguing but, in the future, they will be intriguing enough to boost sales. Or perhaps the relatively poor sales of the issues are attributable to the seasonal nature of the magazine, viz. despite their cover articles, the particular issues would have experienced a decrease in sales volume. Any of the scenarios, if true, would cast serious doubt on the recommendation of shifting the magazine's focus on politics to economics and personal finance.

Regarding the survey cited by the article, we should ask who makes up the Newsbeat reader base and whether those people are included in, or have the same views as, the readers of general interest magazines that were surveyed. This information would help to ascertain the relevance of the survey's results to the decision to change Newsbeat's focus. If Newsbeat readers and those of general interest magazines basically overlap, we can be more certain that the recommendation is reasonable. However, the information would still be a bit insufficient, as we do not know exactly what readers are looking for when reading Newsbeat, for example, what specific issues they want to learn about and what political issues they would like to continue to know on Newsbeat. Also, we should ask whether the survey was reliable, valid, and representative. If the sample was small and biased, consisting mostly of people over concerned about economic issues, it could hardly be representative of most readers of general interest magazines. The researchers could have asked which of the two, economics or politics, is more directly related to readers' life, eliciting the response in favor of economic issues. In that event, even if Newsbeat readers are comparable to those of general interest magazines, there is no guarantee that they are more interested in economic issues than in political ones, calling into question the recommendation of shifting Newsbeat's focus to economics.

This brings us to the final question: whether the editor's opposition is valid. If Newsbeat has a particular appeal to readers, and that appeal happens to be the fact that the magazine focuses on political issues, then the editor would have a fairly strong point. If not, then there is the possibility that the editor's point about the lack of politically focused magazines is irrelevant to the issue at hand. We also need to know what the fact that very few magazines cover politics extensively indicates. This could be evidence that politics is not many readers' major concern any longer, or that they want to learn about politics in other ways. If this should be the case, the editor's opposition would be groundless. This could also be evidence that as one of the few magazines featuring extensive political coverage, Newsbeat will experience an increase in sales volume. Should this be true, the editor's assumption about the correlation between sales volume and coverage of political events would be warranted. Without addressing the editor's position, the publisher cannot reliably recommend that Newsbeat should decrease emphasis on politics in favor of economics and personal finance. It would be even more helpful if we had data demonstrating whether magazines that have featured political events extensively have experienced a decrease or increase in sales after de-emphasis of politics.

In sum, the publisher of Newsbeat has many things to consider before making a shift in the magazine's content. There should be further inquiry into whether the majority of its readers have become uninterested in the political content, whether they are comparable to readers of general interest magazines, and whether the magazine's position as one of the few politically focused magazines has any effect on its attractiveness to potential readers.

54. <u>Promofoods</u> denies a potential health risk caused by its canned tuna (Questions to Be Answered)

Relying on the results that after recalling eight million cans of tuna and testing samples from them, only three of the eight chemicals which generally cause the symptoms of dizziness and nausea were found and on the fact that those three chemicals naturally occur in all canned foods, the author concludes that the cans of tuna were not at all detrimental to people's health. However, some uncertainties surrounding the argument warrant further investigation.

We wonder whether the three chemicals were responsible for the dizziness and nausea reported. Despite the tests finding only the naturally occurring chemicals, the author cannot rule out these chemicals as the culprit simply because they are in all canned foods. It may be the case that even when the three chemicals occur naturally, they cause dizziness and nausea. It may also be the case that the consumers who reported dizziness and nausea had a sensitivity to these chemicals. The company should send out a survey to them to find out if they experience the symptoms when eating other canned products or only when eating Promofood's canned tuna. If they have the symptoms only when consuming Promofoods' canned tuna, the conclusion that the canned tuna did not present a threat to health would be implausible. Even if the eight chemicals most commonly associated with dizziness and nausea can be exonerated, this does not necessarily mean that other chemicals were not responsible for the symptoms. It is highly likely that some of them caused dizziness and nausea. If this should be the case, the conclusion about the innocence of Promofoods' canned tuna would be weakened.

Even assuming chemicals can be ruled out as the reason for the health problems, we still have the question of whether the tuna cans had nothing to do with the dizziness and nausea. They could have played a part in causing the symptoms. The article mentions that the cans were tested by chemists, which implies a very narrow investigation. The problem may have been as simple as defective cans or damage to the cans sustained during transport. Such factors would not be detected by chemical tests, as they are not chemical problems. Without ruling out tuna cans as the cause of the dizziness and nausea, the author cannot fairly conclude that the canned tuna had nothing to do with the health risk. Even assuming that the samples of canned tuna did not cause nausea or dizziness, there is no guarantee that they did not cause other kinds of health risks associated with canned fish products, such as rash, diarrhea, headache, and others. It could be that the consumers did not complain about the symptoms, because they were temporary or not serious. In this case, the conclusion would be undermined. Without information about the packaging of the tuna cans, we cannot determine the soundness of the argument.

Even if chemical contamination and damage to the packaging can be eliminated as factors in health risks of the canned tuna, we still cannot release Promofoods from blame. We want to know whether there are problems with the source materials themselves. Pollutants in the ocean are a serious issue after all, and pollutants within the meat of the fish may have been missed by the testing. It is even possible that the pollutants were not chemical or metallic, but biological, as found in other kinds of sea creatures accidentally canned along with the tuna. Perhaps in a few cans some unsavory sea life caused the nausea and dizziness in those hapless consumers. Even if the samples of recalled tuna did not pose a health risk, this does not necessarily mean that other canned tuna of Promofoods did not, either. The author provides no evidence that the samples are representative of all of Promofoods' canned tuna. The chemists from Promofoods could have reported the test findings in this way to save the company's business. They could also have tested very few samples. They could even have performed very casual tests. Any of the scenarios, if true, would make the testing unreliable and invalid, rendering the argument tenuous. Without accounting for these and other possibilities, the author cannot justifiably absolve Promofoods of its responsibility for the health risk that its canned tuna poses.

In conclusion, it is impossible for Promofoods to wash its hands of health risks including dizziness and nausea before the author investigates all possible avenues of contamination or damage that may have occurred. Failing to do the research would be very irresponsible and has the potential for even greater public health concerns in the future, should the company become too lax with its inquiries.

55. Dura-Sock, Inc. to discontinue its Endure manufacturing process (Questions to Be Answered)

The author recommends that the company Dura-Socks, Inc. become more profitable by ending use of the Endure manufacturing process. To justify the recommendation, the memo mentions a study in which customers buy the company's socks every three months, despite the advertising which claims the socks can last two years. It also cites a survey in the northeastern United States that finds most customers value Dura-Socks' stylish appearance and numerous color options. However, the recommendation raises some questions that warrant further investigation before its implementation.

We must query whether the respondents of the recent study represent Dura-Socks' customers in general. However, there is no data in this regard. The number of respondents could be tiny and may not be representative of all customers who buy Dura-Socks. It may be the case that the majority of study participants who buy the socks do so because they work in professions that quickly wear out their foot apparel, but they prefer Dura-Socks products to other brands that would wear out even faster. On the contrary, Dura-Socks' customers generally work in other professions and wear the socks for at least two years. It may also be the case that even if the respondents buy new Dura-Socks every three months, they will still wear the original ones for two years. In that event, if the Endure process were discontinued, the customers would be less satisfied. Even assuming that the customers did not wear their socks after three months, the Endure process advertised may still motivate them psychologically to purchase the socks. Consumers tend to buy products with extra features, even if they have little use for the features. If the process were terminated, regardless of its actual use, sales could decrease. Should this be true, discontinuation of the Endure process to raise profits would be unwarranted.

We should also consider whether the customers surveyed in the northeastern United States are representative of those in other regions. However, the sample could be small and therefore may not typify Dura-Socks' customers in general. The surveyed cities may be the largest single market, but regional preferences may not all be alike, and the combination of the other markets may outweigh the northeastern region. Perhaps unlike the northeastern United States, other parts of the U.S. are less urbanized, and their people enjoy participating in outdoor sports such as camping and hiking, activities that put the durability of socks to the test. Or perhaps people in other regions are less wealthy and value durability of the socks over their appearance and colors. In addition, the fact that style and color options are the most valued feature does not itself imply that durability is unimportant to consumers. It could be that consumers take it for granted, and that were they denied it, they would buy socks of other brands. Any of the scenarios, if true, would cast serious doubt on the assumption about the representativeness of the survey and on the recommendation of ending the Endure process. If a survey could be conducted to find out what customers prefer across the country, it would allow Dura-Socks to determine whether the Endure process deserves discontinuation or whether people prefer socks manufactured with the Endure process.

Even granting that the recent study and consumer survey are valid and reliable, we still need to investigate whether ceasing use of the Endure process has the potential to turn higher profits. However, discontinuing the process may mean that the company will need to spend money on reconfiguring its factories and changing its advertising campaigns, which can cost a considerable sum, not to mention the fact that the company will be giving up the feature around which the brand is built, causing it to lose dedicated customers. Ending the process may also mean that it will give up a cost-effective process, because the patented process may incur much lower manufacturing costs. Profit is a function of revenue and costs. If such a strategy helps the company to enhance revenues and decrease costs, the claim that discontinuing the process will make the company's business more profitable will be strengthened. Otherwise, it would be invalidated. To decide whether the argument is sound, we need data regarding the revenues and costs before and after the discontinuation of the Endure process.

In conclusion, discontinuation of Dura-Socks' Endure process is a plan that needs to be queried further. At the top of the company's list of priorities before it implements the plan should be figuring out if customers really do not care about the Endure process and if the cost of rebranding the company and changing processes would be reasonable and not negatively affect its profits.

56. Causes of Xanadu National Park's amphibian population decline (Specific Evidence)

In this letter to the editor of an environmental magazine, the author asserts that global pollution of water and air is not responsible for the decrease in the species and numbers of amphibians in Xanadu National Park. Instead, the author blames the decline on the introduction of trout in 1975, which have been known to eat the eggs of amphibians. However, the evidence provided is not adequate for ascertaining the soundness of the argument.

The author must provide evidence that the decline of amphibians in Xanadu was not caused by pollution. The letter states that the number of amphibian species in Xanadu went down from seven in 1975 to just four in 2002 and populations of each species were decimated. The author compares this with the global decline of amphibians, which the author asserts was clearly caused by pollution, and claims that the decline in Xanadu was not the result of pollution. However, no evidence is given to support the claim. Before the claim is accepted, there would need to be a detailed analysis of not only the samples of current air and water, but also records of samples taken from 1975 to 2002 to prove that pollution had no connection to the species die-offs. If the samples are found to be heavily polluted and unhealthy for the amphibians, it is possible that they have died from the pollution. Otherwise, the argument that trout have caused the decline would be strengthened. Without more information about pollution of air and water in Xanadu, we cannot fully evaluate the argument.

The author should also offer evidence that the introduction of trout was the reason for the population drop. However, no information is provided to prove that this is the case. Just because the fish are known to eat amphibian eggs does not necessarily mean they were the direct cause of the drop. It is possible that while trout eat amphibian eggs, they do not eat the eggs of the seven species but those of other species. It is also possible that they were small in number and had only eaten a tiny number of the eggs. It is even possible that not many amphibians had grown from the eggs because of the climate change. Any of the scenarios, if true, would invalidate the claim that the steep decline of the amphibians was attributable to the introduction of trout only. To establish the claim, the author would need to show that the trout consumed amphibian eggs as a primary food source, and that the number of eggs eaten by trout accounted for a significant number of those laid, such that too few amphibians had lived long enough to reach adulthood and maintain their numbers.

Finally, before blaming pollution, trout, or any other alleged reason for the amphibian die-off, the author needs to furnish more information about changes in the park that may have occurred in the span between 1975 and 2002. This is, after all, a considerable amount of time, and since little information is given in the letter about the park, there are countless other possible culprits. For example, the amphibians could have been killed by something introduced to the park later than trout. They could also have left the park for some other place because of the climate change. Even anthropogenic causes other than pollution could have been contributing factors, such as boat tours that disrupt spawning pools. Poaching of the amphibians for pets or for other reasons may have been rampant during the span, targeting mostly three of the species but causing collateral damage to the other four species. In these scenarios, trout could not have been the only cause of the dramatic decline. Without ruling out all other possible explanations, the author cannot convince me that trout were the only reason for the amphibian decline in the park.

In conclusion, if this letter wishes to make a more convincing argument, the author needs to provide data proving that no pollution could have harmed amphibians in Xanadu, that trout could have had a significant impact, and that no other factors could have contributed to the dramatic decline.

57. Causes of Xanadu National Park's amphibian population decline (Alternative Explanations)

In this letter to the editor of an environmental magazine, the author asserts that the introduction of trout begun in 1975, which have been known to eat the eggs of amphibians, is to blame for the decrease in the species and number of amphibians in Xanadu National Park. However, there may be other explanations for this phenomenon.

One possible explanation is that the disappearance of the amphibians from the park occurred due to overpopulation of the animals, rather than predation. The letter itself states that in 1975 there were plenty of each species. It could be that a lack of natural predators caused the amphibians' numbers to grow so large that they overconsumed their natural food source, which then led to massive die-offs and even extinction of three species. It could also be that as a result of overpopulation of the animals, the amphibians of each species had intraspecies fights for food, and killed one another in enormous numbers, with the amphibians of three species having fought the hardest and killed the greatest numbers until they became too few to sustain themselves. It could even be that due to overpopulation, many amphibians of four species and all amphibians of three species migrated to other places, dramatically reducing the numbers of the four species and making the three species disappear altogether. Any of the scenarios, if true, would rule out the possibility that the trout alone caused the decline of four species and demise of three species.

There is also the possibility that the first study in 1975 misidentified some of the species. Since technology and scientific techniques have come such a long way, certain classification systems may have changed, and thus some of the animals, including the three extinct species, that were once classified as amphibians are no longer thought of as such. This would account for the fewer recorded species of amphibians in the 2002 study. Of the four species observed in 2002, many of them were about to die when the first study was conducted but were still recorded. This would explain the dramatic decrease in the number of amphibians in the second study. It may also be the case that in the 1975 census, the study took place at a time when the amphibians were more active and therefore, the researchers detected large numbers of amphibians of seven species. Conversely, the 2002 observation may have taken place at a time when the researchers did not find a large population of amphibians owing to the animals' inactivity and found none of the three species due to their hibernation. Unless there is evidence that misidentification did not lead to the difference in numbers of amphibians between the two studies, it is unfair to assume that the trout alone were responsible for the scenario.

One more possibility is that the decline was the result of poaching or pollution. Perhaps in the span of nearly three decades between the studies, some of the amphibians became popular as pets, or were poached for other reasons. Such activities could have led to the extinction of three species of the amphibians and severe reduction in the numbers of the other four species before measures were taken to combat them, because while the three species were poached, the other four species were damaged. This possibility would be more persuasive if the animals were unique to the park, as this would have made poaching a more lucrative and thus tempting practice. Or perhaps pollution of water and air was the cause. The three species could have been more vulnerable to it than the other four species; therefore, they became extinct and the other four were decimated. This suggests that poaching or pollution, among other explanations, could rival the introduction of trout as the cause.

While the author may be correct in the belief that trout were the cause of the decline in amphibians at Xanadu National Park, there are still other potential explanations, such as overpopulation, misidentification, poaching, or pollution. Without further evidence, the author cannot blame squarely the decline on the introduction of trout.

58. Study of reading preferences of Waymarsh citizens called into question (Specific Evidence)

While lying about their own reading habits seems to make sense intuitively–people wish others to think they are smarter, so they will say they prefer reading Dostoevsky to reading J. K. Rowling–it is premature to conclude that they are misrepresenting their reading habits without first ruling out alternative explanations. To fully assess the claim that the citizens had lied about their reading habits, we need additional evidence.

The author must provide evidence of the reliability and validity of the first study. Relevant information includes how many people were studied, what percentage of the population they comprised, and demographic information indicating if the preference spans the socio-economic spectrum of the city. The sample could have been small and constituted an anomaly, a group of people who happened to prefer literary classics. The respondents could even have been smaller in number, further distorting the results. Perhaps the people reported that they preferred literary classics as reading material simply to seem more educated when they in fact preferred mystery novels. Or perhaps the researchers asked what books the participants preferred rather than what books they read. In such scenarios, the study is neither reliable nor valid, making it unreasonable to draw comparisons between the results of the first study and those of the second study, undermining the argument that the respondents in the first study had misrepresented their reading habits.

While the second study does appear to be more reliable in that it uses hard evidence from libraries rather than self-reported responses, it fails to give information about the demographics of its respondents. The argument would benefit from a comparison between the people who checked out books in the second study and those who had been surveyed in the first study to see if their demographics align. If the two samples had different demographics, it is possible that they had different reading habits. Specifically, the sample of the second study could consist mostly of people who borrowed mystery novels from public libraries, unlike the sample of the first study that could have been largely made up of people who preferred literary classics. In this case, the respondents in the first study might have reported their reading habits accurately. Alternatively, if the two samples had the same demographic makeup, or even included the same people, it is possible that they had similar reading habits. Should this be true, the respondents might have misstated their reading habits in the first study. Without information about the demographics of the respondents, we cannot fully assess the argument.

Finally, other important details left out by the article include the amount of time that has passed between the two studies, and the contexts in which they were performed. If the studies took place far apart from each other chronologically, it would stand to reason that people's reading preferences had changed over time. It is possible that the people had been interested in literary classics, but mystery novels were often adapted into films, which then spurred interest in the genre, a less prominent occurrence in the past. Also, just because the books that the respondents checked out of the public libraries in the second study differed from those that the participants had preferred in the first study does not necessarily mean the respondents in the first study had falsely represented their reading habits. It is possible that they still preferred literary classics, but instead of borrowing them from the public libraries in Waymarsh, they bought them, borrowed them from other libraries, or obtained them in any other way. It is also possible that a few extremely avid mystery novel readers accounted for the discrepancy. It is even possible that mystery novels were more readily available at Waymarsh's public libraries than literary classics since they were easier to stock in terms of price and supply. Such scenarios would weaken the argument. Without information about sales from bookstores or a survey of the participants' personal libraries, the author cannot confidently claim that the respondents in the first study had lied about their reading habits.

To conclude, the argument that the participants in the first study had misrepresented their reading habits is simply not supported by any concrete evidence. To strengthen the argument, the author must show that the first study did not represent a significant portion of the population, whereas the second study did. To better evaluate the argument, we need information about the tastes of Waymarsh readers since the first study.

59. Should the company XYZ use Delany rather than Walsh for laid-off employee assistance? (Specific Evidence)

The author recommends that the company XYZ continue to use Delany Personnel Firm rather than Walsh Personnel Firm for its re-employment services to laid-off workers. To justify the recommendation, the memo mentions that when it used Walsh's service eight years prior, only half of the workers found new employment within a year. It also states that Delany's services helped laid-off workers find new jobs within just six months as compared to Walsh's nine and that Delany has more office locations and staff. However, we find it hard to assess the argument fully due to a lack of solid evidence.

We must have evidence that an isolated occurrence indicates Walsh's inferior service. The memo points out that eight years ago, Walsh was only able to find new work for fifty percent of XYZ's laid-off employees within a year. This statistic is presented with the implication that Delany was, and still is, able to provide a larger percentage of XYZ employees with new jobs within less than a year. Yet, this statistic is eight years old, and does not provide any comparative information whatsoever. It is possible that Delany could only secure new employment for less than fifty percent of unemployed people within more than a year at that time. Even if Walsh did poorly eight years ago, it is possible that factors other than its service had contributed to the scenario: the general economic decline or another factor beyond Walsh's control. Even if its service was to blame for the scenario, there is no guarantee that it still does poorly and will continue to do so in the future. If this is the case, it is unfair to conclude that Delany is superior in serving laid off workers based on just one incident. To decide whose service is consistently superior rather than just occasionally so, we need to look at Walsh's track record compared to Delany's.

In addition, we should have evidence that another possibly isolated incident is indicative of a trend in the performance of the respective companies. The comparison that is given by the memo regarding how long it takes for each service to find new jobs for employees, six months for Delany and nine for Walsh, seems at first to be very persuasive. However, this comparison only applies to a single year, last year to be precise, and as another isolated incident, could be an aberration, unrepresentative of a trend in the performance of the respective companies. Even if Delany did better than Walsh in helping clients find jobs last year, it is possible that it did worse than Walsh in serving XYZ's laid off workers, since we do not know what portion of either company's clients were XYZ's employees to be placed. If neither served few of XYZ's employees, there would be no reliable comparisons. Before we make more reliable comparisons, we also need to make sure that the placed employees are representative of XYZ's laid off employees in general. Otherwise, factors, such as the employees' enterprising efforts to look for jobs, might explain the difference in the time needed to place them. In this case, the argument that Delany is superior to Walsh in helping XYZ's unemployed workers land jobs would be unjustified. Thus, it is unfair to assume that the respective companies' service alone was responsible for the difference in the time it took the clients to secure employment. The clients' qualifications could be more important than the service in helping them find jobs. This could also account for the other scenario last year: those who used Delany's service were able to secure employment much faster than those who did not, because the former group could be a biased sample that happened to be much more qualified than the latter group. Should this be the case, Delany's superiority could be challenged. If the author could establish a link between the reemployment rate and the time it took to find new employment, in a way that presented Delany as having the better of both statistics, then the argument would have a fair bit of weight behind it.

Finally, we need evidence in support of the assumption that a bigger company will always provide a better service. However, the author provides no evidence to substantiate the assumption. On its own, the fact that Delany has more offices and staff members does not really say anything about its effectiveness or superiority to Walsh. Without any supporting evidence, we could just as easily assume the opposite. For example, larger companies usually have to deal with larger rates of inefficiency; therefore, it is equally likely that the staff at Delany are less dedicated to finding new jobs for XYZ's employees than Walsh, and since Delany is a larger company, it will probably have less to lose if its service is unsatisfactory. It is also likely that despite a greater number of offices, Delany's number of employees per office is smaller than Walsh's. It is even likely that Delany largely serves industries and areas where XYZ's laid-off employees seldom seek jobs. Above all, it seems that the author defines superior service only in terms of the speed with which both companies help clients find jobs. However, good jobs involve much more than just having jobs. While Delany may have placed its clients faster, Walsh may have helped them find satisfying jobs in a reasonably longer time. Should this be true, the assumption about Delany's superior service would prove unwarranted and the argument in favor of using Delany rather than Walsh would be undermined.

In sum, to better evaluate the argument, we need extra evidence, including what percentage of XYZ's laid-off workers each service can find new jobs for and how quickly they can be found over a long span of time. If the memo wishes to posit that more staff and offices make Delany a better choice, especially in helping clients find satisfying jobs, it must first explain how that trait makes it superior.

60. Study of reading preferences of Waymarsh citizens called into question (Assumptions)

The author concludes that people had misrepresented their preferences in the first study of the reading habits of Waymarsh citizens which found that the respondents preferred to read literary classics. To support the conclusion, the article posits that, according to a second study, of the most oft checked out books at the public libraries, they in fact preferred to read mystery novels. However, the assumptions that underlie the argument are not based on hard facts and need close examination before we determine its soundness.

The argument is predicated on the assumption that the first study is a reliable and valid one. However, the author offers no evidence that this is true. It is possible that the respondents in the first survey had not answered honestly. If the people being surveyed knew the purpose of the study, there is a chance that many of them would lie about their preferences in order to make themselves, or the populace with which they identify, appear to be more educated or cultured. Also, the researchers could have asked what kind of books the respondents preferred instead of what kind of books they read most often. If the researchers had asked the latter question, the results would accord better with the library results. Furthermore, we do not know the number of citizens surveyed or whether they represented Waymarsh citizens generally. Nor do we know what percentage of the citizens surveyed responded. In either case, the smaller the population involved, the less reliable the survey results. If this should be true, the assumption about the reliability and validity of the first study would prove unwarranted and the argument that it undergirds would collapse. Without more information about the survey's methodology and the people surveyed or making responses, it is impossible to rely on its results.

While the second study does appear to be more credible in that it uses hard evidence from libraries rather than self-reported responses, the author also relies on the assumption that the second study is reliable and valid. However, the author provides no evidence to substantiate this. The article does not indicate how many people were involved in the second study or what portion of the people surveyed responded. The smaller the sample, the less reliable the results. Nor does it show if there are any similarities between the people in each study. For example, we do not know if the participants in the first study are just the library patrons in the second study, making it difficult to say whose reading habits are being misrepresented. Also, we do not know the length of time between the two studies. It is possible that if the studies took place far apart chronologically, the reading preferences of the citizens and the demographic composition of Waymarsh had changed and the second study just reported an outdated set of information. Should this be true, the assumption about the reliability and validity of the second study would prove unwarranted and the argument that it underpins would fall apart. Unless there is evidence that the results of the second study are reliable and valid, it is not fair to assume that the results of the first study were misrepresentation of its respondents' reading preferences.

Finally, the author makes the assumption that just because the books that the respondents checked out of the public libraries in the second study differed from those that the participants had preferred in the first study, the citizens had misrepresented their true reading habits. However, no information is provided to prove that this is the case. It is possible that they still preferred literary classics, but instead of borrowing them from the public libraries in Waymarsh, they bought them, borrowed them from other libraries, or obtained them in any other way. It is also possible that a few extremely avid mystery novel readers accounted for the discrepancy. Perhaps mystery novels took less time to read, and therefore had a higher turnover rate. Or perhaps they were more readily available at Waymarsh's public libraries than literary classics because they were easier to stock in terms of price and supply. Such scenarios would undermine the assumption about the people's reading habits and the argument that the respondents in the first study had lied about their reading habits. Without the true reasons for the participants' library book choices, the author cannot confidently claim that they had given incompatible answers regarding their reading habits in two studies.

The results of the studies appeal to our a priori understanding of the world, in which people will sometimes lie about themselves in order to seem more educated. However, the methodology used in the studies lends itself to questions about the validity of the results. The researchers must take more care with the design of the questions as well as with the analysis of the data. While the conclusion may be true, the studies have reached it on the basis of unsound reasoning.

61. Health Naturally to build a new store in Plainsville (Specific Evidence)

The author argues that Health Naturally should build a new store in Plainsville because this town fits the targeted demographic of people with an interest in healthy living. To support the argument, the article cites the local merchant sales of running shoes and exercise clothing, health club membership and attendance, and the fact that the Plainsville school system requires children to participate in a fitness program that encourages regular exercise. However, these pieces of information are too vague to warrant the assumption that Plainsville residents fit Health Naturally's desired consumer group and we need extra evidence to determine the validity of the argument.

First, the reports by merchants on the sales of exercise clothing and running shoes are not accompanied by any statistics or time-frames. The author assumes that this trend is indicative of an overall mindset of the populace that will continue into the long-term future. However, it is possible that this recent sales trend is nothing more than a short-lived fad, or, depending on the size of the town, a trend that will end once products reach market saturation. The fact that sales of running shoes and exercise equipment are at all-time highs means little by itself. The sales may be miniscule to begin with and still insignificant compared with sales in other equivalent cities. Moreover, all-time highs in these sales do not necessarily mean Plainsville has become "health-conscious" –perhaps people often buy such merchandise to show off rather than use it. Even assuming that the residents have genuine interest in living healthy lives, the author has yet to offer evidence that they will buy enough products of Health Naturally to make the new store profitable. If this should be the case, the argument that Health Naturally should build one of its new stores in Plainsville would be weakened.

In addition, there must be evidence for the assumption that the health club's membership and class attendance is a sign that the entire town follows a healthy lifestyle. However, the assumption could be an overestimation based on a small sample. Gyms and health centers usually cater to middle to higher-income earners, who may make up a smaller percentage of a population. Thus, without information about the sample size, it is entirely likely that the number of members in the health club represents only a small portion of Plainsville's total population, despite an increase in membership and some full classes. The market capacity could be negligible to begin with, so an all-time high in numbers could be an increase of a handful, hardly justifying the opening of a new store. The fact that the weight training and aerobics classes are full is not convincing, either, as it may simply be that the club is too small to accommodate many clients or does not have enough people to teach many classes. The fact that it almost closed for lack of business five years before could also be a cause for concern. Should this be true, the argument would be undermined.

Finally, there should be evidence that because schoolchildren are required to participate in a fitness-for-life program, they will be potential customers in the future. However, compulsory participation does not necessarily mean genuine interest in health and may even generate a reaction against health-conscious living, especially among teenagers. Besides, children may not hold onto every idea that we attempt to imprint on them when they are very young, and while some may well become Health Naturally's customers in the future, there is also the possibility that none of them will. The program may not be successful at present, and even if it is effective now, there is no guarantee that it will be successful in the future. Even assuming that it will prosper in the future, the author cannot be certain that Plainsville's schoolchildren will become Health Naturally's customers as a result. If this is the case, the argument is not sound. In fact, it makes little sense to build a store to serve a market that does not yet exist. In order to use the impact of the program as evidence, the author needs to establish a specific link between children's exercise program and their subsequent healthy lifestyles as adults.

In sum, the assumptions that underlie the argument are based on data that is far too vague to be reliable. We must have more concrete market data to show that the sales of health-related products are not a short-lived fad and more detailed population statistics to see if the income of the Plainsville people justifies the new store. We should also scrutinize the fitness-for-life program to see if it has had any real effect on contributing to the healthy lifestyles of children as they age. Only in this way can we fully assess the claim that a new store of Health Naturally in Plainsville will be very successful.

62. Should the company XYZ use Delany rather than Walsh for laid-off employee assistance? (Assumptions)

The author recommends that the company XYZ continue to use Delany Personnel Firm rather than Walsh Personnel Firm for its re-employment services to laid-off workers. To justify the recommendation, the memo mentions that when it used Walsh's service eight years prior, only half of the workers found new employment within a year. It also states that Delany's services helped laid-off workers find new jobs within just six months as compared to Walsh's nine, and that Delany has more office locations and staff. However, the argument is replete with assumptions and loopholes that we must scrutinize to determine its soundness.

First, the author assumes that an isolated occurrence indicates Walsh's inferior service. The memo points out that eight years ago, Walsh was only able to find new work for fifty percent of XYZ's laid-off employees within a year. This statistic is presented with the implication that Delany was, and still is, able to provide a larger percentage of XYZ employees with new jobs within less than a year. Yet, this statistic is eight years old, and does not provide any comparative information. It is possible that Delany could only secure new employment for less than fifty percent of unemployed people within more than a year at that time. Even if Walsh did poorly eight years ago, it is possible that factors other than Walsh's service could have contributed to the scenario: the general economic decline or another factor beyond Walsh's control. Even if Walsh's service was to blame for the scenario, there is no guarantee that it still does poorly and will continue to do so in the future. If this is the case, it is unfair to conclude that Delany is superior in serving laid-off workers based on just one incident. To decide whose service is consistently superior rather than just occasionally so, we need to look at Walsh's track record compared to Delany's.

Second, the author implies that another possibly isolated incident is indicative of a trend in the performance of the respective companies. The comparison that is given by the memo in terms of how long it takes for each service to find new jobs for employees, six months for Delany and nine for Walsh, seems at first to be very persuasive. However, this comparison only applies to a single year, last year to be precise, and as another isolated incident, could be an aberration, unrepresentative of a trend in the performance of the respective companies. Even if Delany did better than Walsh in helping clients find jobs last year, it is possible that it did worse than Walsh in serving XYZ's laid-off workers, since we do not know what portion of either company's clients were XYZ's employees to be placed. If neither served few of XYZ's employees, there would be no reliable comparisons. Before we make more reliable comparisons, we also need to make sure that the placed employees are representative of XYZ's laid-off employees in general. Otherwise, factors, such as the employees' enterprising efforts to look for jobs, might explain the difference in the time needed to place them. In this case, the argument that Delany is superior to Walsh in helping XYZ's unemployed workers land jobs would be unjustified. Thus, it is unfair to assume that the respective companies' service alone was responsible for the difference in the time it took the clients to secure employment. The clients' qualifications could be more important than the service in helping them find jobs. This could also account for the other scenario last year: those who used Delany's service were able to secure employment much faster than those who did not, because the former group was a biased sample that happened to be much more qualified than the latter group. Should this be the case, Delany's superiority could be challenged. If the author could establish a link between the reemployment rate and the time it took to find new employment, in a way that presented Delany as having the better of both statistics, then the argument would have a fair bit of weight behind it.

Lastly, the author suggests that a bigger company will always provide a better service. However, the author offers no evidence to substantiate this. On its own, the fact that Delany has more offices and staff members does not really say anything about its effectiveness or superiority to Walsh. Without any supporting evidence, we could just as easily assume the opposite. For example, larger companies usually have to deal with larger rates of inefficiency; therefore, it is equally likely that the staff at Delany are less dedicated to finding new jobs for XYZ's employees than Walsh, and since Delany is a larger company, it will probably have less to lose if its service is unsatisfactory. It is also likely that despite a greater number of offices, Delany's number of employees per office is smaller than Walsh's. It is even likely that Delany largely serves industries and areas where XYZ's laid-off employees seldom seek jobs. Above all, it seems that the author defines superior service only in terms of the speed with which both companies help clients find jobs. However, good jobs involve much more than just having jobs. While Delany may have placed its clients faster, Walsh may have helped them find satisfying jobs in a reasonably longer time. Should this be true, the assumption about Delany's superior service would prove unwarranted and the argument in favor of using Delany rather than Walsh would be undermined.

In sum, the assumptions that underlie the argument lack the necessary facts to be warranted. To better evaluate the argument, we need more data on what percentage of XYZ's workers each company can find new jobs for and how quickly they can be found over a long span of time. If the memo wishes to posit that more staff and offices make Delany a better choice, especially in helping clients find satisfying jobs, it must first explain how that trait makes it superior.

63. Health Naturally to build a new store in Plainsville (Assumptions)

The author recommends that the company Health Naturally construct a new health foods store in Plainsville. To justify the recommendation, the memo claims that Plainsville's populace are highly health-conscious and cites three facts to support this: 1) sales of athletic paraphernalia in Plainsville are at an all-time high, 2) the local health club has succeeded in attracting and retaining customers, and 3) the mandatory "fitness-for-life" program through the local schools is indoctrinating a new generation of customers. To determine the soundness of the argument, we need to scrutinize the assumptions that underlie it.

First, the author relies on the assumption that those who work out are generally health-conscious people. However, several lurking variables exist to undermine the strength of such a correlative argument. For example, an upsurge in crime may encourage people to desire a more intimidating physique. In this case, they would value exercise, not necessarily healthy living. Without evidence to demonstrate a definitive link between exercise and overall health-consciousness, the author fails to prove satisfactorily that Plainsville residents are concerned with healthy living.

Next, the author implies that a connection exists between athletic clothing and health food sales. However, the author fails to substantiate this. Several variables other than a health-conscious population could positively affect the sale of athletic apparel while not impacting the sales of Health Naturally products. For example, athletic apparel may be fashionable or less expensive, driving up demand for this good without affecting markets for other health products. Alternatively, the population of Plainsville may be so obese that their only recourse for comfortable clothes lies in the elastic waists of sweatpants and the arch support of running shoes. In any case, however, the author fails to establish a clear link between sales of athletic clothing and health food products.

The author continues by suggesting that the turnaround of a local health club demonstrates the populace's recently discovered dedication to healthy living. However, of more importance than this club's recent reemergence as a viable business is why it was at the brink of bankruptcy in the first place. Five years is simply not long enough to demonstrate an enduring trend; indeed, the erratic nature of such a turnaround indicates volatility rather than stability in the Plainsville market. Thus, while the success of the fitness club may demonstrate a present interest in healthy living, it does not indicate that this interest will last into the future.

Finally, the author assumes that compulsory physical education will secure Plainsville's health-products market into the distant future. However, this takes it for granted that the "fitness-for-life" program impacts lifestyles and that the specific program utilized in Plainsville is effective. Regarding the latter, the author has yet to demonstrate whether Plainsville's program itself is any good. As for the former, the program may be ineffective. Specifically, its compulsory nature may provoke a reaction against health-conscious living, especially among teenagers. In that event, Plainsville's "fitness-for-life" program may not generate a new wave of loyal customers for Health Naturally.

In conclusion, the author founds the argument on doubtful assumptions, undermining its validity. To bolster it, the author must provide experimental evidence by way of a survey of Plainsville residents to show that Plainsville has a health-conscious population that would purchase Health Naturally products. Specifically, the author must offer data demonstrating the reasons for the increased purchase of exercise clothing, the dedication and motivation of club members, and the effectiveness of the school's physical education program.

64. Predators responsible for decline of gazelle population from the Western Palean Wildlife Preserve (Specific Evidence)

Citing the fact that one-hundred lions and one-hundred gazelles were moved from the Western Palean Wildlife Preserve to the East Palean Preserve three years ago due to flooding and that in the three years since the move, the western gazelle has almost completely died out, the author concludes that while the eastern preserve has a climate with slightly less rainfall, the lower precipitation is not the cause, and that the larger number of predators in the eastern preserve must be the cause. However, before we ascertain the validity of the argument, we need some crucial evidence.

The author must provide evidence regarding whether predation has caused the western gazelle to be almost extinct. The article mentions that the eastern preserve has most of the same animals as the western preserve and possesses similar climate. However, no evidence is given as to whether these conditions were the same only at the time of the introduction of the western gazelles or have remained unchanged in the three years since the importing of them. If the conditions have remained the same since the western gazelles were introduced to the East Palean Preserve, it is likely that predation has been a factor in their decline: the one hundred lions that were imported with them may have lost a primary food source, prey animals present in the western preserve but absent in the eastern preserve, and killed most of the gazelles. Otherwise, climate or other factors could have been responsible for the drastic decline, rendering the assumption about predation as the culprit unwarranted. Without more information about what may have been preying upon the western gazelles, the author cannot confidently claim that predation was the cause.

In addition, the author needs to offer evidence that may be used to rule out lower rainfall as a possible cause of western gazelle's decline. Gazelles are herbivorous animals, and since there was already a population of eastern gazelles present when the western gazelles arrived, it is possible that the rainfall that occurred in East Palean Preserve supported just enough grass for only one of the populations. It is also possible that the western gazelles largely relied on a kind of vegetation that required more rainfall and could only be found in the western preserve, or for whatever reason, western gazelle was unable to cope with the dearth of food. In either scenario, lower rainfall could have been responsible for the virtual disappearance of western gazelle, rendering the role of the predators untenable.

There could, of course, be other explanations, but if the article wishes to claim that rainfall had no influence whatsoever, it should provide evidence to show that the climate allowed for a sustainable level of food and other nutriments for both gazelle populations.

Finally, it falls to the author to furnish evidence that factors other than lower rainfall have not contributed to the near disappearance of western gazelle. Making the assertion that the larger number of predators caused the decrease in the western gazelles, the author offers nothing by way of evidence other than an unfounded claim. A more reliable bit of proof would be detailed records of kills made by the predators of both gazelle populations in the preserve to see if the western gazelle population was truly affected by such activity, as compared to deaths by other causes, such as disease or poaching. The assumption that poaching has caused the steep decline would be more convincing if the western gazelles were unique to the East Palean Preserve, as this would have made poaching a more lucrative and thus tempting practice. It could also be that environmental factors, such as air and water pollution, were much more harmful in the eastern preserve and the western gazelles could not withstand them. In these scenarios, the author cannot fairly attribute the die-offs to the larger number of predators, such as lions.

In conclusion, the author lacks solid support for the claim that increased predation rather than regional climate differences must be the cause of the western gazelles' decline. To make the argument more convincing, the author must provide death statistics and detailed records of the climates of both preserves over the full three-year period, which would at least lay the groundwork for a more reliable comparison.

65. Is living in small towns like Leeville healthier than living in big cities like Masonton? (Alternative Explanations)

Relying on the fact that workers in the town of Leeville take fewer sick days and that the incidences of stress related illness in the town are lower than those in the relatively larger town of Masonton, the author posits that the disparity in two respects is due to Leeville's relaxed pace of life. While this may be the case, a number of other factors might explain the facts.

One possible explanation is that workers in Leeville are healthier as a result of factors other than its less stressful life. It may simply be that it has a smaller number of workers. If workers take the same number of sick days on average in both Leeville and Masonton, it is reasonable that those in Leeville would have fewer days of sick leave. Also, if both places have the same number of facilities for exercise and fitness, Leeville workers may have access to a higher number of them and exercise more. They may even have higher physician-resident ratios, more clement weather, and less air pollution. Perhaps they have healthier lifestyles in other respects. For example, they may eat more healthily. Or perhaps they are born healthier than those in Masonton. Any of the scenarios, if true, would rule out Leeville's relaxed pace of life as the sole reason for the fact that its workers take fewer sick days.

Another likely explanation is that the smaller number of sick days taken by Leeville workers is not health-related at all, but instead is the result of other job-related pressures. Specifically, it may be the case that for whatever reason, workers in Leeville do not feel secure in their jobs, and fear that taking time off work may cause their bosses to fire them. Alternatively, it may also be the case that a slowing economy, combined with a system of hourly wages, has made it necessary for people to work as often as possible to make ends meet at home. Perhaps since Leeville is rather small, the businesses in the town report fewer days of sick leave for individual workers because of a cultural sensibility that taking sick leave would make one seem weak. This indicates that factors other than the health benefits of the relatively relaxed pace of life could be responsible for fewer sick days that Leeville workers take.

Regarding the diagnosis of stress-related illness in Leeville, again, since the town is rather small, it could be that the people there do not report stress as an issue because of their unawareness of the issue or because of an aversion to psychological treatment that usually comes with such a diagnosis, whereas their counterparts in Masonton have a better knowledge of the issue and are more willing to have a relevant diagnosis. It could also be that the doctors in Leeville fail to diagnose many stress-related illnesses, whereas those in Masonton can accurately diagnose such cases. It is likely that Leeville and Masonton have different definitions of stress-related illness. It is also likely that Leeville workers are less likely to be laid off, have more say in decision-making, receive higher salaries, or are better at coping with stressful situations. All these scenarios would cast serious doubt on the explanation that the mere comfortable pace of life in Leeville contributes to the diagnosis of much lower rates of stress-related illness there than in Masonton.

While it may very well be the case that Leeville does have a relatively relaxed pace of life which contributes to fewer sick days taken by workers and lower rates of stress-related illness, we should not rule out other possible explanations. Their lifestyles and desire to keep a job or earn more money may be to blame for their disinclination to take sick days and social stigmas or misinterpretation of data for the diagnosis of lower rates of stress-related illness.

66. Changing WWAC radio station's music from rock to a news-and-talk format (Questions to Be Answered)

Relying on a recent decline in listener numbers and some retirees' potential limited interest in music, the author recommends that WWAC radio station change to a talk news format from a rock-music format. However, this recommendation should be based on enough hard evidence to warrant such a change. To determine whether this is the case, we must have answers to some relevant questions.

To begin with, we must know whether there is a connection between the closing of a few local shops selling recorded music and a limited interest in music. However, the author provides no data in this regard. Just because some local shops have closed does not necessarily mean a decrease in local sales of recorded music, because other local shops could experience an increase in sales. Even if there is a drop in local sales of recorded music, there may not be a drop in sales of recorded rock music. Even assuming that there is a decrease in sales of recorded rock music, this does not necessarily indicate a limited interest in music or in rock music in particular. A myriad of other factors might explain this phenomenon. For example, the introduction of the internet may have harmed the sale of music everywhere due to illegal downloading and online music solutions. Therefore, it is highly possible that people are still very much interested in rock music, but simply do not wish to buy it in physical format. Even if listeners have been losing interest in rock-and-roll music, this does not necessarily mean that they prefer 24-hour news. If this should be the case, the assumption about the connection between music sales and people's interest in rock music would prove unjustified, and the argument that the radio station should change from rock-and-roll music to continuous news would collapse. The radio station would do well to conduct surveys to find out if people have lost interest in music or have simply found other ways of obtaining it. If it is found that people have lost interest in music and specifically in rock music, WWAC radio station would be better served by changing its format.

Next, we should know whether a change to a news talk format is the condition necessary for reversing a drop in the number of WWAC's listeners. Yet, the memorandum offers no details in this regard. Just because there is a drop in listener numbers does not necessarily mean there should be a change of the form of radio. The drop could be negligible and normal fluctuations. Also, just because the news talk form of radio has become more and more popular in the area does not necessarily mean it is the only viable option. It could be that while a news and talk format has become increasingly popular, listeners prefer the format of an existing competitor only. Perhaps there is a strategy better than changing to a news and talk format, for example, changing to a music format to the retirees' tastes. Or perhaps listeners have dropped in number because they dislike the time the music is broadcast or because they dislike the music anchor; simply changing the broadcast time or the anchor would accomplish the goal. Or perhaps WWAC has transmission problems; simply repairing the transmission would achieve the outcome. In such scenarios, the claim that a change to the new format may benefit WWAC radio station would be weakened. It would be far more convincing if there were some actual survey data to back up this claim. Without identifying what is responsible for the decline in listener numbers, the author cannot fairly assume that the news talk format is the only strategy for increasing the number of WWAC's listeners.

Finally, we need to know what the retirees' actual tastes are. There is mention of an increase in the population of retirees, but no specific mention of what their actual tastes are except the claim that they may not be interested in music. Just because some local stores selling recorded music have closed does not necessarily mean people have no interest in music. Even if some people have lost interest in music, this does not necessarily mean that the retirees have no interest in music. Considering that most retirees grew up during the rock-and -roll era, it is likely that they would be interested in rock music radio. Until there is a survey to find out, we cannot know for sure. Also, even if the retirees have no interest in rock music, there is no guarantee that they will be interested in the news and talk format of the radio. Perhaps they like other types of music or a mix of music and news. Moreover, there is no mention of the population of the retirees moving to WWAC's area. Even if they favor the talk news format over rock music, there is the chance that their numbers are too small to compensate for the drop in listeners. There is even the chance that population growth resulting from the outside retirees would stop completely. Should this be true, the recommendation of switching to a news and talk format would be unreasonable.

In conclusion, the fundamental element this memorandum lacks in order to support its recommendation is data, specifically survey data. It makes broad claims about the interests of listeners in WWAC's area without providing any proof. A series of listener surveys would help WWAC uncover more about why it has experienced a decline in the number of listeners and assist it in deciding whether to accept the suggestion of changing formats.

67. Monitoring employees' internet use (Questions to Be Answered)

The author recommends that Climpson Industries install software on company computers to detect the internet use of employees, predicting that doing so will help the company to raise productivity and boost the company's profits overall by preventing them from wasting time. To better assess the prediction and its argument, we need answers to some key questions.

We must have the answer to whether workers are wasting time on the internet on personal or recreational activities. The recommendation cites a recent national survey that found that most workers with access to the Internet on the job had used company computers for activities such as banking or playing games. We want to know whether the survey is valid, but there is little data about it. It is entirely possible that the sample is an aberration, with predominantly participants abusing their internet and computer privileges. We also want to know whether the findings of the national survey are true for Climpson employees. It is likely that few Climpson workers participate in such activities. It is also likely that even if some do, they are simply taking a short break before beginning the next task. If this is the case, the national survey is not valid or representative, and the claim that workers in Climpson are wasting time on the internet is groundless. Before taking such an extreme measure as monitoring its employees' computer activity, the company should first consider whether the workers have been wasting time by using the internet for personal or recreational activities.

Also, we should learn whether installing the monitoring software will be the best way to prevent employees from wasting their time. However, the author provides no information in this regard. There is the possibility that employees, if they are indeed wasting time as the author claims, will simply find a way around the software, rendering it moot. Similarly, they may use their own devices as distractions, such as their smartphones or mobile gaming consoles. In either scenario, the monitoring software on the company's computers would be completely useless, rendering the argument gratuitous. The company should thoroughly research the software it plans to use in order to see if it has had a high rate of success at tracking the activity of workers and is resistant to tampering to avoid misrepresentation of its usefulness. Instead of installing the software, the company may monitor workers' internet use by analyzing the search history of the workstation internet browsers. It could accomplish this simply by having someone from its IT department log the activity of workers on the computers to check if such activity involves a significant amount of time on banking or entertainment websites. If it is found that workers spend little time on such activities, installing the monitoring software as the most effective way to stop employees from wasting time on the job would be unfounded.

Finally, we need to know whether the monitoring software will do anything to boost productivity and raise the company's profit overall. Granted that the employees are wasting time on the internet, there is no evidence provided to support the assertion that the monitoring software will help raise productivity and the company's overall profit. It is likely that workers may decide to become less productive in retaliation for what they may view as unfair treatment. Alternatively, they may quit altogether, and the company may have a hard time hiring new workers, thanks in large part to the ability of employees to complain publicly about policies that are perceived to be oppressive. If this should be true, the argument in support of installing the monitoring software for improved productivity would be tenuous. Also, profit is a function of revenue and costs. Installing the software may cost large sums of money, rendering the policy undesirable. To substantiate the assumption about the benefits of installing the monitoring software, the author must account for other factors that may result in less productivity and weigh the costs of taking the course of action against the revenue.

In conclusion, the recommendation is not supported by enough evidence to justify its implementation. To be convinced that this plan would work, we would need solid proof that employees have been abusing computer and internet privileges, along with detailed information about the tracking software's effectiveness. It would also help if we were given data on the revenues and costs associated with installing the monitoring software.

68. Will Sartorian's new alpaca overcoat sell well? (Assumptions)

The author argues that Sartorian, a men's clothing company, should recontinue its line of popular alpaca overcoats. To support the argument, the memo claims that the company can expect a strong demand for the product as a result of its customers' negative response to its discontinuance five years before and of the lack of competition from other sellers. The author then predicts that the demand, together with the overall rise in clothing prices, will help the company to garner more profits from its alpaca coats than in the past. However, to determine the soundness of the argument, we need to examine some important assumptions.

Firstly, the author assumes that a new fabric supplier is a sufficient condition for resuming production of Sartorian's popular alpaca overcoats. However, the author does not provide evidence to substantiate this. The overcoats were popular five years ago, but there is no guarantee that they will still be popular. Given the rapid change of fashion, it is highly likely that they represent something outmoded. If this is true, the company risks wasting money by restarting its manufacturing of this line of products. Also, the company discontinued the business because it was unable to secure reliable supplies of excellent wool fabric. The article simply mentions that it has a new fabric supplier. It is likely that the new supplier will be an unreliable one of alpaca. It is also likely that one supplier will be too small in number to be reliable in providing the required fabric, or that factors other than the supplier were responsible for the unreliability at the time and could still make the alpaca supply unreliable nowadays. Any of these scenarios, if true, would cast serious doubt on Sartorian's plan to resume production of its alpaca overcoats.

Secondly, the author implies that there will be a huge demand for the company's alpaca coats. If there were some relevant statistics, such as consumer demand surveys to back up this claim, it could be more plausible. However, as it stands, the idea sounds a bit incredible in the face of a market that tends to change rather quickly. The protest from its customers when the company stopped producing the alpaca overcoat does not necessarily mean they wanted the product very much; it may have indicated that they were concerned about its after-sales service when it discontinued this line of products, not to mention the possibility that the customers were small in number and did not represent other customers who had also bought the product. Even if this means the customers placed a great value on the products at that time, the same perception may not be there anymore. In this case, the assumption would prove unwarranted. Also, the lack of competition does nothing to help the situation; if anything, it may suggest a decrease in demand for alpaca overcoats. There is even the chance that the plan could backfire completely, as people may perceive the company as backwards or lacking vision due to its backing of a dated style. This could account for the fact that no competitor offers a similar product. If this should be true, the assumption about pent-up customer demand would be unjustified, rendering the argument for resuming production of the alpaca overcoats tenuous.

Finally, the author suggests that a pent-up demand for the company's alpaca overcoats and increase in clothing prices overall will be sufficient to make it gain more profits from the coats than ever before. We have poked holes in the assumption about the high demand, but even if the assumption proves warranted, and clothing prices have risen overall, there is no guarantee that the profitability would exceed that in the past. It is likely that the company profits will remain the same or even decrease. Profit is a function of revenue and costs. Rise in clothing prices overall does not necessarily mean prices for alpaca coats will also increase. It is likely that people will not want to pay for the overcoats at all, much less at higher prices than before. In fact, those who remember the lower cost of the alpaca overcoats in the past may refuse to buy the newer, higher priced ones, sparking a backlash against the product. Should this be the case, the assumption about customers' willingness to pay higher prices for the same product will be unfounded. Even if customers are willing to pay higher prices, the rise may not be significant enough to cover the costs, including costs of purchasing fabric, manufacturing and selling the overcoats, and employing people, among other things; therefore, the company is unlikely to anticipate an increase in profitability. Similarly, the demand may be strong, but it is not strong enough to enable the company to sell large quantities of alpaca coats to boost its profitability. Such scenarios could dramatically raise the costs and make the business unprofitable, rendering the argument implausible.

To conclude, the main assumption that must be examined before the company moves forward with this plan involves whether pent-up demand for its alpaca overcoats exists. The author could obtain it through customer surveys and other market research strategies to see if people are buying comparable items. Included in such surveys could be questions as to whether consumers would be willing to pay higher prices for the new coats. Without relevant information, we cannot fully assess the argument and without a sound argument, the company could incur a huge risk by restarting to sell alpaca overcoats at increased prices.

69. Will Sartorian's new alpaca overcoat sell well? (Questions to Be Answered)

The author argues that Sartorian, a men's clothing company, should recontinue its line of popular alpaca overcoats. To support the argument, the memo claims that the company can expect a strong demand for the product as a result of its customers' negative response to its discontinuance five years before and of the lack of competition from other sellers. The author then predicts that the demand, together with the overall rise in clothing prices, will help the company to garner more profits from its alpaca coats than in the past. However, to determine the soundness of the prediction and its argument, we need answers to some key questions.

Firstly, the author must answer whether a new fabric supplier is a sufficient condition for resuming production of the company's popular alpaca overcoats. However, the author does not provide relevant data. The overcoats were popular five years ago, but there is no guarantee that they will still be popular. Given the rapid change of fashion, it is highly likely that they represent something outmoded. If this is true, the company risks wasting money by restarting its manufacturing of this line of products. Also, the company discontinued the business because it was unable to secure reliable supplies of excellent wool fabric. The article simply mentions that it has a new fabric supplier. It is likely that the new supplier will be an unreliable one of alpaca. It is also likely that one supplier will be too small in number to be reliable in providing the required fabric, or that factors other than the supplier were responsible for the unreliability at the time and could still make the alpaca supply unreliable nowadays. Any of these scenarios, if true, would cast serious doubt on Sartorian's plan to resume production of its alpaca overcoats.

Secondly, the author should answer whether there will be a huge demand for the company's alpaca coats. If there were some relevant statistics, such as consumer demand surveys to back up this claim, it could be more plausible. However, as it stands, the idea sounds a bit incredible in the face of a market that tends to change rather quickly. The protest from its customers when the company stopped producing the alpaca overcoat does not necessarily mean they wanted the product very much; it may have indicated that they were concerned about its after-sales service when it discontinued this line of products, not to mention the possibility that the customers were small in number and did not represent other customers who had also bought the product. Even if this means the customers placed a great value on the products at that time, the same perception may not be there anymore. Also, the lack of competition does nothing to help the situation; if anything, it may suggest a decrease in demand for alpaca overcoats. There is even the chance that the plan could backfire completely, as people may perceive the company as backwards or lacking vision due to its backing of a dated style. This could account for the fact that no competitor offers a similar product. If this should be true, the assumption about pent-up customer demand would be unjustified, rendering the argument for resuming production of the alpaca overcoats tenuous.

Finally, the author needs to answer whether a pent-up demand for the company's alpaca overcoats and increase in clothing prices overall will be sufficient to make it gain more profits from the coats than ever before. We have poked holes in the assumption about the high demand, but even if the assumption proves warranted, and clothing prices have risen overall, there is no guarantee that the profitability would exceed that in the past. It is likely that the company profits will remain the same or even decrease. Profit is a function of revenue and costs. Rise in clothing prices overall does not necessarily mean prices for the alpaca coats will also increase; it is likely that people will not want to pay for the overcoats at all, much less at higher prices than before, even though the overall prices of clothing have increased. In fact, those who remember the lower cost of the alpaca overcoats in the past may refuse to buy the newer, higher priced ones, sparking a backlash against the product. Should this be the case, the assumption about customers' willingness to pay higher prices for the same product will be unfounded. Even if customers are willing to pay higher prices, the rise may not be significant enough to cover the costs, including costs of purchasing fabric, manufacturing and selling the overcoats, and employing people, among other things, so the company is unlikely to anticipate an increase in profitability. Similarly, the demand may be strong, but it is not strong enough to enable the company to sell large quantities of alpaca coats to boost its profitability. Such scenarios could dramatically raise the costs and make the business unprofitable, rendering the argument implausible.

To conclude, the main question that must be answered before the company moves forward with this plan is whether pent-up demand for its alpaca overcoats exists. This could be accomplished through customer surveys and other market research strategies to see if people are buying comparable items. Included in such surveys could be questions as to whether consumers would be willing to pay higher prices for the new coats. Without relevant information, we cannot fully assess the argument and without a sound argument, the company could incur a huge risk by restarting to sell alpaca overcoats at increased prices.

70. The Classical Shakespeare Theatre to attract more audience members by learning from Avon (Questions to Be Answered)

Citing a twenty percent drop in the average audience attendance at the theatre, along with considerably reduced profits, despite more advertising, and a similar program that was implemented two years ago by a nearby theatre called Avon Repertory Company (Avon), which has experienced a ten-percent profit increase since then, the author recommends that the Classical Shakespeare Theatre of Bardville (Shakespeare) start a "Shakespeare in the Park" program in order to increase profits. However, we need answers to some critical questions before we determine whether the company should implement such a plan.

Regarding the decrease in audience size at Shakespeare, we must ask if this has been a continuous trend or a recent phenomenon, and whether twenty percent smaller audience would be enough to significantly affect profits. If the decrease has only occurred recently, then it would be unreasonable to rush into this new program without first investigating why it has happened, since there may be the chance that it is the result of temporary factors, such as sudden changes in the city's population, or a short string of unpopular performances. There may also be the chance that the company has been increasing its ticket prices, improving profits despite a gradual decrease in the size of audience. In either scenario, the new program may not have the predicted result of making the company more profitable and therefore is unwarranted.

While Shakespeare's advertising has increased, we are left to wonder whether the quality of the advertising could be the reason for fewer people visiting the shows. It may be that the advertising is not getting the reach it should as a result of using the wrong medium. For example, perhaps the company has been using traditional posters and billboards for advertising, when it could and should be using the internet and social media platforms to build awareness. It may also be that the advertising has offended some communities recently. It may even be that it has become less and less aesthetically pleasing. Any of the scenarios, if true, would make the recommendation of implementing the program unreasonable. Regardless, it is worth looking into the advertising so that the company does not continue to waste its dwindling profits on useless advertisements.

Concerning the "Free Plays in the Park" program itself, we should figure out whether the program implemented by Avon was the direct cause of its profit increase over the subsequent two years. That is not a short period of time after all, and any number of other factors could have played a part; therefore, it would be advisable to perform due diligence first. As with Shakespeare, Avon's profit increase could have resulted from seasonal changes in the city's population or from a recently hired popular performer. It could also have come from discontinuance of the company's unpopular performances. It could even have come about because the audience's tastes have changed. In such scenarios, there is no guarantee that the company's new program "Free Plays in the Park" alone has contributed to its profit rise, rendering the predicted result unlikely.

Even assuming that Avon's new program is responsible for its profit increase, we need to know whether Shakespeare will benefit from a similar program. Both companies and their new programs may be too different from each other to justify a similar strategy. For example, "Free Plays in the Park" may attract a large audience because it is free and the audience may include many potential customers for its regular shows later, whereas "Shakespeare in the Park" may charge high ticket prices that will only draw a small audience that may include few would-be customers for its regular performances in the future. In that event, it is unfair to suggest to Shakespeare that it should follow the example of the other company that has experienced a ten percent increase in profit. Even if the company can institute a comparable program, there is no guarantee that its profits will increase, because the revenue and costs associated with launching such a program are not given. Should this be true, the argument would be weakened. If the company can become more profitable because of the program "Shakespeare in the Park", the argument would be strengthened. To better evaluate the argument, we need Shakespeare's cost-to-profit projections to see if its program similar to Avon's will be profitable.

To conclude, before adopting the recommendation to put on a "Shakespeare in the Park" program, Shakespeare must first find the root causes of the decrease in audience members and profits. It should also investigate the reach and effectiveness of its advertising, along with the details surrounding the other company's "Free Plays in the Park" program.

71. A new café for <u>Monarch Books</u> (assumptions)

The author recommends that Monarch Books open a café in its store in order to boost profits and compete with Book and Bean, a bookstore and café combined. To justify the recommendation, the article claims that it could remove the children's book section to make space for the café, citing census data showing a considerable decline in the percentage of the people under the age of ten. However, before we determine whether Monarch should undertake such a renovation, we must consider some issues surrounding the argument and its underlying assumptions.

The author assumes that using the space for children's books to open a café in its own store is necessary for Monarch. The article mentions that Monarch has a large customer base and is well-known for its book selection. Yet by recommending major changes, the manager implies that having a wide customer base is meaningless. The article makes no mention of declining profits or a loss of customers, nor does it indicate whether Monarch's readers are interested in having a café in its store, so we must wonder whether spending the money to renovate its location would even be necessary. Should this plan fail, not only would the store lose money from the initial renovation and its damaged reputation of being a bookstore stocking a wide range of books, but it would then need to spend even more money to renovate once again to remove the café and repair its reputation, rendering its business unprofitable. In that event, the assumption about the need for a café in Monarch's store would prove unwarranted and the argument in support of Monarch opening a café in its own store would be gratuitous.

The author also implies that Book and Bean, which already planned to open a combination bookstore and coffee shop in the same city, will benefit from the new store. However, the article gives no evidence that opening such a store would help Book and Bean at all. For all we know, the café in the store could hurt its business by adding a huge maintenance cost to its budget. After all, a bookstore by itself is fairly easy to maintain and all one needs to do is to keep the building at a certain temperature and humidity, but a café has to be constantly cleaned, repaired, and resupplied. As a result, Book and Bean may have been adversely affected by its coffee shop in its store. If this is true, there is no guarantee that Monarch will benefit from a café, not to mention that launching a café will help it to compete with Book and Bean's planned store in the city. In this way, the implication is unsubstantiated. A detailed analysis of the effects of Book and Bean's café on its business is needed before Monarch passes judgement on the benefits of opening one. If there is evidence that Book and Bean has not profited from its café, the author cannot confidently claim that Monarch should open one in its own store. The worst scenario could be that Book and Bean does not open a Collegeville store at all, rendering the assumption unsubstantiated and undermining the argument.

Finally, the author suggests that a trend will continue. The article recommends making room for the café by getting rid of the children's book section, using national census data that shows a decline in the percentage of the population under the age of ten. This assumes that the trend will remain unchanged into the future. However, as we know, census data accounts for past trends and cannot always be trusted to predict future scenarios. Monarch has been in business for over twenty years and is known for its wide selection of books, after all; therefore, if it hopes to stay in business for another twenty years, or even longer, it needs to plan for the real trend. If there is no decrease in the number of children younger than ten in the future, the store may lose much business by replacing its children's book section with a café because doing so may hurt its reputation as a store with a variety of books on every subject and with one section devoted to children's books. Even if there is a drop in the portion of the people below ten, there may not be a drop in the number of children below ten, because the total population could rise. Even assuming that there is an eventual decrease in the number of children under ten, there may be an increase in the number of children above ten. Granted that there is a decline in the number of all the children, there may be no decline in sales of children's books, because children may buy more books on average as a result of factors such as parents' desire to nurture their children's literacy skills through reading or programs that they participate in. Even if the national trend continues, there is no guarantee that it will be true for Monarch where the percentage of the population under age ten may not decrease locally and will remain so in the future. Should this be true, the assumption and the argument that it underlies would be unfounded.

In conclusion, the evidence in the argument needs further scrutiny before Monarch decides to spend a considerable amount of money to add a café to its store. It must consider whether its customer base or profits are under threat and whether the example of Book and Bean is indeed a valid one. It must also take into account the long-term effects of removing its children's section if it is to maintain in the future its reputation for being reader-friendly and having a large selection of books.

72. A new café for Monarch Books (Specific Evidence)

The author recommends that Monarch Books open a café in its store in order to boost profits and compete with Book and Bean, a bookstore and café combined. To justify the recommendation, the article claims that it could remove the children's book section to make space for the café, citing census data showing a considerable decline in the percentage of the people under the age of ten. However, before we determine whether Monarch should undertake such a renovation, we need a significant amount of additional evidence.

The author must provide evidence that using the space for children's books to open a café in its own store is necessary for Monarch. The article mentions that Monarch has a large customer base and is well-known for its book selection. Yet by recommending major changes, the manager implies that having a wide customer base is meaningless. The article makes no mention of declining profits or a loss of customers, nor does it indicate whether Monarch's readers are interested in having a café in its store, so we must wonder whether spending the money to renovate its location would even be necessary. Should this plan fail, not only would the store lose money from the initial renovation and its damaged reputation of being a bookstore stocking a wide range of books, but it would then need to spend even more money to renovate once again to remove the café and repair its reputation, rendering its business unprofitable. In that event, the assumption about the need for a café in Monarch's store would prove unwarranted and the argument in support of Monarch opening a café in its own store would be gratuitous.

The author should also offer evidence that Book and Bean, which already planned to open a combination bookstore and coffee shop in the same city, will benefit from the new store. However, the article gives no evidence that opening such a store would help Book and Bean at all. For all we know, the café in the store could hurt its business by adding a huge maintenance cost to its budget. After all, a bookstore by itself is fairly easy to maintain and all one needs to do is to keep the building at a certain temperature and humidity, but a café has to be constantly cleaned, repaired, and resupplied. As a result, Book and Bean may have been adversely affected by its coffee shop in its store. If this is true, there is no guarantee that Monarch will benefit from a café, not to mention that launching a café will help it compete with Book and Bean's planned store in the city. In this way, the implication is unsubstantiated. A detailed analysis of the effects of Book and Bean's café on its business is needed before Monarch passes judgement on the benefits of opening one. If there is evidence that Book and Bean has not profited from its café, the author cannot confidently claim that Monarch should open one in its own store. The worst scenario could be that Book and Bean does not open a Collegeville store at all, rendering the assumption unsubstantiated and undermining the argument.

Finally, the author needs to furnish evidence that a trend will continue. The article suggests making room for the café by getting rid of the children's book section, using national census data that shows a decline in the percentage of the population under the age of ten. This assumes that the trend will remain unchanged into the future. However, as we know, census data accounts for past trends and cannot always be trusted to predict future scenarios. Monarch has been in business for over twenty years and is known for its wide selection of books, after all; therefore, if it hopes to stay in business for another twenty years, or even longer, it needs to plan for the real trend. If there is no decrease in the number of children younger than ten in the future, the store may lose much business by replacing its children's book section with a café because doing so may hurt its reputation as a store with a variety of books on every subject and with one section devoted to children's books. Even if there is a drop in the portion of the people below ten, there may not be a drop in the number of children below ten, because the total population could rise. Even assuming that there is an eventual decrease in the number of children under ten, there may be an increase in the number of children above ten. Granted that there is a decline in the number of all the children, there may be no decline in sales of children's books, because children may buy more books on average as a result of factors such as parents' desire to nurture their children's literacy skills through reading or programs that they participate in. Even if the national trend continues, there is no guarantee that it will be true for Monarch where the percentage of the population under age ten may not decrease locally and will remain so in the future. Should this be true, the assumption and the argument that it underlies would be unfounded.

In conclusion, the evidence in the argument needs further scrutiny before Monarch Books decides to spend a considerable amount of money to add a café to its store. It must consider whether its customer base or profits are under threat and whether the example of Book and Bean is indeed a valid one. It must also take into account the long-term effects of removing its children's section if it is to maintain in the future its reputation for being reader-friendly and having a large selection of books.

73. Building a jazz club in Monroe (Assumptions)

The author concludes that a jazz club would be a lucrative venture in the city of Monroe. To support the conclusion, the application cites the popularity of jazz music in the area by presenting examples such as a highly-rated jazz radio program, a recent jazz festival, and the famous jazz musicians that reside there. However, before the loan for the proposed jazz club is approved, we need to scrutinize certain assumptions that underlie the argument.

First, the author assumes that attendees at the annual jazz music festival are representative of the local people that enjoy jazz music. The application states that the recent jazz music festival attracted 100,000 people. However, there is no mention of the exact number of people from Monroe; therefore, we do not know the portion, if any at all, of the attendees from Monroe. Census information that showed the population of Monroe and a survey that showed whether locals or tourists comprised a significant percentage of the jazz festival attendees would be evidence needed to evaluate the business-loan applicant's argument. If a large portion of the attendees were from Monroe, it could be proof of popularity of jazz there, making the case for a jazz music club in Monroe more convincing. It is also likely that Monroe is a town of only 100 and few attendees were locals. Should the assumption be false, there is the risk that the author may be overestimating the number of people willing to attend a new jazz club. However, even if the people from Monroe accounted for a considerable portion of the attendees, it is likely that the trend last summer was an aberration and may not continue. Should this be true, the argument would be weakened.

Secondly, the author implies that just because the jazz radio station is the highest rated station in Monroe and a few famous jazz musicians live in Monroe, jazz is popular in the city. However, there is no solid evidence that this is the case. It is possible, especially in the current age of MP3 players and the internet, that it is simply the only radio station that is listened to at all, and that the number of listeners is relatively small. If this is true, then jazz may not be as popular as previously thought, leading to a lack of attendees in the proposed club. Even if the jazz station is popular, there is no guarantee that its listeners would be interested in listening to jazz at the new club. It could even compete with the proposed club for listeners. Either scenario would undermine the case for a new club in Monroe. The author also implies that the local musicians will be able to perform at the new club. The application notes that a few famous jazz musicians own homes in Monroe, but there is no guarantee that they would like to perform at the local jazz club or that locals would be willing to hear them perform. They may perform elsewhere and even at the nearest jazz club but reside in Monroe simply to take advantage of peaceful small-town life. If this is true, their proximity to the club may have no bearing on its success. As a result, the argument for a new jazz club in Monroe will be weakened. If the jazz musicians are willing to play at the club, are appreciated in the area, and do not demand unreasonable compensation for performing at the club, the argument will be strengthened. Lacking relevant evidence, we cannot fully evaluate the potential success of a new jazz club in Monroe.

Finally, the author suggests that a jazz music club in Monroe would be extremely profitable. Granted that jazz is popular in Monroe, we need information regarding whether the proposed jazz music club would dominate the local market just because the nearest jazz club is more than an hour away. The application suggests that people are unwilling to drive over an hour to the closest club. However, it is likely that people are willing to do so because the nearest club is competitive in terms of admission prices, atmosphere, and services. In this case, the assumption raises questions and the argument that it underlies would be undermined. Also, the nationwide study finds that an average jazz fan spends about $1,000 every year on jazz entertainment. However, it could be that the typical fan spends little at jazz music clubs. It could also be that a jazz fan in Monroe spends little on jazz entertainment and even less at jazz music clubs. When the new club is unlikely to receive the revenue, the prediction of an extremely profitable business would be groundless, because profit is a function of revenue and costs. It will become even more groundless if the applicant fails to consider all kinds of costs associated with launching a business. Before touting the profitability of the club, the author must estimate all the costs as well as the revenues.

In conclusion, the assumptions underlying the argument in favor of a new jazz club in Monroe are gratuitous. The potential owner must first provide solid data on the population of Monroe, and the portion of people in the city who both like jazz music and are willing to spend money on going to a jazz club. It would also be in the owner's best interest to contact the local musicians to see if they are willing to play at the club at an affordable rate. Above everything else, the owner must weigh the potential revenue against the costs to make sure that the business would be lucrative.

74. Is living in small towns like Leeville healthier than living in big cities like Masonton? (Assumptions)

Relying on the fact that businesses in the town of Leeville report fewer sick days for individual workers than those in Masonton, that it has a lower proportion of physicians to residents, and that its residents are considerably older on average, the author posits that the disparity in three respects is due to Leeville's relaxed pace of life and concludes that people who want better health and longer lives should relocate to small communities. However, the argument is full of assumptions and loopholes that we must scrutinize before we determine its persuasiveness.

The argument rests on the assumption that the smaller number of sick days reported by businesses in Leeville is a direct result of living in a small town with a more relaxed pace of life. However, the author offers no evidence to substantiate this. A smaller number of reported sick days may not indicate better health. Even if it is an indication of being healthier, there is no guarantee that it has been caused by a cozier pace of life. There is the chance that individual workers in Leeville are generally healthier than their counterparts in Masonton. There is also the chance that the number of days taken off work by individual workers may not be health-related at all, but instead is the result of other job-related pressures. Specifically, it may be the case that for whatever reason, workers in Leeville do not feel secure in their jobs, and fear that taking time off work may cause their bosses to fire them. Alternatively, it may also be the case that a slowing economy, combined with a system of hourly wages, has made it necessary for people to work as often as possible to make ends meet at home. Perhaps since Leeville is rather small, the businesses in the town report fewer days of sick leave for individual workers because of a cultural sensibility that taking sick leave would make one seem weak. Should this be true, the assumption about Leeville workers' fewer sick days would be unsubstantiated. Even if the assumption is warranted, the author also assumes that health of both Leeville workers and Masonton workers represents that of their respective residents. However, this is not necessarily true. Without establishing that this is true, the author cannot make any reliable comparisons about the overall health of both towns' inhabitants, not to mention the effect of town size on health.

The argument is also based on the assumption that the lower ratio of physicians to residents in Leeville has been caused by its relaxed pace of life. However, this need not be the case. A lower ratio of physicians to residents does not necessarily mean being healthier. Even if it means better health, there is no guarantee that it is a result of a more relaxed tempo of life. It is possible that the town could only afford one physician for its one thousand residents. It is also possible that few physicians would like to work there because of its low salaries and living standards. It is even possible that the residents there go to the nearby Masonton for physical examination and treatments because of its lower charges and better doctors. Perhaps they eat a more nutritious diet and exercise more. Or perhaps they have fewer visits to doctors because of Leeville's better air quality. In such scenarios, they do not need more than one physician. Any of the scenarios, if true, would invalidate the assumption that Leeville residents need a smaller proportion of physicians to residents because its less stressful lifestyle makes its people healthier. Even if the assumption is warranted, there is no guarantee that Leeville is representative of small communities and Masonton big cities. In this case, the argument would be weakened.

Finally, the argument relies on the assumption that the population considerably older on average in Leeville has resulted from its less stressful lifestyle. However, the author provides no evidence to establish this. It may simply be the case that Leeville is a popular town for people to retire in. It may also be the case that since the town is small, a few very old citizens tend to raise the average age of the town considerably, but most citizens live a shorter life on average than those in Masonton. Even if its people have longer lives on average than Masonton's, their average lifespans may still be shorter than those of other big city residents. Even assuming that its people have longer lives on average than big city inhabitants, this may not hold true for all other small communities. Granted that Leeville's relaxed pace of life is responsible for fewer sick days of its individual workers, a lower proportion of physicians to residents, and the significantly older age on average of its residents and that the claim holds true for all small communities, this does not necessarily mean that all those seeking longer and healthier lives should relocate to small communities, because the author overlooks other factors that are needed to enjoy such lives, such as jobs, housing, and schools. If a small community is unable to provide enough well-paying jobs, affordable housing, and good schools, its people may not be able to make a living, not to mention having better health and greater longevity, rendering the argument in support of relocating to small communities gratuitous.

While it may very well be the case that Leeville does have a relatively relaxed pace of life which contributes to fewer sick days reported by businesses, a lower proportion of physicians to residents, and longer lives on average, the author should not hastily assume that this is true. Even if this is true, we still need evidence that Leeville and Masonton are representative of small communities and big cities respectively and that longer and healthier lives require nothing more than a relaxed pace of life in a small community. Since no evidence is given to corroborate this, we should scrutinize the assumptions to better assess the argument that they underlie.

75. Building a jazz club in Monroe (Questions to Be Answered)

The author concludes that a jazz club would be a lucrative venture in the city of Monroe. To support the conclusion, the application cites the popularity of jazz music in the area by presenting examples such as a highly-rated jazz radio program, a recent jazz festival, and the famous jazz musicians that reside there. However, before the loan for the proposed jazz club is approved, we need answers to some questions.

Firstly, we must ask whether attendees at the annual jazz music festival are representative of the local people that enjoy jazz music. The application states that the recent jazz music festival attracted 100,000 people. However, there is no mention of the exact number of people from Monroe; therefore, we do not know the portion, if any at all, of the attendees from Monroe. Census information that showed the population of Monroe and a survey that showed whether locals or tourists comprised a significant percentage of the jazz festival attendees would be evidence needed to evaluate the business-loan applicant's argument. If a large portion of the attendees were from Monroe, it could be proof of popularity of jazz there, making the case for a jazz music club in Monroe more convincing. It is also likely that Monroe is a town of only 100 and few attendees were locals. However, even if the people from Monroe accounted for a considerable portion of the attendees, it is likely that the trend last summer was an aberration and may not continue. Should this be true, the prediction would be very unreasonable.

Secondly, we should ask whether the local musicians will be able to perform at the new club. The application notes that a few famous jazz musicians own homes in Monroe, but there is no guarantee that they would like to perform at the local jazz club or that locals would be willing to hear them perform. They may perform elsewhere and even at the nearest jazz club but reside in Monroe simply to take advantage of peaceful small-town life. If this is true, their proximity to the club may have no bearing on its success. As a result, the argument for a new jazz club in Monroe will be weakened. If the jazz musicians are willing to play at the club, are appreciated in the area, and do not demand unreasonable compensation for performing at the club, the argument will be strengthened. Lacking relevant evidence, we cannot fully evaluate the potential success of a new jazz club in Monroe.

Thirdly, we need to ask whether the fact that the jazz radio station is the highest rated station in Monroe indicates that jazz is popular in the city. However, the author provides no information about this. It is possible, especially in the current age of MP3 players and the internet, that it is simply the only radio station that is listened to at all, and that the number of listeners is relatively small. As with the previous contention, population data and music preference surveys could help us appraise this counterargument. It would also help if the author could provide the ratings for all radio stations in Monroe, so that we could have a clearer picture of how much more popular the jazz station is than the other radio stations. If the difference in ratings is small, then it would weaken the case for starting a club that plays jazz music exclusively. Even if the jazz station is popular, there is no guarantee that its listeners would be interested in listening to jazz at the new club. It could even compete with the proposed club for listeners. Either scenario would undermine the case for a new club in Monroe.

Finally, we lack the answer to whether a jazz music club in Monroe would be extremely profitable. Assuming that jazz is popular in Monroe, we need information regarding whether the proposed jazz music club would dominate the local market just because the nearest jazz club is more than an hour away. The application suggests that people are unwilling to drive over an hour to the closest club. However, it is likely that people are willing to do so because the nearest club is competitive in terms of admission prices, atmosphere, and services. In this case, the argument would be undermined. Also, the nationwide study finds that an average jazz fan spends about $1,000 every year on jazz entertainment. However, it could be that the typical fan spends little in jazz music clubs. It could also be that a jazz fan in Monroe spends little on jazz entertainment and even less in jazz music clubs. When the new club is unlikely to receive the revenue, the prediction of a profitable business would be groundless, because profit is a function of revenue and costs.

It will become even more groundless if the applicant fails to consider all kinds of costs associated with launching a business. Before touting the significant profitability of the club, the author must estimate all the costs as well as the revenues.

In conclusion, before receiving approval of this loan, the potential owner must first provide solid data on the population of Monroe, and the portion of people in the city who both like jazz music and are willing to spend money on going to a jazz club. It would also be in the owner's best interest to contact the local musicians to see if they are willing to play at the club at an affordable rate. Above everything else, the owner must weigh the potential revenue against the costs to make sure that the business would be lucrative.

76. Is living in small towns like Leeville healthier than living in big cities like Masonton? (Alternative Explanations)

Relying on the fact that businesses in the town of Leeville report fewer sick days for individual workers than those in Masonton, that it has a lower proportion of physicians to residents, and that its residents are considerably older on average, the author posits that the disparity in three respects is due to Leeville's relaxed pace of life. While this may be the case, other possible explanations are worth exploring, including a desire to keep a job or earn more money, physicians' concerns and the residents' needs, and the residents' genes and lifestyles, among other things.

Regarding the days taken off work by individual workers, there are two explanations for the disparity. One possible explanation is that Leeville has a smaller number of workers. If workers take the same number of sick days on average in both Leeville and Masonton, it is reasonable that those in Leeville would have fewer days of sick leave. Another likely explanation is that the days taken off work by individual workers may not be health-related at all, but instead is the result of other job-related pressures. Specifically, it may be the case that for whatever reason, workers in Leeville do not feel secure in their jobs, and fear that taking time off work may cause their bosses to fire them. Alternatively, it may also be the case that a slowing economy, combined with a system of hourly wages, has made it necessary for people to work as often as possible to make ends meet at home. Perhaps since Leeville is rather small, the businesses in the town report fewer days of sick leave for individual workers because of a cultural sensibility that taking sick leave would make one seem weak. This indicates that factors other than the health benefits of the relatively relaxed pace of life could be responsible for reporting fewer days of sick leave in Leeville.

When it comes to the physician-resident ratios, a myriad of other factors might explain the disparity. It is possible that Leeville could only afford one physician for its one thousand residents. It is also possible that few physicians would like to work there because of its low salaries and living standards. Perhaps the residents there eat a more nutritious diet and exercise more; therefore, they are healthier and do not need more than one physician. Or perhaps they go to the nearby Masonton for physical examination and treatments because of its lower charges and better doctors. All such scenarios would obviate the need for more than one physician. On the contrary, it is likely that Masonton is much richer and has the money to hire as many physicians as it wants for its citizens. It is also likely that physicians enjoy working there for its hefty jobs and good life quality. The citizens there could care little about their eating and do little exercise; therefore, they are less healthy and need more physicians. They could also be more inclined to see a doctor. All such factors, rather than the relaxed lifestyle of Leeville, could contribute to the difference in the number of physicians each city has.

With respect to average ages, many factors besides Leeville's less stressful lifestyle might be the reasons for the disparity. It could be that Leeville, with agreeable weather and few crimes, is a popular town for people to retire in. It could also be that since the town is small, a few very old citizens that have recently relocated there raise the average age of the town considerably. At the same time, many young residents may be moving outside of Leeville. It could even be that Leeville has fewer incidences of disease as a result of less air pollution in the town. Above everything else, the residents may be genetically programmed to live longer, healthier lives. All such scenarios would rule out the relaxed pace of life in Leeville as the sole factor in contributing to its residents' better health and greater longevity. Conversely, Masonton may be a popular town for young people who choose to work there for its plentiful good jobs. It may also have higher rates of disease because of its severe air pollution. Most importantly, many of its citizens may be less fortunate in genetics, having genes that promise shorter lifespans, or they tend to have less reasonable regimens, leading to many young deaths. Should this be true, the difference in residents' ages of both places is attributable to factors other than the less stressful pace of life in Leeville.

While it may very well be the case that Leeville does have a relatively relaxed pace of life which contributes to longer, healthier lives, we should not rule out other possible explanations. Once we have explored all the possibilities, we will be able to decide whether the author should recommend small towns to people seeking health and longevity.

77. Shortening work shifts to reduce the number of <u>on-the-job accidents</u> (Alternative Explanations)

In this memo, the author, a vice president of a manufacturing company, cites a statement by experts that claims fatigue and sleep deprivation are major factors responsible for a great number of on-the-job accidents. The vice president also gives an example from its competitor, Panoply Industries, which already has work shifts shorter by one hour with an alleged successful result. Relying on the statement and the example, the author claims that Panoply's better safety record is attributable to its shorter work shifts. Yet, other explanations could also account for the facts.

One possible cause of the accidents reported by workers at the newly opened factory could be insufficiently trained staff. Factories can be dangerous places even for very experienced workers; large and powerful automated machines care little about what is in their way after all, so accidents are prone to happen. It is possible that the new factory purchased many new machines and hired many new workers during the previous year. Therefore, it could be that it had more untrained workers than Panoply who could not operate the machines properly or follow safety instructions. It could also be that the machines were not adequately maintained. If the workers in the company being discussed were less experienced than those at Panoply, this could account for the disparity in accidents that occurred in the respective factories. It is also possible that the factory has many more workers than Panoply, thereby reporting more on-the-job accidents. This scenario could also rival shorter work shifts as an explanation for the difference in the number of reported accidents.

It may also be the case that the problem with work shifts is something other than their length. They could be spaced too closely together, meaning that days off during the week are too apart. This is similar to the argument made in the memo regarding a need for shorter shifts and accounts for the fact that even if shifts are shorter, the human body needs days off between workdays to heal. Having to work day after day in a dangerous environment, regardless of how long the shift is, can take a heavy toll on a person's body. Perhaps the new factory's workers were allowed to take no breaks within a shift whereas their counterparts at Panoply were allowed to take several breaks. Or perhaps their workload per capita was much heavier than that of Panoply workers. Or perhaps their negative feelings towards work shifts made them more willing to report on-the-job accidents in the past year whereas those at Panoply did not bother to do so, since they would be rewarded for reporting fewer accidents. These scenarios would also rule out shorter work shifts as the only explanation for the smaller number of on-the-job accidents reported at Panoply.

Granting that sleep deprivation is the root cause, it may be that work has nothing to do with workers' exhaustion, but their choice of activities after work does. It is no secret that factory work is considered a blue-collar job, and in blue-collar society, going out drinking with colleagues after work is a common activity, whether for the comradery or for the relief alcohol brings after a long day on the job. Such behavior, if pursued nightly, may lead to chronic sleep-deprivation in its own right, work hours notwithstanding. The trend of the factory last year could also be an aberration when many workers went out drinking to adapt to the new environment whereas those at Panoply did not go out drinking very often, because they had adjusted to the blue-worker environment. Unless there is evidence that longer work shifts alone have contributed to more accidents, employees' after-work activities could be another explanation.

In conclusion, various other factors might explain the greater number of accidents at the author's factory in the memo. Poorly trained or inexperienced staff that are unprepared for the dangerous work environment, weekends that are few and far between, and recreation activities which go late in the night have equal chances of being root causes.

78. Shortening work shifts to reduce the number of on-the-job accidents at Butler (Specific Evidence)

The author concludes that Butler Manufacturing can make each of its work shifts shorter by one hour in order to reduce the number of on-the-job accidents, which the author claims has been a result of sleep deprivation. To support the conclusion, the article cites a government study that reports fatigue and sleep deprivation are major factors responsible for the aforementioned issues, as well as a separate factory, Panoply Industries, which has work shifts that are one hour shorter and thirty percent fewer accidents. Unfortunately, the author does not provide enough evidence to bolster the argument, and to fully assess it, we need extra evidence.

Firstly, the comparison showing a thirty percent more accidents at Butler is not made with any context that justifies a change in scheduling. We do not know how many accidents this number represents, nor how far it deviates from the normal number of accidents in previous years. If the number of accidents that occurred at Panoply during the past year was ten, then thirty percent more at Butler would mean only three extra incidences. Even if a difference of thirty percent represents a significant number, the trend last year could have been an aberration and may not continue. It would also help to know the severity of the accidents to see if immediate action is truly warranted. Moreover, the fact that the accidents were self-reported could skew the results because workers at Butler may have been more willing to report the accidents whereas those at Panoply did not bother to do so. Should this be true, the need for shortening work shifts to reduce the number of on-the-job accidents may be unjustified. To better evaluate the argument, we need more information about Butler's thirty percent more accidents during the past year.

Even assuming that Butler's greater number of accidents represent a significant disparity and severity, nothing is mentioned by the article to explain why they have happened. It is not known if fatigue or sleep deprivation was the sole cause, or other factors, such as poor safety standards, machine malfunctions, or simply having many more workers, especially untrained workers, contributed to more accidents. If the cause is something other than worker fatigue, then reducing the number of work hours will hardly help. Even assuming that worker fatigue was the culprit, it may not have been the workload that was causing it, but rather after -work activities that led to lost sleep. Without ruling out these explanations, the author cannot reliably conclude that longer work shifts were responsible for more on-the-job accidents. Even if Butler needs to reduce its time of each work shift, there is no guarantee that its employees will use the extra hour to rest or one more hour will be enough for its employees to have adequate rest. In this case, the claim that Butler can enhance its safety record by implementing shorter work shifts to give its workers adequate rest would be undermined.

Finally, regarding the case of Panoply, no information provided shows that its shorter work shifts have any connection to its fewer on-the-job accidents in a single year. Without proof that it had its own issues with worker fatigue or evidence that it too decreased its work hours, leading to a reduction in related accidents, the case does not stand well as an example; the scenario in the past year may have been an anomaly and may not be representative of its performance in other years. Even accepting the case does not guarantee that the same policy will be successful at Butler, since there is no established similarity between the two plants. It is likely that Panoply's workers need one more hour to get adequate amounts of rest each day whereas Butler's employees have had enough rest. It is also likely that Panoply's workers use the extra hour to have a rest, whereas their Butler counterparts will use it to go out drinking and therefore become even more exhausted. If this should be true, the argument that Butler should emulate Panoply to reduce the number of on-the-job accidents would be weakened.

In conclusion, in order to decide whether Butler will succeed by shortening its work shifts, we must have proof that the greater number of accidents at Butler in the previous year, as compared to Panoply, was not an isolated occurrence and represented a considerable gap and severity. Also, we should uncover the root cause of the accidents in order to implement an appropriate work schedule. Finally, we need to determine whether Panoply and Butler factories bear enough similarities for Panoply's work-shift policy to achieve the desired effect at Butler.

79. Shortening work shifts to reduce the number of on-the-job accidents at Butler (Questions to Be Answered)

The author recommends that Butler Manufacturing make each of its work shifts shorter by one hour in order to reduce the number of on-the-job accidents, which the author claims has been a result of sleep deprivation. To justify the recommendation, the article cites a government study that reports fatigue and sleep deprivation are major factors responsible for the aforementioned issues, as well as a separate factory, Panoply Industries, which has work shifts that are one hour shorter and thirty percent fewer accidents. However, we need answers to a number of questions before we determine the soundness of the recommendation.

We must know whether the accidents were significant in number and serious. However, the comparison showing a thirty percent more accidents at Butler is not made with any context that justifies a change in scheduling. We do not know how many accidents this number represents, nor how far it deviates from the normal number of accidents in previous years. If the number of accidents that occurred at Panoply during the past year was ten, then thirty percent more at Butler would mean only three extra incidences. Even if a difference of thirty percent represents a significant number, the trend last year could have been an aberration and may not continue. It would also help to know the severity of the accidents to see if immediate action is truly warranted. Moreover, the fact that the accidents were self-reported could skew the results because workers at Butler may have been more willing to report the accidents whereas those at Panoply did not bother to do so. Should this be true, the recommendation of shortening work shifts is unlikely to have the predicted result of enhancing safety record by giving workers adequate rest, rendering the argument invalid.

Even assuming that Butler's more accidents represent a significant disparity and severity, we should know whether longer work shifts alone were responsible for the greater number of accidents. However, nothing is mentioned by the article to explain why they happened. It is not known if fatigue or sleep deprivation was the sole cause, or other factors, such as poor safety standards, machine malfunctions, or simply having many more workers, especially untrained workers, contributed to more accidents. If the cause is something other than worker fatigue, then reducing the number of work hours will hardly help. Even assuming that worker fatigue was the culprit, it may not necessarily be the workload that was causing it, but rather after -work activities that led to lost sleep. Without ruling out these explanations, the author cannot reliably conclude that worker fatigue was responsible for more on-the-job accidents. Even if Butler needs to reduce its time of each work shift, there is no guarantee that its employees will use the extra hour to rest or one more hour will be enough for its employees to have adequate rest. In this case, the claim that Butler can enhance its safety record by making each work shift shorter by one hour would be undermined.

Finally, regarding the case of Panoply, we need to know whether its smaller number of accidents resulted from its shorter work shifts. However, no information provided shows that its shorter work shifts have any connection to its fewer on-the-job accidents in a single year. Without proof that it had its own issues with worker fatigue or evidence that it too decreased its work hours, leading to a reduction in related accidents, the case does not stand well as an example; the scenario in the past year may have been an anomaly and may not be representative of its performance in other years. Even accepting the case does not guarantee that the same policy will be successful at Butler, since there is no established similarity between the two plants. It is likely that Panoply's workers need one more hour to get adequate amounts of rest each day whereas Butler's employees have had enough rest. It is also likely that Panoply's workers use the extra hour to have a rest whereas their Butler counterparts will use it to go out drinking and therefore become even more exhausted. If this should be true, the recommendation that Butler should emulate Panoply to reduce the number of on-the-job accidents would be unfounded.

In conclusion, in order to decide whether Butler Manufacturing will succeed by shortening its work shifts by one hour, we must have proof that the greater number of accidents at Butler in the previous year, as compared to Panoply, was not an isolated occurrence and represented a significant gap and severity. Also, we should uncover the root cause of the accidents in order to implement an appropriate work schedule. Finally, we need to determine whether Panoply and Butler factories bear enough similarities for Panoply's work-shift policy to achieve the desired effect at Butler.

80. Reducing in-store imported cheese inventory (Assumptions)

The author recommends that a chain of cheese stores improve profits by ceasing to stock many of its imported cheeses and instead focus on domestic ones. However, the argument is based on many assumptions that we must examine closely to determine whether it is convincing.

The author assumes that the newest store is representative of the entirety of locations the chain has across the United States. The memo states that the best-selling cheeses at one location last year were all domestic. This fact by itself does sound convincing. However, they may only account for a smaller portion of the total sales volume of the store. Even if they make up a great portion of the total sales, a myriad of factors might explain this phenomenon. It could be the case that the new location had some sort of sale on those particular cheeses, that customers in that region simply preferred those cheeses, or that the store was new and did not yet begin to stock many imported cheeses. In such scenarios, sales and customers' preferences of the newest store may not typify those of the chain's other stores. It could also be the case that the trend last year was an aberration and may not continue. In contrast, it could be that many customers in other parts of the country do not like cheddar cheeses but prefer imported cheeses. If this should be true, the recommendation of stopping stocking many imported cheeses and concentrating on domestic cheeses to increase profits would be unjustified. Customer surveys and more recent sales figures would go a long way toward evaluating the argument.

Next, the author implies that the subscribers to the magazine Cheeses of the World are comparable to this chain's potential customers. The memo mentions that the survey found a popularity trend among its subscribers that favors domestic cheeses. But there is no survey data comparing the magazine readers to all the cheese-eaters in the entire nation. The survey results could be a gross misrepresentation. Then, the question arises as to whether the subscribers to this magazine constitute a considerable portion of this chain's customers or at least are similar to them. If yes, then the survey would be something worthy of consideration regarding the stocking recommendation. Also, we would like to know whether the survey is reliable and valid. The sample could have been a small group of self-selecting subscribers who tended to prefer domestic cheeses to imported ones. The researchers could have asked questions such as "Which do you prefer in terms of prices, domestic cheeses or imported cheeses?" In either scenario, the survey results would not be valid. Unless the survey is reliable, valid, and representative, the surveyed subscribers could not represent potential cheese buyers of this chain, the recommendation would be unreasonable, and the argument would be undermined.

Finally, the author suggests that discontinuing the chain's inventory of many varieties of imported cheese will improve its profits. However, even assuming that there is a nation-wide preference for domestic cheeses to imported cheeses, there could be price hikes by suppliers in the face of increasing demand, which may offset any expenses saved by removing imported stock. The chain should look into whether this could occur, and to what extent its stores would be affected. Also, stopping stocking imported cheeses may hurt the chain's reputation as a seller of imported cheeses as well as domestic cheeses. Customers may value the variety and choice of its stocked cheeses. Even if they prefer domestic cheeses, they may buy some imported cheeses at the same time. In this case, by discontinuing stock of imported cheeses, the chain may lose profits instead. In addition, the author needs to find out the profit margins of imported cheeses versus domestic cheeses. If imported cheeses have higher profit margins than those of domestic cheeses, the proposed course of action would be undesirable, because the expenses saved from reducing inventory of imported cheeses may be much less than loss of revenue that may result from stocking them. The author even fails to consider better options for improving profits. Perhaps expenses for stocking imported cheeses only account for a small portion of the total costs whereas those for renting the business space a significant part of the costs. In this case, it would be much more profitable to move to cheaper locations instead. Any of the scenarios, if true, would invalidate the assumption about increased profitability of and the argument for focusing on domestic cheeses.

While it may benefit the company to stock primarily domestic cheeses, as it stands, the argument in favor of the measure lacks the necessary scrutiny to assuage all concerns about it. The possibility exists that the measure will backfire, and unless the aforementioned issues are addressed, it would not be prudent to go forward with the author's recommendation.

81. Reducing in-store <u>imported cheese</u> inventory (Specific Evidence)

The author recommends that a chain of cheese stores improve profits by ceasing to stock many of its imported cheeses and instead focus on domestic ones. However, the argument in support of this measure lacks the necessary evidence to substantiate itself. To fully assess the argument, we need extra evidence.

We must have evidence that the newest store is representative of the entirety of locations the chain has across the United States. However, no relevant information is provided. The author states that the best-selling cheeses at one location last year were all domestic. This fact by itself does sound convincing. However, they may only account for a smaller portion of the total sales volume of the store. Even if they make up a great portion of the total sales, a myriad of factors might explain this phenomenon. It could be the case that the new location had some sort of sale on those particular cheeses, that customers in that region simply preferred those cheeses, or that the store was new and did not yet begin to stock many imported cheeses. In such scenarios, sales and customers' preferences of the newest store may not typify those of the chain's other stores. It could also be the case that the trend last year was an aberration and may not continue. In contrast, it could be that many customers in other parts of the country do not like cheddar cheeses but prefer imported cheeses. If this should be true, the recommendation of stopping stocking many imported cheeses and concentrating on domestic cheeses to increase profits would be unjustified. Customer surveys and more recent sales figures would go a long way toward evaluating the argument.

Next, we should have evidence that the subscribers to the magazine Cheeses of the World are comparable to this chain's potential customers. However, no information is offered in this respect. The memo mentions that the survey found a popularity trend among its subscribers that favors domestic cheeses. But there is no survey data comparing the magazine readers to all the cheese-eaters in the entire nation. The survey results could be a gross misrepresentation. Then, the question arises as to whether the subscribers to this magazine constitute a considerable portion of this chain's customers or are at least similar to them. If yes, then the survey would be something worthy of consideration regarding the stocking recommendation. Also, we would like to know whether the survey is reliable and valid. The sample could have been a small group of self-selecting subscribers who tended to prefer domestic cheeses to imported ones. The researchers could have asked questions such as "Which do you prefer in terms of prices, domestic cheeses or imported cheeses?" In either scenario, the survey results would not be valid. Unless the survey is reliable, valid, and representative, the surveyed subscribers could not represent potential cheese buyers of this chain, the recommendation would be unreasonable, and the argument would be undermined.

Finally, we need evidence that discontinuing the chain's inventory of many varieties of imported cheese will improve its profits. However, the author provides no data in this regard. Even assuming that there is a nationwide preference for domestic cheeses to imported cheeses, there could be price hikes by suppliers in the face of increasing demand, which may offset any expenses saved by removing imported stock. The chain should look into whether this could occur, and to what extent its stores would be affected. Also, stopping stocking imported cheeses may hurt the chain's reputation as a seller of imported cheeses as well as domestic cheeses. Customers may value the variety and choice of its stocked cheeses. Even if they prefer domestic cheeses, they may buy some imported cheeses at the same time. In this case, by discontinuing stock of imported cheeses, the chain may lose profits instead. In addition, the author needs to find out the profit margins of imported cheeses versus domestic cheeses. If imported cheeses have higher profit margins than those of domestic cheeses, the proposed course of action would be undesirable, because the expenses saved from reducing inventory of imported cheeses may be much less than loss of revenue that may result from stocking them. Furthermore, the author even fails to consider better options for improving profits. Perhaps expenses for stocking imported cheeses only account for a small portion of the total costs whereas those for renting the business space a significant part of the costs. In this case, it would be much more profitable to move to cheaper locations instead. Any of the scenarios, if true, would invalidate the assumption about increased profitability of and the argument for focusing on domestic cheeses.

While it may benefit the company to stock primarily domestic cheeses, as it stands, the argument in favor of the measure lacks the necessary scrutiny to assuage all concerns about it. The possibility exists that the measure will backfire, and unless the aforementioned issues are addressed, it would not be prudent to go forward with the author's recommendation.

82. KNOW radio station to shift to a 24-hour news format (Assumptions)

The author recommends that KNOW radio station change to a 24-hour news format from a rock-music format in order to attract older listeners and guarantee a good future. To justify the recommendation, the article states that the number of listeners over the age of fifty has risen, while the total number of listeners has gone down. It also cites reduced sales of recorded music in the area, along with success of continuous news stations in neighboring cities. However, the argument is based on many assumptions that we must scrutinize before we ascertain its soundness.

The first assumption that underlies the argument is that the decline in local music sales is indicative of a limited interest in rock-and-roll music and of a preference for continuous news. However, decreased sales of recorded music do not necessarily mean people's interest in rock-and-roll music has also decreased. The reported decrease in sales could be inaccurate and negligible. Even if there is a drop in local sales of recorded music, there may not be a drop in sales of recorded rock music. Even assuming that there is a decrease in sales of recorded rock music, this does not necessarily indicate a limited interest in rock music. A myriad of other factors might explain this phenomenon. For example, the introduction of the internet may have harmed the sale of music everywhere due to illegal downloading and online music solutions. Therefore, it is highly possible that people are still very much interested in rock music, but simply do not wish to buy it in physical format. Even if listeners have been losing interest in rock-and-roll music, this does not necessarily mean that they prefer 24-hour news. If this should be the case, the assumption about the connection between music sales and people's interest in rock music would prove unjustified, and the argument that the radio station should change from rock-and-roll music to continuous news would collapse. The radio station would do well to conduct surveys to find out if people have lost interest in music or have simply found other ways of obtaining it.

The second assumption that undergirds the argument is that the popularity of 24-hour news radio in neighboring cities is an indication of the possible success of such programming in KNOW's case. Even if people are no longer interested in rock-and-roll music, this does not necessarily mean that they would like to switch to the 24-hour news format. They may prefer rock-and-roll music in a different format or a mix of rock-and-roll music and news. They may even stop listening to the radio altogether. Moreover, just because the all-news format is popular in neighboring cities does not necessarily mean it will be popular with KNOW's listeners. The author implies that the major difference between KNOW and all-news stations in nearby cities is the rock-and-roll programming versus the continuous news programming. However, KNOW may have transmission problems while all-news stations in neighboring cities may have excellent transmission. Also, KNOW's listeners may have tastes different from those of all-news stations' listeners. Either of the scenarios, if true, would invalidate the assumption that KNOW can emulate the all-news stations. Thus, the author's plan to change KNOW's format may fail outright due to lack of listener interest. Otherwise, the plan to change KNOW's format stands a better chance of success. To better assess the argument, we need evidence that KNOW and the all-news stations are sufficiently alike in ways that might affect listeners' interest in similar programming.

The third assumption that underpins the argument is that listeners over the age of 50 prefer news radio to rock-and-roll music. The article mentions an increase in the number of people over the age of 50, along with a decline of listeners overall, and states that this plan to change programming is an attempt to appeal to those older listeners. This comes with the implication that listeners in this age demographic like continuous news better than rock-and-roll music. However, this is not supported by any hard data. It could be that given their age and possible exposure to rock-and-roll music, people in this group prefer rock-and-roll music to continuous news that requires much time and energy. The author also suggests that the number of older listeners will be great enough to compensate for the overall loss of listeners and secure KNOW's future in case they are interested in the suggested programming. Again, no information is provided to establish this. Even if older listeners are interested in the 24-hour news format, they may be outnumbered by younger listeners who prefer rock-and-roll music. Moreover, the author suggests that KNOW's programming is the sole factor in its decline in the number of listeners. However, factors such as transmission problems and unpopular anchors might explain the decline. If this should be the case, the assumption about older listeners' preference would prove unwarranted, and the argument in support of switching to 24-hour news would be undermined.

In conclusion, the fundamental assumptions on which this memorandum bases its recommendation are groundless. The assumption that the decline of local music sales means a preference for continuous news is unwarranted. So is the implication that the success of continuous news radio in neighboring cities has some bearing on KNOW's locale. There is also nothing given to support the assumption that older listeners prefer 24-hour news to rock-and-roll music. As it stands, this plan runs a very high risk of failure.

83. KNOW radio station to shift to a 24-hour news format (Questions to Be Answered)

The author concludes that KNOW radio station should change to a 24-hour news format from a rock-music format in order to attract older listeners and become more lucrative. To support the conclusion, the article states that the number of listeners over the age of fifty has risen, while the total number of listeners has gone down. It also cites decreased sales of recorded music in the area, along with success of continuous news stations in neighboring cities. However, we need answers to some questions before we determine whether KNOW should go forward with this plan.

We must investigate whether the decline in local music sales is indicative of a limited interest in rock-and-roll music and of a preference for continuous news. However, the author provides no data in this regard. Decreased sales of recorded music do not necessarily mean people's interest in rock-and-roll music has also decreased. The reported decrease in sales could be inaccurate and negligible. Even if there is a drop in local sales of recorded music, there may not be a drop in sales of recorded rock music. Even assuming that there is a decrease in sales of recorded rock music, this does not necessarily indicate a limited interest in rock music. A myriad of other factors might explain this phenomenon. For example, the introduction of the internet may have harmed the sale of music everywhere due to illegal downloading and online music solutions. Therefore, it is highly possible that people are still very much interested in rock music, but simply do not wish to buy it in physical format. Even if listeners have been losing interest in rock-and-roll music, this does not necessarily mean that they prefer 24-hour news. If this should be the case, the assumption about the connection between music sales and people's interest in rock music would prove unjustified, and the argument that the radio station should change from rock-and-roll music to continuous news would collapse. The radio station would do well to conduct surveys to find out if people have lost interest in music or have simply found other ways of obtaining it.

We should also conduct research into whether the popularity of 24-hour news radio in neighboring cities is an indication of the possible success of such programming in KNOW's case. Even if people are no longer interested in rock-and-roll music, this does not necessarily mean that they would like to switch to the 24-hour news format. They may prefer rock-and-roll music in a different format or a mix of rock-and-roll music and news. They may even stop listening to the radio altogether. Moreover, just because the all-news format is popular in neighboring cities does not necessarily mean it will be popular with KNOW's listeners. The author implies that the major difference between KNOW and all-news stations in nearby cities is the rock-and-roll programming versus the continuous news programming. However, KNOW may have transmission problems while all-news stations in neighboring cities may have excellent transmission. Also, KNOW's listeners may have tastes different from those of all-news stations' listeners. Either of the scenarios, if true, would invalidate the assumption that KNOW can emulate the all-news stations. Thus, the author's plan to change KNOW's format may fail outright due to lack of listener interest. Otherwise, the plan to change KNOW's format stands a better chance of success. To assess the argument properly, we need evidence that KNOW and the all-news stations are sufficiently alike in ways that might affect listeners' interest in similar programming.

Finally, we need to inquire whether listeners over the age of fifty prefer the all-news format and whether their number is significant as a group, since they are the demographic which the plan intends to attract. The article mentions an increase in the number of people over 50, along with a decline of listeners overall, and states that this plan to change programming is an attempt to appeal to those older listeners. This comes with the implication that listeners in this age demographic like news radio better than rock-and-roll music. However, we do not know whether this is the case, and thus need additional data to evaluate the programming targeting them. It could be that given their age and possible exposure to rock-and-roll music, people in this group prefer rock-and-roll music to continuous news that requires much time and energy. The author also suggests that the number of older listeners will be great enough to compensate for the overall loss of listeners and increase profits in case they are interested in the suggested programming. Again, no information is provided to establish this. Even if older listeners are interested in the 24-hour news format, they may be outnumbered by younger listeners who prefer rock-and-roll music. Moreover, the author suggests that KNOW's programming format is the sole factor in the decline in its number of listeners and its profitability. However, factors such as transmission problems and unpopular anchors might explain the decline. Even if switching formats is justified, it is unfair to assume that KNOW will be more profitable than ever before we weigh the revenue against all the costs, including the costs associated with the switching itself. If this should be the case, the assumption about older listeners' listening preference would prove unjustified, and the argument in support of changing the radio's programming would be undermined.

In conclusion, KNOW must address some serious questions before it can take any action regarding the plan. To fully evaluate the argument, we would benefit from information about the link, if any exists, between local music sales and programming preferences in KNOW's broadcasting area and about the similarity between the listening preferences of local audience and those of listeners in neighboring cities. We also need data by way of a survey of older listeners to find out if they would be more inclined to listen to 24-hour news than to rock-and-roll music.

84. Reducing operating hours at Movies Galore to cut expenses (Assumptions)

The author concludes that in order to reverse the drop in its profits, the movie-rental chain, Movies Galore, should reduce operating expenses by closing earlier and cutting down its overall inventory. To support the conclusion, the memorandum presents an example of one of the store locations in Marston having already experienced success with these policies. However, the argument is full of assumptions and loopholes that require scrutiny with extra evidence.

For one thing, the author assumes that reducing operating costs is sufficient and necessary for stopping the company's fall in profits. However, the assumption is not supported with any evidence. It is not even implied or shown that operating costs comprise the most significant expense of the company, and thus, without specific financial data, there is no guarantee that the proposed policies of closing earlier and reducing its stock in each store will have any effect on the company's performance. It could be just as likely that the cost of renting the business space constitutes the greatest expense, and if this should be true, reducing operating hours and stock would be far less effective than simply moving to a cheaper location. This would mesh well with the plan of reducing Movies Galore's inventory, as it would no longer need as much space. Even if decreasing operating expenses will reverse the decline in profits, this does not necessarily mean that it is the only option. The author gratuitously assumes that raising rental rates to boost profits is not feasible. However, raising prices may be a good option if customers could accept a reasonable rise in price because they rent the movies of the chain for their wide selection as well as for their low prices. A slight increase in rental prices is unlikely to damage its reputation for offering bargains. While it may not be a good strategy for the downtown store to raise its prices, because there are many competitors around, the other stores could raise their rental rates, because the demand there for rented movies may be very strong and there may be few competitors around. Even if raising rental prices is not viable, this does not necessarily mean that there are no other ways to boost profits than decreasing operating costs by cutting the company's hours and stock. Other initiatives, such as customer loyalty programs, which could offer discounts after a certain number of rentals, may also work to attract more business to the stores. Should this be true, it would be unjustifiable to assume that the only method to save the company's profits is to implement the operating expense reduction plan.

For another, the author implies that just because the store in downtown Marston dramatically reduced its operating expenses by closing earlier and replacing its stock of older movies, the policies have been successful and there will not be any consequences in the future. However, the author provides no evidence to substantiate this. The new policies were only implemented at the Marston location one month ago, which is hardly enough time to yield any significant data. It is possible that they caused the company's profits to decrease instead of increasing. It is also possible that the trend last month was an aberration and will not continue. Either of the scenarios would cast serious doubt on the assumption about the success of the downtown store in boosting profits. In addition, the consequences of cutting stock will become most apparent as society's tastes in movies change over time. For example, so-called "classic" movies often experience revivals in popularity, and thus the store could lose out if it reduced its stock of older movies. Therefore, it is entirely possible that the revenue lost because of closing earlier and only stocking newer movies would outweigh the savings in decreased operating expenses, invalidating the claim that reducing operating costs would boost profits. All these scenarios would undermine the assumption about the success of the policies and the recommendation of implementing them at all other stores.

Even granting that the policies have been successful at the downtown Marston store, the author also suggests that the same level of success, if any at all, will be experienced at all other locations. The specific traits of this downtown store need to be analyzed and compared to each of the other nine locations in order to see if there are certain qualities of the nearby areas, such as population density and average income, that may affect customers' ability to rent from the stores. If these factors are found to be consistent across all locations, then the plan stands a better chance of working. However, there is no information given by the author about the specific circumstances of this particular location and considering that it is located in a downtown area, the new policies may have drastically different levels of success in less populated areas. It is possible that the people in downtown Marston do not rent movies very often, regardless of what the store has in stock. However, if other areas have a different customer demographic, people may rent movies frequently. It is also possible that in other locations most people rent movies between 6:00 p.m. and 9:00 p.m. and prefer movies released more than five years ago. If this is true, it is unfair to assume that just because the policies have succeeded in the downtown location, they will automatically succeed in all other locations, rendering the argument unconvincing.

In conclusion, the assumptions made by the author to support the plan to cut the hours of operation and stop stocking movies older than five years are not warranted. To substantiate the assumptions, the author must provide concrete evidence that no methods other than reducing operating expenses are available to Movies Galore for enhancing its profits, that the policies have succeeded in the downtown Marston store, and that the downtown location is similar enough to other locations for the same methods to be applied elsewhere.

85. Reducing operating hours at Movies Galore to cut expenses (Questions to Be Answered)

The author recommends that in order to stop the drop in its profits, the movie-rental chain, Movies Galore, reduce operating expenses by closing earlier and cutting down its overall inventory. To justify the recommendation, the memorandum presents an example of one of the store locations in Marston having already experienced success with these policies. Yet, we need answers to certain questions surrounding the argument prior to the plan's approval.

To begin with, the author must answer whether reducing operating costs is sufficient and necessary for stemming the company's decline in profits. Before attempting to fix the problem, the author should determine whether operating expenses comprise the largest percentage of costs for the company. Without specific financial data, there is no guarantee that the proposed policies will have any effect on the company's performance. Alternative costs, such as licensing fees and losses due to unreturned movies, should be investigated. If they constitute the greatest expense, reducing operating hours would be far less effective than decreasing the alternative costs. While a shortening of operating hours and reduction of inventory do have the potential to save on the company's costs, they may not necessarily be the only way of increasing profits. The author gratuitously assumes that raising rental rates to boost profits is not feasible. However, raising prices may be a good option if customers could accept a reasonable rise in price because they rent the movies of the chain for their wide selection as well as for their low prices. A slight increase in rental prices is unlikely to damage its reputation for offering bargains. While it may not be a good strategy for the downtown store to raise its prices, because there are many competitors around, the other stores could raise their rental rates, because the demand there for rented movies may be very strong and there may be few competitors around. Even if raising rental prices is not viable, this does not necessarily mean that there are no other ways to boost profits than decreasing operating costs by cutting the company's hours and stock. Other initiatives, such as customer loyalty programs, which could offer discounts after a certain number of rentals, may also work to attract more business to the stores. Should this be true, it would be unjustifiable to assume that the only method to save the company's profits is to implement the operating expense reduction plan.

In addition, the author should answer whether just because the store in downtown Marston dramatically reduced its operating expenses by closing earlier and replacing its stock of older movies, the policies have been successful and there will not be any consequences in the future. However, the author provides no information in this regard. The new policies were only implemented at the Marston location one month ago, which is hardly enough time to yield any significant data. It is possible that they caused the company's profits to decrease instead of increasing. It is also possible that the trend last month was an aberration and will not continue. Either of the scenarios would cast serious doubt on the assumption about the success of the downtown store in boosting profits. In addition, the consequences of cutting stock will become most apparent as society's tastes in movies change over time. For example, so-called "classic" movies often experience revivals in popularity, and thus the store could lose out if it reduced its stock of older movies. Therefore, it is entirely possible that the revenue lost because of closing earlier and only stocking newer movies would outweigh the savings in decreased operating expenses, invalidating the claim that reducing operating costs would boost profits. All these scenarios would undermine the assumption about the success of the policies and the recommendation of implementing them at all other stores.

Even granting that the policies have been successful at the downtown Marston store, the author needs to answer whether the same level of success, if any at all, will be experienced at all other locations. The specific traits of this downtown store need to be analyzed and compared to each of the other nine locations in order to see if there are certain qualities of the nearby areas, such as population density and average income, that may affect customers' ability to rent from the stores. If these factors are found to be consistent across all locations, then the plan stands a better chance of working. However, there is no information given by the author about the specific circumstances of this particular location, and considering that it is located in a downtown area, the new policies may have drastically different levels of success in less populated areas. Perhaps the people in downtown Marston do not rent movies very often, regardless of what the store has in stock. However, if other areas have a different customer demographic, people may rent movies frequently. Or perhaps in other locations most people rent movies between 6:00 p.m. and 9:00 p.m. and prefer movies released more than five years ago. If this is true, it is unfair to assume that just because the policies have succeeded in the downtown location, they will automatically succeed in all other locations, rendering the argument unconvincing.

In conclusion, before determining whether reducing operating costs by closing earlier and only stocking newer movies is a viable means of boosting profits, the author must give due consideration to the chain's primary costs and to the applicability of the downtown Marston example to the other locations. Also, the author should conduct an analysis of alternative options in terms of reducing costs and improving profits as a matter of due diligence.

86. Should Acme require all of its employees to take the Easy Read Course? (Questions to Be Answered)

This recommendation from the personnel director to the president of Acme Publishing Company claims that productivity at the company could be improved if all employees were required to take the Easy Read Speed-Reading Course, a three-week seminar. To support the claim, the article states that at other companies one graduate of the course was able to read a five-hundred-page report in two hours, and that another graduate went from assistant manager to vice president in less than a year. It also notes that the cost, five-hundred dollars per employee, is not significant in comparison to the potential benefits the course may provide. Yet we need answers to certain questions raised about the argument before we determine whether the company should follow the advice.

We must ask whether reading faster contributes to a company's productivity. However, there is no data in this regard. The article states that the course teaches one to absorb more information each day, but does nothing to support this notion, nor links faster information absorption to the application of such information. It may be the case that employees who can read faster can memorize more quickly but take longer to process that information and thus take no less time to apply it than normal. Without more data, nothing can be said for certain. Besides, the alleged successful experience of the companies should be scrutinized. Since we do not have any information about how reading faster helps with productivity, the employee that read a five-hundred-page report is irrelevant until we know what her purpose for reading was, and how well she applied what she read to her job. As for the employee whose career advanced within a year, we should consider if the promotion was related to the employee's reading ability or was the result of other factors. Perhaps the person was already in line for the promotion. Or perhaps the two employees were already excellent readers before taking the course. Should that be the case, then the Easy Read course may have had no bearing on that promotion. Any of the scenarios, if true, would cast serious doubt on the assumption about the connection between speed reading and increased productivity and on the recommendation of taking the course.

In addition, we should investigate whether the potential benefits of the course will outweigh the costs to implement it. Since the author has yet to establish the connection between speed reading and better productivity, it is unjustifiable to claim that Acme will benefit a great deal from the course. Even if it will be able to improve its productivity, we need a complete cost-benefit analysis to determine whether the benefits will outstrip the costs. It is possible that the costs will outweigh the benefits. While the program's five-hundred-dollar fee per employee seems insignificant, the total costs of all the employees may be a huge amount. The dollar-value of the gain in productivity would need to be compared with the total costs of the program for all employees. Moreover, it is likely that many employees in Acme may not be able to leave work to participate in the course for three weeks and if they do, the company's operations may be disrupted. Consequently, instead of boosting its productivity, the course could decrease Acme's productivity considerably. This decrease, together with the significant expense for the course, could far outweigh the benefits of the course. If this should be the case, the assumption about the net benefits of the course would be unwarranted and the recommendation would be unjustified. To better assess the argument, we need an in-depth cost-benefit analysis of participating in the course.

Finally, we need to know whether just because many other companies have benefited greatly from the course, Acme will also benefit from it. Acme may not be similar enough to other companies to stand to benefit from the course. It is possible that other companies have many people who have no basic reading skills and read very slowly; therefore, the course primarily concerned with basic reading and fast reading has been a good fit for them. On the contrary, Acme's employees may be mostly proficient readers and have no need for the course. Even if the course teaches reading skills that they may find marginally useful, the course materials may not focus on the type of reading they are engaged in at work, reducing the benefits for them. Also, the author does not specify how other companies' employees have participated in the course. Perhaps they have taken the course without leaving their companies, only some people in the same company have taken the course at the same time, and they have chosen to take one component of the course each time when they could leave work. Should this be true, requiring all of Acme's employees to take the course would be a waste of their time and money and make a dent in the company's productivity, undermining the argument.

In conclusion, the advice to require all of Acme's employees to take the Easy Read course begs many questions: whether there is a link between fast reading and productivity, whether the cost of sending all employees to take this course can be justified by higher productivity, and whether Acme will benefit from the course. The president of Acme must have answers to these questions before deciding to accept the recommendation. Otherwise, the company could end up wasting much money and many man-hours on a useless training program.

87. Does Buzzoff provide better pest control services than Fly-Away? (Questions to Be Answered)

The loss of products at the company's Palm City fast-food warehouse is regrettable and definitely warrants investigation, yet based on the information provided by the memo, we need answers to certain questions before assessing the plan to choose Buzzoff Pest Control Company over Fly-Away Pest Control Company for all of the company's pest control services.

To better evaluate the recommendation, we must find out if Fly-Away was to blame for the higher amount of pest damage at the Palm City warehouse. However, other than the value of the lost product, there are no other details about the cause of damage at all. We do not know what pests caused the damage, nor the methods that Fly-Away had been using to prevent pests. Perhaps the warehouse was the victim of a unique species of insect that was resistant to insecticide or other standard pest prevention methods. Or perhaps the loss was the fault of the previous service provider Buzzoff but the amount of loss was not discovered until last month. Or perhaps the greater amount of loss at the Palm City warehouse was the result of the mistake of the warehouse operators, such as an accidental damaging of passive pest control equipment like rat traps. While the value of the lost product at the Palm City warehouse was greater than that at the Wintervale warehouse, the percentage of loss relative to the total value of the warehouse storage at the former may be much lower than that at the latter. Any of the scenarios, if true, would cast serious doubt on the assumption that Fly-Away's inferior performance has contributed to the greater amount of pest damage at the Palm City warehouse and on the argument that Buzzoff should replace Fly-Away for more of the company's pest control services.

Even if Fly-Away was responsible for the pest damage at the Palm City warehouse, we should know whether Fly-Away and Buzzoff are basically similar to each other in environment and other conditions relevant to pest control. Both provide pest control services, but, other than that, they could differ vastly. The Palm City warehouse may be significantly larger than the Wintervale warehouse. If this were true, that could mean that the losses that allegedly occurred because of Fly-Away's incompetence would not seem so high as to warrant the cancellation of future business using its service. The Palm City warehouse may also have more species of pests unique to it that Fly-Away must tackle. It may even be that the food stored at the Palm City warehouse is more vulnerable to pests than that in Wintervale, or that the climate near the Palm City warehouse makes it more difficult to kill the pests. Should this be true, the assumption about comparability of both pest control service companies proves unsubstantiated and the argument against continuing to use Fly-Away's service would collapse.

Even assuming that Fly-Away and Buzzoff are essentially the same, we need to discover if returning to Buzzoff for all the company's pest control services will save more money. However, we do not know how much the two pest control companies are being paid as compared to the amount of damage done each month. The memo does mention that Fly-Away's charge for service is significantly lower; thus, there is the possibility that continuing to use its service would be the best cost-saving measure, especially if the Palm City warehouse was an isolated incident. The assumption about Buzzoff's ability to save more money could be further undermined if Buzzoff's service at the Wintervale warehouse last month was also an aberration and its service in future months will be worse than Fly-Away's. Also, if Buzzoff cannot tackle certain species of pests peculiar to the warehouse in Palm City whereas Fly-Away can, using Buzzoff's service is likely to waste rather than save money. Moreover, if the contract with Fly-Away is terminated before expiry, the author's company may need to pay compensation. In such scenarios, returning to Buzzoff for all the company's pest control services to save money would be unjustified. Unless there is evidence that the difference in the prices charged by both companies is smaller than the money possibly saved from use of Buzzoff for pest control services, the author cannot confidently claim that Buzzoff rather than Fly-Away should be used for all pest control services to best save money.

In conclusion, to determine the soundness of the argument, we must have answers to questions regarding whether the higher amount of pest damage at the Palm City warehouse was a direct result of negligence and incompetence of Fly-Away and whether the Palm City warehouse is similar to its Wintervale counterpart in ways that might affect the effect of their service on pest control. We must also have answers to questions regarding detailed comparisons of the losses and environment between both pest control services.

88. Is <u>Alpha</u> a superior construction company? (Assumptions)

The recommendation that a company use the construction company Alpha in lieu of Zeta does seem compelling at first, considering Alpha's stable workforce as well as the lower construction and maintenance costs and lower energy consumption of the Alpha building. However, the argument is based on many assumptions that call for scrutiny before we ascertain its soundness.

The threshold assumption made by the author is that the higher construction cost of

Zeta's building makes Zeta a less attractive choice than Alpha. However, this is not necessarily true. The author neglects the possibility that despite identical floor plans of both buildings, Zeta's building has used high-quality materials and will thus be worth the higher costs in the long run, because it may be safer and last longer. For example, Zeta may have installed a piece of expensive but necessary equipment for the safety of the building whereas Alpha may have chosen not to. It may also have erected the building in a region that requires much higher labor costs. It may even be the case that Zeta's building was furnished whereas Alpha's was not. Any of the scenarios, if true, would cast serious doubt on the assumption that just because Zeta's building cost more, Alpha should take precedence over Zeta when it comes to the bid for the new building project. Even if Zeta's building cost more in construction, this does not necessarily mean that its bid for the new building project will involve higher construction cost than Alpha's bid, because there is the possibility that the new project will use lower-end building materials and cheaper labor. If this should be the case, the argument that Alpha, rather than Zeta, should be considered for the new building project would be undermined.

Also, the author implies that Zeta's higher maintenance expenses and higher energy consumption resulted from its poor performance. However, this need not be the case. A myriad of other factors might explain the higher expenses. It is possible that whereas Alpha's building was situated in an area of good weather and free of natural disasters, Zeta's building was located in a region known for bad weather, earthquakes, and hurricanes, increasing the need for maintenance of all kinds, including that of roofing and framing of the building, among other things. It is also possible that the local government requires Zeta's building to have annual housing renovation whereas Alpha's building can do the renovation if it wants to. It is even possible that Zeta's higher maintenance costs were only for last year. Any of the scenarios, if true, would cast serious doubt on the assumption that Zeta's poor performance has caused the higher maintenance expenses of its building. In addition, factors other than Zeta's incompetence could account for the higher energy consumption of its building. Perhaps Zeta's building was in an area much colder than that of Alpha's, requiring more energy for heating. Or perhaps it has been serving many more people than Alpha's. Or perhaps the residents of the Zeta building have been using less energy-efficient appliances. In such scenarios, Zeta's performance is not to blame. Unless there is relevant evidence, the author cannot fairly assume that Zeta's performance was responsible for the higher maintenance costs and higher energy consumption of its building. Even if Zeta is inferior to Alpha in terms of maintenance costs and energy consumption of one building up to now, there is no guarantee that this will be the case in the future, invalidating the argument of using Alpha rather than Zeta for the new project.

Finally, the author suggests that Alpha's stable workforce is somehow indicative of superior performance. Yet there is no evidence provided to substantiate this. There is no mention of Zeta's workforce which could be more stable than Alpha's. Therefore, it would seem that mentioning this piece of information is unfair, unless it has a significant effect on which company should be chosen, in which case it would help the author's argument to state specifically what benefits there are to be gained from the companies' respective workforces. Also, a competent workforce may be more important than a stable workforce, as long as it does not adversely affect the new building project. If Alpha has a workforce that is competent as well as stable, it would be an advantage in its bid for the project. The memo offers no details in this respect; therefore, the author cannot justifiably recommend that the company use Alpha rather than Zeta in its new building project. Unless the author can provide some hard data to show that a low employee turnover contributes to better performance, for example, constructing a building of higher quality, it seems to be an irrelevant point.

While the initial information given certainly makes Alpha a tempting choice in the bid for the company's new construction project, the author must provide clear evidence that Alpha's building will be superior to Zeta's, based not just on the previous projects, but on the new plan as well. Furthermore, the author needs to offer better justification for the inclusion of worker turnover as a relevant point in deciding between the two construction companies.

89. Does Buzzoff provide better pest control services than Fly-Away? (Alternative Explanations)

The loss of products at the company's Palm City fast-food warehouse is regrettable and definitely warrants investigation, yet based on the information provided by the memo, damages at the warehouses could be attributed to many factors other than the negligence of Fly-Away Pest Control Company.

The aberration last month is one possible explanation. The contract with Fly-Away was signed recently and the pest damage tally was made last month. It could be the case that pest control takes some time to have effects but Fly-Away did not have the time for starting its work until late last month, because the contract was signed less than a month ago. It could also be the case that the pest damage is attributable to the previous service provider Buzzoff Pest Control Company, but the amount of damage was not discovered until last month. It could even be the case that last month the mistake of the warehouse operators, such as an accidental damaging of passive pest control equipment like rat traps, has contributed to the pest damage. Any of the scenarios, if true, would rule out Fly-Away's negligence as the sole factor in its greater pest damage at the Palm City warehouse it serviced.

The warehouse conditions are another likely explanation. The warehouse that Fly-Away serviced may be significantly larger than the one that Buzzoff serviced. This means that it may be as dutiful as Buzzoff, but more damage may occur as it has to deal with more pests. Also, the climate of the area where Fly-Away's warehouse is located may make it more vulnerable to pest damage. For example, the area could be warmer than the area where Buzzoff's warehouse is situated and therefore more easily infested with pests. It could also be that because of the climate, the warehouse was the victim of a unique species of insect that was resistant to insecticide or other standard pest prevention methods. Should this be the case, the warehouse conditions could be another factor that might explain the difference in pest damage.

The food conditions are still another possible explanation. As for the difference in value between the damaged products at the two warehouses, perhaps each warehouse stored the same amount of food, but the types of food were different and worth different amounts. Thus, the quantity of food damaged may have been the same at both warehouses, but the value of the products lost would be radically different, as is described in the memo. For example, Fly-Away's warehouse may have stored more expensive items or food that was more vulnerable to pest attack. The author also overlooks the possibility that something other than food in the warehouse has attracted pests that are extremely damaging to the food whereas it is absent at the warehouse that Buzzoff serviced. Such scenarios would rule out the possibility that Buzzoff is superior to Fly-Away merely because it is less negligent.

In sum, unless there is evidence for the claim that the higher amount of damage at the Palm City warehouse was a direct result of the negligence of Fly-Away, the author cannot fairly conclude that other factors were not responsible for the difference in pest damage, such as the aberration last year, warehouse conditions, and food conditions. To rely on an unsubstantiated claim would be to risk wasting the company's money.

90. Does Buzzoff provide better pest control services than Fly-Away? (Assumptions)

The loss of products at the company's Palm City fast-food warehouse is regrettable and definitely warrants investigation, yet based on the information provided by the memo, there do appear to be many assumptions underlying the suggested plan to cease hiring the Fly-Away Pest Control Company for services in favor of the costlier Buzzoff Pest Control Company, despite the lower loss of products at the Wintervale warehouse the latter serviced.

The author suggests that the greater worth of food destroyed by pest damage at the Palm City warehouse is the fault of Fly-Away. However, other than the value of the lost product, there are no other details about the cause of damage at all. We do not know what pests caused the damage, nor the methods that Fly-Away had been using to prevent pests. Perhaps the warehouse was the victim of a unique species of insect that was resistant to insecticide or other standard pest prevention methods. Or perhaps the loss was the fault of the previous service provider Buzzoff but the amount of loss was not discovered until last month. Or perhaps the greater amount of loss at the Palm City warehouse was the result of the mistake of the warehouse operators, such as an accidental damaging of passive pest control equipment like rat traps. While the value of the lost product at the Palm City warehouse was greater than that at the Wintervale warehouse, the percentage of loss relative to the total value of the warehouse storage at the former may be much lower than that at the latter. Any of the scenarios, if true, would cast serious doubt on the assumption that Fly-Away's inferior performance has contributed to the greater amount of pest damage at the Palm City warehouse and on the argument that Buzzoff should replace Fly-Away for more of the company's pest control services.

Building on the suggestion that Fly-Away was responsible for the pest damage at the Palm City warehouse, the author implies that Fly-Away and Buzzoff are basically similar to each other in environment and other conditions relevant to pest control. Both provide pest control services, but, other than that, they could differ vastly. The Palm City warehouse may be significantly larger than Wintervale's. If this were true, that could mean that the losses that allegedly occurred because of Fly-Away's incompetence would not seem so high as to warrant the cancellation of future business using its service. The Palm City warehouse may also have more species of pests unique to it that Fly-Away must tackle. It may even be that the food stored at the Palm City warehouse is more vulnerable to pests than that in Wintervale, or that the climate near the Palm City warehouse makes it more difficult to kill the pests. Should this be true, the assumption about comparability of both pest control service companies proves unsubstantiated and the argument against continuing to use Fly-Away's service would collapse.

Even if the implication is valid, the author also assumes that the relatively lower loss at the Wintervale warehouse means that returning to Buzzoff for all the company's pest control services will save more money. However, we do not know how much the two pest control companies are being paid as compared to the amount of damage done each month. The memo does mention that Fly-Away's charge for service is significantly lower; thus, there is the possibility that continuing to use its service would be the best cost-saving measure, especially if the Palm City warehouse was an isolated incident. The assumption about Buzzoff's ability to save more money could be further undermined if Buzzoff's service at the Wintervale warehouse last month was also an aberration and its service in future months will be worse than Fly-Away's. Also, if Buzzoff cannot tackle certain species of pests peculiar to the warehouse in Palm City whereas Fly-Away can, using Buzzoff's service is likely to waste rather than save money. Moreover, if the contract with Fly-Away is terminated before expiry, the author's company may need to pay compensation. If this should be true, returning to Buzzoff for all the company's pest control services to save money would be unjustified. Unless there is evidence that the difference in the prices charged by both companies is smaller than the money possibly saved from use of Buzzoff for pest control services, the author cannot confidently claim that Buzzoff rather than Fly-Away should be used for all pest control services to best save money.

In conclusion, to better evaluate the argument, we need evidence that the higher amount of loss at the Palm City warehouse was a direct result of negligence and incompetence of Fly-Away, and that the Palm City warehouse is similar to its Wintervale counterpart in ways that might affect the effect of their service on pest control. We also need information by way of detailed comparisons of the losses and environment between both pest control services. The potential loss of products and thus profits that may result from using Buzzoff's service rather than Fly-Away's could make the assumptions underlying the argument very risky to bet on.

91. Should businesses hire only people who need less than six hours of sleep per night? (Questions to Be Answered)

Relying on the finding that advertising firms whose executives reported requiring sleep of no more than six hours each night achieved higher profit margins and faster growth, the author recommends that companies only employ people who need less than six hours of sleep every night. However, we need answers to certain questions to fully assess the recommendation.

The author must inform us whether the study results are statistically reliable. However, there is only one study, which, from a scientific perspective, is far from sufficient to support any claims about the efficacy of sleeping less. The executives studied may have had individual predispositions that allowed them to function better with less sleep, making them the exception rather than the rule. They may also have been old people who tended to sleep less. They may even have chosen to report the need for less sleep time for fear that needing more sleep time will be considered a sign of weakness. Another major issue with the study is the sample size and number of respondents. The sample of 300 participants seems impressive, but it could be tiny if the executives totaled 10, 000. We just do not know. If just a negligible number of them have responded, they might not be representative of the participants, let alone of all advertising executives. All such scenarios would render the study invalid and unrepresentative, undermining the recommendation of hiring only employees who need to sleep for fewer than six hours per night. Further studies should be conducted to see if the results of this single study can be corroborated.

The author should also tell us whether a correlation between events means a causation between them. However, there is no evidence that the higher profit margins and growth of the companies were a direct result of the amount of sleep their advertising executives got each night. For all we know, those companies may have had favorable market shares or products with quality superior to that of their competitors'. They may also have had more productive employees or better technologies. If this is true, the author has yet to establish the connection between the advertising executives' amount of sleep every night and their companies' success. Otherwise, the article's entire premise is invalid. Without extra information, it is impossible to know for sure, and therefore it is not fair to assume that the advertising executives who slept less are to thank for the beneficial results.

Building on the implication that the advertising executives' amount of sleep each night is responsible for their firms' prosperity, the author needs to answer whether what is true for one position in one industry will also be true for other positions and other industries. However, the assumption is based on a study of advertising executives only and makes no mention of any other positions and other industries and their relationship to sleep. We have no information on the particular duties of advertising executives and factors unique to their work that are affected by sleep or the lack thereof. Such factors could be nonexistent in other positions and could lead to severe fatigue among workers that perform more physically demanding jobs. They could also be absent in other industries that require a different schedule and a different profile of employees. The assumption underlies the claim that all positions in all industries will benefit from employing people who only need to sleep for fewer than six hours. However, the scenarios noted above indicate that such an assumption is unsubstantiated, thereby rendering the claim invalid and the recommendation unreasonable. Further investigation should be made into other positions in the company and into other types of business to see if the findings for advertising executives apply to other positions and other industries.

In conclusion, this recommendation relies on a vague correlation that requires further analysis. If we are to take the study's results as a factor on which to base hiring practices, there need to be more studies that find similar results, as well as studies that take into account many factors, in order to rule out possible contributing factors aside from sleep times. It would also help if we knew more details about how sleep affects the performance in specific job fields beyond the executive level and in other industries.

92. Adopting honor codes similar to Groveton's (Alternative Explanations)

The author posits that the adoption of an academic honor code by Groveton College was the underlying cause of a reduction in cases of cheating among students there. In this system, students agree not to cheat, and promise to report any incidences of cheating they have detected to a faculty member. This new system allegedly resulted in a decrease in cheating, down to only fourteen cases from an original thirty under the old system, over a five-year period. Yet there are many unexplored explanations for these results.

One very obvious alternative explanation is that students simply chose not to report it when they witnessed one another cheating. That is one fatal flaw with the honor code system, because it relies on students to be honest in their actions and reporting. Students often hesitate to report their classmates' cheating and have felt less and less inclined to report cheating each year since adoption of the honor code. In this situation, there would not necessarily be fewer incidences of cheating, just fewer reported cases, which are supported by the small amount of data provided. Of course, most students of Groveton in the survey would lie by saying that they would prefer an honor system in order to perpetuate a system from which they directly benefited. Without relevant evidence, the author could not reliably conclude that merely the honor code was responsible for the decrease in the number of cases of cheating at Groveton.

It may also be the case that the lower number of cheating cases was the result of performance of a new student body. Perhaps the new students entered Groveton with much better academic performance and were more intelligent than those in previous years. Or perhaps the students worked much harder than those that had enrolled before them. It is likely that due to new education techniques at the junior high and high school level, incoming students to Groveton College were better equipped to handle their coursework and thus did not need to rely on cheating to pass their classes. It is also likely that the new students were less adept at detecting their classmates' cheating than both teachers and previous students who had been more experienced at recognizing cheating. If this were true, it would certainly result in lower reported rates of cheating.

Lastly, there is the possibility that, in response to the high amount of cheating, the teachers at Groveton College believed their coursework to be too demanding, and thus lowered the difficulty, which led to a subsequent decline in students' need to cheat. It would account for the gradual decrease in cheating cases, as teachers would need a few semesters to fine tune their curriculums. It is also possible that over the years students took an increasing number of courses on academic integrity and chose to cheat less and less while the honor code was in place. Such a scenario could also be responsible for decreasing cases of cheating among students. Without ruling out these possible explanations, the author could not reasonably assume that the honor code alone contributed to Groveton College's success with combating cheating.

In sum, there are many alternative explanations for the decline in cheating at Groveton College aside from the new honor code. It could be that the students' ability to cheat was protected under the honor code system, or that they had no real need of it due to their academic ability. The illusion of its success may have even been the result of easier coursework. Without more data, all these reasons hold the potential to account for the facts presented in the article and thus warrant further investigation.

93. Adopting honor codes similar to Groveton's (Questions to Be Answered)

The author recommends that all colleges and universities adopt an honor code similar to that of Groveton college, relying on the fact that Groveton has experienced a decrease in the reported cases of cheating over a period of five years, on a recent survey which found that a majority of students would be less inclined to cheat with an honor code in place, and on the prediction that the code will certainly contribute to a remarkable drop in cheating among college students. However, before we determine whether any other college or university should adopt such an honor code, we need answers to certain questions.

First, the argument raises the question of whether the honor code has been successful. The system in which teachers monitored students found thirty cases of cheating, whereas in the newer student-reporting system, only twenty-one cases were reported in the first year, and then only fourteen five years later. This begs the question of whether there has been a reduction in the number of cases of cheating because the honor code was in place, or whether cheating has decreased for other reasons. For example, students often hesitate to report their classmates' cheating. They may simply have become more and more reluctant to report cheating each year since adoption of the honor code. They may also have been less adept at detecting their classmates' cheating than teachers and former students who had been more experienced. Potential cheaters may even have chosen not to cheat during the period regardless of the honor code. If one of the scenarios turns out to be true, we will need to reinvestigate Groveton's "success" before other universities adopt a similar honor code.

Secondly, the question arises of whether the survey is reliable, valid, and representative. The recent survey of Groveton's students found that most reported that they would not cheat with an honor code in place. However, since these answers were self-reported by the students, it is safe to assume that they would give answers on the survey that would benefit them the most. This raises the question of whether the honor code is reliable at all, since it obviously works in favor of dishonest students. Perhaps most students answered that the honor code would make them less likely to cheat because it made cheating easier, and therefore they hoped to keep it by falsely claiming that it would make them less inclined to cheat. This indicates that the participants of the survey may be an anomaly consisting mostly of people who hope to benefit from the honor code. Even if the respondents are representative of Groveton students, there is no guarantee that they will do as they have claimed in the survey. Besides, the researchers could have asked the irrelevant question of whether an honor code is better than none, instead of how it compares to the old system of teacher monitoring. In all such scenarios, the survey is neither valid nor representative, rendering the recommendation and its argument gratuitous.

Lastly, there is of course the question of the cultural differences among all universities and colleges that may affect the success rate of an honor code system. For example, Groveton could be a small school where the honor code is easily implemented and naturally efficacious, whereas at larger universities it would be hard to implement the code, and even if implemented, the code would be less effective. Groveton students could be more likely to report cheating, or less likely to cheat with an honor code in place, than students in other universities and colleges. Even if it has worked in Groveton, this does not necessarily mean that it will work in other colleges and universities. It may very well be that the honor code would contribute to lower cases of cheating in Groveton but would lead to no significant changes or even an increase in cheating at other institutions, rendering unreasonable the author's prediction of a significant decline in cheating among college students. All this is incumbent on the willingness of students to follow the honor code, and currently there is no accurate measure of this variable. Even if the code will be effective in other colleges and universities, there is the possibility that some universities and colleges may have had in place an honor code comparable to Groveton's, thereby making a new one redundant. If Groveton is typical in respects relevant to the incidence of cheating, it will be plausible for other universities and colleges to enforce a similar honor code. Otherwise, the recommended action would be indefensible.

In conclusion, the adoption of an honor code across all universities and colleges requires further analysis in the areas of its actual success rate, not only at Groveton, but at other institutions as well. Furthermore, surveys of student opinions of the system change should be disregarded as those who wish to cheat will skew the results, since they stand to benefit from an honor code system. Finally, there should be further testing of the honor code system nationally and internationally to see if institutional differences will affect the willingness of students to report on one another.

94. Using UltraClean in our hospital system (Assumptions)

The author recommends offering UltraClean hand soap at all hand-washing stations for both visitors and staff throughout a hospital system to eliminate severe patient infections. To justify the recommendation, the memo cites a controlled lab study, in which a concentrated solution of extra-strength UltraClean reduced forty percent more harmful bacteria than the soap currently used by the hospitals. It also presents a more recent test of regular strength UltraClean at its Worktown hospital that supposedly experienced a twenty percent reduction in patient infection compared to its other hospitals. However, the argument is replete with assumptions and loopholes that require scrutiny before we determine its validity.

The author assumes that the results of the laboratory test are applicable to all hospitals. However, the effectiveness of the soap in a controlled lab compared to that of the soap in a real-world hospital environment is not necessarily the same. We have no information either about the types of bacteria used in the lab experiment or about the amount of extra-strength UltraClean required to kill forty percent more harmful bacteria than the normal hand soap. Perhaps the bacteria used were in a weakened state due to the controlled environment. Or perhaps a substantial amount of UltraClean was applied for an extended length of time. In either scenario, the author cannot be certain that UltraClean alone was responsible for the results. In this case, the assumption about the possibility of generalizing the test findings to the hospitals is unjustified, because the hospitals may have different kinds of more harmful bacteria and other sources of infection such as viruses. Without more information about the study, its results cannot be used to support the argument that UltraClean should be offered at hand-washing stations throughout the hospital system to eliminate serious patient infections.

The author also implies that the regular-strength UltraClean was the sole factor in the lower number of infections. Yet there is no information provided to support the assumption, nor is there any information with which to determine whether the Worktown hospital is exactly the same as, or different from, the other hospitals. It is possible that the Worktown hospital had better air-filtration systems or better sanitation protocols. It is also possible that much fewer patients were present when the test was conducted. Even if some patients were present, they might have used the liquid hand soaps currently supplied in the hospital rather than the regular-strength UltraClean in the test. Perhaps the hospital reported twenty-percent fewer cases of patient infection but more cases of serious patient infection. Or perhaps it reported fewer cases to help to promote UltraClean or to seem outstanding in preventing patient infection. Even if the hand soap lowered patient infection, a twenty percent reduction may not have been significant. For example, if the other hospitals had reported an average of 5 cases of patient infection, the hospital in Worktown could have reported 4, with a difference of only 1 patient, a number that is negligible. Should this be true, the assumption would prove unjustified. Unless there is evidence that regular-strength UltraClean was responsible for the decrease in patient infections, especially serious infections and that other hospitals throughout the system are comparable to the Worktown hospital, the author cannot justifiably claim that UltraClean should be offered at hand-washing stations throughout the hospital system.

Even granting that the laboratory test and the recent Worktown test are valid, the author also suggests that having UltraClean at all hand soap stations will do anything to prevent serious infections. Even if using UltraClean can reduce infections caused by harmful bacteria, it may not reduce infections caused by other factors such as viruses. Even if UltraClean can decrease ordinary infections, there is no guarantee that it will be able to prevent any serious infections. Even assuming that UltraClean is effective at reducing serious infections, this does not necessarily mean that it should be supplied at all hand soap stations as the only option, because some hospitals may have no severe infections and there may be equally efficacious but cheaper alternatives, for example, the liquid hand soaps being used in the hospitals. Even if UltraClean should be used, the author does not distinguish between extra-strength UltraClean and regular-strength UltraClean. If the former is to be supplied, it may be even more expensive. However, it is possible that doctors, nurses, and patients need extra-strength UltraClean but visitors only need regular-strength UltraClean. In these scenarios, the assumption about the extensive use of UltraClean would prove unwarranted and the argument would collapse.

In sum, the author's recommendation that all hospitals provide UltraClean hand soap at handwashing stations for visitors and staff is based on unjustified assumptions. The lab test and the hospital test have used different versions of the soap and do not provide any clear proof that either of them had any effect on bacteria or infections. This fact, coupled with the lack of any consideration of other contributing factors in the test results, makes the argument highly suspect.

95. Using UltraClean in our hospital system (Alternative Explanations)

The author claims that a twenty-percent reduction in patient infections at a hospital in Worktown resulted from the use of regular-strength UltraClean hand soap by visitors, nurses, and doctors. However, various explanations, aside from the hand soap, could account for the lower number of infections.

Firstly, it could simply be the case that the Worktown hospital did not receive a significant number of patients with serious illnesses or injuries during the period in which the experiment took place. Since the people who usually get infections at hospitals are those with open wounds or compromised immune systems, the lack of such patients could conceivably be the cause of the lower number of infections, and in such a scenario the kind of hand soap used would be irrelevant. It could also be that even if the Worktown hospital had many patient infections, the hospital did not report them to seem outstanding in preventing patient infections. In this event, the brand of hand soap would be of little consequence.

It may also be the case that the explanation was not the kind of soap used, but how frequently people in the hospital washed their hands. After all, the only real function that hand soaps have regarding sanitation is that they provide a lubricating agent which makes it harder for matter to bond to one's skin and makes it easier for microbes to be removed with water. However, any property that could effectively kill large amounts of bacteria would be equally harmful to a person's skin. Therefore, it is far more likely that people at the Worktown hospital simply washed their hands more often, which removed more infectious bacteria from their hands. During the test, while doctors, nurses, and visitors used regular-strength UltraClean at the Worktown hospital, the patients might have washed their hands with the liquid hand soaps currently supplied in the hospital. This indicates that washing hands often with common hand soaps might have contributed to the reduction in patient infections.

Finally, there is a possibility that the sanitation protocol, rather than the brand of hand soap provided, was responsible for the reduction in infections. In many cases, infection is the result of unchanged sheets and bandages, physical contact, a bad air filtration system or just a dirty environment in general. It is possible that the Worktown hospital was better at keeping a clean environment for its patients than the other hospitals. It is also possible that few visitors came to the hospital during the test whereas other hospitals received many visitors during this period of time. It is even possible that the doctors, nurses, and visitors at the hospital were healthier than their counterparts at other hospitals in the group. Thus, the hospital may have had fewer cases of patient infection to report. These scenarios would rule out the possibility that the UltraClean soap alone would have bearing on infection rates.

To conclude, the memo does not address all factors that could have contributed to the twenty-percent reduction in infection cases at the Worktown hospital. Other potential factors include but are not limited to the following: the number of seriously ill or injured patients throughout the duration of the test, hand-washing frequency, and the overall hygiene of the hospital. Unless these and other explanations are ruled out, the author cannot confidently claim that the hospital group should take action on the basis of the explanation given in the memo.

96. Wearing helmets may not actually be good for bicycle safety (Questions to Be Answered)

Reasoning that the increase in helmet usage over a ten-year period by bicyclists has led to a two-hundred percent increase in bicycle-related accidents because bicyclists ride less safely as a result of an increased sense of security from wearing helmets, the author recommends that the government try to educate them on bicycle safety related to the factors other than helmet use. However, the argument raises some questions to which we must have answers before we determine its soundness.

The author must answer whether the respondents of the two studies are representative of bicyclists nationwide. However, with reference to the studies, no clear details are given by the newsletter. One study only mentions the increase in the number of cyclists who wear helmets, which was self-reported, and the other study the 200 percent increase in bike accidents. The self-reported data may not have been reliable, because the respondents may have reported wearing helmets simply to appear that they are responsible and safety-conscious. In this case, there could be no increase or even decrease in the number of people who wear helmets, invalidating the claim that more helmet usage by bicyclists over a decade has resulted in a dramatic rise in bike-related accidents. The respondents may also be an aberration, consisting mostly of youths who take more risks, distorting the results. Either of the scenarios would make the respondents unrepresentative of all bicyclists nationwide. Besides, the increase in accidents is not combined with any other data, such as the actual number of bike related accidents before and now. It is possible that there were only a small number of accidents ten years prior, and thus a two-hundred percent increase would still be a relatively insignificant number of accidents overall. If this should be true, then the recommendation of educating people about bike safety instead of telling them to wear helmets would be unfounded.

Also, the author should address the question of whether the cause of the accidents is the feeling of safety bestowed by the helmets. Yet, no information about the real cause of the accidents is given. Perhaps the increase in the number of accidents is the result of an aging population of drivers that cannot see as well or react as quickly as their younger selves. Or perhaps the increase is attributable to roads in bad condition or the weather conditions. Or perhaps increasing numbers of people riding bikes now are responsible for the rise in accidents. If the number of bicyclists wearing helmets had been misrepresented, not wearing helmets could also have been the culprit in bike accidents. Any of the scenarios, if true, would render the assumption about the reasons for the rise in accident numbers unwarranted and invalidate the argument that the government should focus on education about bicycle safety in ways other than encouraging or requiring helmet use. Without more information about exactly what has happened in each case from post-accident interviews or traffic camera footage, it would be very illogical to simply link the cause to a feeling of safety that may not exist.

Finally, the author needs to respond to the question of whether all the bike-related accidents have involved serious injuries and the proposed course of action of government will be adequate to prevent them. However, the author offers no data in this regard. The newsletter mentions that the goal of the government's new focus will be to reduce the number of serious injuries from bike accidents but does not differentiate between the seriousness of the accidents. Even if there has been an increase in bike-related accidents, and the number may even be significant, it is possible that most of them are minor, or even involve no injury at all. In this case, the assumption about the severity of injuries would prove unwarranted, and the argument for the government to concentrate on education about bicycle safety regarding necessary factors other than helmet use would collapse. More importantly, the number of severe accidents may have decreased thanks to the increase in the wearing of helmets. If this is the case, then it is possible that the helmets are to thank and should not be ignored by the government. Also, just because wearing helmets fails to prevent bike-related accidents does not necessarily mean education about other factors required for bike safety will help to reduce the number of severe bicycle-related accidents. For example, it is unlikely to be effective when the cause is road conditions. Perhaps education about bike safety often helps riders decrease the number of minor accidents. In that event, the argument is undermined. Without more information about the severity of the bike accidents over the past decade, the author cannot justifiably recommend focus on education about other factors essential for bicycle safety.

In conclusion, to determine the reasonableness of the recommendation, we must first have more data to show that the two-hundred percent increase in accidents represents a significant number of accidents, and that an increased feeling of safety from wearing a helmet was the direct cause of the accidents. Furthermore, there should be an investigation into the severity of injuries to see if it is necessary for the government to focus its bike-related safety education on factors such as a false sense of security rather than helmet use.

97. Using UltraClean in our hospital system (Specific Evidence)

The author recommends that a group of hospitals offer UltraClean, an antibacterial hand soap, at all hand-washing stations throughout its hospital system in order to eliminate severe patient infections. To justify the recommendation, the memo cites a laboratory study that found UltraClean reduced harmful bacteria populations 40 percent more than the hand soaps being used. It goes on to say that a recent test of the soap at one hospital resulted in fewer cases of patient infection than at any other hospitals in the group. However, there is a lack of evidence that we can rely on to assess the argument.

We must have evidence of the laboratory test as a reliable and valid study. However, the test does not provide any solid data with which we can determine UltraClean's effectiveness in a real-world setting, where larger numbers of and more kinds of bacteria, in addition to other sources of patient infection such as viruses, are present. The author assumes that the laboratory test of the hand soap is a valid and reliable study but provides no information about the types of bacteria used in the lab experiment, about exactly what kind of bacteria UltraClean was 40 percent better at killing or about the amount of extra-strength UltraClean required to kill forty percent more harmful bacteria than the normal hand soap. Perhaps the bacteria used were in a weakened state due to the controlled environment. Or perhaps a substantial amount of UltraClean was applied for an extended length of time. If this is the case, the argument that UltraClean should be offered throughout the hospital system to eliminate serious infections will be undermined. However, if it could be shown that extra strength UltraClean is effective at killing a wide range of harmful bacteria and viruses in a realistic setting, the argument would be more convincing.

We should also have proof that the regular-strength UltraClean at the Worktown hospital was the sole factor in the lower number of infections. Yet there is no information provided to support the assumption, nor is there any information with which to determine whether the Worktown hospital is the same as, or different from, the other hospitals. It is possible that the Worktown hospital had better air-filtration systems or better sanitation protocols. It is also possible that much fewer patients were present when the test was conducted. Even if some patients were present, they might have used the liquid hand soaps currently supplied in the hospital rather than the regular-strength UltraClean in the test. Perhaps the hospital reported twenty-percent fewer cases of patient infection but more cases of serious patient infection. Or perhaps it reported fewer cases to help to promote UltraClean or to seem outstanding in preventing patient infection. Even if the hand soap lowered patient infection, a twenty percent reduction may not have been significant. For example, if the other hospitals had reported an average of 5 cases of patient infection, the hospital in Worktown could have reported 4, with a difference of only 1 patient, a number that is negligible. Should this be true, the brand of hand soap used would be of little consequence. Unless there is evidence that regular-strength UltraClean was responsible for the decrease in patient infections, especially serious infections, and that other hospitals throughout the system are comparable to the Worktown hospital, the author cannot justifiably claim that UltraClean should be offered at hand-washing stations throughout the hospital system.

Even granting that the laboratory test and the recent Worktown test are valid, we still need evidence that supplying UltraClean at all hand soap stations will do anything to prevent serious infections. Even if using UltraClean can reduce infections caused by harmful bacteria, it may not reduce infections caused by other factors such as viruses. Even if UltraClean can decrease ordinary infections, there is no guarantee that it will be able to prevent any serious infections. Even assuming that UltraClean is effective at reducing serious infections, this does not necessarily mean that it should be supplied at all hand soap stations as the only option, because some hospitals may have no severe infections and there may be equally efficacious but cheaper alternatives, for example, liquid hand soaps being used in the hospitals. Even if UltraClean should be used, the author does not distinguish between extra-strength UltraClean and regular-strength UltraClean. If the former is to be supplied, it may be even more expensive. However, it is possible that doctors, nurses, and patients need extra-strength UltraClean but visitors only need regular-strength UltraClean. If this should be the case, the assumption about the extensive use of UltraClean would prove unwarranted and the argument would collapse.

In conclusion, the author should provide more hard data relevant to the effectiveness of UltraClean, such as anti-microbial properties in a real hospital environment, as well as details to show that the experiments in both the lab and the Worktown hospital were conducted appropriately. Furthermore, the author must establish a stronger connection between the use of UltraClean and the prevention of serious patient infections, perhaps by way of a study of its use by patients who have already contracted minor infections.

98. Wearing helmets may not actually be good for bicycle safety (Specific Evidence)

Reasoning that the increase in helmet usage over a ten-year period by bicyclists has led to a two-hundred percent increase in bicycle-related accidents because bicyclists ride less safely as a result of an increased sense of security from wearing helmets, the author recommends that the government try to educate them on bicycle safety related to the factors other than helmet use. To better assess the argument, we need extra evidence.

The author must provide evidence that the respondents of the two studies are representative of bicyclists nationwide. However, with reference to the studies, no clear details are given by the newsletter. One study only mentions the increase in the number of cyclists who wear helmets, which was self-reported, and the other study the 200 percent increase in bike accidents. The self-reported data may not have been reliable, because the respondents may have reported wearing helmets simply to appear that they are responsible and safety-conscious. In this case, there could be no increase or even decrease in the number of people who wear helmets, invalidating the claim that more helmet usage by bicyclists over a decade has resulted in a dramatic rise in bike-related accidents. The respondents may also be an aberration, consisting mostly of youths who take more risks, distorting the results. Either of the scenarios would make the respondents unrepresentative of all bicyclists nationwide. Besides, the increase in accidents is not combined with any other data, such as the actual number of bike related accidents before and now. It is possible that there were only a small number of accidents ten years prior, and thus a two-hundred percent increase would still be a relatively insignificant number of accidents overall. If this should be true, then the recommendation of educating people about bike safety instead of telling them to wear helmets would be unfounded.

Next, the author should offer evidence that the accidents are a result of the feeling of safety bestowed by the helmets. Yet, no information about the real cause of the accidents is given. Perhaps the increase in the number of accidents is the result of an aging population of drivers that cannot see as well or react as quickly as their younger selves. Or perhaps the increase is attributable to roads in bad condition or the weather conditions. Or perhaps increasing numbers of people riding bikes now are responsible for the rise in accidents. If the number of bicyclists wearing helmets had been misrepresented, not wearing helmets could also have been the culprit in bike accidents. Any of the scenarios, if true, would render the assumption about the reasons for the rise in accident numbers unwarranted and invalidate the argument that the government should focus on education about bicycle safety in ways other than encouraging or requiring helmet use. Without more information about exactly what has happened in each case from post-accident interviews or traffic camera footage, it would be very illogical to simply link the cause to a feeling of safety that may not exist.

Finally, the author needs to furnish evidence that all the bike-related accidents have involved serious injuries and the proposed course of action of government will be adequate to prevent them. However, the author offers no data in this regard. The newsletter mentions that the goal of the government's new focus will be to reduce the number of serious injuries from bike accidents but does not differentiate between the seriousness of the accidents. Even if there has been an increase in bike-related accidents, and the number may even be significant, it is possible that most of them are minor, or even involve no injury at all. In this case, the assumption about the severity of injuries would prove unwarranted, and the argument for the government to concentrate on education about bicycle safety regarding necessary factors other than helmet use would collapse. More importantly, the number of severe accidents may have decreased thanks to the increase in the wearing of helmets. If this is the case, then it is possible that the helmets are to thank and should not be ignored by the government. Also, just because wearing helmets fails to prevent bike-related accidents does not necessarily mean education about other factors required for bike safety will help to reduce the number of severe bicycle-related accidents. For example, it is unlikely to be effective when the cause is road conditions. Perhaps education about bike safety often helps riders decrease the number of minor accidents. In that event, the argument is undermined. Without more information about the severity of the bike accidents over the past decade, the author cannot justifiably recommend focus on education about other factors essential for bicycle safety.

In conclusion, to ascertain the soundness of the argument, we must first have more study data to show that the two-hundred percent increase in accidents represents a significant number of accidents, and that an increased feeling of safety from wearing a helmet was the direct cause of the accidents. Furthermore, there should be an investigation into the severity of injuries to see if it is necessary for the government to focus its bike-related safety education on factors such as a false sense of security rather than helmet use.

99. Should Acme require all of its employees to take the Easy Read Course? (Specific Evidence)

This recommendation from the personnel director to the president of Acme Publishing Company claims that productivity at the company could be improved if all employees were required to take the Easy Read Speed-Reading Course, a three-week seminar. To support this claim, the article states that at other companies one graduate of the course was able to read a five-hundred-page report in two hours, and that another graduate went from assistant manager to vice president in less than a year. It also notes that the cost, five-hundred dollars per employee, is not significant in comparison to the potential benefits the course may provide. Yet the evidence given is inadequate for full evaluation of the argument.

There must be evidence of a clear link between speed reading and productivity. The article states that the course teaches one to absorb more information each day, but does nothing to support this notion, nor links faster information absorption to the application of such information. It may be the case that employees who can read faster can memorize more quickly but take longer to process that information and thus take no less time to apply it than normal. Without more data, nothing can be said for certain. Besides, the alleged successful experience of the companies should be scrutinized. Since we do not have any information about how reading faster helps with productivity, the employee that read a five-hundred-page report is irrelevant until we know what her purpose for reading was, and how well she applied what she read to her job. As for the employee whose career advanced within a year, we should consider if the promotion was related to the employee's reading ability or was the result of other factors. Perhaps the person was already in line for the promotion. Or perhaps the two employees were already excellent readers before taking the course. Should that be the case, then the Easy Read course may have had no bearing on that promotion. Any of the scenarios, if true, would cast serious doubt on the assumption about the connection between speed reading and increased productivity and on the recommendation of taking the course.

In addition, there should be evidence regarding whether the potential benefits of the course will outweigh the costs to implement it. Since the author has yet to establish the connection between speed reading and better productivity, it is unjustifiable to claim that Acme will benefit a great deal from the course. Even if it will be able to improve its productivity, we need a complete cost-benefit analysis to determine whether the benefits will outstrip the costs. It is possible that the costs will outweigh the benefits. While the program's five-hundred-dollar fee per employee seems insignificant, the total costs of all the employees may be a huge amount. The dollar-value of the gain in productivity would need to be compared with the total costs of the program for all employees. Moreover, it is likely that many employees in Acme may not be able to leave work to participate in the course for three weeks and if they do, the company's operations may be disrupted. Consequently, instead of boosting its productivity, the course could decrease Acme's productivity considerably. This decrease, together with the significant expense for the course, could far outweigh the benefits of the course. If this should be the case, the assumption about the net benefits of the course would be unwarranted and the recommendation would be unjustified. To better assess the argument, we need an in-depth cost-benefit analysis of participating in the course.

Finally, there needs to be evidence regarding whether just because many other companies have benefited greatly from the course, Acme will also benefit from it. Acme may not be similar enough to other companies to stand to benefit from the course. It is possible that other companies have many people who have no basic reading skills and read very slowly; therefore, the course primarily concerned with basic reading and fast reading has been a good fit for them. On the contrary, Acme's employees may be mostly proficient readers and have no need for the course. Even if the course teaches reading skills that they may find marginally useful, the course materials may not focus on the type of reading they are engaged in at work, reducing the benefits for them. Also, the author does not specify how other companies' employees have participated in the course. Perhaps they have taken the course without leaving their companies, only some people in the same company have taken the course at the same time, and they have chosen to take one component of the course each time when they could leave work. Should this be true, requiring all of Acme's employees to take the course would be a waste of their time and money and make a dent in the company's productivity, undermining the argument.

In conclusion, the recommendation is in dire need of more statistical support both in the actual amount of productivity gained from having employees that can speed read and in how the example employees are connected to the notion of increased productivity. Perhaps more importantly, the results of a comparison of the training program's costs for all employees and the value of the increase in productivity, if any exists, would help us evaluate the argument.

100. Should <u>Acme</u> require all of its employees to take the Easy Read Course? (Questions to Be Answered)

This recommendation from the personnel director to the president of Acme Publishing Company claims that productivity at the company could be improved if all employees were required to take the Easy Read Speed-Reading Course, a three-week seminar. To support the claim, the article states that at other companies one graduate of the course was able to read a five-hundred-page report in two hours, and that another graduate went from assistant manager to vice president in less than a year. It also notes that the cost, five-hundred dollars per employee, is not significant in comparison to the potential benefits the course may provide. Yet the company must ponder some crucial questions before it adopts the recommendation.

The president must consider whether there is a link between speed reading and productivity. However, there is no data in this regard. The article states that the course teaches one to absorb more information each day, but does nothing to support this notion, nor links faster information absorption to the application of such information. It may be the case that employees who can read faster can memorize more quickly but take longer to process that information and thus take no less time to apply it than normal. Without more data, nothing can be said for certain. Besides, the alleged successful experience of the companies should be scrutinized. Since we do not have any information about how reading faster helps with productivity, the employee that read a five-hundred-page report is irrelevant until we know what her purpose for reading was, and how well she applied what she read to her job. As for the employee whose career advanced within a year, we should consider if the promotion was related to the employee's reading ability or was the result of other factors. Perhaps the person was already in line for the promotion. Or perhaps the two employees were already excellent readers before taking the course. Should that be the case, then the Easy Read course may have had no bearing on that promotion. Any of the scenarios, if true, would cast serious doubt on the assumption about the connection between speed reading and increased productivity and on the recommendation of taking the course.

In addition, the president should investigate whether the potential benefits of the course will outweigh the costs to implement it. Since the author has yet to establish the connection between speed reading and better productivity, it is unjustifiable to claim that Acme will benefit a great deal from the course. Even if it will be able to improve its productivity, we need a complete cost-benefit analysis to determine whether the benefits will outstrip the costs. It is possible that the costs will outweigh the benefits. While the program's five-hundred-dollar fee per employee seems insignificant, the total costs of all the employees may be a huge amount. The dollar-value of the gain in productivity would need to be compared with the total costs of the program for all employees. Moreover, it is likely that many employees in Acme may not be able to leave work to participate in the course for three weeks and if they do, the company's operations may be disrupted. Consequently, instead of boosting its productivity, the course could decrease Acme's productivity considerably. This decrease, together with the significant expense for the course, could far outweigh the benefits of the course. If this should be the case, the assumption about the net benefits of the course would be unwarranted and the recommendation would be unjustified. To better assess the argument, we need an in-depth cost-benefit analysis of participating in the course.

Finally, the president needs to know whether just because many other companies have benefited greatly from the course, Acme will also benefit from it. Acme may not be similar enough to other companies to stand to benefit from the course. It is possible that other companies have many people who have no basic reading skills and read very slowly; therefore, the course primarily concerned with basic reading and fast reading has been a good fit for them. On the contrary, Acme's employees may be mostly proficient readers and have no need for the course. Even if the course teaches reading skills that they may find marginally useful, the course materials may not focus on the type of reading they are engaged in at work, reducing the benefits for them. Also, the author does not specify how other companies' employees have participated in the course. Perhaps they have taken the course without leaving their companies, only some people in the same company have taken the course at the same time, and they have chosen to take one component of the course each time when they could leave work. Should this be true, requiring all of Acme's employees to take the course would be a waste of their time and money and make a dent in the company's productivity, undermining the argument.

In conclusion, the recommendation is in dire need of more statistical support both in the actual amount of productivity gained from having employees that can speed read and in how the example employees are connected to the notion of increased productivity. Perhaps more importantly, the results of a comparison of the training program's costs for all employees and the value of the increase in productivity, if any exists, would help us evaluate the argument.

101. Restricting showerhead water flow in <u>Sunnyside Towers</u> (Specific Evidence)

Relying on the recent change to low-flow showerheads in three of the buildings in an apartment complex by the name of Sunnyside Towers, the author claims that modifying the rest of the twelve buildings will help to increase the Sunnyside Corporation's profits due to saving costs on water. Before we determine the validity of the argument, we need some crucial evidence.

We must have evidence concerning whether after modification of showerheads, water will be saved in the first three of the buildings. The letter starts by mentioning that the showerheads only allow one-third the normal flow of water, and that there has not yet been any data on water usage before and after the change. Even if there has been data for the first month since the installation, we are not sure that it will be representative of the water use of the three buildings in the future. It is possible that if less water flows through the showerheads, and, as the letter mentions, the pressure is lower, the tenants may use the shower for a longer period. It is also possible that future tenants will use more water per capita, or that other uses of water will rise. In such scenarios, there may be no net change in their water use or there may be even an increase; thus, there would be no financial savings. Even if there will be financial savings, there is no guarantee that the savings will be significant. In that event, the prediction of profits as a result of modifying showerheads in the first three buildings would be gratuitous. To determine whether there will be a drop in water use, we need information about actual water usage before and after the adjustment.

Conceding that the showerheads will lower the cost of water, we should have evidence regarding whether the complaints about low water pressure involve serious issues. It is possible that there have been only a few residents since the adjustment, so there are only a few complaints. This may mean a high percentage of complaints. It is also possible that many have complaints, but they do not bother to report them. The worst scenario would be that many who have heard about the showerhead problem have chosen not to live in the buildings. Even if there have been only a few complaints about low water pressure and no problems with showers during the first month since the adjustment, there is the possibility that in the future many more complaints will be made, that many more problems with showers will be reported, and that many more tenants will vacate because they are displeased. In this case, the argument for financial savings and the prediction of the profits will be tenuous. If the complaints do not involve serious issues, and there are no issues other than the complaints, the argument for saving money and the prediction of the profit would be strengthened.

Even accepting that there is no issue other than the few complaints that do not involve serious problems, we also need evidence regarding whether change to low-flow showerheads to restrict water flow throughout the rest of the buildings will boost the profits of the company further. Profit is a function of revenues minus costs. The potential costs as well as financial savings should be considered. It is likely that the cost to modify all the showerheads in the entire twelve-building complex will not be offset by the savings on water, not to mention any problems that may require fixing down the line; while there have not been any major issues with showers yet, there may be unforeseen difficulties in the future. It is also likely that the adjustment will cost much more on average in the rest of the buildings than in the first three buildings. It is even likely that the rates charged by water companies will rise. Any of the scenarios, if true, would undermine the prediction of further increase in profits. Otherwise, there would be a better case for the prediction. However, without information about the costs of adjusting the showerheads and future rates, we cannot ascertain the soundness of the prediction and its argument.

In conclusion, the owner of Sunnyside Towers should rethink the decision to modify all the apartments' showerheads with the new low-flow model, as there is not enough data to support the claim that it will save on water and increase profits. To better evaluate the argument, we need a cost-benefit analysis that incorporates room for future maintenance expenditures and higher rates.

102. Restricting showerhead water flow in Sunnyside Towers (Assumptions)

Relying on the change to low-flow showerheads the week before in three of the buildings in an apartment complex by the name of Sunnyside Towers, the author claims that modifying the rest of the twelve buildings will help to increase the Sunnyside Corporation's profits due to saving costs on water. Before we determine the validity of the argument, we need to examine some key assumptions that underlie it.

The author implies that after modification of showerheads, water will be saved in the first three of the buildings. However, since there has not yet been any data on water usage before and after the change, the assumption is not warranted. Even if there has been data for the first week since the installation, we are not sure that it will be representative of the water use of the three buildings during the rest of the first month. It is possible that if less water flows through the showerheads, and, as the letter mentions, the pressure is lower, the tenants will use the shower for a longer period. It is also possible that future tenants will use more water per capita, or that other uses of water will rise. In such scenarios, there may be no net change in their water use or there may be even an increase; thus, there would be no financial savings. Even if there will be financial savings, there is no guarantee that the savings will be significant. In that event, the prediction of profits as a result of modifying showerheads in the first three buildings would be gratuitous.

Building on the implication that the showerheads will lower the cost of water, the author assumes that the complaints about low water pressure do not involve serious issues. However, there is no evidence that this is true. It is possible that there have been only a few residents since the adjustment, so there are only a few complaints. This may mean a very high percentage of complaints, given the adjustment made just one week before. It is also possible that many have complaints, but they do not bother to report them. The worst scenario would be that many who have heard about the showerhead problem have chosen not to live in the buildings. Even if there have been only a few complaints about low water pressure and no problems with showers during the first week, there is the possibility that during the rest of the first month after the adjustment many more complaints will be made, that many more problems with showers will be reported, and that many more tenants will vacate because they are displeased. In this case, the argument for financial savings and the claim regarding the profits will be tenuous. If the complaints do not involve serious issues, and the trend of the first week continues into the rest of the first month, the argument for saving money and the claim concerning the profits would be strengthened.

Granted that there is no issue other than the few complaints that involve no serious problems, the author also suggests that change to low-flow showerheads to restrict water flow throughout the rest of the buildings will further boost the profits of the company. However, the author provides no evidence to substantiate this. Profit is a function of revenues minus costs. The potential costs as well as financial savings should be considered. It is likely that the cost to modify all the showerheads in the entire twelve-building complex will not be offset by the savings on water, not to mention any problems that may require fixing down the line; while there have not been any major issues with showers yet, there may be unforeseen difficulties in the future. It is also likely that the adjustment will cost much more on average in the rest of the buildings than in the first three buildings. It is even likely that the rates charged by water companies will rise. Any of the scenarios, if true, would undermine the prediction of further increase in profits. Otherwise, there would be a better case for the prediction.

In conclusion, the owner of Sunnyside Towers should rethink the decision to modify all the apartments' showerheads with the new low-flow model, as there is not enough data to support the claim that it will save on water and increase profits. To better evaluate the argument, we need a cost-benefit analysis that incorporates room for future maintenance expenditures and higher rates.

103. Should Happy Pancake House replace butter with margarine? (Assumptions)

Relying on the fact that after the replacement of butter with margarine in Happy Pancake House restaurants in the southwestern United States, only about 2 percent of customers have made formal complaints and on reports that some customers asking for butter but receiving margarine instead have not complained, the author recommends that Happy Pancake House take similar action in its restaurants in the rest of the country to eliminate the costs of buying butter. However, before we determine whether the company should implement this plan, we should scrutinize the assumptions that underlie the argument.

The author assumes that just because only about two percent of customers have complained formally about the change from butter to margarine, ninety-eight percent of them are satisfied with the change. However, the author provides no evidence to substantiate this. It is likely that customers who have complained formally account for a much larger portion of those who have asked for butter. It is also likely that many customers have complained informally, for example, on social networking sites. It is even likely that only two percent care enough to complain directly to the company, whereas the others are unhappy, but do not wish to spend the time complaining about the change. In such scenarios, the company risks angering this silent majority, who may decide to stop eating at Happy Pancake House once all locations switch to margarine. Furthermore, the replacement may have happened too recently to yield significant feedback, alerting Happy Pancake House to a potentially much higher rate of negative response to the replacement later. In that event, the assumption of a ninety-eight percent satisfaction rate is unfounded and the recommendation of replacing butter with margarine in other parts of the United States is unlikely to have the predicted result of saving money on butter.

The author also implies that the absence of complaints among customers when given margarine instead of butter results from their inability to distinguish between the two, or from the fact they use the word "butter" to refer to both butter and margarine. If the latter scenario is the case, then the company has little to worry about; but if the former scenario turns out to be true, it could lead to a backlash once the company replaces all butter with margarine and more customers become dissatisfied. It is likely that the customers can tell the difference, but do not see it as something worth complaining about; after all, it is not the waiters' fault. However, the mention of this point by the author implies that the restaurant chain intends to make the change from butter to margarine without informing its customers, which has the potential for lawsuits, should it be discovered that it is lying about what it is serving. Also, the phrase "a number of customers" is vague. We just do not know the percentage of such customers. If a number of customers account for a small percentage of all the customers, this may indicate little impact of the change on customers. Otherwise, this may mean a significant impact on the customers. Even if the number indicates a tiny portion, it could be that the servers report such a small figure to the management simply to seem competent at providing service and avoid punishment. In that event, the recommendation would be unfounded, and the argument undermined.

Finally, the author suggests that the cost of butter is a significant expense and worth avoiding in all its restaurants in the country. While butter accounts for a portion of the costs, other factors such as operating expenses may constitute a much greater percentage of the total costs. Should this be the case, replacement of butter with margarine may not be the ideal option for saving costs. We should, therefore, inquire what specific factors comprise the greatest expenses of the restaurant chain to see where butter fits in that list. Also, even if we grant that the claims made by the author regarding the locations in the Southwestern US are true, this does not necessarily mean that the same will be true in the rest of the country. People in other parts of the country may care more about whether they eat butter or margarine than those in the Southwestern US, and therefore may be more inclined to complain about the change. They may also have more choices regarding breakfast restaurants. They may even be able to pay less for buying butter than for purchasing margarine. Any of the scenarios, if true, could cause the demographic outside the southwest to decide to take their business elsewhere and seriously impact the company's revenues, rendering the argument gratuitous.

In sum, all the assumptions underlie the claim that the company should extend its strategy of replacing butter with margarine throughout the country. However, to substantiate the assumptions, the author must provide additional evidence. If Happy Pancake House wishes to be certain that this change has not significantly affected its business, it should check its recent profits and customer traffic compared to those of the past and do further customer surveys on their satisfaction with the change.

104. Should Happy Pancake House replace butter with margarine? (Questions to Be Answered)

Relying on the fact that after the replacement of butter with margarine in Happy Pancake House restaurants in the southwestern United States, only about 2 percent of customers have made complaints and on reports that some customers asking for butter but receiving margarine instead have not complained, the author concludes that Happy Pancake House should take similar action in its restaurants in the southeast and northeast to become significantly more profitable. However, before the chain accepts this recommendation, it would do well to consider answers to the following questions.

First, we must ask if the two percent of customers that have complained represent all of those who are unhappy with the replacement of butter with margarine. This percentage point does not necessarily mean, as the memorandum suggests, that ninety-eight out of one hundred are happy with the change. It could be that those who have complained account for a much larger portion of customers who have asked for butter. It could also be that only two percent care enough to complain directly to the company, while the others are unhappy, but do not wish to spend the time complaining about the change. On the other hand, if the statistics are reliable, then it would be a fairly persuasive factor to implement the change. Furthermore, the replacement may have happened too recently to yield significant feedback, alerting Happy Pancake House to a potentially much higher rate of negative response to the replacement later. If this should be true, the assumption of a ninety-eight percent satisfaction rate would be unfounded and the recommendation of replacing butter with margarine in other parts of the United States would be unlikely to have the predicted result of saving money on butter and boosting profits. To better evaluate the argument, we need a customer survey to see if people are truly happy with the change.

We should also ask if the servers' claims about the lack of complaints when customers receive margarine after asking for butter are reliable. We wonder whether this phenomenon is the result of an unwillingness to say anything or whether it is indeed evidence that customers cannot tell the difference between butter and margarine when given the latter. It is likely that they can tell the difference, but do not see it as something worth complaining about. If this is the case, then they may decide to start complaining if this "mistake" becomes a permanent change. Also, the phrase "a number of customers" is vague. We just do not know the percentage of such customers. If a number of customers account for a small percentage of all the customers, this is not something to worry about. Otherwise, this may mean something serious for the company. It is also likely that the servers report a small number of complaints to the management to seem competent at providing service and avoid punishment. In that event, the recommendation is unfounded.

Finally, we need to ask if the cost of butter is a significant expense to affect the company's profitability. While butter accounts for a portion of the costs, other factors such as operating expenses may constitute a much greater percentage of the total costs. Should this be the case, replacement of butter with margarine may not be the ideal option for improving profitability considerably. We should, therefore, inquire what specific factors comprise the greatest expenses of the restaurant chain to see where butter fits in that list.

Also, just because one part of the country has succeeded in adopting the strategy does not necessarily mean the rest of the country will automatically do well in utilizing the strategy. It may be that the cost of butter is not the same in all regions of the country, depending on factors such as availability and customer demand: it could be more expensive than margarine in the southwestern US but cheaper than margarine in other places. It may also be that cultural differences will affect people's inclination to complain, and there are regional preferences of butter to margarine or vice versa. It may even be that this part has fewer choices regarding breakfast restaurants. In this case, the recommendation is unreasonable. To better assess the recommendation, we should investigate the correlation between the cost of butter and the company's profitability and the applicability of the strategy to other parts of the country.

In sum, the success of the plan for Happy Pancake House to replace butter with margarine in order to save money and increase profits hinges on whether its customers are willing to complain, whether the information about their ability to distinguish between the two is correct, and whether the cost of butter is a considerable expense. Answers to these questions are pivotal in evaluating the strategy. If customers can tell the difference between butter and margarine, and if they do decide to start complaining once the change takes place, especially across the country, this may have serious negative consequences, mainly in the form of a decrease in customers coming to eat at the chain.

105. Mandatory driver's education course at Centerville High School for students (Assumptions)

The author recommends that Centerville High School sponsor a mandatory driving course. To justify the recommendation, the letter states that there have been several accidents involving teenagers in the town, that parents are too busy to teach their children how to drive, and that the cost of the two driving schools in the town is too expensive for some parents. However, we should examine closely the assumptions that underlie the argument to determine its soundness.

The author assumes that the accidents involving the teenage drivers were a result of poor driving ability, hence the driving course suggestion, yet provides no evidence that this is the case. It may be that the accidents were caused by the other drivers, or even due to wildlife on the road. If this should be true, the assumption about the connection between accidents and driving ability would be unwarranted and the recommendation that Centerville High School sponsor a mandatory driving course would be unjustified. Without proof that poor driving knowledge alone caused the accidents, assuming that the program will do anything to prevent future accidents would be baseless. On the other hand, if it is shown that Centerville High School students were indeed at fault, specifically because they did not know how to drive properly, it would go a long way toward supporting the recommendation. Even if the accidents have been caused by the teenagers' poor driving ability, the author also assumes that the accidents in the past two years are part of a trend of incidents which could be eliminated by the program. If evidence of such a trend is available, such as a comparison of car accidents with teenagers involved not just in the two years mentioned, but also in previous years, then there would be a stronger case for implementing the mandatory driving course. However, as it stands, no such evidence is provided; therefore, it is fair to assume that the accidents in the past two years were nothing but an aberration and may not continue, rendering the recommendation unreasonable.

Next, the author implies that the proposed driving course will be the only effective strategy for preventing future accidents, if a trend of accidents exists at all. We would like to know why this is the case. The drivers involved in the accidents may not have come from the school or even the city; few teenager drivers may have been involved; the accidents may have been too small in number to be called a serious problem and may have caused minor or no injuries or damages; where the funding for the program should come from may be uncertain. Any of the scenarios, if true, would invalidate the assumption about the necessity and effectiveness of a mandatory school-sponsored course. Even if this course will be effective, the author cannot confidently claim that it is the only viable option. Perhaps the number of driving accidents in the city has been declining, and the instruction offered by the two driving schools is responsible for the scenario. For Centerville students who are involved in serious accidents because of lack of driving skills, they may need to take the course there. For Centerville teenagers involved in the accidents because they drive without a license, parents may have no time to teach them how to drive, but they can educate them about the consequences of driving without a license and help to ensure that they will drive legally. Figuring out if there are any alternative measures would give us more to work with when we determine if the mandatory course is the best and only solution. Unless there is evidence that other options are not viable, the author cannot justifiably claim that taking the driver's education course at Centerville High School is the only feasible course of action.

Finally, the author suggests that the parents are typical in Centerville. This letter mentions that some parents complained that their children must receive some instruction on how to drive from people other than the parents. We want to know whether a few people made many complaints, or many people made some complaints. Perhaps only two or three parents complained. The letter also says that some parents cannot afford the instruction offered by the two driving schools in the city. This again raises the question of whether these parents are representative of all parents in Centerville. It could be that these parents are in the minority and constitute an anomaly. Such scenarios would cast serious doubt on the assumption about the representativeness of the parents and on the argument in support of a mandatory driving course established by Centerville High School. However, if the parents are typical of those of Centerville in general, then that may provide the foundation of a sound argument.

In conclusion, the argument in favor of having Centerville High School sponsor a mandatory driving course is not well-supported. There needs to be solid proof that the accidents which have already occurred were the fault of students with poor driving ability from the high school, and that the course is the only way of avoiding such accidents. It would also help to know whether parents in the town cannot afford lessons which are currently available at the driving schools.

106. Should Happy Pancake House replace butter with margarine? (Specific Evidence)

The author recommends that Happy Pancake House replace butter with margarine at all of its restaurants throughout the southeast and northeast USA in order to save costs and increase profits. To justify the recommendation, the memorandum states that in its restaurants in the southwestern USA, only about two percent of people have complained and that according to reports by servers there, some customers do not complain when given margarine instead of butter. Yet the memo lacks evidence in several key areas, making it difficult to assess the argument.

We must have evidence regarding whether the fact that only two percent of customers have complained truly represents a ninety-eight percent satisfaction rate. However, the author provides no data in this regard. It could be that those who have complained account for a much larger portion of customers who have asked for butter. It could also be that only two percent care enough to complain directly to the company, while the others are unhappy, but do not wish to spend the time complaining about the change. It could even be that the replacement has happened too recently to yield significant feedback, alerting Happy Pancake House to a potentially much higher rate of negative response to the replacement later. If this should be true, the assumption of a ninety-eight percent satisfaction rate would be unfounded and the recommendation of replacing butter with margarine in other parts of the United States would be unlikely to have the predicted result of saving money on butter and boosting profits. To better evaluate the argument, we need a detailed customer survey asking about their specific preferences and opinions regarding the change from butter to margarine.

We should also have evidence regarding the absence of complaints among customers when given margarine instead of butter. The unwillingness to say anything may extend to the customers who seemingly cannot tell the difference between butter and margarine when given the latter. Since this point is based on reports by servers and not on any hard evidence by way of a survey, it is not a piece of very useful information. It is likely that customers can tell the difference, but do not see it as something worth complaining about; after all, it is not the waiters' fault if the restaurant does not have any butter. Also, if customers use the word "butter" to refer to both butter and margarine, there will be nothing to worry about. If they are unwilling to complain, it could lead to a backlash once the company replaces all butter with margarine and more customers become dissatisfied.

Moreover, the phrase "a number of customers" is vague. We just do not know the percentage of such customers. If a number of customers account for a small percentage of all the customers, this may indicate little impact of the change on customers. Otherwise, this may mean a significant impact on the customers. There is even the possibility that the servers report a small number of complaints to the management to seem competent at providing service and avoid punishment. In that event, the recommendation would be unfounded.

Finally, we need evidence regarding whether the cost of butter is a significant expense to affect the company's profitability. While butter accounts for a portion of the costs, other factors such as operating expenses may constitute a much greater percentage of the total costs. Should this be the case, replacement of butter with margarine may not be the ideal option for improving profitability. We should, therefore, inquire what specific factors comprise the greatest expenses of the restaurant chain to see where butter fits in that list. Also, just because the new strategy is effective in one part of the country does not necessarily mean it will be effective in other parts as well. It may be that the cost of butter is not the same in all regions of the country, depending on factors such as availability and customer demand. The memorandum claims that the change will save the chain money on the purchase of butter and will thus result in higher profits yet does not offer any relevant figures to show that butter is significantly more expensive than margarine, or that it is more expensive than margarine at all. Nor is there any information regarding the potential loss of customers if they cease to come to the restaurant if butter is no longer served. This may be an especially important point if regional preferences are different throughout the country, a data point for which no information is given. Nor do we know whether this region has fewer choices regarding breakfast restaurants. Should it be vastly different from other parts of the country in these respects, the recommendation is unreasonable. To better assess the argument, we should investigate the correlation between the cost of butter and the company's profitability and the applicability of the strategy to other parts of the country.

In sum, we need extra evidence to evaluate the argument before the chain implements the plan to replace butter with margarine at all of its locations throughout the country. We must determine whether customers are truly satisfied with the change that has already taken place in the southwestern locations, whether customers can distinguish between butter and margarine, and whether any regional differences would affect the cost of butter and the company's profits in its absence.

107. Mandatory driver's education course at Centerville High School for students (Specific Evidence)

The author recommends that Centerville High School sponsor a mandatory driving course. To justify the recommendation, the letter states that there have been several accidents involving teenagers in the town, that parents are too busy to teach their children how to drive, and that the cost of the two driving schools in the town is too expensive for some parents. However, before we determine whether the school board should implement this mandate, we need additional evidence.

We must have evidence that the accidents involving the teenage drivers were a result of poor driving ability, hence the driving course suggestion, yet the author provides no information in this regard. It may be that the accidents were caused by the other drivers, or even due to wildlife on the road. If this should be true, the assumption about the connection between accidents and driving ability would be unwarranted and the recommendation that Centerville High School sponsor a mandatory driving course would be unjustified. Without proof that poor driving knowledge alone caused the accidents, assuming that the program will do anything to prevent future accidents would be baseless. On the other hand, if it is shown that Centerville High School students were indeed at fault, specifically because they did not know how to drive properly, it would go a long way toward supporting the recommendation. Even if the accidents have been caused by the teenagers' poor driving ability, the author also assumes that the accidents in the past two years are part of a trend of incidents which could be eliminated by the program. If evidence of such a trend is available, such as a comparison of car accidents with teenagers involved not just in the two years mentioned, but also in previous years, then there would be a stronger case for implementing the mandatory driving course. However, as it stands, no such evidence is provided; therefore, it is fair to assume that the accidents in the past two years were nothing but an aberration and may not continue, rendering the recommendation unreasonable.

We should also have evidence that the proposed driving course will be the only effective strategy for preventing future accidents if a trend of accidents exists at all. We would like to know why this is the case. The drivers involved in the accidents may not have come from the school or even the city; few teenager drivers may have been involved; the accidents may have been too small in number to be called a serious problem and may have caused minor or no injuries or damages; where the funding for the program should come from may be uncertain. Any of the scenarios, if true, would invalidate the assumption about the necessity and effectiveness of a mandatory school-sponsored course. Even if this course will be effective, the author cannot confidently claim that it is the only viable option. Perhaps the number of driving accidents in the city has been declining, and the instruction offered by the two driving schools is responsible for the scenario. For Centerville students who are involved in serious accidents because of lack of driving skills, they may need to take the course there. For Centerville teenagers involved in the accidents because they drive without a license, parents may have no time to teach them how to drive, but they can educate them about the consequences of driving without a license and help to ensure that they will drive legally. Figuring out if there are any alternative measures would give us more to work with when we determine if the mandatory course is the best and only solution. Unless there is evidence that other options are not viable, the author cannot justifiably claim that taking the driver's education course at Centerville High School is the only feasible course of action.

Finally, we need evidence that the parents are typical in Centerville. This letter mentions that some parents complained that their children must receive some instruction on how to drive from people other than the parents. We want to know whether a few people made many complaints, or many people made some complaints. Perhaps only two or three parents complained. The letter also says that some parents cannot afford the instruction offered by the two driving schools in the city. This again raises the question of whether these parents are representative of all parents in Centerville. It could be that these parents are in the minority and constitute an anomaly. Such scenarios would cast serious doubt on the assumption about the representativeness of the parents and on the argument in support of a mandatory driving course established by Centerville High School. However, if the parents are typical of those of Centerville in general, then that may provide the foundation of a sound argument.

In conclusion, the argument in favor of having Centerville High School sponsor a mandatory driving course is not well-supported. There needs to be solid proof that the accidents which have already occurred were the fault of students with poor driving ability from the high school, and that the course is the only way of avoiding such accidents. It would also help to know if parents in the town truly cannot afford lessons which are currently available at the driving schools.

108. Should high school teachers assign homework less frequently as Marlee teachers do? (Specific Evidence)

Relying on a survey of high school math and science teachers which shows that Marlee students get better grades overall and have a lower chance of repeating a school year even though they are assigned homework less frequently than their Sanlee counterparts, the author recommends that teachers in her district emulate those in Marlee district and assign homework only two times or less each week. However, the evidence supporting the argument is sorely lacking, making it difficult for us to assess it fully.

There must be evidence that high schools in Marlee and Sanlee represent those in the author's area. However, there is a dearth of data to suggest that this is the case. The survey could be invalid and unreliable. Perhaps many Sanlee teachers have reported assigning homework more frequently to show that they have a better understanding of how students learn. Should this be true, the survey would be invalid. While the comparison between Marlee and Sanlee seems compelling at first glance, these are only two districts, and their high schools may not be an accurate representation of other high schools. Furthermore, the only classes covered by the survey were math and science, which are only a fraction of the subjects that students must take in school. The author's area and other subjects may assign homework more often and report higher grades. Should this be the case, the assumption about the representativeness of Marlee and Sanlee districts would be unjustified and the argument that the teachers in the author's area should follow Marlee's homework schedule would be undermined. An in-depth study across more school districts and more subjects with actual figures would be a far better metric by which to evaluate the proposed change.

There should also be evidence that grades in math and science represent students' overall performance. Because math and science classes are the only subjects surveyed, it is impossible to know if the lower grades and repeat rates at Sanlee are isolated to the students in those classes, or if they apply to all students at the school in general. It may be that despite receiving homework assignments more frequently, students in other subjects at Sanlee perform very well compared to those at Marlee, but without any data, it cannot be implied that students perform uniformly in all subjects. In this case, the assumption about the representativeness of grades in math and science would prove unwarranted and the argument would be gratuitous. A more detailed survey investigating students' comparative performance in other classes as well as in math and science classes would give a clearer picture of this issue.

Even if we grant that there is a huge gap in academic performance between Sanlee and Marlee students, there needs to be evidence regarding whether this disparity is the result of the difference in how often teachers in each district assign homework. It is possible that students in Sanlee schools are academically inferior to begin with. It is also possible that they seldom do their homework, that they experience stricter grading than Marlee students, or that their teachers are less efficacious than those of Marlee schools. Even if they do their homework, it may be easy and only take a few minutes to finish each time, whereas Marlee students may be assigned challenging homework and spend much more time on it every time. It is even possible that Marlee students are assigned more homework each time or do homework even on days when they have no assignments, ending up doing more homework each week. Similarly, the two districts may have different policies for deciding whether a student should repeat a year of school. Any of the scenarios, if true, would weaken the connection between less frequent homework and better grades. Without ruling out other feasible explanations, the author cannot justifiably claim that the gap in students' academic performance is attributable to the difference in frequency with which teachers assign homework.

To conclude, the assumption that assigning homework less frequently will result in higher grades and lower cases of students repeating a year is simply not supported by sufficient evidence. To fully evaluate the argument, we must have evidence by way of a detailed survey of a large number of high schools and subjects in different districts and comparative information about teaching quality of those schools. We must also know specifically which students were surveyed at the Sanlee and Marlee schools to determine the given examples' relevance to the argument.

109. Mandatory driver's education course at Centerville High School for students (Questions to Be Answered)

The author recommends that Centerville High School sponsor a mandatory driving course. To justify the recommendation, the letter states that there have been several accidents involving teenagers in the town, that parents are too busy to teach their children how to drive, and that the cost of the two driving schools in the town is too expensive for some parents. However, before we determine whether the school board should implement this mandate, we need answers to certain questions.

To begin with, we must ask whether the accidents involving the teenage drivers were a result of poor driving ability, hence the driving course suggestion, yet the author provides no information in this regard. It may be that the accidents were caused by the other drivers, or even due to wildlife on the road. If this should be true, the assumption about the connection between accidents and driving ability would be unwarranted and the recommendation that Centerville High School sponsor a mandatory driving course would be unjustified. Without proof that poor driving knowledge alone caused the accidents, assuming that the program will do anything to prevent future accidents would be baseless. On the other hand, if it is shown that Centerville High School students were indeed at fault, specifically because they did not know how to drive properly, it would go a long way toward supporting the recommendation. Even if the accidents have been caused by the teenagers' poor driving ability, the author also assumes that the accidents in the past two years are part of a trend of incidents which could be eliminated by the program. If evidence of such a trend is available, such as a comparison of car accidents with teenagers involved not just in the two years mentioned, but also in previous years, then there would be a stronger case for implementing the mandatory driving course. However, as it stands, no such evidence is provided; therefore, it is fair to assume that the accidents in the past two years were nothing but an aberration and may not continue, rendering the recommendation unreasonable.

Next, we wonder if the proposed driving course will be the only effective strategy for preventing future accidents, if a trend of accidents exists at all. We would like to know why this is the case. The drivers involved in the accidents may not have come from the school or even the city; few teenager drivers may have been involved; the accidents may have been too small in number to be called a serious problem and may have caused minor or no injuries or damages; where the funding for the program should come from may be uncertain. Any of the scenarios, if true, would invalidate the assumption about the necessity and effectiveness of a mandatory school-sponsored course. Even if this course will be effective, the author cannot confidently claim that it is the only viable option. Perhaps the number of driving accidents in the city has been declining, and the instruction offered by the two driving schools is responsible for the scenario. For Centerville students who are involved in serious accidents because of lack of driving skills, they may need to take the course there. For Centerville teenagers involved in the accidents because they drive without a license, parents may have no time to teach them how to drive, but they can educate them about the consequences of driving without a license and help to ensure that they will drive legally. Figuring out if there are any alternative measures would give us more to work with when we determine if the mandatory course is the best and only solution. Unless there is evidence that other options are not viable, the author cannot justifiably claim that taking the driver's education course at Centerville High School is the only feasible course of action.

Finally, we need to consider whether the parents are typical in Centerville. This letter mentions that some parents complained that their children must receive some instruction on how to drive from people other than the parents. We want to know whether a few people made many complaints, or many people made some complaints. Perhaps only two or three parents complained. The letter also says that some parents cannot afford the instruction offered by the two driving schools in the city. This again raises the question of whether these parents are representative of all parents in Centerville. It could be that these parents are in the minority and constitute an anomaly. Such scenarios would cast serious doubt on the assumption about the representativeness of the parents and on the argument in support of a mandatory driving course established by Centerville High School. However, if the parents are typical of those of Centerville in general, then that may provide the foundation of a sound argument.

In conclusion, the argument in favor of having Centerville High School sponsor a mandatory driving course leaves many questions that must be answered prior to any final decision. Knowing the exact cause of accidents and how many parents are unable to afford the currently available instruction of the two driving schools would certainly be a good start. Aside from that, discovering other possible solutions would at least provide a baseline with which to compare each one's potential efficacy rather than relying on one alone.

110. Should high school teachers assign homework less frequently as Marlee teachers do? (Assumptions)

Relying on a recent statewide survey of high school math and science teachers which shows that Marlee students get better grades overall and have a lower chance of repeating a school year even though only 25 percent of Marlee teachers reported having assigned homework three to five times each week, versus 86 percent of Sanlee teachers, the author recommends that teachers in the entire state of Attra assign homework only two times or less each week. However, the argument is full of assumptions and loopholes that we must examine closely before we determine its soundness.

The first assumption that underlies the argument is that high schools in Marlee and Sanlee districts represent other high schools in the state. However, the author provides no supporting data. The survey could be invalid and unreliable. 86 percent of the teachers could have represented few people, whereas 25 percent a large number of people. Even assuming that 86 percent involves a large population, whereas 25 percent a small one, there is no guarantee that Sanlee students have been assigned homework more frequently. Perhaps many Sanlee teachers have reported assigning homework more frequently to show that they have a better understanding of how students learn. Should this be true, the survey would be invalid. Also, while the comparison between Marlee and Sanlee seems compelling at first glance, these are only two districts, and may not be an accurate representation of all high schools in the state. Furthermore, the only classes covered by the survey were math and science, which are only a fraction of the subjects that students must take in school. Other districts and other subjects may assign homework more often and report higher grades. Should this be the case, the assumption about the representativeness of Marlee and Sanlee districts would be unjustified and the argument that the teachers in other high schools in the state should follow Marlee's homework schedule would be undermined. An in-depth study across more subjects and school districts with actual figures would be a far better metric by which to evaluate the proposed change.

The second assumption that buttresses the argument is that grades in math and science represent students' overall performance. However, because math and science classes are the only subjects surveyed, it is impossible to know if the lower grades and repeat rates at Sanlee are isolated to the students in those classes, or if they apply to all students at the school in general. It may be that despite receiving homework assignments more frequently, students in other subjects at Sanlee perform very well compared to those at Marlee, but without any data, it cannot be implied that students perform uniformly in all subjects. In that event, the assumption about the representativeness of grades in math and science would prove unwarranted and the argument would be gratuitous. A more detailed survey investigating students' comparative performance in other classes as well as in math and science classes would give a clearer picture of this issue. It may also be that the results of the recent survey are an anomaly and with homework assigned as often, high school math and science students in Sanlee used to be superior in academic performance to their counterparts in Marlee. In this case, the argument would be weakened.

Even if we grant that there is a huge gap in academic performance between students in Sanlee and those in Marlee, the author also assumes that this disparity is the result of the difference in how often teachers in each district assign homework. However, the author offers no evidence that this is true. It is possible that students in Sanlee schools are academically inferior to begin with. It is also possible that they seldom do their homework, that they experience stricter grading than Marlee students, or that their teachers are less efficacious than those of Marlee schools. Even if they do their homework, it may be easy and only take a few minutes to finish each time, whereas Marlee students may be assigned challenging homework and spend much more time on it every time. It is even possible that Marlee students are assigned more homework each time or do homework even on days when they have no assignments, ending up doing more work each week. Similarly, the two districts may have different policies for deciding whether a student should repeat a year of school. Any of the scenarios, if true, would weaken the connection between less frequent homework and better grades. Without ruling out other feasible explanations, the author cannot justifiably claim that the gap in students' academic performance is attributable to the difference in frequency with which teachers assign homework.

To conclude, the assumption that assigning homework less frequently will result in higher grades and lower cases of students repeating a year is simply unwarranted. To fully evaluate the argument, we must have evidence by way of a detailed survey of a large number of schools and subjects in different districts and comparative information about teaching quality of those schools. We must also know specifically which students were surveyed at the Sanlee and Marlee schools to determine the given examples' relevance to the argument.

111. Adopting honor codes similar to Groveton's (Specific Evidence)

The author recommends that all colleges and universities adopt an honor code similar to that of Groveton college, relying on the fact that Groveton has experienced a decrease in the reported cases of cheating over a period of five years, as well as a recent survey which found that a majority of students would be less inclined to cheat with an honor code in place. Yet, to better assess the argument, we need additional evidence.

First, we must have evidence regarding whether Groveton's honor code has been successful. The system in which teachers monitored students found thirty cases of cheating, while in the newer student-reporting system, only twenty-one cases were reported in the first year, and then only fourteen five years later. This begs the question of whether there has been a reduction in the number of cases of cheating because the honor code was in place, or whether cheating has decreased for other reasons. For example, students often hesitate to report their classmates' cheating. They may simply have become more and more reluctant to report cheating each year since adoption of the honor code. They may also have been less adept at detecting their classmates' cheating than teachers and former students who had been more experienced. Potential cheaters may even have chosen not to cheat during the period regardless of the honor code. If one of the scenarios turns out to be true, we will need to reinvestigate Groveton's "success" before other universities adopt a similar honor code. If the author could provide more information about the five years after the first, as well as details of each case, we would be able to better determine the efficacy of the honor code.

Secondly, we should have evidence regarding the validity, reliability, and representativeness of the recent survey of Groveton's students in which most reported that they would not cheat with an honor code in place. However, since these answers were self-reported by the students, it is safe to assume that they would give answers on the survey that would benefit them the most. This raises the question of whether the honor code is reliable at all since it obviously works in favor of dishonest students. Perhaps most students answered that the honor code would make them less likely to cheat because it made cheating easier, and therefore they hoped to keep it by falsely claiming that it would make them less inclined to cheat. This indicates that the participants of the survey may be an anomaly consisting mostly of people who hope to benefit from the honor code. Even if the respondents are representative of Groveton students, there is no guarantee that they will do as they have claimed in the survey. Besides, the researchers could have asked the irrelevant question of whether an honor code is better than none, instead of how it compares to the old system of teacher monitoring. In all such scenarios, the survey is neither valid nor representative, rendering the argument unreasonable. Thus, a more useful piece of data to support this point would be the performance of the students who answered in favor of the honor code. If they seemed to be underperforming students before the honor code, then this might be a sign that they took advantage of the system to cheat.

Lastly, we need proof that there do not exist any significant differences among all universities and colleges that may affect the success rate of an honor code system. For example, Groveton could be a small school where the honor code is easily implemented and naturally efficacious, whereas at larger universities it would be hard to implement the code and even if implemented, the code would be less effective. Groveton students could be more likely to report cheating, or less likely to cheat with an honor code in place, than students in other universities and colleges. Even if it has worked in Groveton, this does not necessarily mean that it will work in other colleges and universities. All this is incumbent on the willingness of students to follow the honor code, and currently there is no accurate measure of this variable. Even if the code will be effective in other colleges and universities, there is the possibility that some universities and colleges may have had in place an honor code comparable to Groveton's, thereby making a new one redundant. If Groveton is typical in respects relevant to the incidence of cheating, it will be plausible for other universities and colleges to enforce a similar honor code. Otherwise, the recommended action would be indefensible.

In conclusion, the adoption of an honor code across all universities and colleges requires further analysis in the areas of its actual success rate, not only at Groveton, but at other institutions as well. Furthermore, surveys of student opinions of the system change should be disregarded as those who wish to cheat will skew the results, since they stand to benefit from an honor code system. Finally, there should be further testing of the honor code system nationally and internationally to see if institutional differences will affect the willingness of students to report on one another.

112. Cutting funding for the Grandview Symphony (Questions to Be Answered)

The author recommends that the Grandview Symphony's funding be completely removed from the following year's budget in light of what the author views as a newfound self-sufficiency to prevent a city budget deficit. To justify the recommendation, the memo cites a two-hundred percent increase in private donations and a doubling in attendance at the symphony's park concert series last year. It also notes the plan by the symphony to increase ticket prices in the following year. Yet before we determine whether the city of Grandview should withdraw its financial support to the symphony, we should have answers to certain questions.

One important question to consider is whether the increase in private donations is significant or even remotely close to covering the operating costs of the Grandview Symphony. It may certainly be possible for private donations to fully support the symphony, but without accurate data showing how much was previously donated versus the costs of running the symphony, a two-hundred percent increase is a meaningless statistic. The private contributions before last year may have been very small and therefore an increase of two-hundred percent may not be significant. Even if the contributions were significant, they may not be adequate for operating the symphony, not to mention the possibility that they could help prevent a city budget deficit that may be many, many times the symphony budget. Also, the trend last year could have been an aberration and may not continue. For example, the contributions could decrease dramatically this year and even more dramatically next year. Perhaps the city has provided the greatest amount of funding for the symphony last year, boosting private contributions for it. Therefore, if the city ceases funding for the symphony, private contributions may diminish as well. If the increase in donations has not been significant and is unlikely to sustain, the argument that the symphony can fully support itself and has no need for city funding next year would be gratuitous.

Another question to answer is whether the increase in attendance at the concerts-in-the-park series is grounds for elimination of funding for the symphony. As with the increase in private donations, the article does not cite any specific numbers regarding previous attendance, nor do we know how important this particular series of concerts is compared to other performances put on each year by the symphony. If the attendance had been negligible before last year, a double attendance may not be significant. If the series accounts for a small portion of all of the symphony's events annually, it may contribute a small amount to the funding for the symphony, not to mention that for the city budget deficit. We also want to know whether the attendance requires paying for tickets. If the attendance is free of charge, the series may increase the costs instead of increasing the revenue. If the city's funding helps promote the series and offset most of its costs, the argument for eliminating its funding for the symphony would be weakened. Even if the doubling of attendance means a significant rise in the number of attendees, the trend last year could have been an anomaly and may not hold true next year. Any of the scenarios, if true, would invalidate the claim that the symphony has no need for city funding next year.

Still another question to address is whether the plan by the symphony to increase ticket prices for next year, coupled with a double increase in its private contributions and one hundred percent increase in attendance at its park concert series, would guarantee that it will be self-sufficient and warrant elimination of both funding for it and a city budget deficit. We would like to know whether raising ticket prices is a good option. As with private contributions and concert attendance, no concrete data is provided regarding current ticket revenues and potential increase for next year. If the amount of rise is too small, it will be meaningless for the symphony's operation. If the audience and the benefactors refuse to accept the rise, the symphony could not rely on this new source of funding. Even if the symphony can rely on the increase in ticket prices for next year, there is no guarantee that this increase, together with that in private contributions and concert attendance, will be enough to make up for the eliminated budget. Even assuming that increased revenue from these sources will be equal to the removed budget, this does not necessarily mean that the symphony will be self-sustaining, because it had been struggling financially before last year, which implies that the current city budget for it has been inadequate. Should this be the case, the argument for not including funding for the symphony in next year's city budget would be unjustified.

In sum, before the city of Grandview decides to cancel its financial support of the symphony, there must be a more in-depth investigation of the figures regarding the change in private contributions and attendance, along with how these and other factors may have influenced the symphony's decision to increase ticket prices. There should also be information about exactly what portion of the city budget the symphony funding makes up in order to ascertain if cutting the funding would have any effect on preventing a city budget deficit.

113. Should high school teachers assign homework less frequently as Marlee teachers do? (Questions to Be Answered)

Relying on a recent statewide survey of high school math and science teachers which shows that Marlee students get better grades overall and have a lower chance of repeating a school year even though only 25 percent of Marlee teachers reported having assigned homework three to five times each week, versus 86 percent of Sanlee teachers, the author recommends that teachers in the entire state of Attra assign homework only two times or less each week. However, we must have answers to some questions before we determine whether this plan should be implemented at every high school in the state.

We wonder whether high schools in Marlee and Sanlee districts represent other high schools in the state. However, the author provides no supporting data. The survey could be invalid and unreliable. 86 percent of the teachers could have represented few people, whereas 25 percent a large number of people. Even assuming that 86 percent involves a large population, whereas 25 percent a small one, there is no guarantee that Sanlee students have been assigned homework more frequently. Perhaps many Sanlee teachers have reported assigning homework more frequently to show that they have a better understanding of how students learn. Should this be true, the survey would be invalid. Also, while the comparison between Marlee and Sanlee seems compelling at first glance, these are only two districts, and may not be an accurate representation of all high schools in the state. Furthermore, the only classes covered by the survey were math and science, which are only a fraction of the subjects that students must take in school. Other districts and other subjects may assign homework more often and report higher grades. Should this be the case, the assumption about the representativeness of Marlee and Sanlee districts would be unjustified and the argument that the teachers in other high schools in the state should follow Marlee's homework schedule would be undermined. An in-depth study across more subjects and school districts with actual figures would be a far better metric by which to evaluate the proposed change.

We also wonder whether grades in math and science represent students' overall performance. Because math and science classes are the only subjects surveyed, it is impossible to know if the lower grades and repeat rates at Sanlee are isolated to the students in those classes, or if they apply to all students at the school in general. It may be that despite receiving homework assignments more frequently, students in other subjects at Sanlee perform very well compared to those at Marlee, but without any data, it cannot be implied that students perform uniformly in all subjects. In that event, the assumption about the representativeness of grades in math and science would prove unwarranted and the argument would be gratuitous. A more detailed survey investigating students' comparative performance in other classes as well as in math and science classes would give a clearer picture of this issue. It may also be that the results of the recent survey are an anomaly and with homework assigned as often, high school math and science students in Sanlee used to be superior in academic performance to their counterparts in Marlee. In this case, the argument would be weakened.

Even if we grant that there is a huge gap in academic performance between students in Sanlee and those in Marlee, we must ask whether this disparity is the result of the difference in how often teachers in each district assign homework. However, the author offers no evidence that this is true. It is possible that students in Sanlee schools are academically inferior to begin with. It is also possible that they seldom do their homework, that they experience stricter grading than Marlee students, or that their teachers are less efficacious than those of Marlee schools. Even if they do their homework, it may be easy and only take a few minutes to finish each time, whereas Marlee students may be assigned challenging homework and spend much more time on it every time. It is even possible that Marlee students are assigned more homework each time or do homework even on days when they have no assignments, ending up doing more homework each week. Similarly, the two districts may have different policies for deciding whether a student should repeat a year of school. Any of the scenarios, if true, would weaken the connection between less frequent homework and better grades. Without ruling out other feasible explanations, the author cannot justifiably claim that the gap in students' academic performance is attributable to the difference in frequency with which teachers assign homework.

To conclude, the assumption that assigning homework less frequently will result in higher grades and lower cases of students repeating a year raises too many questions to be accepted at face value. To fully evaluate the argument, we must have information by way of a detailed survey of a large number of schools and subjects in different districts and comparative information about teaching quality of those schools. We must also know specifically which students were surveyed at the Sanlee and Marlee schools to determine the given examples' relevance to the argument.

114. Cutting funding for the Grandview Symphony (Specific Evidence)

The author predicts that the Grandview Symphony will be able to support itself without the city government's budget in light of its potentially more revenue from increased audiences and raised ticket prices. To justify the prediction, the memo cites a new conductor who has attracted high-profile guest performers, in turn doubling private donations and bringing attendance to record-highs at the symphony's park concert series. It also notes the symphony's ability to increase ticket prices. However, the author does not provide sufficient evidence to make a compelling case for the argument.

We must have evidence regarding the size and sustainability of donations. The doubling of donations, while sounding like a huge increase in revenue, may not account for much without specific financial details regarding how much the symphony generally gets in donations. It is likely that the symphony generally receives next to nothing in donations, and since we also do not know how much it costs to run the symphony, nor how much the symphony relies on the financial support from the city, it is not fair to infer that it is now self-sufficient. A detailed financial breakdown of costs and revenues would be a good way to determine the validity of the author's claim here. Even if the doubling means a significant increase, there is no guarantee that the trend will last into the future. Perhaps the city has provided the greatest amount of funding for the symphony last year, boosting private contributions for it. Therefore, if the city ceases funding for the symphony, private contributions may diminish as well. Thus, a survey that asks the respective parties their reasons for donating would certainly help to find out if this increase can continue. If the increase in donations has not been significant and is unlikely to sustain, the assumption about the possibility of the symphony as "an established success" is unwarranted, and the argument for eliminating city funding for it is unfounded.

We should also have evidence that the increase in attendance at the concerts-in-the-park series is a good reason for elimination of city funding for the symphony. However, the memo does not cite any specific numbers regarding previous attendance, nor do we know how important this particular series of concerts is compared to other performances put on each year by the symphony. If the attendance had been negligible one year before, new highs may not be significant. The information about the series would be very persuasive if it comprised the majority of the symphony's viewership, but alternatively, it may also be that it is a relatively minor performance; without more details it is impossible to know for sure. We also want to know whether the attendance requires paying for tickets. If the attendance is free of charge, the series may increase the costs instead of increasing the revenue. If the city's funding helps promote the series and offset most of its costs, the argument for eliminating its funding for the symphony would be weakened. Even if new highs mean a significant rise in the number of attendees, the trend last year could have been an anomaly and may not hold true in the future. Any of the scenarios, if true, would invalidate the claim that the symphony has been successful and therefore has no need for city funding in the future.

Finally, we need evidence that the new conductor is single-handedly responsible for the turnaround in donations and attendance and that increasing ticket prices is a viable course of action. While it is certainly possible that the conductor and the guest performers have been a contributing factor, the benefactors and audience members may have other reasons for donating and attending. Even if the conductor and the guest performers have been responsible for the increase in donations and attendance, it is also possible that they require higher salaries and costlier venues, only perform for the park concert series that may account for a small fraction of the symphony's annual events, and will work with the symphony only for one year. If this is the case, it is likely that with increased operating costs, the high attendance cannot sustain, entailing more funding from the city, rendering the argument for funding elimination unpersuasive. Even if the trend regarding donations and concert attendance last year continues, there is no guarantee that the symphony can increase ticket prices. The audience and the benefactors may not accept the increase, making this option an unreliable source of funding. Even if the symphony can rely on the increase in ticket prices in the future, there is no guarantee that the increase will result in much revenue, because it may be insignificant. Even if the increase is considerable, there is no guarantee that more revenue from larger audiences and higher ticket prices will be enough to make up for the eliminated budget. There may still be a huge gap between the symphony's total revenue and the city budget. Should this be the case, the argument for removal of funding for the symphony from the city budget would be unjustified.

In sum, before the city of Grandview decides to cancel its financial support of the symphony, the author must first provide a number of pieces of key evidence, perhaps by way of a survey of donors and attendees asking their reasons for increased contributions and attendance. Also, a record of attendance that compares all events over time would help to determine if the concerts-in-the-park series accounts for a significant portion of attendees. Lastly, a complete analysis of the symphony's costs and revenues and its ability to increase ticket prices would yield evidence that can be used to assess the argument.

115. Should roller skaters invest in high-quality protective and reflective gear? (Assumptions)

The author concludes that investing in high-quality protective gear and reflective equipment will significantly lessen the risk of roller-skaters being seriously injured in an accident. To support the conclusion, the article cites a hospital statistic, which states that 75 percent of roller-skaters who went to the emergency room after an accident in streets or parking lots had not been wearing any protective equipment or any light-reflecting material. However, the argument is full of assumptions and loopholes that we must examine closely to determine its soundness.

The author assumes that the people who went to the emergency room after roller-skating accidents in streets or parking lots are indicative of all roller-skaters. While the fact that 75 percent of roller skaters who went to the hospital had not been wearing any protective or preventative gear when they had accidents in streets or parking lots may seem like clear evidence in support of safety equipment, the author goes too far in assuming that they represent all roller-skaters. In fact, the author offers no evidence that this is the case. It is possible that the people who had accidents in streets or parking lots, inherently more dangerous areas for roller skating, only accounted for a tiny fraction of the people who went to the emergency room after roller-skating accidents and only represented a small percentage of all roller-skaters. Therefore, the people who went to the emergency room after roller-skating accidents in the more dangerous areas do not typify roller-skaters in general. It could be that most people skate-board in comparatively safer places such as parks or backyards. It could also be that many people do not go to the emergency room after a skate-boarding accident. If this should be true, the assumption about the representativeness of the roller-skaters would prove unwarranted and the argument that roller-skaters should purchase high-quality protective gear to mitigate severe injuries in accidents would be gratuitous.

Next, the author implies that skate-boarders' lack of gear and equipment is solely responsible for their injuries. However, this need not be the case. It is likely that bad weather conditions have contributed to the injuries. For example, skate-boarders could not have seen what was going around them because of the weather. It is also likely that skaters' lack of skill has been responsible for them. It is even likely that their carelessness was to blame for the injuries. Any of the scenarios, if true, would rule out gear and equipment as the only factor correlated with the risk of roller skating injuries. While 75 percent of roller skaters who had accidents in streets or parking lots had not been wearing any protective gear or reflective equipment, it could be that the 25 percent of roller skaters who had been wearing protective gear were injured just as severely as they, rendering the connection between wearing gear and equipment and the risk of roller skating injuries tenuous, undermining the argument for investing in protective and preventative gear to help roller-skaters significantly decrease serious injuries in accidents.

Even granting that not wearing protective gear and reflective equipment has caused injuries, the author also suggests that only severe injuries have occurred. However, this is not necessarily the case. We do not know the severity of the injuries of those admitted to the emergency room; thus, it is not justifiable to imply that all those admitted suffered serious injuries. While hospital statistics seem useful in determining the need for protective equipment, since there is no data with which to compare the severity of injuries involving roller-skaters who were wearing protective gear with that involving those who were not, it is not fair to infer that only the skate-boarders with severe injuries go to the emergency room for treatment. Perhaps people skate-board for relaxation during evenings and weekends and go to the emergency room after an accident when other medical service is not available, whether they have severe or minor injuries. Should this be true, the assumption about the severity of injuries would be unwarranted, rendering the argument for investing in protective gear and equipment to prevent serious injuries unfounded.

Finally, the author takes it for granted that people should invest in high-quality protective and preventative equipment. However, the author provides no evidence to substantiate this. Even if skate-boarders go to the emergency room for treatment of serious injuries, this does not necessarily mean that they could be prevented through wearing high-quality protective clothing and light-reflecting material. It is possible that, depending on the nature of the accidents, such as getting hit by a car versus simply falling down, protective gear would be either completely useless or very helpful. Even if safety gear may contribute to preventing serious injuries in some cases, since we do not have information about the limits of protective clothing, it is not fair to assume that wearing such gear will prevent serious injuries in all cases. Also, the author overlooks other strategies that may help roller-skaters achieve the same results. For example, ordinary protective equipment, such as a piece of white cloth, may be as beneficial as a piece of much more expensive light-reflecting equipment. If roller-skaters often have serious accidents in streets or parking lots, they may simply avoid such places and engage in the activity in safer places with simple protective equipment. They may also avoid injury by doing warming up exercise before starting to skate. In such scenarios, investing in high-quality protective gear could be a waste of money. Unless there is evidence that no alternative strategies are viable, the author cannot justifiably assume that it is necessary for all roller-skaters to make the investment.

In sum, the assumptions that underlie the argument are too vague to support it. If the author is wrong, then many roller skaters may gain a false sense of security because of the protective gear they wear and may end up behaving more carelessly as a result, which could in turn lead to the same severe injuries that the author wishes to prevent.

116. Cutting funding for the Grandview Symphony (Assumptions)

The author recommends that the Grandview Symphony's funding be completely removed from the city's budget in light of what the author views as a newfound self-sufficiency. To justify the recommendation, the memo cites a new conductor who has attracted high-profile guest performers, in turn tripling private donations and bringing attendance to record highs at the symphony's outdoor summer concert series. However, the argument is full of assumptions and loopholes that we must scrutinize to determine its soundness.

The author assumes that tripling of private contributions justifies the city's elimination of funding for the symphony. However, the author provides no evidence to substantiate this. We need information regarding the size and sustainability of donations. The tripling of donations, while sounding like a huge increase in revenue, may not account for much without specific financial details regarding how much the symphony generally gets in donations. It is likely that the symphony generally receives next to nothing in donations, and since we also do not know how much it costs to run the symphony, nor how much the symphony relies on the financial support from the city, it is not fair to infer that it is now self-sufficient. A detailed financial breakdown of costs and revenues would be a good way to determine the validity of the author's claim here. Even if the tripling means a significant increase, there is no guarantee that the trend will last into the future. Perhaps the city has provided the greatest amount of funding for the symphony in the past two years, boosting private contributions for it. Therefore, if the city ceases funding for the symphony, private contributions may diminish as well. Thus, a survey that asks the respective parties their reasons for donating would certainly help to find out if this increase can continue. If the increase in donations has not been significant and is unlikely to sustain, the assumption about the possibility of the symphony having succeeded in finding an audience is unwarranted, and the argument for eliminating city funding for it is unfounded.

The author also implies that the dramatic increase in attendance at the outdoor summer series is a good reason for elimination of funding for the symphony. However, the memo does not cite any specific numbers regarding previous attendance, nor do we know how important this particular series of concerts is compared to other performances put on each year by the symphony. If the attendance had been negligible two years before, new highs may not be significant. The information about the series would be very persuasive if it comprised the majority of the symphony's viewership, but alternatively, it may also be that it is a relatively minor performance; without more details it is impossible to know for sure. We also want to know whether the attendance requires paying for tickets. If the attendance is free of charge, the series may increase the costs instead of increasing the revenue. If the city's funding helps promote the series and offset most of its costs, the argument for eliminating its funding for the symphony would be weakened. Even if new highs mean a significant rise in the number of attendees, the trend in the past two years could have been an anomaly and may not hold true in the future. Any of the scenarios, if true, would invalidate the claim that the symphony has successfully found an audience and therefore has no need for city funding in the future.

Even granting that the symphony has experienced considerable increase in private donations and concert attendance in the past two years, the author also suggests that the new conductor is single-handedly responsible for the turnaround in donations and attendance. While it is certainly possible that the conductor and the guest performers have been a contributing factor, the benefactors and audience members may have other reasons for donating and attending. Even if the conductor and the guest performers have been responsible for the increase in donations and attendance, it is also possible that they require higher salaries and costlier venues, only perform for the outdoor summer series that may account for a small fraction of the symphony's annual events, and will work with the symphony only for two years. If this is the case, it is likely that with increased operating costs, the high attendance cannot sustain, entailing more funding from the city, rendering the argument for funding elimination unpersuasive. Also, no concrete data is provided regarding what portion of the full funding private contributions and revenues from the outdoor summer series account for. It is possible that both sources of revenues combined only constitute a small portion of the funding required for the symphony to remain in business. Even if they are great enough for full funding of the symphony, it is likely that either source or both will decrease or disappear altogether. If this should be the case, the assumption that the symphony will be self-sufficient would be unwarranted and the argument that the city can stop funding the symphony would be undermined.

In sum, before the city of Grandview decides to cancel its financial support of the symphony, the author must first provide a number of key pieces of evidence to substantiate the argument's assumptions, perhaps by way of a survey of donors and attendees asking their reasons for increased contributions and attendance. Also, a record of attendance that compares all events over time would help to determine if the outdoor summer series accounts for a significant portion of attendees. Lastly, a complete analysis of the symphony's costs and revenues would yield evidence that can be used to assess the argument.

117. More healthful lifestyles in Forsythe (Assumptions)

The author concludes that the new lifestyles adopted by the citizens of Forsythe are more healthful than before. To support the conclusion, the article presents survey results in which the citizens' eating habits align more closely with government nutritional recommendations than ten years before. It also cites a fourfold increase in the sale of foods that contain kiran, which has been shown by a study to reduce cholesterol, and a decrease in the sales of sulia, a food which the healthiest citizens tend to avoid. However, to determine the soundness of the argument, we need to scrutinize the assumptions that underlie it.

First, the author assumes that the respondents are representative of the entire population of the town. Yet no concrete evidence is provided to substantiate this. If the survey finding is to be accepted as evidence, it needs to provide more information about the sample, such as the number of people and demographics of the citizens surveyed, the specific questions asked, and how they have been asked. Without relevant information, it is possible that the only people questioned were those that already fell into the healthiest portion of the populace. The sample could be very small and an anomaly, whereas the town residents in general still keep the lifestyle ten years before. It is also possible that the respondents misrepresented their lifestyles simply to seem health conscious, further skewing the results. In this case, the assumption about the representativeness of the respondents would prove unwarranted and the claim that the citizens of Forsythe have become more health-oriented would be invalid. Unless the survey is valid, reliable, and representative, the author cannot substantiate the claim.

Even granting that the survey was properly administered, the author also implies that following the government recommendations more closely is the same as living a healthier lifestyle. However, government recommendations usually only cover the bare minimum requirements; therefore, there is the possibility that these health recommendations are for people living at the poverty level. If this is true, the recommendations as a metric may be inadequate for measuring the relative healthiness of an entire populace. Perhaps the citizens' dietary habits are less wholesome today than ten years ago. Thus, the author has yet to establish the connection between aligning more with the government recommendations and adopting a more healthful lifestyle. Unless these recommendations are better explained, how closely the citizens of Forsythe follow them is irrelevant to this argument.

Finally, the author suggests that increased consumption of kiran and decreased consumption of sulia are proof of a healthier lifestyle. However, the author needs to furnish evidence that this is true. It could be the case that the residents of Forsythe do not have high cholesterol levels and therefore do not need to consume kiran. Even if consumption of kiran may make them healthier, there is no guarantee that a fourfold increase will be adequate, since the amount could have been very small to begin with. Also, the fact that the healthiest citizens tend to avoid sulia does not necessarily mean that it is unhealthy; it could be that it simply is not palatable. In that event, the assumption about kiran and sulia would be gratuitous. Even if more consumption of kiran and less consumption of sulia indicate a more healthful lifestyle, kiran and sulia are only two foods and by no means the only sources of nutrition the citizens eat. It could also be the case that the citizens now have a less healthy lifestyle overall because they eat much more unhealthy food and exercise much less than before. Any of the scenarios, if true, would invalidate the claim that the people of Forsythe have followed more wholesome lifestyles. Without further information about the two particular foods, their consumption would be irrelevant.

In conclusion, the author makes a few assumptions that underlie the claim that Forsythe citizens have lived more healthful lives. If the assumptions are to be considered valid, there must first be more specific details about the survey of dietary habits, particularly regarding the sample. Furthermore, there should be more information about the government guidelines for nutritional eating, such as whom the guidelines are meant for and what standard of health they are designed to meet. Lastly, there needs to be evidence that kiran and sulia have been significant staples in the diets of Forsythe citizens and that they have the stated effects on consumers' nutritional health.

118. Increased demand for heating oil (Questions to Be Answered)

The author predicts an increased demand for heating oil throughout the next five years. To justify the prediction, the memo states that most homes in the northeastern United States have always used oil as their primary fuel for heating, and that climate forecasters have predicted a cold weather trend, based on 90 days of below-normal temperatures last heating season, which will continue for years into the future. It also notes that the population in this region has grown recently, with a large number of new homes being built to address the issue. However, we must have answers to certain questions before we determine whether the prediction and its argument are sound.

We must ask whether homeowners may use any alternative heating sources instead of oil, and whether this competition would affect the demand for heating oil. The author assumes that because oil has been the traditional choice of fuel for heating, it will remain so in the future. However, various other options may become more popular in the future for various reasons. For example, the push for green energy alternatives could make oil fall out of popularity, or a newer and cheaper source of energy may be discovered that would render oil obsolete. There is even the possibility that some people, especially old people, will leave this part of the country for the south during winters, decreasing the need for heating oil. If this should be the case, the prediction of a growing demand for heating oil during the next five years would be unjustified. To determine whether the prediction is well-founded, we need to know how oil will fare in its competition with other heating sources in the future.

We should also consider whether the climate prediction will hold true for as long as the forecasters have claimed. The memo suggests that the climate trends will continue. However, the author provides no evidence to substantiate this. The trend in the last heating season could have been an aberration and may not continue. Even if the trend persists, this does not necessarily mean there will be an increased demand for heating oil, since the memo does not indicate whether in the 90 days when the region underwent below-normal temperatures, residents used more heating oil. It is possible that the region experienced no more demand for heating oil during this period. Also, there is no guarantee that the prediction of forecasters would be accurate. With the onset of climate change, there may be a chance that the cold weather periods will shorten significantly in the near future, leading to a decrease in the demand for heating systems of all kinds. Even assuming that the weather pattern will last for as long as the forecasters have claimed, there may not be an increasing demand for heating oil because it may have become so expensive at some point that people will switch to other means of heating. Any of the scenarios, if true, would make the prediction unreasonable.

Finally, we wonder whether new homes have the potential to be future heating oil users. The article notes that new homes are being built in the region for the growing population. However, there is no detailed information about the number of new homes being built. It is possible that the number is indeed great, but few will be occupied such that there is no need for heating of any kind. It is also possible that the houses are better-insulated or few of them rely on oil for heating. While new homes may become future users of heating oil, the article does not specifically state that these houses are built with heating systems that use oil as fuel. It may be the case that these houses will utilize electric heating or water radiators instead. If they are built with heating systems that do use heating oil, then this would lend support to the prediction that heating oil will experience increased demand. Otherwise, the prediction would be implausible. Without more information about the designs of these houses, it is impossible to say for certain.

To conclude, the argument raises the following questions: Are there any alternative sources of heat that could compete with heating oil? How certain are we that the alleged weather trend will continue? Are the new homes under construction being built with heating systems that use heating oil? Unless we have answers to these questions, we cannot fully assess the author's prediction and argument.

119. Increased demand for heating oil (Specific Evidence)

The author predicts an increased demand for heating oil throughout the next five years. To justify the prediction, the memo states that most homes in the northeastern United States have always used oil as their primary fuel for heating, and that climate forecasters have predicted a cold weather trend, based on 90 days of below-normal temperatures last heating season, which will continue for years into the future. It also notes that the population in this region has grown recently, with a large number of new homes being built to address the issue. However, we must have additional evidence before we determine whether the argument is sound.

We must have evidence that because oil has been the traditional choice of fuel for heating, it will remain so in the future. However, the article does not provide any data to support this prediction. There remains the possibility that people may cease using oil in favor of alternative energy sources. The push for green energy alternatives could make oil fall out of popularity, or a newer and cheaper source of energy may be discovered that would render oil obsolete. There is even the possibility that some people, especially old people, will leave this part of the country for the south during winters, decreasing the need for heating oil. If this should be the case, the prediction of a growing demand for heating oil during the next five years would be unjustified. To determine whether the prediction is well-founded, we need to know how oil will fare in its competition with other heating sources in the future.

We should also have evidence regarding the potential that the climate prediction will hold true for as long as the forecasters have claimed. The memo suggests that the climate trends will continue. However, the ninety-days of below-average temperatures during the last heating season are not given with any context with which to determine the possibility of their continuance. The trend in the last heating season could have been an aberration and may not continue. Even if the trend persists, this does not necessarily mean there will be an increased demand for heating oil, since the memo does not indicate whether in the 90 days when the region underwent below-normal temperatures, residents used more heating oil. It is possible that the region experienced no more demand for heating oil during this period. Also, there is no guarantee that the prediction of forecasters would be accurate. With the onset of climate change, there may be a chance that the cold weather periods will shorten significantly in the near future, leading to a decrease in the demand for heating systems of all kinds. Even assuming that the weather pattern will last for as long as the forecasters have claimed, there may not be an increasing demand for heating oil because it may have become so expensive at some point that people will switch to other means of heating. Any of the scenarios, if true, would make the prediction unreasonable.

Finally, we need evidence regarding whether new homes have the potential to be future heating oil users. The article notes that new homes are being built in the region for the growing population. However, there is no detailed information about the number of new homes being built. It is possible that the number is indeed great, but few will be occupied such that there is no need for heating of any kind. It is also possible that the houses are better-insulated or few of them rely on oil for heating. While new homes may become future users of heating oil, the article does not specifically state that these houses are built with heating systems that use oil as fuel. It may be the case that these houses will utilize electric heating or water radiators instead. If they are built with heating systems that do use heating oil, then this would lend support to the prediction that heating oil will experience increased demand. Otherwise, the prediction would be implausible. Without more information about the designs of these houses, it is impossible to say for certain.

To conclude, the author does not provide adequate evidence to support the argument. To better evaluate the argument, we must have information by way of surveys of consumers' future preferences and detailed consumer reports of the preferred method of heating. Also, we should have meteorological reports over a longer period than just one season to determine if there is indeed a cold weather trend that could continue. Finally, we need blueprints of the new homes which are being built to show whether they will contribute at all to an increase in the demand for heating oil.

120. Should Grove College remain all-female? (Assumptions)

The author argues that Grove College, an all-female institution, should not convert itself into a co-ed institution in order to boost student morale and secure continued financial support from alumnae. To support the argument, the article cites a survey of students in which 80 percent of the respondents favored keeping the college all-female, and an alumnae survey pointing to a majority view of its respondents in favor of preserving the status quo. Yet, to fully evaluate the argument, we need to examine its numerous assumptions.

Regarding the student survey, the author makes the assumption that the respondents represent a majority of all the college's students. However, the author does not offer any data to back it up. 80% of the respondents may have been an insignificant number. It is possible that only a small percentage of students filled out the survey, specifically new students that took a keen interest in the college's history. It is also possible that the survey was administered after the college's students were educated about its tradition of all-female education. In either scenario, this survey would not be a very useful metric for measuring total student morale. Even if the survey is valid and reliable, there is no guarantee that admitting only female students will boost morale among students, since it is impossible to determine how a co-ed policy would impact the morale of all students before Grove adopts the policy and analyzes the morale of its male students as well as that of its female students. In that event, the assumption about the representativeness of the respondents would prove unwarranted and the argument that the college should preserve its tradition of all-female education would collapse.

On a similar note, the author implies that the alumnae survey is a reliable one. Likewise, the author makes no mention of the specific number of people questioned nor the number of respondents compared to all the alumnae. More than half of the respondents could have been a very small number. The sample could have been a tiny one, with only a few respondents who happened to place a great value on the college's long tradition of all-female education. It could also have consisted mostly of alumnae who have made no or small donations to the college. Should this be the case, assuming that the respondents are representative of the entire body of alumnae could lead to undesirable consequences, for example, alienating alumnae whose financial support most likely has far greater implications for the college, viz. those who have made the largest contributions. Even if the survey is reliable and valid and the assumption is substantiated, there is no guarantee that the college can persuade its alumnae to contribute financially to it, because student morale is just one of the many factors in attracting alumnae's financial support. In this way, the argument that the assumption undergirds falls apart.

With both surveys in question, the author still assumes that the opinions of most faculty members are less important than either those of the student respondents or those of the alumnae respondents. However, the author provides no evidence to substantiate this. We do not know the number of faculty members who attended the meeting, but it could be that the survey involving faculty members had a large and possibly representative sample. The faculty members are also key stakeholders of the college. They may have a better understanding of its application and future enrollments and care about it as much as or even more than students and alumnae. Also, faculty morale that arises from a co-ed policy may affect how alumnae will make financial contributions to the college. Enhanced faculty morale may result in improved instruction which may in turn boost morale among students, particularly among the largest contributors, who could continue to donate large sums to the college. If this should be true, the assumption about the relative importance of faculty members' opinions would be unwarranted and the argument would be gratuitous. Without taking into account the opinions of most faculty members, the author cannot confidently claim that Grove College should preserve its tradition of admitting no male students.

To conclude, this article makes a few assumptions in favor of not changing Grove College's female-only status. With such a weak argument, the college risks making a blind decision that could cost it financial support and lead to a disgruntled student body and faculty. If the author can provide more accurate data from the surveys, showing majorities of respondents in both categories leaning against the decision to change the school status, then there would be a stronger case for the argument.

121. Should Grove College remain all-female? (Questions to Be Answered)

The author argues that Grove College, an all-female institution, should not convert itself into a co-ed institution in order to boost student morale and secure continued financial support from alumnae. To support the argument, the article cites a survey of students in which 80 percent of the respondents favored keeping the college all-female, and an alumnae survey pointing to a majority view of its respondents in favor of preserving the status quo. However, to better assess the recommendation, we need answers to some key questions.

Regarding the student survey, we wonder whether the respondents represent a majority of all the college's students. However, the author does not offer any data to back it up. 80% of the respondents may have been an insignificant number. It is possible that only a small percentage of students filled out the survey, specifically new students that took a keen interest in the college's history. It is also possible that the survey was administered after the college's students were educated about its tradition of all-female education. If this should be the case, then this survey would not be a very useful metric for measuring total student morale. Even if the survey is valid and reliable, there is no guarantee that admitting only female students will boost morale among students, since it is impossible to determine how a co-ed policy would impact the morale of all students before Grove adopts the policy and analyzes the morale of its male students as well as that of its female students. In that event, the recommendation that the college preserve its female-only status would be unfounded.

On a similar note, we also want to know whether the alumnae survey is a reliable one. Likewise, the author makes no mention of the specific number of people questioned nor the number of respondents compared to all the alumnae. More than half of the respondents could have been a very small number. The sample could have been a tiny one, with only a few respondents who happened to place a great value on the college's long tradition of all-female education. It could also have consisted mostly of alumnae who have made no or small donations to the college. If the alumnae had responded as students and later responded as alumnae, it would be interesting to see if they kept their answers consistent on the surveys or their opinions changed over time. If their answers were inconsistent, the surveys could not have been valid or reliable. Should this be the case, assuming that the respondents are representative of the entire body of alumnae could lead to undesirable consequences, for example, alienating alumnae whose financial support most likely has far greater implications for the college, viz. those who have made the largest contributions. Even if the survey is reliable and valid and the assumption is substantiated, there is no guarantee that the college can persuade its alumnae to contribute financially to it, because student morale is just one of the many factors in attracting alumnae's financial support. In this way, the recommendation would not be reasonable.

With both surveys in question, it would be useful to find out if the opinions of most faculty members are less important than either those of the student respondents or those of the alumnae respondents. However, the author provides no evidence in this regard. We do not know the number of faculty members who attended the meeting, but it could be that the survey involving faculty members had a large and possibly representative sample. The faculty members are also key stakeholders of the college. They may have a better understanding of its application and future enrollments and care about it as much as or even more than students and alumnae. Also, faculty morale that arises from a co-ed policy may affect how alumnae will make financial contributions to the college. Enhanced faculty morale may result in improved instruction which may in turn boost morale among students, particularly among the largest contributors, who could continue to donate large sums to the college. If this should be true, the assumption about the relative importance of faculty members' opinions would be unwarranted and the argument would be gratuitous. Therefore, without taking into account the opinions of most faculty members, the author cannot justify the recommendation that Grove College preserve its tradition of admitting no male students.

To conclude, we must have answers to the questions raised by the argument in favor of not changing Grove College's female-only status. If the author can provide more accurate data from the surveys, showing majorities of respondents in both categories leaning against the decision to change the school status, then there would be a stronger case for the argument. However, unless such data is offered, it remains highly suspect.

122. Increased demand for heating oil and investment in Consolidated (Questions to Be Answered)

Predicting an increased demand for heating oil, the author recommends that a client invest in Consolidated Industries, a home heating oil seller. To justify the recommendation, the letter states that the northeastern United States has always used oil as the primary fuel for heating, and that climate forecasters at Waymarsh University have predicted a cold weather trend, based on 90 days of below-average temperatures last year, which will continue for years into the future. It also notes that a large number of new homes have been constructed in the past year. However, we must have answers to certain questions before we determine whether the recommendation and its argument are sound.

We must ask whether homeowners may use any alternative heating sources instead of oil, and whether this competition would affect the demand for heating oil. The author assumes that because oil has been the traditional choice of fuel for heating, it will remain so in the future. However, various other options may become more popular in the future for various reasons. For example, the push for green energy alternatives could make oil fall out of popularity, or a newer and cheaper source of energy may be discovered that would render oil obsolete. If this is the case, oil is unlikely to remain the main heating fuel. The letter also points out that many new homes have been constructed in the region in the past year. However, there is no information about the number of new homes built and how many of them will use oil as their major fuel for heating. If few of them are sold and occupied, few of them rely on oil for heating, or they are better insulated, the prediction of a growing demand for heating oil would be unjustified. Unless there is relevant evidence, the author cannot confidently claim that oil will remain the main heating fuel in the future, rendering the prediction of an increasing demand for heating oil unreasonable and the argument for investment in Consolidated implausible.

We should also consider the potential that the climate prediction will hold true for as long as the forecasters have claimed. The letter suggests that the climate trends will continue. However, the author provides no evidence to substantiate this. The trend in the past year could have been an aberration and may not continue, not to mention the likelihood that ninety days of below-average temperatures last year did not require more heating oil than in other years. Also, there is no guarantee that the prediction of forecasters would be accurate. With the onset of climate change, there may be a chance that the cold weather periods will shorten significantly in the near future, leading to a decrease in the demand for heating systems of all kinds. Even assuming that the weather pattern will last for as long as the forecasters have claimed, there may not be an increasing demand for heating oil because it may have become so expensive at some point that people will switch to other means of heating. There is even the possibility that some people, especially old people, will leave this part of the country for the south during winters, decreasing the need for heating oil. Even if there is a rising demand for heating oil in this region, the demand for heating oil in other parts of the country may decrease. Any of the scenarios, if true, would make the recommendation of investment in Consolidated unconvincing.

Even granting the two previous points, we wonder whether Consolidated is the only major retailer in this market worth investing in. It is likely that Consolidated does not have a track record of success in its business operations. It is also likely that even if the retail sale of home heating oil is one of its major business operations, it is not profitable, since its business scale is too small, its operating costs are enormous, and its stores are few and have inconvenient locations. Besides, there may be some other companies that do as well as or even better than Consolidated in the same industry, but the author makes no mention of them, or at least does not give reasons for them not being worthy investments. Even if Consolidated has been successful in its retail sale of home heating oil, there may be better investment opportunities in other industries. Should this be the case, the argument for investment in Consolidated would fall apart.

To conclude, the assumptions on which the argument is based are not warranted. In this case, there is a chance that investors would be placing their money in a dying industry, or at the very least in a single company when other options are available but unmentioned. Unless we have answers to the questions noted above, we cannot fully evaluate the recommendation and its argument.

123. More healthful lifestyles in Benton (Questions to Be Answered)

The author predicts that the new lifestyles adopted by the citizens of Benton City will help them soon keep its obesity rate far below the national average. To justify the prediction, the article cites a survey in which the citizens' eating habits align more closely with government nutritional recommendations than ten years before. It also cites a fourfold increase in the sale of foods that contain kiran, which has been shown by studies to reduce cholesterol, and a decrease in the sales of sulia, a food which the healthiest citizens tend to avoid. However, to better assess the prediction, we need answers to certain questions.

First, we must find out whether the survey respondents are representative of the whole population of Benton. Specifically, we would benefit from having more information about the sample, such as the number of people and demographics of the citizens surveyed, the specific questions asked, and how they have been asked. Without relevant information, it is possible that the only people questioned were those that already fell into the healthiest portion of the populace. This could be a very small sample and an anomaly, whereas most citizens keep the lifestyle ten years before. It is also possible that the respondents misrepresented their lifestyles simply to seem health conscious, further skewing the results. The assumption about the representativeness of the survey respondents underlies the claim that the citizens of Benton have become more health-oriented. However, unless the survey is valid, reliable, and representative, the claim could not be substantiated. Even if the claim is justified, there is no guarantee that the obesity rate in the city will be far below the national average shortly, because there is no evidence given that merely healthier eating habits of Benton residents will contribute to a significant drop in its obesity rate. In this case, the prediction would be unreasonable.

Even granting that the survey was properly administered, this raises the question of whether following the government recommendations more closely is the same as living a healthier lifestyle. After all, government recommendations usually only cover the bare minimum requirements; therefore, there is the possibility that these health recommendations are for people living at the poverty level. If this is true, the recommendations as a metric may be inadequate for measuring the relative healthiness of an entire populace. Perhaps the citizens' dietary habits are less wholesome today than ten years before. Thus, the author has yet to establish the connection between aligning more with the government recommendations and adopting a more healthful lifestyle. Unless these recommendations are better explained, how closely the citizens of Benton follow them is irrelevant to this argument. Even if following the government recommendations more closely indicates a healthier lifestyle, this does not necessarily mean that the obesity rate in the city will be much lower than the national average shortly, because a healthier lifestyle today may be still unwholesome if the original one was very unhealthy. In that event, the prediction would be unfounded.

Finally, we wonder whether increased consumption of kiran and decreased consumption of sulia are proof of a healthier lifestyle. However, the article lacks data in this regard. It could be the case that the residents of Benton do not have high cholesterol levels in their blood and therefore do not need to consume kiran. Even if consumption of kiran may make them healthier, there is no guarantee that a fourfold increase will be adequate, since the amount could have been very small to begin with. Also, the fact that the healthiest citizens tend to avoid sulia does not necessarily mean that it is unhealthy; it could be that it simply is not palatable. Should this be true, the assumption about kiran and sulia would be gratuitous. Even if more consumption of kiran and less consumption of sulia indicate a more healthful lifestyle, kiran and sulia are only two foods and by no means the only sources of nutrition the citizens eat. It could also be the case that the citizens now have a less healthy lifestyle overall because they drink or eat much more unhealthy food and exercise much less than before. Any of the scenarios, if true, would undermine the claim that the people of Benton have followed more wholesome lifestyles and the prediction that Benton residents' obesity rate will be far below the national average in a short time because of their more healthful lifestyles. Without further information about the two particular foods, their consumption would be irrelevant.

In conclusion, if the prediction made by the article is to be taken as valid, there must first be more specific details about the survey of dietary habits, particularly regarding the sample. Furthermore, there should be more information about the government guidelines for nutritional eating, such as whom the guidelines are meant for and what standard of health they are designed to meet. Lastly, there needs to be evidence that kiran and sulia have been significant staples in the diets of Benton citizens, that they have the stated effects on consumers' nutritional health and that there is a link between healthier lifestyles and lower obesity rate.

124. Should Bargain Brand Cereals start selling other low-priced foods? (Questions to Be Answered)

The author recommends that Bargain Brand Cereals, a company that sells very low-priced cereal, start selling other low-priced foods in light of its success with selling cereal. To justify the recommendation, the memo states that Bargain Brand has been able to outperform its competitors and maintain profits despite keeping its prices constant while the competitors have lowered prices. Yet we must have answers to some questions before we determine whether Bargain Brand's board of directors should implement the proposed plan.

While Bargain Brand's success is commendable, the exact reasons for it are not clearly described by this memo. Thus, the question arises of whether it was the competitively low prices at which it sold its cereal or some other reason that attracted consumers to its brand. It is possible that it has superior quality control, wider distribution, or better after-sales service. Even if its low prices drew customers away from its competitors, there is no guarantee that this policy will continue to be effective as its competitors introduce their special bargain brands. Knowing this is important to the memo's suggestion, because if the brand's popularity is based on some other factor, the recommendation that it should expand into other low-priced food products would be unreasonable. Therefore, information about reasons for Bargain Brand's success would go a long way toward helping us evaluate the author's recommendation.

Next, there is the question regarding Bargain Brand's continued success and sustainability, or to be more precise: Can Bargain Brand maintain low prices on other products as it has with its first product? It is not known how exactly Bargain Brand has been able to sell its first product at prices lower than other companies; perhaps it is a result of good relationships with suppliers, among other things. However, it is possible that the same strategy will not be as effective with other foods, perhaps because of the cost from suppliers, or even the perceived value of certain foods. For example, selling cereal, a staple, cheap may not affect its perceived quality in the eyes of consumers so much as that of other foods, such as meat or fruit. It is also possible that as the top-selling companies further lower their prices, the customers would return to their products. Should Bargain Brand begin facing heavy competition when selling new food products, it may no longer be able to avoid raising prices in order to maintain a competitive edge, decreasing its sales and making its profits diminish even further. In such scenarios, its move may be warrantless. Without information about sustainability of the low-pricing strategy for its line of other products, we cannot fully evaluate the recommendation.

Finally, the memo's implication of Bargain Brand's success with cereal as a reason for expansion leaves one wondering if expansion is a necessary move for the company to make. The author assumes that expansion into other low-priced food products is the only route to growing the company. However, the author provides no evidence to substantiate this. It is possible that Bargain Brand is making a profit that may be small and dwindling. It is also possible that the company can reap large profits without ever expanding outside its area of expertise. It is even possible that other barriers such as regional laws and regulations make it almost impossible to enter other markets. In such scenarios, it stands to reason that unless there is a present need to add new foods to its product line, doing so is not a priority. Even assuming this strategy is the only viable one, there is no guarantee that the company will succeed by marketing other low-priced food products as soon as possible. It may take a long time to establish the company and get ready for such an option. Should this be true, the recommendation would be hardly reasonable. Absent information about the necessity of the company's move, we simply cannot say for certain.

To conclude, Bargain Brand's board of directors needs answers to certain questions before considering the recommendation honestly. To wit, they must know the exact reasons for Bargain Brand's competitive success and profits, as well as whether this strategy is sustainable for not only its current product, but also those they wish to expand into. Furthermore, they must identify a specific motivating factor for expanding into other markets in order to justify the cost and risk of implementing this plan.

125. Should Bargain Brand Cereals start selling other low-priced foods? (Assumptions)

The author recommends that Bargain Brand Cereals, a company that sells very low-priced cereal, start selling other low-priced foods in light of its success with selling cereal. To justify the recommendation, the memo states that Bargain Brand has been able to outperform its competitors and maintain profits despite keeping its prices constant while the competitors have lowered prices. However, the argument is full of assumptions and loopholes that we must scrutinize to ascertain its validity.

The author assumes that Bargain Brand's low prices were the most significant reason which attracted customers. Yet there is no evidence that this is the case. It is possible that some other factors were responsible for its attraction, such as superior quality control or wider distribution. It is also possible that its after-sales service has been better. Perhaps it has had a greater variety of products. Or perhaps it has been advertising heavily. Any of the scenarios, if true, would render the assumption unwarranted. In that event, the recommendation that supports utilizing the same strategy of low pricing to expand into other food products as soon as possible may not result in the same competitive advantages but may lead to disastrous failures, rendering the argument unconvincing. Even if Bargain Brand's low prices drew customers away from its competitors, there is no guarantee that this policy will continue to be effective as its competitors introduce their special bargain brands. In this case, the assumption about the role of low prices in its attraction would be unwarranted and the argument undermined.

The author also implies that because Bargain Brand's competitors were unable to compete in the past, Bargain Brand will be able to outcompete them in the future. It is not impossible, but the memo does not provide enough proof to make this implication a certainty. The company could be making a profit that is small and dwindling, indicating its inability to sustain the competition. Even if it has been more successful than its rivals in the past year, one year could be too short to establish that it has outperformed its rivals. There is no guarantee that it will continue to succeed, given the volatile market. It could be that as the top-selling companies further lower their prices, the customers would return to their products. Should Bargain Brand begin facing heavy competition when selling new food products, it may no longer be able to avoid raising prices in order to maintain a competitive edge, decreasing its sales and making its profits diminish even further. If this should be true, the assumption that Bargain Brand will continue to beat its rivals would prove unwarranted and the argument in favor of expanding into other products as soon as possible would fall apart.

Finally, the author suggests that Bargain Brand will be able to implement its lower-price policy when selling other food products. However, this could be a risky attempt, because the author does not give any information about which low-priced foods Bargain Brand plans to expand into, nor if these foods will cost more or less than cereal. It could be that unlike cereal, a staple, other low-priced products take much longer and much more money to promote. Thus, there is a chance that the cost of expanding into other foods may hurt the company's ability to maintain low prices, which supposedly is its main selling point, leading to an overall decrease in sales and profits. There is also a chance that other barriers such as regional laws and regulations will make it almost impossible to enter other markets. There is even a chance that the plan will have worse consequences if implemented too soon. In such scenarios, the assumption would not be justified, and the argument would be implausible.

To summarize, the memo makes a number of assumptions that could contribute to financial disaster for Bargain Brand, should they prove to be false. We do not know what specific factor drew customers to the company's cereal in the first place, nor do we have enough information to determine if Bargain Brand will be able to maintain competitively low prices while netting profits, particularly when it expands into other foods.

126. Increased demand for heating oil and investment in Consolidated (Questions to Be Answered)

Predicting an increased demand for heating oil, the author recommends that a client invest in Consolidated Industries, a home heating oil seller. To justify the recommendation, the letter states that the northeastern United States has always used oil as fuel for heating, and that local weather forecasters have predicted a cold weather trend, based on twenty days of below-average temperatures last year, which will continue for years into the future. It also notes that a large number of new homes have been constructed in the past year. However, we must have answers to certain questions before we determine the soundness of the recommendation and its argument.

We must ask whether homeowners may use any alternative heating sources instead of oil, and whether this competition would affect the demand for heating oil. The author assumes that because oil has been the traditional choice of fuel for heating, it will remain so in the future. However, various other options may become more popular in the future for various reasons. For example, the push for green energy alternatives could make oil fall out of popularity, or a newer and cheaper source of energy may be discovered that would render oil obsolete. If this should be the case, the prediction of a growing demand for heating oil would be unjustified, not to mention the possibility of a large growth. Moreover, we need to consider whether new homes have the potential to be future heating oil users. The article points out that many new homes have been built in the region in the past year. However, there is no detailed information about the number of new homes built. It is possible that the number is indeed great, but few will be occupied such that there is no need for heating of any kind. It is also possible that the houses are better-insulated or few of them rely on oil for heating. While new homes may become future users of heating oil, the article does not specifically state that these houses have been built with heating systems that use oil as fuel. It may be the case that these houses will utilize electric heating or water radiators instead. If they are built with heating systems that do use heating oil, then this would lend support to the prediction that heating oil will experience an increased demand. Without more information about the designs of these houses, it is impossible to say for certain.

We should also investigate whether the trend in the past year will continue. The article notes that the region had only twenty days of below-average temperatures in the past year. However, there is no detailed information about how much the residents needed heating oil. It is likely that they needed little heating of any kind. Even if they needed some heating, they may have used no oil as fuel. Even assuming they needed much heating oil, the trend in the past year could have been an aberration and may not continue. Besides, the local weather forecasters' prediction could be inaccurate. With the onset of climate change, there may be a chance that the cold weather periods will shorten significantly in the near future. Even assuming that the climate prediction will hold true for as long as the forecasters have claimed, there may not be an increasing demand for heating oil because it may have become so expensive at some point that people will switch to other means of heating. There is even the possibility that some people, especially old people, will leave this part of the country for the south during winters, decreasing the need for heating oil. Even if there is a rising demand for heating oil in this region, the demand for heating oil in other parts of the country may decrease. Any of the scenarios, if true, would make the prediction of a large increase in the demand for heating oil unjustified and the recommendation of investment in Consolidated unconvincing. Without relevant data, we cannot properly evaluate the recommendation and its argument.

Even granting the two previous points, we wonder whether Consolidated is the only major retailer in this market worth investing in. It is likely that Consolidated does not have a track record of success in its business operations. It is also likely that even if the retail sale of home heating oil is one of its major business operations, it is not profitable, since its business scale is too small, its operating costs are enormous, and its stores are few and have inconvenient locations. Besides, there may be some other companies that do as well as or even better than Consolidated in the same industry, but the author makes no mention of them, or at least does not give reasons for them not being worthy investments. Even if Consolidated has been successful in its retail sale of home heating oil, there may be better investment opportunities in other industries. Should this be the case, the argument for investment in Consolidated would fall apart.

To conclude, the assumptions on which the argument is based are not warranted. In this case, there is a chance that investors would be placing their money in a dying industry, or at the very least in a single company when other options are available but unmentioned. Unless we have answers to the questions noted above, we cannot fully assess the recommendation and its argument.

127. Increased demand for heating oil and investment in Consolidated (Specific Evidence)

Predicting an increased demand for heating oil, the author recommends that a client invest in Consolidated Industries, a home heating oil seller. To justify the recommendation, the letter states that the northeastern United States has always used oil as fuel for heating, and that local weather forecasters have predicted a cold weather trend, based on twenty days of below-average temperatures last year, which will continue for years into the future. It also notes that a large number of new homes have been constructed in the past year. However, we must have additional evidence before we determine the soundness of the recommendation and its argument.

We must have evidence regarding whether homeowners may use any alternative heating sources instead of oil, and whether this competition would affect the demand for heating oil. The author assumes that because oil has been the traditional choice of fuel for heating, it will remain so in the future. However, various other options may become more popular in the future for various reasons. For example, the push for green energy alternatives could make oil fall out of popularity, or a newer and cheaper source of energy may be discovered that would render oil obsolete. If this should be the case, the prediction of a growing demand for heating oil would be unjustified. Moreover, we need to consider whether new homes have the potential to be future heating oil users. The article points out that many new homes have been built in the region in the past year. However, there is no detailed information about the number of new homes built. It is possible that the number is indeed great, but few will be occupied such that there is no need for heating of any kind.

It is also possible that the houses are better-insulated or few of them rely on oil for heating. While new homes may become future users of heating oil, the article does not specifically state that these houses have been built with heating systems that use oil as fuel. It may be the case that these houses will utilize electric heating or water radiators instead. If they are built with heating systems that do use heating oil, then this would lend support to the prediction that heating oil will experience an increased demand. Without more information about the designs of these houses, it is impossible to say for certain.

We should also have evidence regarding whether the trend in the past year will continue. The article notes that the region had only twenty days of below-average temperatures in the past year. However, there is no detailed information about how much the residents needed heating oil. It is likely that they needed little heating of any kind. Even if they needed some heating, they may have used no oil as fuel. Even assuming they needed much heating oil, the trend in the past year could have been an aberration and may not continue. Besides, the local weather forecasters' prediction could be inaccurate. With the onset of climate change, there may be a chance that the cold weather periods will shorten significantly in the near future. Even assuming that the climate prediction will hold true for as long as the forecasters have claimed, there may not be an increasing demand for heating oil because it may have become so expensive at some point that people will switch to other means of heating. There is even the possibility that some people, especially old people, will leave this part of the country for the south during winters, decreasing the need for heating oil. Even if there is a rising demand for heating oil in this region, the demand for heating oil in other parts of the country may decrease. Any of the scenarios, if true, would make the prediction of an increase in the demand for heating oil unjustified and the recommendation of investment in Consolidated unconvincing. Without relevant data, we cannot properly evaluate the recommendation and its argument.

Even granting the two previous points, we need evidence regarding whether Consolidated is the only major retailer in this market worth investing in. It is likely that Consolidated does not have a track record of success in its business operations. It is also likely that even if the retail sale of home heating oil is one of its major business operations, it is not profitable, since its business scale is too small, its operating costs are enormous, and its stores are few and have inconvenient locations. Besides, there may be some other companies that do as well as or even better than Consolidated in the same industry, but the author makes no mention of them, or at least does not give reasons for them not being worthy investments. Even if Consolidated has been successful in its retail sale of home heating oil, there may be better investment opportunities in other industries. Should this be the case, the argument for investment in Consolidated would fall apart.

To conclude, the assumptions on which the argument is based are not warranted. In this case, there is a chance that investors would be placing their money in a dying industry, or at the very least in a single company when other options are available but unmentioned. Unless we have additional evidence, we cannot fully assess the argument.

128. Should Grove College remain all-female? (Questions to Be Answered)

The author argues that Grove College, an all-female institution, should not convert itself into a co-ed institution in order to boost student morale and secure continued financial support from alumnae. To support the argument, the article cites a survey of students in which 80 percent of the respondents favored keeping the college all-female, and an alumnae survey pointing to a majority view of its respondents in favor of preserving the status quo. However, to better assess the recommendation, we need answers to some key questions.

Regarding the student survey, we wonder whether the respondents represent a majority of all the college's students. However, the author does not offer any data to back it up. 80% of the respondents may have been an insignificant number. It is possible that only a small percentage of students filled out the survey, specifically new students that took a keen interest in the college's history. It is also possible that the survey was administered after the college's students were educated about its tradition of all-female education. If this should be the case, then this survey would not be a very useful metric for measuring total student morale. Even if the survey is valid and reliable, there is no guarantee that admitting only female students will boost morale among students, since it is impossible to determine how a co-ed policy would impact the morale of all students before Grove adopts the policy and analyzes the morale of its male students as well as that of its female students. In that event, the recommendation that the college preserve its female-only status would be unfounded.

On a similar note, we also want to know whether the alumnae survey is a reliable one. Likewise, the author makes no mention of the specific number of people questioned nor the number of respondents compared to all the alumnae. More than half of the respondents could have been a very small number. The sample could have been a tiny one, with only a few respondents who happened to place a great value on the college's long tradition of all-female education. It could also have consisted mostly of alumnae who have made no or small donations to the college. If the alumnae had responded as students and later responded as alumnae, it would be interesting to see if they kept their answers consistent on the surveys or their opinions changed over time. If their answers were inconsistent, the surveys could not have been valid or reliable. Should this be the case, assuming that the respondents are representative of the entire body of alumnae could lead to undesirable consequences, for example, alienating alumnae whose financial support most likely has far greater implications for the college, viz. those who have made the largest contributions. Even if the survey is reliable and valid and the assumption is substantiated, there is no guarantee that the college can persuade its alumnae to contribute financially to it, because student morale is just one of the many factors in attracting alumnae's financial support. In this way, the recommendation would not be reasonable.

With both surveys in question, it would be useful to find out if the opinions of most faculty members are less important than either those of the student respondents or those of the alumnae respondents. However, the author provides no evidence in this regard. We do not know the number of faculty members who attended the meeting, but it could be that the survey involving faculty members had a large and possibly representative sample. The faculty members are also key stakeholders of the college. They may have a better understanding of its application and future enrollments and care about it as much as or even more than students and alumnae. Also, faculty morale that arises from a co-ed policy may affect how alumnae will make financial contributions to the college. Enhanced faculty morale may result in improved instruction which may in turn boost morale among students, particularly among the largest contributors, who could continue to donate large sums to the college. If this should be true, the assumption about the relative importance of faculty members' opinions would be unwarranted and the argument would be gratuitous. Therefore, without taking into account the opinions of most faculty members, the author cannot justify the recommendation that Grove College preserve its tradition of admitting no male students.

To conclude, we must have answers to the questions raised by the argument in favor of not changing Grove College's female-only status. If the author can provide more accurate data from the surveys, showing majorities of respondents in both categories leaning against the decision to change the school status, then there would be a stronger case for the argument. However, unless such data is offered, it remains highly suspect.

129. Should <u>Top Dog</u> stores advertise in Exotic Pets Monthly? (Assumptions)

The author recommends that Top Dog Pet Stores begin placing ads in the magazine Exotic Pets Monthly. To justify the recommendation, the memo cites another pet store, Fish Emporium, as an example, stating that five years prior, its sales increased by fifteen percent following its ads in the magazine. It also mentions that the Fish Emporium stores in Gulf City, the city in which Top Dog is based, saw a sales increase of even more than fifteen percent. However, the author makes too many assumptions to warrant the notion that placing ads in the magazine will cease the decline in sales of Top Dog and lead to an increase in its profits.

The author implies that between Fish Emporium and Top Dog there is an equivalency in ways that might affect the impact of advertising. However, we have almost no details about the products these companies sell, nor do we know whether there are any differences in their management decisions or costs of operation. If the assumption is correct, and the two companies are similar in these ways, then the plan stands a much better chance of succeeding; if not, then there is a chance that these differing factors could make any amount of advertising irrelevant. For example, advertising may have a great impact on Fish Emporium's customers, whereas it may have a negligible effect on Top

Dog's because they sell different products. Similarly, it may be that Exotic Pets Monthly used to be very popular when it carried Fish Emporium's ads, whereas it is seldom read today. Any such differences between the two companies would render the assumption about their comparability unwarranted. Unless there is evidence that the two companies are sufficiently alike in ways that may affect the impact of ads, the author cannot justifiably claim that Top Dog should follow Fish Emporium's example in placing ads.

Even granting that the two companies are similar, the author also assumes that Fish Emporium has succeeded as a result of the advertising and location. However, the author offers no evidence to substantiate this. Just because it experienced a sales increase of fifteen percent overall and of over fifteen percent in Gulf City after its advertising in the magazine does not necessarily mean that merely advertising and location were responsible for the sales increase. A myriad of other factors might explain the overall increase. It is possible that Fish Emporium was becoming popular because it was selling a unique product. It is also possible that at the time, the economy was booming and the demand for Fish Emporium's products increased. Similarly, there may be any number of reasons for the greater increase in Gulf City. It is likely that Gulf City stocked most of the popular product. It is also likely that the magazine that carried the advertising was better received there. It is even likely that its sales employees in Gulf City were much more competent. Any of the scenarios, if true, would cast serious doubt on the assumption about the causal relationship between Fish Emporium's success and its advertising and location. Even if the assumption is justified, this does not necessarily mean Top Dog can achieve the same level of success that Fish Emporium experienced five years ago. There could have been any number of significant market changes since then, such as changing consumer demands or even a decreased readership of Exotic Pets Monthly. This would make any advertising a costly waste of money, as there would be few additional customers as a result of it.

Finally, the author suggests that by taking out ads in the same magazine, Top Dog will be able to stop its sales decline and make a profit again. The author assumes that just because some of Fish Emporium's increased sales took place in Gulf City, Top Dog's location there will have any effect on its sales. We do not know precisely of which products Fish Emporium sold more, nor do we know what products Top Dog sells, so it is unjustifiable to assume that Top Dog will be able to sell any more of its products than it has in the past. Perhaps Top Dog's sales volume in Gulf City has peaked and there would be little further improvement despite advertising. Or perhaps Top Dog's poor sales are attributable to factors, such as incompetent sales employees or after-sales service, that advertising has no effect on. Or perhaps other ways of advertising are more effective and affordable than having the magazine carry its ads. In such scenarios, Top Dog would not benefit from the advertising. Even if Top Dog can succeed after placing the ads, there is no guarantee that the sales increase will be adequate for reversing the lately sales drop and making a profit. It is likely that a sales increase of a little more than fifteen is far from enough for making up for the significant decrease in sales. Should this be true, the assumption would be unwarranted and the argument that supports advertising in the same magazine would be undermined. Profit is a function of revenue and costs. Without an analysis of revenues relative to costs, the author cannot reliably conclude that Top Dog's sales increase will be significant enough to yield a profit.

In conclusion, it is questionable whether taking out ads in Exotic Pets Monthly will positively affect Top Dog's profits. The assumptions that underlie the argument simply ignore too many factors to be valid, such as the differences between Top Dog and Fish Emporium, the changes that may have occurred in the five years since Fish Emporium's success, and the consumer preferences in Gulf City.

130. Should Top Dog stores advertise in Exotic Pets Monthly? (Specific Evidence)

The author recommends that Top Dog Pet Stores begin placing ads in the magazine Exotic Pets Monthly. To justify the recommendation, the memo cites another pet store, Fish Emporium, as an example, stating that five years prior, its sales increased by fifteen percent following its ads in the magazine. It also mentions that the Fish Emporium stores in Gulf City, the city in which Top Dog is based, saw a sales increase of even more than fifteen percent. However, there is a lack of evidence to support the idea that placing ads in the magazine will cease the decline in sales of Top Dog and lead to an increase in its profits.

The author must provide evidence that Fish Emporium and Top Dog are essentially similar so that they would be equally affected by the same kind of advertising. However, we have almost no details about the products these companies sell, nor do we know whether there are any differences in their management decisions or costs of operation. If the assumption is correct, and the two companies are similar in these ways, then the plan stands a much better chance of succeeding; if not, then there is a chance that these differing factors could make any amount of advertising irrelevant. For example, advertising may have a great impact on Fish Emporium's customers whereas it may have a negligible effect on Top Dog's because they sell different products. Similarly, it may be that Exotic Pets Monthly used to be very popular when it carried Fish Emporium's ads whereas it is seldom read today. Any such differences between the two companies would render the assumption about their comparability unwarranted. Unless there is evidence that the two companies are sufficiently alike in ways that may affect the impact of ads, the author cannot justifiably claim that Top Dog should follow Fish Emporium's example in placing ads.

Even granting that the two companies are similar, the author should offer evidence that Fish Emporium has succeeded as a result of the advertising and location. However, we have no data in this regard. Just because it experienced a sales increase of fifteen percent overall and of over fifteen percent in Gulf City after its advertising in the magazine does not necessarily mean that merely advertising and location were responsible for the sales increase. A myriad of other factors might explain the overall increase. It is possible that Fish Emporium was becoming popular because it was selling a unique product. It is also possible that at the time, the economy was booming and the demand for Fish Emporium's products increased. Similarly, there may be any number of reasons for the greater increase in Gulf City. It is likely that Gulf City stocked most of the popular product. It is also likely that the magazine that carried the advertising was better received there. It is even likely that its sales employees in Gulf City were much more competent. Any of the scenarios, if true, would cast serious doubt on the assumption about the causal relationship between Fish Emporium's success and its advertising and location. Even if the assumption is justified, this does not necessarily mean Top Dog can achieve the same level of success that Fish Emporium experienced five years ago. There could have been any number of significant market changes since then, such as changing consumer demands or even a decreased readership of Exotic Pets Monthly. This would make any advertising a costly waste of money, as there would be few additional customers as a result of it.

Finally, the author needs to substantiate the claim regarding the part that advertising and Gulf City may play in stopping Top Dog's sales decline and enabling it to make a profit again. The author assumes that just because some of Fish Emporium's increased sales took place in Gulf City, Top Dog's location there will have any effect on its sales. We do not know precisely of which products Fish Emporium sold more, nor do we know what products Top Dog sells, so it is unjustifiable to assume that Top Dog will be able to sell any more of its products than it has in the past. Perhaps Top Dog's sales volume in Gulf City has peaked and there would be little further improvement despite advertising. Or perhaps Top Dog's poor sales are attributable to factors such as incompetent sales employees or after-sales service that advertising has no effect on. Or perhaps other ways of advertising are more effective and affordable than having the magazine carry its ads. In such scenarios, Top Dog would not benefit from the advertising. Even if Top Dog can succeed after placing the ads, there is no guarantee that the sales increase will be adequate for reversing the lately sales drop and making a profit. It is likely that a sales increase of a little more than fifteen is far from enough for making up for the significant decrease in sales. Should this be true, the assumption would be unwarranted and the argument that supports advertising in the same magazine would be undermined. Profit is a function of revenue and costs. Without an analysis of revenues relative to costs, the author cannot reliably conclude that Top Dog's sales increase will be significant enough to yield a profit.

In conclusion, the memo does not offer enough evidence to support the recommendation that Top Dog start advertising in Exotic Pets Monthly. The author must establish a sufficient similarity between Top Dog and Fish Emporium, show that no serious market changes have occurred in the five years since Fish Emporium's success, and provide evidence that being based in Gulf City will somehow contribute to Top Dog's more sales.

131. Reducing Balmer Island moped accidents by learning from Torseau (Questions to Be Answered)

The author suggests that in order to decrease the number of moped accidents during the summer months by 50 percent on Balmer Island, it place a limit on the number of mopeds that each moped rental company can rent out per day during the summer season, specifically from 50 to 30. To justify the suggestion, the letter presents the neighboring island of Torseau as an example of having successfully implemented the policy, as it was able to achieve the same reduction in moped accidents after taking the course of action. However, we must have answers to certain questions before we determine whether the same result would indeed occur if Balmer Island places its own caps.

We want to know whether the use of mopeds on Balmer during the summer season is responsible for the moped-pedestrian accidents and whether reducing the number of moped rentals will decrease the number of accidents. However, the author offers no information in this regard. The letter simply states that the population increases to a huge number on Balmer during the summer months and that there are accidents involving mopeds and pedestrians. Yet we do not know if other factors, such as malfunctioning traffic lights, unclear road signs, alcohol or drug abuse, lack of road maintenance and lack of convenient sidewalks, contribute to these accidents. If they do, the assumption would be unwarranted. Without ruling out these and other alternative possibilities, the author cannot confidently claim that decreasing the number of moped rentals at any given time will decrease the number of accidents. Nor do we know Balmer's original population. If we are speaking of an increase of only a few hundred people, the author cannot reliably conclude that moped accidents will rise considerably. Similarly, we just do not know what portion of the new people are moped operators or pedestrians. If few of them rent a moped, they may have little impact on the number of moped accidents. Also, merely enforcing limits on moped rentals may be ineffective. The author needs to assure us that other conditions in Balmer that serve to increase the accident rate will not change. For example, people may buy mopeds instead of renting them in response to the enforcement of moped rentals, or pedestrians may increase in large numbers. Either scenario might lead to a higher rate of moped accidents. Unless there is relevant evidence, it is unfair to assume that use of mopeds has contributed to moped-pedestrian accidents in Balmer and restricting the number of moped rentals will attain the desired reduction in accidents.

We also wonder whether success of a policy on moped rentals on Torseau is proof that such a policy will be effective on Balmer as well. However, the two places may be too different from each other to justify implementing the same policy. We do not know of many circumstances that might have played a role in the accidents on Torseau. For example, we do not have information on the weather and population of Torseau or what the moped rental limits were in that area last year. It is likely that Torseau had very fine weather and experienced no population increase. It could very well be the case that Torseau receives comparatively few visitors during summertime relative to their overall population, thus decreasing the number of potential accidents and easily meeting the statistical requirement of a 50 percent reduction. It is also likely that few people rented mopeds last year. It is even likely that it enforced higher moped rental standards. For example, outlets might have been only allowed to rent newer mopeds to their patrons. Therefore, factors other than limits on the number of moped rentals might have contributed to its fifty percent decrease in moped accidents. Balmer, with its population possibly exploding during the summer months and possibly different causes of moped accidents, could find it difficult to replicate the results. Even if they have the same reasons for moped accidents and enforce similar measures, there is no guarantee that Balmer will be able to enforce them as effectively as Torseau has done. For example, people on Torseau may prefer to rent mopeds, whereas people on Balmer may prefer to own mopeds. Should this be the case, the prediction would prove unjustified. Unless there is evidence that the two islands are similar enough to warrant the implementation of the same policy, the author cannot reliably predict that one island's success in decreasing moped accidents will automatically carry over to the other.

Of course, we need the answer to whether alternative solutions exist aside from simply limiting the number of rentable mopeds. Even if Balmer enforces similar restrictions on moped rentals, there is no guarantee that the overall number of moped rentals will drop, because the companies could satisfy the demand by opening more rental shops instead of supplying more rental mopeds at each shop. In this case, the assumption that restricting the number of moped rentals is the only course of action proves gratuitous. It is likely that alternative solutions exist and can be as effective or even more effective. Driver safety awareness programs could be released before and during the summer season; certain lanes could be designated as moped lanes for the duration of the summer months. There is even the possibility of simply reducing the speed limit so that riders would be forced to slow down. Many other alternatives could be suggested, ones that would help reduce moped accidents and allow the moped rental companies to continue to do business and make profits during peak travel months. Should this be true, the argument would be weakened. Without accounting for alternative solutions, the author cannot reasonably claim that limiting the number of rental mopeds is the only viable policy.

In conclusion, we need more information about the example of Torseau to see if the moped rental cap would be as effective on Balmer. There is a possibility that other factors such as a difference in population and other extenuating circumstances have been responsible for the decrease in accidents on Torseau. It is also important to consider other means of reducing accidents, ones that would not negatively impact the moped businesses on Balmer that probably rely on summer tourism for most of their income. Without answers to relevant questions, we cannot fully assess the argument.

132. Should High-intensity lighting be installed in Amburg? (Questions to Be Answered)

Relying on the assumption that the city of Belleville has had success in reducing vandalism via high-intensity lighting in its business district and on the fact that Amburg also has a problem with vandalism in its business district, the author recommends that Amburg have a similar addition of high-intensity lighting with the money currently used on bicycle patrols to reduce crime. To assess the recommendation properly, we must have answers to certain questions about the effect of high-intensity lighting on vandalism in Belleville and on crimes in Amburg and about the cost of implementing the course of action. The answers may either weaken or strengthen the claim that high-intensity lighting will be effective.

We must have the answer to whether high-intensity lighting is effective in reducing vandalism in Belleville. The article mentions that almost immediately after Belleville installed high-intensity lighting in its central business district last October, vandalism dropped. The author assumes that this is an indication that high-intensity lighting alone was responsible for the decrease in vandalism. However, the author provides no evidence to substantiate this. It is likely that cameras had just been installed to record vandalism. It is also likely that a law that metes out harsh punishment to vandalism had been enacted at the same time. It is even likely that police patrols had just been instituted there. Any of the scenarios, if true, would cast serious doubt on the assumption that high-intensity lighting only contributed to the decrease in vandalism. Even if it was responsible for the drop in vandalism, since the author gives no statistics about the amount of vandalism decline, it could be that the decline was negligible. Even assuming that the decline was significant, it is possible that the effect of high-intensity lighting may not last. Perhaps since the initial drop, the perpetrators of vandalism have become habituated to the lighting and are no longer discouraged from committing crime by it. In this way, the recommendation of installing it throughout Amburg to reduce crime considerably would be unfounded.

We should also have the answer to whether high-intensity lighting will be effective in Amburg. High-intensity lighting may have been efficacious in curbing vandalism in Belleville, but this does not necessarily mean it would carry the intended result in Amburg. It is likely that the people behind vandalism in Belleville were deterred by police patrols on bicycles rather than by high-intensity lighting. If Amburg's citizens are not deterred by a police presence in the area, it is possible that the addition of this lighting will not deter them. It is also possible that the bicycle patrols were instituted too recently in Amburg for their effects to be observed. It is even possible that the bicycle patrols have been effective in Amburg, but the incidence of vandalism remains unchanged because at the same time, other factors have been contributing to an increase in the rate of vandalism. Should this be the case, the assumption that Belleville and Amburg are similar enough to justify the same course of action would be groundless, rendering the recommendation invalid. Even if high-intensity lighting is good at controlling vandalism in Amburg, this does not necessarily mean that it is the ideal way to tackle other crimes. Similarly, other crimes may be best deterred by a police presence. If this should be true, the assumption that just because high-intensity lighting is effective at combating vandalism, it is effective at tackling other crimes, would be gratuitous and the prediction of its effect on considerably reducing crime rates in Amburg would be unreasonable.

Even granting that high-intensity lighting is a method superior to bicycle patrols, we need the answer to whether the money being used to pay for the bicycle patrols will be sufficient to cover the costs of installing enough lights to effectively dissuade criminal activity. If the cost of installing the high-intensity lights is significantly more than paying for bicycle patrols, thus leading to poor implementation, then there would not be much of a chance of the plan being very effective. Should this be true, the recommendation is unlikely to have the predicted result and would not be plausible. Also, the author assumes that there are but two options, either high-intensity lighting or bicycle patrols, for reducing crime in Amburg. However, there are other equally efficacious and affordable means. For example, social programs may educate young people about vandalism and other crimes and help reduce crime rates among them. In that event, the recommendation of installing high-intensity lighting throughout Amburg to reduce crime rates substantially could lead to enormous amounts of wasted money.

If the two cities' situations are completely different, the argument will not be tenable. However, if the sources of vandalism are similar and comparable measures were previously taken in Belleville, installing high-intensity lighting will be a reasonable course of action for Amburg as well. The cost of installation is also a significant point of contention, since the money to be used to pay for the lights may be much more than that which was used for the bike patrols.

133. Should Acme require all of its employees to take the Easy Read course? (assumptions)

This recommendation from the personnel director to the president of Acme Publishing Company claims that productivity at the company could be improved if all employees were required to take the Easy Read Speed-Reading Course, a three-week seminar. To support the claim, the article states that at another company one graduate of the course was able to read a five-hundred-page report in two hours, and that another graduate went from assistant manager to vice president in less than a year. It also notes that the cost, five-hundred dollars per employee, is not significant in comparison to the potential benefits the course may provide. Yet the argument is rife with assumptions and loopholes that we must scrutinize to determine its soundness.

The author assumes that a link exists between speed reading and improved productivity. However, there is no evidence that this is the case. The article states that the course teaches one to absorb more information each day, but does nothing to support this notion, nor links faster information absorption to the application of such information. It may be the case that employees who can read faster can memorize more quickly but take longer to process that information and thus take no less time to apply it than normal. Without more data, nothing can be said for certain. Besides, the alleged successful experience of the companies should be scrutinized. Since we do not have any information about how reading faster helps with productivity, the employee that read a five-hundred-page report is irrelevant until we know what her purpose for reading was, and how well she applied what she read to her job. As for the employee whose career advanced within a year, we should consider if the promotion was related to the employee's reading ability or was the result of other factors. Perhaps the person was already in line for the promotion. Or perhaps the two employees were already excellent readers before taking the course. Should that be the case, then the Easy Read course may have had no bearing on that promotion. Any of the scenarios, if true, would cast serious doubt on the assumption about the connection between speed reading and increased productivity and on the recommendation of taking the course.

The author also implies that the potential benefits of the course will outweigh the costs to implement it. However, this is not necessarily so. Since the author has yet to establish the connection between speed reading and better productivity, it is unjustifiable to claim that Acme will benefit a great deal from the course. Even if it will be able to improve its productivity, we need a complete cost-benefit analysis to determine whether the benefits will outstrip the costs. It is possible that the costs will outweigh the benefits. While the program's five-hundred-dollar fee per employee seems insignificant, the total costs of all the employees may be a huge amount. The dollar-value of the gain in productivity would need to be compared with the total costs of the program for all employees. Moreover, it is likely that many employees in Acme may not be able to leave work to participate in the course for three weeks and if they do, the company's operations may be disrupted. Consequently, instead of boosting its productivity, the course could decrease Acme's productivity considerably. This decrease, together with the significant expense for the course, could far outweigh the benefits of the course. If this should be the case, the assumption about the net benefits of the course would be unwarranted and the recommendation would be unjustified. To better assess the argument, we need an in-depth cost-benefit analysis of participating in the course.

Finally, the author suggests that just because many other companies have benefited greatly from the course, Acme will also benefit from it. This need not be the case. Acme may not be similar enough to other companies to stand to benefit from the course. It is possible that other companies have many people who have no basic reading skills and read very slowly; therefore, the course primarily concerned with basic reading and fast reading has been a good fit for them. On the contrary, Acme's employees may be mostly proficient readers and have no need for the course. Even if the course teaches reading skills that they may find marginally useful, the course materials may not focus on the type of reading they are engaged in at work, reducing the benefits for them. Also, the author does not specify how other companies' employees have participated in the course. Perhaps they have taken the course without leaving their companies, only some people in the same company have taken the course at the same time, and they have chosen to take one component of the course each time when they could leave work. Should this be true, requiring all of Acme's employees to take the course would be a waste of their time and money and make a dent in the company's productivity, undermining the argument.

In conclusion, the recommendation is in dire need of more statistical support both in the actual amount of productivity gained from having employees that can speed read and in how the example employees are connected to the notion of increased productivity. Perhaps more importantly, the results of a comparison of the training program's costs for all employees and the value of the increase in productivity, if any exists, would help us better evaluate the argument.

134. Cutting funding for the Grandview Symphony (Questions to Be Answered)

The author recommends that the Grandview Symphony's funding be completely removed from the following year's budget in light of what the author views as a newfound self-sufficiency. To justify the recommendation, the memo cites a two-hundred percent increase in private donations and a doubling in attendance at the symphony's park concert series last year. It also notes the plan by the symphony to increase ticket prices in the following year. Yet before we determine whether the city of Grandview should withdraw its financial support to the symphony, we should have answers to certain questions.

One important question to consider is whether the increase in private donations is significant or even remotely close to covering the operating costs of the Grandview Symphony. It may certainly be possible for private donations to fully support the symphony, but without accurate data showing how much was previously donated versus the costs of running the symphony, a two-hundred percent increase is a meaningless statistic. The private contributions before last year may have been very small and therefore an increase of two-hundred percent may not be significant. Even if the contributions were significant, they may not be adequate for operating the symphony. Also, the trend last year could have been an aberration and may not continue. For example, the contributions could decrease dramatically this year and even more dramatically next year. Perhaps the city has provided the greatest amount of funding for the symphony last year, boosting private contributions for it. Therefore, if the city ceases funding for the symphony, private contributions may diminish as well. If the increase in donations has not been significant and is unlikely to sustain, the argument that the symphony can fully support itself and has no need for city funding in the future would be gratuitous.

Another question to answer is whether the increase in attendance at the concerts-in-the-park series is grounds for elimination of funding for the symphony. As with the increase in private donations, the article does not cite any specific numbers regarding previous attendance, nor do we know how important this particular series of concerts is compared to other performances put on each year by the symphony. If the attendance had been negligible before last year, a double attendance may not be significant. If the series accounts for a small portion of all of the symphony's events annually, it may contribute a small amount to the funding for the symphony. We also want to know whether the attendance requires paying for tickets. If the attendance is free of charge, the series may increase the costs instead of increasing the revenue. If the city's funding helps promote the series and offset most of its costs, the argument for eliminating its funding for the symphony would be weakened. Even if the doubling of attendance means a significant rise in the number of attendees, the trend last year could have been an anomaly and may not hold true next year. Any of the scenarios, if true, would invalidate the claim that the symphony can prosper without city funding in the future.

Still another question to address is whether the plan by the symphony to increase ticket prices for next year, coupled with a double increase in its private contributions and one hundred percent increase in attendance at its park concert series, would guarantee that it will be self-sufficient and warrant elimination of funding for it. We would like to know whether raising ticket prices is a good option. As with private contributions and concert attendance, no concrete data is provided regarding current ticket revenues and potential increase for next year. If the amount of rise is too small, it will be meaningless for the symphony's operation. If the audience and the benefactors refuse to accept the rise, the symphony could not rely on this new source of funding. Even if the symphony can rely on the increase in ticket prices for next year, there is no guarantee that this increase, together with that in private contributions and concert attendance, will be enough to make up for the eliminated budget. Even assuming that increased revenue from these sources will be equal to the removed budget, this does not necessarily mean that the symphony will be self-sustaining, because it had financial difficulties for many years, which implies that the current city budget for it has been inadequate. Should this be the case, the argument for not including funding for the symphony in next year's city budget would be unjustified.

In sum, before the city of Grandview decides to cancel its financial support of the symphony, there should be a more in-depth investigation of the figures regarding the change in private contributions and attendance, along with how these and other factors may have influenced the symphony's decision to increase ticket prices.

135. Using supplements derived from beneficia to prevent colds and reduce absenteeism by emulating East Meria (Questions to Be Answered)

Relying on a study which reports that in an area called East Meria, people only visit the doctor for cold-related issues once or twice a year, while at the same time consuming large amounts of a plant called beneficia, the author recommends that people in West Meria take the supplement derived from beneficia to reduce absences from school and work. Yet we must have answers to some key questions in order to see if the recommendation will be successful.

The author must answer whether a connection exists between the consumption of beneficia and the low number of cold-related doctor visits in East Meria. However, no data is provided in this regard. There is the possibility that the study involves a small sample and is not statistically reliable and the people surveyed are not representative of the general population of East Meria. There is also the possibility that people in East Meria simply do not see as much of a need to go to the hospital if they have a cold, save for the most serious situations. If they do not go to the doctor when they have a cold, then it will be very difficult to determine any effect that eating beneficia may have on their likelihood of being absent from school or work. If the connection is to be established, there needs to be more data on the actual number of colds contracted by the people in the area on a yearly basis, which can then be compared to the number of cold-related hospital visits. Assuming that the people in East Meria do get colds less often, it raises the question of whether beneficia is directly responsible for this. There could be a wide range of other factors that contribute to such a phenomenon, like naturally strong immune systems, hygienic practices, or even other foods. It could even be that the people in East Meria cannot afford to see a doctor for more than once or twice a year for the treatment of colds and choose to buy some medicine from OTC. In such scenarios, the author cannot justifiably assert that consuming beneficia will do anything to help prevent colds. If the author can provide clear evidence that beneficia has some properties which prevent colds, it would lend much support to the argument in favor of taking the supplement.

Even assuming there is a connection between beneficia consumption and fewer colds, the author should also answer whether taking the nutritional supplements derived from beneficia works as well as eating beneficia. Even if the connection between beneficia consumption and the low number of cold-related doctor visits in East Meria can be established, this does not necessarily mean that it will hold true in West Meria. The people in West Meria may be allergic to beneficia, already consume too much beneficia, find beneficia too expensive, or have other equally effective ways to prevent colds. Even if consuming beneficia will contribute to fewer colds in West Meria, there is no guarantee that the nutritional supplements derived from beneficia will be equally effective. Since the nutritional supplements are not the plant beneficia itself, taking the supplements may not be able to prevent colds, because it is likely that the contents of the plant other than those contained in the supplements are responsible for the effect, rendering the recommendation of taking the nutritional supplements unreasonable. Even if taking them is as effective at reducing colds as eating beneficia, the author needs to offer evidence that the daily use of the supplements is necessary. There is the possibility of negative health effects resulting from an overdose of the supplements. It stands to reason, then, that without detailed analysis of the contents of the supplements, the suggestion that students and employees take them every day carries a high chance of causing unforeseen health problems even worse than colds, making the recommendation unfounded.

Even if the daily consumption of the nutritional supplements derived from beneficia is able to prevent colds, the author needs to answer whether preventing colds can reduce absenteeism. However, the author only states that colds are offered most often as the reason for absenting oneself from school and work. Just because colds are the reason given most frequently does not necessarily mean they are the real reason. It is possible that students or employees give colds as the reason because they are the most acceptable reason. It is also possible that using colds as the reason requires no medical proof whereas other excuses often require some form of proof. It is even possible that students or employees are absent because they are not motivated to study or work. In such scenarios, no connection between colds and absences has been established. Even if such a connection is substantiated, there is no guarantee that there exists the link of absenteeism to colds. Perhaps colds cause absences, but they may not cause absenteeism, chronic absence that could result from economic factors or chronic health problems. Therefore, preventing colds does not necessarily lower absenteeism. Without relevant evidence, we cannot fully evaluate the recommendation of taking the nutritional supplements derived from beneficia daily to prevent colds and decrease absenteeism.

In conclusion, we should have answers to relevant questions to determine the soundness of the recommendation. We must know if there are truly fewer cases of the cold in East Meria, and if this lower number of incidences is the result of beneficia consumption. Also, we should have detailed lab research into the chemical contents of the nutritional supplements derived from beneficia to ensure that there is no component that may cause undue harm. Finally, we need proof of the connection between colds and absenteeism.

136. Building a jazz club in Monroe (Questions to Be Answered)

The author relies on a variety of statistics from marketing research to predict that a jazz club would be a lucrative venture in the city of Monroe. However, closer inspection of the evidence reveals that the prediction and its argument raise some questions to which we must have answers before we determine the plausibility of the argument.

Firstly, the author must answer whether the new jazz music club in Monroe would dominate the local market just because the nearest jazz club is more than sixty miles away and Monroe's annual jazz festival is popular. The new club may not be able to do so, because people could be willing to drive over 60 miles to the closest club for its better admission prices, atmosphere, and services. If this should be true, the prediction of a profitable new jazz club would be unreasonable. Even assuming that people are unwilling to drive over 60 miles to the nearest club, we may still debate how strong Monroe's jazz market is. The applicant notes that there is adequate evidence that jazz is popular in Monroe, but for all we know, Monroe could be a town of just 100 people. The vast majority of the attendees may have been tourists who were there for the festival and may not be the regular customers of the new jazz club. The attendance of 100,000 people last summer may have been an aberration and the trend may not continue. If this should be the case, the prediction and its argument would be further invalidated. Without census information about the population of Monroe and a survey that shows whether locals or tourists comprised a significant percentage of the jazz festival attendees, the author cannot convince me of the large scale of Monroe's jazz market, nor can we determine whether the prediction and its argument are reasonable.

Secondly, the author should answer whether the local musicians will be able to perform at the new club. The application notes that a few famous jazz musicians own homes in Monroe, but there is no guarantee that they would like to perform at the local jazz club or that locals would be willing to hear them perform. They may perform elsewhere and even at the nearest jazz club but reside in Monroe simply to take advantage of peaceful small-town life. If this is true, their proximity to the club may have no bearing on its success. As a result, the argument for a new jazz club in Monroe will be weakened. If the jazz musicians are willing to play at the club, are appreciated in the area, and do not demand unreasonable compensation for performing at the club, the argument will be strengthened. Lacking relevant evidence, we cannot fully evaluate the potential success of a new jazz club in Monroe.

Thirdly, the author needs to answer whether the fact that the jazz radio station is the highest rated station in Monroe indicates that jazz is popular in the city. It is possible, especially in the current age of MP3 players and the internet, that it is simply the only radio station that is listened to at all, and that the number of listeners is relatively small. As with the previous contention, population data and music preference surveys could help us appraise this counterargument. It would also help if the author could provide the ratings for all radio stations in Monroe, so that we could have a clearer picture of how much more popular the jazz station is than the other radio stations. If the difference in ratings is small, then it would weaken the case for starting a club that plays jazz music exclusively. Even if the jazz station is popular, there is no guarantee that its listeners would be interested in listening to jazz at the new club. It could even compete with the proposed club for listeners. Either scenario would undermine the case for a new club in Monroe.

Finally, the author has to inform us whether the proposed jazz club in Monroe would be extremely profitable. Assuming that jazz is popular in Monroe, we need information regarding the profitability of the new jazz music club. The nationwide study finds that an average jazz fan spends about $1,000 every year on jazz entertainment. However, it could be that the typical fan spends little in jazz music clubs. It could also be that a jazz fan in Monroe spends little on jazz entertainment and even less in jazz music clubs. When the new club is unlikely to receive the revenue, the prediction of a profitable business would be groundless, because profit is a function of revenue and costs. It will become even more groundless if the applicant fails to consider all kinds of costs associated with launching a business. Before touting the significant profitability of the club, the author must estimate all the costs as well as the revenues.

In conclusion, before receiving approval of this loan, the potential owner must first provide solid data on the population of Monroe, and the portion of people in the city who both like jazz music and are willing to spend money on going to a jazz club. It would also be in the owner's best interest to contact the local musicians to see if they are willing to play at the club at an affordable rate. Above everything else, the owner must weigh the potential revenue against the costs to make sure that the business would be lucrative.

137. Disappearance of large mammal species on the Kaliko Islands (Alternative Explanations)

The author concludes that humans' excessive hunting was the cause of mass extinctions of large mammals on the Kaliko Islands. To support the conclusion, the article states that archaeological findings indicate that early humans depended on both fishing and hunting for survival, and that archaeologists have discovered many sites where fish bones were discarded and simple tools that were good for hunting. However, other explanations could also account for the mammal species' extinction.

One explanation for the extinction of mammals in the Kaliko Islands could be extreme changes in weather or natural disasters. Little information is given by the article about the geographic nature of the islands or their climate; therefore, there is the possibility that over the three-thousand-year span there had been a miniature ice-age, a drought, a severe weather phenomenon such as a hurricane, a volcano eruption, or any other natural disaster that killed off at once or gradually most of the large mammals in the islands before the humans could hunt them. This would explain the lack of mammal bones among the fish bones in the discard piles that were discovered, if the fish bones had been discarded by the humans. This would also rule out normal hunting as the sole factor in the extinction of the mammals, not to mention excessive hunting.

It may also be the case that the mammals died off from a lack of resources. The article describes them as being large, and while we do not know exactly what they ate, it is safe to assume that they needed to consume huge amounts of food to survive. Since the introduction of humans, who would probably kill off any threatening predators and compete for food sources on which the mammals depended for their subsistence, it is likely that the population of large mammals was not sustainable and starved to death. It could also be that the animals and plants that the mammals consumed decreased dramatically for some reason. It could even be that the humans forced the mammals to leave their territory by intruding on their natural habitat. These scenarios would account for the long period of time it took for them to die out, as over-hunting by humans has generally led to extinction over a much shorter period.

Finally, there remains the possibility that the mammals of the Kaliko Islands did not all die, but simply migrated to other islands or to the mainland. As mentioned earlier, the information provided by the article does not give much insight into the location or historical weather patterns of the islands; therefore, it could be that during a particularly cold period, a land bridge was formed between the islands across which the mammals, for whatever reason, decided to migrate and they did not return, making most of the large species extinct in the Kaliko Islands. This would also rule out the possibility that humans' excessive hunting contributed to the mammals' die-off there.

In conclusion, there are many other potential explanations for the disappearance of the large mammals of the Kaliko Islands besides excessive hunting. Factors such as extreme climate change or natural disasters, loss of habitat or resources, or even simple migrations could equally account for their alleged extinction from the islands.

138. Using fish oil supplements to prevent colds and reduce absenteeism by emulating East Meria (Questions to Be Answered)

Relying on a study which reports that in an area called East Meria, people only visit the doctor for cold-related issues once or twice a year, while at the same time consuming large amounts of fish, the author recommends that people in West Meria take a nutritional supplement derived from fish oil to prevent colds and reduce absences from school and work. Yet we must have answers to some key questions in order to see if the recommendation and its argument are indeed sound.

The author must answer whether a connection exists between the consumption of fish and the low number of cold-related doctor visits in East Meria. However, no data is given in this regard. There is the possibility that the study involves a small sample and is not statistically reliable and the people surveyed are not representative of the general population of East Meria. There is also the possibility that people in East Meria simply do not see as much of a need to go to the hospital if they have a cold, save for the most serious situations. In such scenarios, the connection is groundless. If the connection is to be established, there needs to be more data on the actual number of colds contracted by the people in the area on a yearly basis, which can then be compared to the number of cold-related hospital visits. Assuming that the people in East Meria do get colds less often, there is still no real proof provided to show that their consumption of fish is the cause. There could be a myriad of other factors that contribute to such a phenomenon, like naturally strong immune systems, hygienic practices, or even other foods. It could even be that the people in East Meria cannot afford to see a doctor for more than once or twice a year for the treatment of colds and choose to buy some medicine from OTC. Unless there is evidence that some chemical in fish can help the human body resist the colds, the author cannot justifiably assert that consuming fish will do anything to help prevent sickness.

Even assuming there is a connection between fish consumption and fewer colds, the author should also answer whether taking the nutritional supplement derived from fish oil works as well as eating fish. Even if the connection between fish consumption and the low number of cold-related doctor visits in East Meria can be established, this does not necessarily mean that it will hold true in West Meria. The people in West Meria may be allergic to fish, already consume too much fish, find fish too expensive, or have other equally effective ways to prevent colds. Even if consuming fish will contribute to fewer colds in West Meria, there is no guarantee that taking the nutritional supplement derived from fish oil will be equally effective. Since the nutritional supplement simply comes from fish oil, it is likely that taking it will not be able to prevent colds, as it is different from fish in contents, rendering the recommendation of taking the nutritional supplement unreasonable. Even if taking it is as effective at reducing colds as eating fish, the author needs to offer evidence that its daily use is necessary. There is the possibility of negative health effects resulting from an overdose of the supplement. It stands to reason, then, that without detailed analysis of the contents of the supplement, the suggestion that students and employees take it every day carries a high chance of causing unforeseen health problems even worse than colds, making the recommendation unfounded.

Even if the daily consumption of the nutritional supplement derived from fish oil is able to prevent colds, the author needs to answer whether preventing colds can reduce absenteeism. However, the author only states that colds are offered most often as the reason for absenting oneself from school and work. Just because colds are the reason given most frequently does not necessarily mean they are the real reason. It is possible that students or employees give colds as the reason because they are the most acceptable reason. It is also possible that using colds as the reason requires no medical proof whereas other excuses often require some form of proof. It is even possible that students or employees are absent because they are not motivated to study or work. In such scenarios, no connection between colds and absences has been established. Even if such a connection is substantiated, there is no guarantee that there exists the link of absenteeism to colds. Perhaps colds cause absences, but they may not cause absenteeism, chronic absence that could result from economic factors or chronic health problems. Therefore, preventing colds does not necessarily lower absenteeism. Without relevant evidence, we cannot fully evaluate the recommendation of taking the supplement from fish oil daily to prevent colds and decrease absenteeism.

In conclusion, we should have answers to some key questions before we determine the soundness of the recommendation and argument. We must know if there are truly fewer cases of the cold in East Meria, and if this lower number of incidences is the result of fish consumption. Also, we should have detailed lab research into the chemical contents of the nutritional supplement to ensure that there is no component that may cause undue harm. Finally, we need proof of the connection between colds and absenteeism.

139. Shortening work shifts to reduce the number of on-the-job accidents at Alta (Questions to Be Answered)

The author recommends that Alta Manufacturing reduce each work shift by one hour in order to decrease the number of accidents, which the author claims has been a result of sleep deprivation. To justify the recommendation, the memo cites a claim by experts that fatigue caused by sleep deprivation is a major factor contributing to the aforementioned issue, as well as a separate factory which has work shifts that are one hour shorter and thirty percent fewer accidents. To ascertain the soundness of the recommendation and its argument, we need answers to some key questions.

We must know whether Alta employees' inadequate sleep was responsible for its accidents. However, it is not specified whether Alta's accidents were related to sleep deprivation at all. Sleep deprivation is a probable cause of accidents, but it is unlikely the only one. Perhaps Alta's higher accident rate resulted from its laxer safety education and regulations. Or perhaps its equipment was out of date or not very safe. Or perhaps it had more inexperienced workers. Above all, the trend in the past year may have been an aberration and may not continue. Even if it persists, thirty percent more on-the-job accidents may not be significant if Panoply had a small number of accidents. For example, if Panoply had three such accidents last year, Alta would have just about one more accident. Any of the scenarios, if true, would invalidate the recommendation that Alta should reduce its work shifts' time by an hour to help its workers have enough sleep to lower its number of on-the-job accidents. In order to decide whether shortening the work shifts by an hour is a reasonable argument, more details of Alta's on-the-job accidents are needed.

We should also know whether the work shifts' length has any effect on employees' sleep at Alta. The author assumes that if the work shifts are shorter, the employees will get adequate amounts of sleep, but there is nothing to indicate that the length of the work shifts is interfering with the employees' sleep in the first place. They may already have enough sleep, making it unnecessary to reduce the number of hours for each shift to allow them to have enough sleep. Furthermore, there is nothing to support the assumption that if they have an extra hour, the employees will use that hour to sleep. Some employees may have small children to care for, or other jobs or obligations to keep them busy. Others may spend the extra hour going out drinking, staying up very late. Even if they use the extra time to sleep, it is likely that one more hour will be inadequate. Thus, while Panoply's employees may need one extra hour for proper sleep to reduce its on-the-job accidents, it is unfair to assume that shortening each work shift by one hour will help Alta's employees have adequate amounts of sleep and lower the number of on-the-job accidents.

Finally, we need to know whether reducing time of the work shifts will have any adverse effects. There is nothing in the article to indicate shorter shifts will increase production or provide other benefits to the employees. It is possible that cutting time would reduce the wages of the employees and have unintended consequences. Instead of the employees being happier or less tired, they could be stressed out due to a decrease in their earnings. The stress could cause lack of sleep and concentration and possibly increase the accidents in the workplace. It is also possible that the original work shift enables the employees to be very productive, but the proposed shorter work shift would make them much less productive and hurt Alta's profitability. Should this be the case, the recommendation of shortening each work shift by one hour will probably not be popular with the employees or the company and is likely to fail. A survey of the employees themselves could provide insights into why there were so many more accidents at Alta than at Panoply and help the company identify tailored strategies.

In conclusion, we need to take answers to these questions into consideration when we determine whether the argument to make each work shift shorter by one hour is credible. There needs to be a direct connection between the accidents at Alta and the lack of sleep. Another issue is whether an extra hour off work will translate into more sleep for the employees. Still another issue is whether the strategy will have any severe negative consequences. Finding the exact cause of the work accidents, making sure the employees have enough experience and training, and checking to make sure the equipment is safe to use can all help us evaluate this recommendation.

140. Should non-residents be allowed on the Committee for a Better Oak City? (Questions to Be Answered)

The author recommends limiting membership of the Committee for a Better Oak city to residents of the city only. To justify the recommendation, the letter claims that the committee's decision-making process is hindered by allegedly foolish objections, and that only those who pay taxes in the city know how to best spend those tax dollars on improvements. However, we need answers to some questions before determining whether the suggested limitation will allow the committee to make Oak City a better place in which to live and work.

We must know whether the objections raised by non-resident committee members were foolish and whether the committee's failure to make important decisions was something bad for the city. The author assumes that the recent meetings were unable to make important decisions merely due to unwise objections raised by non-resident committee members. However, there is no evidence in this regard. In what way were these objections foolish? What does the members' non-resident status have to do with this particular issue? Since we do not know what the committee was discussing, nor the exact nature of the objections, the determination that they were foolish is not very helpful for the author's argument. It is likely that the issues discussed were complicated and the decisions took more than one meeting to finalize. It is also likely that committee members' opinions changed back and forth. It is even likely that the objections were in fact valid, despite the author calling them "foolish"; then whether the committee members are residents of Oak City is irrelevant. Any of the scenarios, if true, would cast serious doubt on the assumption that the oppositions of the non-resident members were "foolish" and hindered the committee's ability to make important decisions. Even if the oppositions impeded the committee's ability to make significant decisions, this does not necessarily mean that it was something bad. Perhaps the oppositions made the discussion of the issues thorough and might result in well-considered decisions, benefiting the city in the long term. If the committee membership were restricted to residents only, the committee could miss such valid objections and fail to make Oak City a better place in some ways. In this case, the recommendation is unlikely to have the predicted result and therefore unfounded.

In addition, we should know whether only people who live in Oak City and pay taxes understand how the money could be used. This begs the question: does living in the city and paying taxes afford one knowledge of civil budgetary spending? To be sure, living in a city may allow one to be more aware of what improvements are needed, but that does not necessarily mean that one also knows how to go about improving it. While people who work in the city but reside somewhere else may not know much about everyday life in the city, they may have a good understanding of the business and politics of the city by reading about the topics or by using their relevant knowledge of their own cities. Even if they do not have a full knowledge of such issues, they may know where money could be best used to improve the city. For example, as local employees, they may understand the labor market and business-related things. They may also understand what non-residents have access to in addition to jobs. They may even be experts on civil budgetary spending. All of the scenarios, if true, would invalidate the recommendation that the committee should only have residents as members because only they know how the money could be utilized, severely weakening the argument. If the non-resident committee members do not have the required expertise, then the letter's case would be strengthened.

Finally, we need to know whether the removal of non-resident members will allow the committee to make Oak City a better place. This leaves us wondering: How? Even granting that these non-resident members have been obstructing the committee's ability to make decisions, this does not necessarily mean that those decisions are good ones. Without more information about precisely what decisions are being made, there is no way to evaluate what effect they will have on Oak City's status for residents and workers. Even assuming that non-residents members have been making invalid objections, there is no guarantee that the committee composed of resident members only will be able to make Oak City a better place. It is likely that resident members have little knowledge of civil budgetary spending. It is also likely that the expertise needed for making decisions that would make the city a better place involves issues related to nonresidents who work in the city, and therefore non-resident members may provide relevant knowledge. In either scenario, the recommendation of restricting committee membership to residents is unlikely to have the predicted result that the reformed committee can enhance the city as a place for non-residents as well as residents.

In conclusion, the recommendation in the letter raises many questions regarding how the objections raised by non-resident members have hindered the committee, the connection, or lack thereof, between living in Oak City and a member's ability to budget spending, and whether the non-resident members have been the primary cause of the committee's previous inability to improve Oak City. Without first knowing the answers to such questions, we cannot fully evaluate the argument that limiting membership on the Committee for a Better Oak City will positively affect the committee's ability to improve the city.

141. Building a new golf course and resort hotel in Brindleburg (Questions to Be Answered)

While it is understandable that Brindleburg wishes to improve its economy, this is no grounds for entertaining the unwarranted assumptions made by the author of this memo. The example of Seaside Vista may be enticing, with its increased tourism, many more new business loan applications, and higher tax revenues. However, we need answers to certain questions before we determine whether a new golf course and resort hotel will help Brindleburg.

One question is whether tourists are attracted by Seaside Vista's new golf course and hotel. However, this is not backed up by any evidence. Its visitors have increased 20% in number over the past two years, but numerous factors could be responsible for the scenario. Other features, such as a growing national economy, a shift in the location preferences of travelers, or travel marketing efforts may have had significant effects on this development. If this should be true, the assumption that Seaside Vista's new golf course and resort hotel alone have contributed to increased tourism would prove unjustified and the recommendation of following Seaside Vista's example would be groundless. Without more details about the tourists themselves and the reasons for their choices, we have no way of knowing why Seaside Vista has experienced the influx of visitors. Even if the new golf course and hotel have contributed to its increase in visitors, the increase could be insignificant since the number might have been very small to begin with and the trend of increase may not continue, undermining the argument for emulating Seaside Vista.

Another question is whether in Seaside Vista, the dramatic rise in new business loan applications this year and increase in tax revenue over the past two years have no other root causes than the golf course and resort hotel. Significant increase in new business loan applications may mean the businesses needed much money but does not necessarily mean new businesses have opened. Even if new businesses have opened, this year could be an aberration and the increase may have little connection to the new golf course and resort hotel. Also, it is unfair to claim that a significant portion of the new tax revenues have been contributed by the allegedly higher numbers of tourists alone. Seaside Vista could have implemented a stricter policy of tax collecting, raised its tax rates, or created a new type of tax. Or it could simply have had an improved economy. At the same time, while tax revenues have increased, the revenues may be insignificant if they were small to begin with and the trend of increase may not persist. Without ruling out such scenarios, the author cannot reliably conclude that the new golf course and hotel only have led to a substantial rise in new business loan applications and more tax revenues.

Even if Seaside Vista is able to prove that all of its recent benefits have common ties to the new hotel and golf course, still another question is whether Brindleburg and Seaside Vista are similar enough for the plan to be worth Brindleburg's considerable expense. There is no guarantee that this is the case. It is likely that visitors go to Brindleburg simply to shop rather than play golf. It is also likely that they go there to hike. It is even likely that the need for golf and resorting has been fulfilled by Seaside Vista. Any of the scenarios, if true, would weaken the assumption that Brindleburg can reap the same benefits by adding a golf course and resort hotel. Even if it can follow Seaside Vista's example, this does not necessarily mean that the plan will be the most effective way to better its economy since the true cause of its present economic situation has not been identified. There is no guarantee that the project will generate enough tax revenues to be used for funding public improvements. Therefore, the recommendation may not have the predicted result, rendering the argument unconvincing.

To conclude, without answers to these questions, we cannot determine whether the recommendation is plausible. The city could run significant financial risks, should Brindleburg choose to follow the memo's recommendation. The costs of building new facilities as large as a golf course and resort hotel may even lead to reduced tax income, as the town would likely need to increase taxes temporarily to pay for them, which would deter citizens from starting any businesses in the area.

142. Should Appian Roadways be hired to construct access roads for shopping malls? (Questions to Be Answered)

The author recommends that Appian Roadways rather than Good Intentions Roadways be chosen to construct access roads for shopping malls. To justify the recommendation, the memo suggests that the latter provides roads of lesser quality because a section of a road it worked on two years ago is in poor condition. It also notes that the former purchased new machinery and hired a new manager. While this may be true, in order to compare the two stretches of roads and the quality of the respective companies' work, we need answers to certain questions regarding the representativeness and use of the two sections in question. Also, we need to look closely at the new equipment and staff of Appian Roadways to check for relevance.

We must know whether the road sections in question are representative of the whole roads. A stretch of Route 101, paved by Good Intentions, is in poor condition after just two years. On the contrary, a stretch of Route 40, paved by Appian, is still in good condition after more than four years. Relying on these factoids, the author assumes that Appian provides roads that will not need to be repaired for four years. However, looking at just a section of Route 40 does not give a complete picture of the road, nor does looking at just a section of Route 101. Other sections of both roads could be in any state of disrepair. For example, other areas of Route 40 could be cracked with many potholes, whereas those of Route 101 in good condition. If this should be the case, the assumption about the relative quality of roads paved by the two companies and about the access roads to be built by Appian would prove unwarranted and the recommendation of hiring Appian rather than Good Intentions to construct access roads for shopping malls would be gratuitous.

Moreover, we should know whether the road sections under discussion have been heavily used. When comparing two sections of roads, the author does not take into account the actual use of these roads. If Route 101 is in a high-traffic area, it may be used more frequently. Naturally, more frequent use will lead to quicker deterioration. If Route 40 is in a more residential or rural area, it may stay in better condition longer. Should this be the case, it is unfair to assume that just because two road sections paved by two different companies are in different condition, the companies' comparative quality alone has contributed to the current road condition respectively. Therefore, the recommendation of using Appian instead of Good Intentions may be unfounded. The company that builds shopping malls presumably wants its access roads to be used heavily. Before it decides whether Appian or Good Intentions is the better choice for this project, it is necessary to assess the locations and usage of the roads built by them to better understand why the areas of the roads are in their current condition.

Finally, we need to know whether factors other than road usage and the work of the two companies have been responsible for the current condition of the road sections. The author offers no information in this respect. Perhaps the section of Route 101 paved by Good Intentions is located in an earthquake area or has experienced very bad weather during the two years since its completion, whereas such scenarios have been absent on the section of Route 40 paved by Appian since four years before. Should this be the case, the author cannot reliably conclude that Appian is the better choice for construction of the access roads for shopping malls. Also, Appian's new equipment or quality control manager may be irrelevant unless they will have any direct bearing on construction quality of the access roads for shopping malls. If they help it build better roads than Good Intentions, the case for hiring it would be strengthened. However, Good Intentions may have the same equipment and a more competent quality control manager. It may also have better trained workers. Such scenarios would undermine the argument for using Appian rather than Good Intentions for the access roads. Above all, the author fails to consider choices other than Appian and Good Intentions, further undermining the argument. To better assess the recommendation, we must know whether factors such as weather and equipment play a key part in constructing good roads.

In short, Good Intentions should not be penalized because its work appears to be of a lower quality based on one section of one road whose bad condition could have been attributable to frequency of use or other aggravating factors beyond its control. The company in question should do extensive research to further understand the locations and daily traffic of these roads as well as the conditions of other roads each company has paved. Only then can it be confident that its mall access roads will be built properly.

143. Should high-intensity lighting be installed in Amburg? (Specific Evidence)

Relying on the assumption that the city of Belleville has had success in reducing vandalism via high-intensity lighting in its central business district and on the fact that Amburg also has a problem with vandalism in its business district, the author recommends that Amburg have a similar addition of high-intensity lighting to reduce crime and revitalize the declining neighborhoods. To assess the argument properly, we must have extra evidence regarding the effect of high-intensity lighting on vandalism in Belleville and on crimes in Amburg and regarding the cost of implementing the course of action. The additional evidence may either weaken or strengthen the claim that high-intensity lighting will be effective.

We must have evidence relevant to the effect of high-intensity lighting on Belleville's vandalism. The article mentions that one month after Belleville installed high-intensity lighting in its central business district last October, vandalism dropped. The author assumes that this is an indication that high-intensity lighting alone was responsible for the decrease in vandalism. However, the author provides no evidence to substantiate this. It is likely that cameras had just been installed to record vandalism. It is also likely that a law that metes out harsh punishment to vandalism had been enacted at the same time. It is even likely that police patrols had just been instituted there. Any of the scenarios, if true, would cast serious doubt on the assumption that high-intensity lighting only contributed to the decrease in vandalism. Even if it was responsible for the drop in vandalism, since the author gives no statistics about the amount of vandalism decline, it could be that the decline was negligible. Even assuming that the decline was significant, it is possible that the effect of high-intensity lighting may not last. Perhaps since the initial drop, the perpetrators of vandalism have become habituated to the lighting and are no longer discouraged by it from committing crime. In this way, the recommendation of installing it throughout Amburg to reduce crime considerably would be unfounded.

We should also have evidence regarding whether high-intensity lighting will be effective in Amburg. High-intensity lighting may have proved helpful in curbing vandalism in Belleville, but this does not necessarily mean it will work in Amburg. It is likely that the people behind vandalism in Belleville were deterred by police patrols on bicycles rather than by high-intensity lighting. If Amburg's citizens are not deterred by a police presence in the area, it is possible that the addition of this lighting will not deter them. It is also possible that the bicycle patrols were instituted too recently in Amburg for their effects to be observed. It is even possible that the bicycle patrols have been effective in Amburg, but the incidence of vandalism remains unchanged because at the same time, other factors have been contributing to an increase in the rate of vandalism. Should this be the case, the assumption that Belleville and Amburg are similar enough to justify installing high-intensity lighting in Amburg would be groundless, rendering the recommendation invalid. Even if high-intensity lighting is good at controlling vandalism in Amburg, this does not necessarily mean that it is the ideal way to tackle other crimes. Similarly, other crimes may be best deterred by a police presence. If this should be true, the assumption that just because high-intensity lighting is effective at combating vandalism, it is effective at tackling other crimes, would be gratuitous and the prediction of its effect on revitalizing the declining neighborhoods in Amburg would be unreasonable.

Even granting that high-intensity lighting is a method superior to bicycle patrols, we need evidence regarding whether Amburg has sufficient funding to cover the costs of installing enough lights to effectively dissuade criminal activity. If the cost of installing the high-intensity lights is significantly more than paying for bicycle patrols, thus leading to poor implementation, then there would not be much of a chance of the plan being very effective. In that event, the recommendation of using high-intensity lighting instead of bicycle patrols throughout Amburg to reduce crime is unlikely to have the predicted result and could lead to enormous amounts of wasted money. Also, the author assumes that installing high-intensity lighting will be adequate for revitalizing the declining neighborhoods. However, revitalizing involves factors other than crimes, such as investment and employment. Therefore, reducing crime rates in Amburg by adding the lighting may be inadequate for making its business district thrive, not to mention the deteriorating neighborhoods outside the business district. Without relevant data, we cannot fully assess the argument.

To determine the soundness of the argument, we need additional evidence. If the two cities' situations are completely different, the argument will not stand. However, if the sources of vandalism are similar and comparable measures were previously taken in Belleville, installing high-intensity lighting will be a reasonable course of action for Amburg as well.

144. Reducing Balmer Island moped accidents by learning from Torseau (Assumptions)

The author recommends that during the summer months, Balmer Island reduce the number of moped rentals at each moped and bicycle rental outlet from 50 to 30 per day in order to decrease the number of accidents involving mopeds and pedestrians. To justify the recommendation, the letter cites Torseau, a neighboring island, as an example of having effectively implemented such a policy last year. Drawing this analogy to dictate a policy could be useful in reducing accidents, but there would be major negative consequences if the assumptions should prove unwarranted.

The author assumes that the use of mopeds on Balmer during the summer season is responsible for the moped-pedestrian accidents and that reducing the number of moped rentals will decrease the number of accidents. However, the author offers no evidence to substantiate this. The letter simply states that the population doubles on Balmer during the summer months and that there are accidents involving mopeds and pedestrians. Yet we do not know if other factors, such as malfunctioning traffic lights, unclear road signs, alcohol or drug abuse, lack of road maintenance and lack of convenient sidewalks, contribute to these accidents. If they do, the assumption would be unwarranted. Without ruling out these and other alternative possibilities, the author cannot confidently claim that decreasing the number of moped rentals at any given time will decrease the number of accidents. Nor do we know Balmer's original population. If we are speaking of an increase of only a few hundred people, the author cannot reliably conclude that moped accidents will rise considerably. Similarly, we just do not know what portion of the new people are moped operators or pedestrians. If few of them rent a moped, they may have little impact on the number of moped accidents. Also, merely enforcing limits on moped rentals may be ineffective. The author needs to assure us that other conditions in Balmer that serve to increase the accident rate will not change. For example, people may buy mopeds instead of renting them in response to the enforcement of moped rentals, or pedestrians may increase in large numbers. Either scenario might lead to a higher rate of moped accidents. Unless there is relevant evidence, it is unfair to assume that use of mopeds has contributed to moped-pedestrian accidents in Balmer and restricting the number of moped rentals will attain the desired reduction in accidents.

The author also implies that success of a policy on moped rentals on Torseau is proof that such a policy will be effective on Balmer as well. However, the two places may be too different from each other to justify implementing the same policy. We do not know of many circumstances that might have played a role in the accidents on Torseau. For example, we do not have information on the weather and population of Torseau or what the moped rental limits were in that area last year. It is likely that Torseau had very fine weather and experienced no population increase. It is also likely that few people rented mopeds last year. It is even likely that it enforced higher moped rental standards. For example, outlets might have been only allowed to rent newer mopeds to their patrons. Therefore, factors other than limits on the number of moped rentals might have contributed to its fifty percent decrease in moped accidents. Balmer, with its population doubled during the summer months and possibly different causes of moped accidents, could find it difficult to replicate the results. Even if they have the same reasons for moped accidents and enforce similar measures, there is no guarantee that Balmer will be able to enforce them as effectively as Torseau has done. Unless there is evidence that the two islands are similar enough to warrant the implementation of the same policy, the author cannot fairly claim that one island's success in decreasing moped accidents will automatically carry over to the other.

Finally, the author suggests that limiting the number of rental mopeds is the only viable solution to the moped accidents. However, this is not necessarily the case. Even if Balmer enforces similar restrictions on moped rentals, there is no guarantee that the overall number of moped rentals will drop, because the companies could satisfy the demand by opening more rental shops instead of supplying more rental mopeds at each shop. In this case, the assumption would be gratuitous, and the argument would fall apart. It is likely that alternative solutions exist and can be as effective or even more effective. Driver safety awareness programs could be released before and during the summer season; certain lanes could be designated as moped lanes for the duration of the summer months. There is even the possibility of simply reducing the speed limit so that riders would be forced to slow down. Many other alternatives could be suggested, ones that would help reduce moped accidents and allow the moped rental companies to continue to do business and make profits during peak travel months. Should this be true, the assumption that restricting the number of rental mopeds is the only course of action would be unwarranted, rendering the argument unjustified.

In short, it is unreasonable to assume that the proposed moped rental limits will help Balmer to prevent moped accidents. We do not have enough information to be certain that the number of mopeds is the cause of these accidents, nor do we have enough data on Torseau's accidents to compare the two islands properly. Unless we have additional evidence, we cannot fully evaluate the argument to determine whether such a measure will necessarily help Balmer.

145. Will the new seafood restaurant in Bay City be successful? (Questions to Be Answered)

The author relies on marketing data concerning the potential popularity of seafood in Bay City to conclude that a new Captain Seafood restaurant located there would be popular and profitable. To determine the validity of the conclusion and its argument, we need to address some key questions.

The author must answer whether a 30 percent increase in seafood consumption in Bay City restaurants justifies the opening of the Captain Seafood restaurant that specializes in seafood. While the increase is worth looking at, it does not indicate with any certainty that people will be willing to eat at the new seafood-focused restaurant. A 30 percent increase may not be significant if the consumption five years before was very small or even negligible. Also, there is no guarantee that the trend of increase will continue. Even if seafood consumption continues to increase, the rise may not be significant enough to sustain a new restaurant that concentrates on seafood. It is equally likely that people will prefer to eat at the restaurants they are familiar with or will simply prefer the specific seafood dishes that those locations offer to those of the new restaurant. This could be especially true in the case of families, as one or more members may not wish to eat seafood and would feel alienated at a restaurant that specializes in seafood. If this should be true, the new seafood restaurant would be unnecessary, rendering the prediction of a profitable seafood-focused restaurant in the city unreasonable.

The author should also address a question regarding the two-income family factoid: whether the information suggests that just because a family eats out more often, it will for some reason want to eat at the new restaurant. A national survey has found that double-come families eat fewer home-cooked meals recently, but such a trend may not continue, nor may it be true for the people in Bay City. It is likely that the residents in Bay City eat as many home-cooked meals as before or even more home-cooked meals than before. In this case, the prediction would be unjustified. Even assuming that the residents there have fewer home-cooked meals than before, this does not necessarily mean that they eat out more often; perhaps they rely on catering services and delivered meals more. Even if they eat out more, it is possible that they do not consume seafood. Even if they consume seafood, it is possible that they will not do it at the new restaurant. These families, though benefiting from having a little extra money, may have no room in their budgets for new restaurants; they may, instead, prefer to stick with what they know they like to avoid wasting money. In that event, the finding that two-income families dine out more than before may not benefit a sit-down restaurant that only serves seafood, invalidating the suggestion of operating a profitable restaurant that features seafood. Also, the article mentions that these families are more health food oriented, which seems to imply that seafood is healthy, or is at least perceived as such. However, there is no evidence for this in the article; seafood may be more often contaminated with pollutants such as mercury and other harmful chemicals. Without any information about the proposed Captain Seafood menu, the author cannot justifiably assume that people will perceive its seafood as healthy. If this restaurant uses much frozen seafood, ingredients with questionable additives, or artificial elements, health-conscious consumers will not be interested. Therefore, the idea is unfounded that the new restaurant will succeed based on the implication that seafood is healthy.

Finally, the author needs to respond to the question of whether the new seafood-focused restaurant will be quite profitable, but no evidence is provided in this regard. It is likely that the new restaurant will be unprofitable. This likelihood could account for the fact that no current restaurant in the city serves only seafood. Profit is a function of revenue and costs. The new restaurant can anticipate some revenues from double-income families if they dine in it, but its revenues may not be able to cover its costs, rendering it unprofitable. We do not know the costs of launching and promoting the restaurant and obtaining healthy seafood. Nor do we know how many families will eat at the new restaurant, how often they will, and how much they are willing to pay. In this case, the prediction of a profitable seafood-focused restaurant in Bay City is unreasonable. Moreover, it is possible that there were some city restaurants whose specialty was seafood, but they closed because of unprofitable business. It is also possible that the demand for seafood in the city has been fulfilled by the currently operating restaurants that do not specialize in seafood. If this city has no seafood restaurants, it is possible that the dishes are fusions, or dishes that only include some elements from the sea. If this is true, a restaurant wholly dedicated to seafood may not be popular or profitable, obviating the need for the new Captain Seafood restaurant in Bay City.

In sum, the argument is in dire need of further research into the profitability of starting a new restaurant that specializes in seafood in terms of the willingness of Bay City residents to eat at such a restaurant instead of the current restaurants that serve seafood as well as other dishes. It would also help if evidence could be provided showing that the incomes of the families in Bay City are sufficient to fit in another restaurant option. Lastly, the connection between healthy eating and seafood needs considerable explanation by way of current scientific data and a survey showing consumer perceptions regarding seafood's healthiness.

146. Litter and vandalism in Central Plaza blamed on skateboarders (Questions to Be Answered)

The author recommends that skateboarding be no longer banned in Central Plaza. To justify the recommendation, the letter asserts that lifting the skateboarding ban would somehow reduce litter and vandalism, citing Monroe Park as an example, and even enable Central Plaza to return to its previously high levels. However, we need answers to some relevant questions before we determine the soundness of the recommendation.

We must know whether banning skateboarding alone contributed to the modest increase in visitor numbers in Central Plaza. The article mentions that the city council voted to prohibit skateboarding on the grounds that skateboarders were the cause of the litter and vandalism that discouraged patronage. However, since the ban, the number of visitors has not significantly increased. Relying on this, the author assumes that prohibiting skateboard shenanigans has contributed to such a slight increase in the number of visitors. However, the author furnishes no evidence to substantiate this. The result may have something to do with the location and facilities of Central Plaza. It is possible that the area is not attractive to visitors for some other reason. In this place where local businesses operate, the businesses may not be very popular with the local citizens. If the economy is not thriving, it is also possible that people are relocating or taking jobs elsewhere, leaving them less time to visit the plaza. The scenarios, if true, would undermine the assumption that banning skateboarding was responsible for the modest increase in the number of visitors and make the recommendation gratuitous.

We should also know whether banning skateboarding has no effect on littering and vandalism. Although skateboarding has been banned, littering and vandalism are still prevalent in Central Plaza. On the basis of this, the author implies that banning skateboarding in Central Plaza contributed to the prevalence of litter and vandalism. However, the author offers no evidence to validate this. It is possible that there could have been more vandalism and litter without the ban. It is also possible that it may take a longer time to see the effect. If this should be true, the assumption about the connection between banning skateboarding and prevalence of litter and vandalism would be unfounded. Similarly, the author assumes that just because skateboarding and absence of vandalism and litter coincide in Monroe Park, allowing skateboarding there is responsible for the absence. However, the author has yet to establish the connection between the two events. It is possible that police patrols have deterred vandalism and litter. It is also possible that people in Monroe Park are well-educated about undesirable consequences of vandalism and litter. Either of the scenarios would invalidate the claim that Monroe Park has no problem with vandalism or litter because it permits skateboarding, rendering the recommendation of lifting the city's ban on skateboarding in the plaza unreasonable.

Finally, we need to know whether Central Plaza can return to its previous glory by lifting the prohibition on skateboarding. The term "former glory" is not clearly defined, so it is difficult for us to assess the validity of the claim. The author needs to define it in more precise, possibly quantifiable terms. Even assuming that Central Plaza's "former glory" means its previously best levels, we need evidence to substantiate the claim. The author must demonstrate that Monroe Park and Central Plaza are sufficiently similar to each other to warrant the same policy of allowing skateboarding. However, it is possible that the two places are too different from each other to expect that the policy will benefit Central Plaza in the same way. For example, Central Plaza may have no funding for police patrols to prevent vandalism or litter, whereas Monroe Park has police patrols. In addition, lifting the ban on skateboarding in Central Plaza may eliminate vandalism and litter, but the situation could be far from its former glory. The city may also need to advertise Central Plaza, and attract popular shops or eateries to the plaza, among other things, to make its business return to its previously high levels. If this is the case, the recommendation of lifting the ban on skateboarding in Central Plaza to achieve the outcome awaits further inquiry.

When a skate shop owner lobbies for skateboarding in public places, one has to question the intentions. It is entirely possible that the argument stems from self-interest and a desire for more business. Who can blame the owner? None. But if the owner could give us more information, including other reasons why Central Plaza is not popular, facts about who is littering and vandalizing the area, and evidence of similarities between Central Plaza and Monroe Park, we would be able to better evaluate the recommendation.

147. Stimulating economy of Dillton (Alternative Explanations)

This newspaper article asserts that two new factories have opened in Dillton, a city whose economy is not doing well. Despite offering incentives to businesses and the resulting new factories' employment of over 1,000 people, the unemployment rate has not changed. The article presents only one explanation for this: out-of-town workers are employed by these new factories. It is irresponsible for a journalistic publication to print something this explicit, especially when there is more than one likely explanation for the phenomenon.

One possibility is that other local businesses have closed or left Dillton, resulting in a loss of employment, due to the financial situation of the city. If we already know the city's economy is not in good shape, we can assume that businesses are failing. Two new factories have opened, but three others that were already there could have stopped operations or left the city. It is entirely possible that an equivalent number of residents have lost their jobs while the new factories are hiring others, because it is unreasonable to assume that the new factories account for the flow of all the workers in the town. This might explain why two new factories employ more than 1,000 people, but the unemployment rate of the city has not improved.

Another possibility is that the existing businesses are adversely affected by the new factories. Because of its economic problems, the city has made substantial efforts to bring in new businesses; a tax reduction and relocation grants have been put into place. These measures will undoubtedly be successful in attracting new businesses but may not benefit the residents or existing businesses within the city. Tax cut could lead to fewer jobs in the departments and organizations funded by the government and in turn affect the private sector by decreasing people's ability to consume and their jobs in it. Tax cut and relocation grants also enable the two new factories to outperform similar factories and even other businesses in shaving costs or boosting revenues, causing them to lay off workers in response. If the difference between the number of jobs gained in the new factories and that of jobs lost in current businesses is zero, the city's overall unemployment percentage could remain the same.

Still another possibility has to do with the city's record of unemployed residents. Perhaps the two factories are staffed with Dillton residents, but the residents, who were unemployed before they were hired by the factories, are still recorded as unemployed before they work at the factories for some time. In addition, because the general economic situation is not favorable, some residents who do not work but are not included in the group of unemployed people may begin to look for jobs actively at the time, and are categorized as unemployed workers, increasing the city's number of unemployed residents and raising its unemployment rate. There is even the chance that the city redefines unemployment and records more jobless residents. Any of the scenarios, if true, would rule out the possibility that the new factories have employed only non-Dillton workers.

It is likely that the two new factories in Dillton have only hired workers from other cities. However, based on what little information we have to work with, there are at least three other plausible explanations for the common, albeit puzzling, situation.

148. Building a HobCo Hobby Shop in <u>Grilldon</u> (Questions to Be Answered)

The author recommends a location for a new HobCo Hobby Shop in southeastern Grilldon, reasoning that this store will be a successful one because the location is ideal in the region. However, we need answers to some questions before we determine the soundness of the recommendation.

We must ask whether the respondents are representative of the area residents. The researchers polled local residents and discovered that 88 percent of the respondents would welcome a hobby shop in southeastern Grilldon. However, we do not know how many residents were targeted for this research or what questions the researchers asked. If the number of respondents only made up a very small percentage of the area residents, their opinion was unlikely to be typical of that of all the residents. Nor do we know how many respondents were counted. 88 percent is a staggering statistic, but if only 50 people participated, the number would not be significant. Furthermore, we wonder what questions were asked in the poll. If asked whether they welcomed a hobby shop, the respondents might have answered "Yes." However, this is not the same as welcoming HobCo. Even if they welcomed HobCo, there is no guarantee that they would spend money in the HobCo store to be opened. Without more information about the poll results, we cannot fully evaluate the recommendation.

Next, we should inquire whether southeastern Grilldon is an ideal location for a new HobCo store. Citing an increase of 300 percent in hobby business in the last decade, the author predicts that the next HobCo store will attract many hobby customers. One question that the claim raises is whether an increase of 300 percent represents something significant. We do not know. If it rose from 5 customers to 20 customers, it is not impressive. If it rose from 50 to 200, it is. Another question that the claim raises is whether the trend of thriving business will continue. No evidence is provided in this regard. It is entirely possible that hobby business will decline in Grilldon and even vanish altogether. Still another question that the claim raises is why southeastern Grilldon does not already have at least one hobby shop. Grilldon is supposedly in an area of the country in which the hobby industry thrives, but there are no hobby shops in southeastern Grilldon now. It could be that local residents' need for hobby shops has been satisfied in other ways, for example, by hobby shops in nearby areas. It could even be that the need has been met online. If this is true, the author cannot confidently claim that southeastern Grilldon is a suitable place for a new HobCo shop. Besides, southeastern Grilldon may be a poor place where people cannot afford hobbies. The residents may welcome a hobby shop, but they will not patronize it, because it is beyond their means, as evidenced by the absence of one in this region. The memo seems confident that a new HobCo shop will do well in this area but fails to offer relevant evidence. Answers to the above questions are critical for our assessment of the author's claim that HobCo stands to benefit from opening an additional shop in southeastern Grilldon.

Finally, we wonder whether the retiree population of Grilldon, another selling point used in the memo, will be potential customers for the HobCo shop in the region. Although the retiree population is described as "a very large population", we just do not know the size. Even if the number of retirees is significant, the author cannot justifiably assume that they will be willing to spend their money and leisure time on hobbies, because they may need to take care of their grandchildren. Even assuming that they are willing to do so, they may not allocate money or time to hobbies that HobCo focuses on. It is possible that HobCo is specialized in hobbies for young people. It is also possible that southeastern Grilldon is far away from the location where retirees live, making it difficult for them to commute. Therefore, the author may need to investigate other hobby shops in the region to compare their products and services to HobCo's. The poll cited by the author could be helpful in this respect, but again, we have no information about who has been asked or the number of respondents. While a senior citizen community may want to shop at this hobby store, it is just as likely that senior centers will organize other activities. In that event, the assumption that the new shop may benefit from the city's large retiree population would prove unwarranted, rendering the recommendation gratuitous.

In conclusion, we cannot determine whether the recommendation of opening a HobCo shop in southeastern Grilldon will have the predicted result, as the argument stands now. To better evaluate the argument, we need information about the polling of residents, the region's relationship with hobby shops, and the retiree demographic of the town. While the recommendation seems viable in theory, the company would benefit from asking more questions and gathering more relevant information.

149. Do teens eating the most family meals have better behaviors? (Questions to Be Answered)

The author recommends that adolescents take part in family meals at least seven times each week. To justify the recommendation, the article cites a study of over 5,000 students in the Appleton school district, wherein nearly thirty percent reported having at least seven meals per week with their families, and the students who reported having the most family meals per week experienced decreased likelihood that they would use harmful substances like drugs, tobacco, and alcohol. It also notes that family meals helped them experience fewer mental disorders such as low self-esteem and depression and avoid academic performance issues. While these findings are interesting at first glance, we need answers to some questions about the study before we determine whether the recommendation is sound.

A foundational question that must be answered is whether the sample of the cited study is representative of all adolescents of the Appleton school district. In any study that is conducted, a sample large enough to be representative of the total population is necessary in order to reasonably apply any findings to people beyond the participants. In this case, the newsletter reports that over 5,000 adolescents from the district were surveyed. However, we are not told exactly how many young people there are in the district; therefore, it is possible that this number comprises a significant portion of the youth population, or an irrelevantly small one. Should the former be the case, it would make the data worthy of further research; yet if the latter were true, then the study would be statistically unreliable. Even if the participants surveyed are representative of Appleton adolescents, there is no guarantee that they typify adolescents in other places as well. Without information about the sample size relative to the target population, the author cannot fairly assume that the sample represents adolescents in general.

Another question that should be addressed has to do with the percentage of young people that have had the most meals with their families each week and are most unlikely to have had bad behaviors like taking illegal drugs. The study findings show that only around 30 percent of teens ate meals with their families at least seven times each week, and that only the ones who ate the most meals were least likely to consume illegal drugs, tobacco, and alcohol. However, we do not know the percentage of teens who reported having the most family meals per week. If they accounted for only 1 percent of the 5,000 surveyed, then the findings would be statistically insignificant. Alternatively, a relatively large percentage would make for a more compelling data set. Even if the number of adolescents who reported eating the most family meals and having no bad behaviors was significant, there is the possibility that they did so simply to make themselves socially acceptable, whereas in fact they have not eaten many family meals each week and have had bad behaviors. There is also the possibility that the teens' memory was unreliable and misrepresented the number of family meals they had each week and their use of illegal drugs, tobacco, and alcohol. Either of the scenarios would invalidate the data set and the claim that teens will benefit greatly from eating family meals at least seven times a week.

Finally, regarding the connection between a high number of family meals and reduced instances of bad behavior and mental issues, it begs the question of whether the meals themselves were the cause at all. No information is given about the families of the students surveyed and about the Appleton school district itself. The connection could have been a correlation rather than a causation. The support of the students' families and the wealth of the area could have played a great role in the good behavior and mental health of the adolescents in the study. If Appleton were revealed to be a rich school district and the students' families loving and supportive, then the connection between family meals and the alleged benefits would be tenuous at best. Otherwise, there would be a stronger case for the connection. Even if the link between family meals and fewer cases of bad behavior and mental issues is valid for adolescents in the Appleton school district, there is no guarantee that it is valid for adolescents in other places. Even if having more family meals a week can address adolescents' bad behaviors and mental issues noted in the article, there is no guarantee that this can address their other bad behaviors as well. Should this be true, the assumption that more family meals were responsible for lower rates of adolescents' bad behaviors in general would prove unwarranted, rendering the recommendation implausible.

In summary, there are many questions surrounding the study and answers to them would help us better assess the recommendation. As the case currently stands, too little information is provided regarding the sample size of the study and the percentage of young people in the study who received the benefits. Furthermore, there is no clear evidence linking the benefits to frequent family meals in particular.

150. Fighting allergy symptoms with Nosinia (Questions to Be Answered)

The author recommends that the herb Nosinia be used to help people relieve their severe allergy symptoms but leaves many questions to be addressed surrounding the study the article uses as support. We need answers to these questions to better assess the recommendation.

The author must answer whether the sample is representative of people with allergies in general. It is standard practice in medical science, or any form of research for that matter, that studies are conducted multiple times on a large number of test subjects. However, in the newsletter, the researchers conducted a study of the comparative effect of Nosinia and a placebo on only 95 men and women. Also, the newsletter does not state that of the 95 people, how many of them took either Nosinia or the placebo. The sample could have been too small, and the participants that took Nosinia could have been even smaller. In such scenarios, the sample may not offer relevant data and is unlikely to be representative of people with allergies, weakening the claim regarding Nosinia's benefits. Furthermore, we do not know whether the 95 people have been randomly selected. If not, they might constitute an aberration. For example, they might have been mostly stakeholders of Nosinia, reporting only its positive effects. Or their particular physical constitution might have made their bodies responsive to the medicine. Any such scenarios would cast serious doubt on the claim regarding Nosinia's positive effect on allergy. Without information about the representativeness of the study participants, the author cannot justifiably recommend treating allergies with Nosinia, let alone severe allergy symptoms.

Even granting that the sample size and demographics are acceptable, the effect of Nosinia on severe allergy symptoms is still highly suspect. The men and women in the study suffered from seasonal allergies to ragweed pollen and reported no significant relief after taking the placebo and Nosinia. Yet the researchers found that Nosinia was more effective than the placebo at relieving the most serious symptoms. However, no evidence is provided to substantiate the claim. Even if it was better than the placebo as a treatment, there is no guarantee that it was any good, since we do not know how effective the placebo was. Even assuming it was efficacious, this does not necessarily mean that it will work better than prescription medications, rendering the recommendation gratuitous. Nor do we know the number of participants with the most severe allergy symptoms. If only a few had them, the number could be statistically insignificant. The group with the most serious allergies could have been an anomaly and factors other than Nosinia could have been responsible for the relief. The participants' gender and age could have played a part. The point of time could also have been a factor. The researchers made a comparison between Nosinia and the placebo recently in participants with seasonal allergies. It is entirely possible that the particular point of time, with its specific weather, rather than some other factor, has affected the efficacy of Nosinia. Such scenarios would further call into question the validity and reliability of the study.

Even if Nosinia was effective at treating the most severe allergies to ragweed pollen, the author should also answer whether it is applicable to serious allergies in general. It is possible that it may not apply to the most severe allergies to other sources. Even assuming it was effective in offering relief for all the most serious allergy symptoms, there is no guarantee that it will provide relief for serious allergy symptoms in general, rendering the recommendation unreasonable. We must ask whether there was a control group that differed from the experimental group in just one respect: taking Nosinia. If this was the experimental design, the author could be more confident of Nosinia's efficacy. Otherwise, the claim regarding Nosinia's effect of relieving severe allergy symptoms would be but a groundless overgeneralization. Therefore, without clarification of Nosinia's efficacy regarding serious allergy to ragweed pollen and regarding serious allergy in general, the author cannot confidently recommend it based on the findings of the study.

Finally, the author needs to answer whether self-reported "feeling healthier" constitutes evidence that the herb had the intended effect. Specifically, the effectiveness was measured by the feelings of relief as reported by the men and women in the study. However, allergies are caused by the body's reaction to allergens, such as the ragweed pollen in the study, and therefore the effectiveness of Nosinia should have a quantifiable explanation regarding the mechanism of relief. Simply stating that the people in the study "felt healthier" after taking Nosinia and using that as justification for recommending it as a treatment could hardly be plausible. To make things worse, the poll was done at the end of the study, an issue that needs to be addressed to convince us of the effect of Nosinia, because some other lurking factors might have helped the subjects cure severe allergy symptoms that they were experiencing. For example, the seasonal allergy may have disappeared by the end of the season, while the study was still in progress. Perhaps the subjects had unknowingly taken some other medicine that cured the allergy by the end of the study. Or perhaps they reported "feeling healthier" just to receive compensation that producers of Nosinia might have promised. Without ruling out these and other factors that could have made the participants more likely to report feeling better, the author cannot reasonably conclude that Nosinia should be used to fight severe allergy symptoms. Without information about the efficacy of Nosinia relative to prescription medications, the author cannot confidently recommend the former over the latter for relieving severe allergy symptoms.

To conclude, the sample size of the Nosinia study is likely far too small and the methods are likely far too vague to glean any useful data about the herb's effectiveness. Likewise, there is no scientific explanation given for the supposed effects of the herb on the participants' symptoms. Before the author clarifies these issues, we wonder how such a recommendation has ended up in a health newsletter in the first place.

151. Do teens eating the most family meals have better behaviors? (Alternative Explanations)

In this article from the website Science News Today, the author claims that adolescents who take part in family meals at least seven times each week are less likely to use harmful substances like drugs, tobacco, and alcohol, and more likely to demonstrate higher self-esteem, lower rates of depression, and better academic performance. The claim is based on a study of over 5,000 students, wherein nearly thirty percent reported having at least seven meals each week with their families. While these findings are interesting at first glance, other factors could be equally viable explanations.

One alternative factor could be self-discipline. It is a common perception that young people are naturally rebellious and willing to engage in maladaptive behaviors. However, it is entirely possible that the adolescents surveyed simply, of their own volition, did not partake in use of drugs, tobacco, or alcohol. It is also possible that they intentionally stayed away from environments and people that might have bad influences on them and cause them to try stuff like illegal drugs. It is even possible that they made every effort to learn about unacceptable behaviors and ways to prevent them. In such scenarios, those surveyed chose not to engage in bad behaviors. Even if they did not have many family meals, they could still succeed in making good decisions. Thus, one should not be too quick to assume that the young people in the study were only reliant on eating with their families in order to make sensible decisions. Without relevant evidence, it is unfair to rule out self-discipline as one of the explanations.

Another likely factor is good parenting that may have an even greater effect on keeping young people on the straight and narrow. For example, it may be that the parents of the teens in the study had exemplary behavior and served as models for their children. It may also be that they often educated their children about bad behaviors and ways to stay away from them. It may even be that they were attentive to their children's needs and provided proper support and guidance as needed. If this is the case, children would probably conduct themselves well and would not engage in unacceptable behaviors. While good parenting may affect youth development positively, few would be surprised when young people from "broken homes" fall prey to drug abuse and alcoholism. Thus, the survey findings may have been the result of nurturing parents rather than simply eating together.

Still another possible factor is the communities in which the teens who were surveyed live. However, we know little about this. It is likely that growing up in affluent communities is a major factor in the lack of illicit activities, production of outstanding students, and general mental well-being of the people living there. The converse is also true, with poverty-stricken areas having high rates of teen drug use, abysmal academic performance, and depression. Therefore, it is possible that the teens were simply afforded the luxuries of wealthy communities, such as high-quality education and well-policed neighborhoods, and raised in an environment that fostered good mental health. In this case, the survey findings may have arisen from the adolescents' living areas rather than from having many meals with their families.

While eating together may have some positive effects on teen behavior, based on the vague information given in the article, we should not put too much stock in the claims surrounding family meals. After all, numerous socio-economic factors may have more significant effects on young people's behaviors. Such factors include but certainly are not limited to young people's personal decisions, parental support, and the financial stability of both the household and the community.

152. Declining donations to educational institutions (Alternative Explanations)

Citing a poll of 200 charitable organizations that found that donations to educational institutions decreased by 3 percent, whereas donations to international aid groups and environmental groups rose respectively by 30 percent and 23 percent and assuming that economic indicators suggest that potential donors have more disposable income, the author concludes that the decline of donations to educational institutions is due to people valuing education less than in the past. While this is an easy assumption to make, other factors could also have contributed to the decline.

One alternative explanation could be that educational institutions simply do not need the financial support any longer. This is evidenced by the fact that potential donors have greater sums of disposable income. Having more spendable money suggests higher incomes, and if this is true, that means more taxes paid to the government. Since the majority of educational institutions are supported by public funds, when wages – and by proxy, taxes – increase, so do the budgets of public schools. The same goes for private educational institutions, which tend to raise tuition as the economy improves. Thus, there may hardly be any need for people to donate money to schools if they are already paying more money in taxes to support them. Also, different original amounts of funding might account for the discrepancy in donation rates. It is likely that international aid groups and environmental groups respectively had a much smaller amount to begin with than educational institutions and therefore were more in need of donations. There is even the chance that they received much fewer donations from unpolled charitable organizations and other sources than educational institutions. This would explain why they had a much greater rise in donations than educational groups.

A similar line of reasoning could be that people have lost their trust in charities related to education. A major issue of education is the stagnation of teacher salaries against increasing salaries for those in administrative roles in schools. Citizens, while having plenty of disposable income, may perceive their donated funds as being mismanaged and not benefiting teachers, who deserve more financial reward than any other members of the education system. It is, therefore, perfectly reasonable that donors would cease offering any more money to organizations which largely benefit employees other than teachers. However, this does not necessarily mean that people care any less about education than they did before; they simply do not want to prop up a broken system. This would also explain the drop in donations to educational institutions.

One more different reason for the decline in donations to educational institutions could be greater concern for global and environmental issues. As mentioned in the article, there was an increase in money given to international aid groups and environmental groups. This could suggest that people believe the protection of the environment and the alleviation of foreign suffering are more pressing issues than education. Yet this does not necessarily mean that education and the other two issues are mutually exclusive. People could care as much about education as in the past, or even more so; the amount of money donated to schools does not necessarily reflect people's overall concern for learning. In fact, having more disposable income is an indicator of having higher education, since bachelor's and even professional master's degrees are often necessary for higher incomes. Thus, the disparity in donation rates might also be explained by people's more concern for global and environmental issues and less concern for educational issues rather than by their decreased concern for educational groups than in the past.

To conclude, the author needs to provide evidence that a decline in donations to educational institutions is indicative of a decrease in the value people place on education. Without evidence by way of reliable and valid surveys of donor perceptions of education in the past and at present, the author cannot rule out other possibilities. Perhaps the institutions no longer need the financial support. Or perhaps people believe that educational institutions would misuse the donations. Or perhaps the increase in donated money to non-educational institutions indicates that people have increased concern for relevant issues.

153. Rising Relannian dairy prices (Alternative Explanations)

The author concludes that farmers in Relanna are artificially increasing the price of cream in order to enhance their profits because cream in local markets costs double the price two years ago. To support the conclusion, the letter cites a 25 percent increase in the number of dairy farms in the last ten years. It also states that new milking technology has increased the efficiency of milking, reducing milking times and the need for human labor. Finally, it cites data from the local Department of Agriculture, which indicates a lower labor cost at most dairy farms than ten years before. However, there may be other explanations for the spike in the price of cream.

To begin with, decreased supply of cream may account for the significant increase in its price. While Relanna has more dairy farms today than ten years ago, the number could have halved compared with two years ago, the number producing cream could have become even smaller, and those still producing cream could have halved their production, significantly reducing the supply of cream and increasing its price. Also, while new technology has greatly facilitated milk production in Relanna, there may not be an equal increase in the efficiency of cream production. Meanwhile, the local government could have begun to impose a quota system that regulates the amount of cream the dairy farms could produce two years ago. It could even be that more people were beginning to consume cream. Any of the scenarios, if true, would cast serious doubt on the claim that farmers are raising their profits by inflating the price of cream.

In addition, increasing costs associated with cream production could be factors in the spike of cream prices. Feed costs that have been rising may be one factor. Despite an improvement in milk extraction technology, the process of turning milk into cream may still be costly. While labor costs at most dairy farms are lower now than ten years ago, this does not necessarily mean that those for producing cream have decreased. They may remain the same, or even have increased as workers demand much higher salaries now than two years ago. It may even be that the government has stopped the support of prices that it provided two years ago to the dairy farms that produced cream. Naturally, all such scenarios would explain a higher price paid by the consumer in stores, since creameries will pass on the increased cost to their customers. Again, the dramatic rise in cream price is not attributable only to the possibility that farmers are artificially raising the price of cream to boost their profits.

Finally, it is likely that local markets take advantage of lower cost products to charge customers more and reap the benefits of the dairy farmers' improvements. For the sake of argument, let us say that the cost of cream has decreased along with the cost of milk due to decreased dairy labor costs and more efficient milk production technology. This would mean that farmers would be able to sell more of their products at a lower price to local markets. However, since local markets are the final distributors, they can decide at what price the cream will be sold, and customers will have no choice but to pay it. It is possible that to receive more profits, they have recently increased the price of cream one hundred percent against two years ago. Therefore, a simple explanation for higher cream prices could be that local markets, rather than the farmers, are the ones inflating prices in an attempt to increase their profits. It is also possible that to enable farmers to receive more benefits, the government has recently begun to regulate the price of cream by doubling it on the basis of the price two years ago, another scenario that might explain the increase in the price of cream.

While it is possible that farmers are trying to increase their profits on cream by inflating its price, other factors could provide reasons for the doubling in the price of cream at Relannian markets. Reduced supply of cream could be one reason. Rising costs of cream production could be another. Finally, it may be the distributors themselves rather than the farmers that are inflating the prices of cream. It would be helpful to have data on cream production specifically rather than just data on milk production.

154. Uses of Dodecan pemchints (Alternative Explanations)

When explaining the finding of a pemchint, a musical instrument used by Dodecan people, among hunters' tools at a site that was miles away from the nearest Dodecan settlement, the author concludes that while pemchints were previously found among other instruments exclusively at ritualistic or celebratory sites, this new discovery implies that the pemchint was used to ward off dangerous wildlife. Yet there are several other explanations for this outlier pemchint.

One very simple explanation for finding the pemchint along with hunters' tools could be that it was used to honor a kill. Hunters could have brought it on hunts or have created it shortly after a kill. It is clearly stated in the article that pemchints were made from hollow pieces of bone, shell, or wood. It is, therefore, likely that a hunter, having recently taken down an animal, crafted a pemchint from the slain creature's bones. This also correlates with the other hunters' tools which were found with the pemchint, as such tools would likely be necessary for the removal of the bones and skin required to create the instrument. The article also mentions that pemchints were likely used in rituals and celebrations due to their discovery among other musical instruments at ceremonial sites. It is, thus, possible that the pemchint was thereafter used as a part of some kind of ritual to honor the animal which it had killed. It is also possible that hunters used other musical instruments at the celebration, but they only buried the pemchint with their tools and forgot to bury the other instruments. This would help resolve the paradox regarding the pemchint's location and surroundings.

Another likely reason that the pemchint was found with hunters' tools has to do with its durability. The article notes that it remained with the tools in the location, whereas other musical instruments were not found there. The pemchint, perhaps as a musical instrument to attract target animals before hunting, might have been buried with hunters' tools and other musical instruments as a celebration after hunting. It might have survived because it was specially treated and well-preserved as an important symbol with hunting tools. It might also have remained in existence because it was made of bone or shell. On the contrary, the other musical instruments made of materials with little durability and constant exposure to air and humidity might have decayed with time. This could account for the fact that it was left only with hunters' tools.

A final reason for discovering the pemchint with hunters' tools so far from the nearest Dodecan settlement could be that it was discarded with other items by travelers. Perhaps a small group of Dodecans were ranging out in the wilderness and set upon by some large predator or encountered extreme weather and were forced to flee for their lives. Certainly, in such a scenario, travelers could have initially brought with them items they thought were important, such as hunting and ceremonial tools, including the pemchint. However, when the heat of the moment overtook them, the unfortunate Dodecans could have simply dropped what was in their hands and run for their lives. The article does not state whether any human remains were found nearby, so it is possible that the items were dropped in a panic. This would also explain why the pemchint was found with hunters' tools.

To summarize, the author makes a very quick assumption when suggesting that the pemchint was only used to scare off predators. It is equally likely that from the bones of an animal that was recently hunted, the pemchint was created and used as a part of a hunter's ritual. There is also the possibility that the pemchint continued to exist, whereas the other musical instruments decayed. Finally, it may have been a part of the personal possessions of travelers who were forced to abandon their items in the face of some unknown emergency. Without more information about the site in which the pemchint was found, it is almost impossible to know for certain why it was there in the first place.

155. Link between health and stair usage (Alternative Explanations)

The author concludes that the exercise that residents of stairs-only buildings have increases their health and longevity. To support the conclusion, the article cites the findings of a study on people in stairs-only buildings and people that live in buildings with both stairs and elevators: people in the former live three years longer than the residents in the latter. It also relies on a study of elderly residents living in buildings with elevators who visit the doctor twice as many times as their stairs-only counterparts. Last of all, it presents the findings of patient questionnaires in which residents of stairs-only buildings scored higher than those of buildings that had elevators. However, for these findings, there may be reasons other than being forced to use the stairs on a daily basis.

The fact that people who live in buildings with only stairs have longer lifespans than people with access to elevators may have nothing to do with stairs. It may be the case that the people who choose to live in buildings that only have stairs live healthier lifestyles overall. They may prefer to eat healthier food and exercise more frequently and thus their lifespan may be extended as a consequence of a sum of their habits. This is further supported by the findings of the questionnaires, on which stairs-only residents scored higher on overall health factors than their elevator-using counterparts. Thus, the choice of living in a building without an elevator may be an effect of their lifestyle choices which lengthen their lives, rather than the cause itself.

Next, the fact that elderly residents of buildings with elevators need more visits to the doctor may be the result of preexisting medical conditions that require them to have access to an elevator. For instance, an elderly person who has a bad back, or is confined to a wheelchair, will have no choice but to take an elevator. Such a condition will also account for the increased frequency of doctor visits in order to monitor their condition and ensure that no complications arise. Their counterparts that live in stairs-only buildings may be relatively younger and do not need the regular visits that advanced age demands. In addition, though one group has twice as many doctor visits as the other one, we do not know if one or two individuals make many visits, or perhaps a wide range of people pay numerous visits. If the former is true, the author cannot reliably conclude that stair usage contributes to better health of residents living in buildings with only stairs.

Finally, it may be the case that the people who live in stairs-only buildings have higher income levels and therefore live a better life than those who reside in buildings with elevators. This may seem counterintuitive at first, since an elevator is an added feature, until one considers that the majority of apartment buildings with elevators are large towers with small apartments. This could mean that wealthier citizens live in larger apartments in buildings with fewer floors, whereas less wealthy citizens live in small efficiencies in 20-plus-floor buildings that require an elevator to get to the higher floors. In such a case, the wealthier residents have no need of an elevator since they live in buildings with fewer floors and have access to better food and healthcare due to their superior salaries, enjoying longer and healthier lives. This scenario also rules out stair usage as the only factor in promoting health and longevity.

In sum, the finding for the health benefits of living in buildings without elevators is compelling but by no means the only explanation for the difference in health between residents of buildings with elevators and those of buildings with only stairs. There could be differences in the lifestyles of the residents, especially in terms of diet or exercise. The elderly residents of buildings with elevators may have preexisting conditions which preclude the use of stairs. Equally likely is the difference in income levels between residents of buildings that have elevators and those of buildings that do not. The author needs to provide more information about these demographic factors before making any final claim regarding the overall benefits of living in a building that only has stairs.

156. Palean baskets found in Lithos (Specific Evidence)

Citing a discovery in the ancient village of Lithos of a woven basket with a pattern that was formerly thought to be unique to the village of Palea, located across the Brim River from Lithos, the author concludes that such baskets were also made by non-Palean cultures since the river is too deep and wide to cross without boats and there is no evidence of Palean boats found. However, the argument is highly suspect, and we need additional evidence before we ascertain its soundness.

One piece of evidence that we must have is proof of the river's historical impassability. The article's focus on the width and depth of the river considers only a very narrow view of transportation in the ancient world. While it may have been too difficult to cross without a boat at the exact location of the village of Palea, there could have been shallower and less broad areas at other sections of the river that allowed trade. Also, the fact that the river is very deep and wide today does not necessarily mean that it was so during the prehistoric era. If further geological data could show that the river was as impassable during the prehistoric era as it is today in all regions in which Palean people are known to have lived, it could help to substantiate the author's assumption about the origin of the Palean baskets. Thus, without evidence to suggest that crossing the river was totally impossible, the author cannot justifiably conclude that the Palean baskets were also made by non-Palean people.

Another piece of evidence that we should have is research showing that Palea itself had no boats or other means of naval travel. There is the possibility that the Paleans did have boats in the past. Just because no boats have been found does not necessarily mean that they never existed. A lack of excavation on the part of the archaeologists could be to blame for this, or perhaps the materials which the Paleans used to build the boats decayed too quickly to be preserved. Regardless, a current lack of boats found is no evidence that they never existed at all. Should this be true, the author cannot confidently claim that "Palean" baskets were also made by non-Palean cultures. More extensive excavations of Palean archeological sites that turn up no evidence of boats or boat-making apparatuses would strengthen the author's argument considerably. Even if Palea had had no boats, the people could have crossed the river by other means, for example, via a bridge, a scenario that would weaken the argument. Without relevant evidence, we cannot fully assess the argument.

A final bit of evidence required to evaluate the argument is proof that people of Lithos did not have their own boats or obtain the basket in any other way. Even if there were no areas of the river shallow or narrow enough to cross, and the Paleans themselves did not have naval capabilities, the article does not mention whether people of Lithos had boats or acquired the basket by other means. If they had boats, they could have made contact themselves with the Paleans; then they could have received as a gift, bought, stolen, or obtained in any other way the discovered basket, and brought it back to Lithos. Besides, they could have found and taken home one Palean basket that had drifted to a place accessible to the people of Lithos, for example, the riverbank on the side of Lithos. They could also have obtained one from another culture that had been in close contact with both Palea and Lithos. In such scenarios, the argument would be undermined. Since the article focuses on only the basket pattern and not on other similarities between the two peoples, there is no way of knowing whether they did not have contact. If the author wishes to make a solid claim that Lithos' baskets were original creations, she needs to provide evidence that Lithos was equally incapable of boat travel and had no contact with other cultures that might have traded with Palea.

In conclusion, the argument does not provide nearly enough evidence to fairly claim that the basket found in Lithos did not come from Palea. If we were to believe the claim, we would need more examples of this type of basket found in Lithos and more research into the Palean village to prove that there were no links between the two societies.

157. Study of rhesus monkeys and humans finds link between birth order and stimulation (Alternative Explanations)

The author concludes that birth order has an influence on the stimulation that individuals experience. To support the conclusion, the letter cites a study that found that firstborn infant rhesus monkeys produced far more cortisol when they encountered a new monkey and that first-time mothers also had far more cortisol than mothers of a few children. It also mentions that similar to the monkeys, firstborn humans produce large amounts of cortisol in stimulating situations. The explanation based on birth order, while not invalid on its own, is not the only one that could account for the facts.

One alternative explanation for the test results could be that the increase in cortisol levels is purely coincidental. According to the letter, the study measured cortisol levels of infant monkeys encountering other monkeys that they had not seen before. This scenario is far too vague to offer any real data since there is no way of knowing if the spike in cortisol production was simply a coincidence or a result of birth order. With a tiny sample of eighteen rhesus monkeys, the finding could be an anomaly. It is possible that the firstborn infant monkeys studied happen to be a group of monkeys producing high cortisol levels as a result of their interaction with unfamiliar monkeys, whereas other firstborn infant monkeys tend to produce average cortisol levels in such situations. Similarly, without information about the sample of firstborn humans, the spike in cortisol levels could be simply a coincidence. The firstborn humans studied could produce elevated cortisol levels as a result of a conditioned response: for some reason, they may not have become accustomed to their mothers' absences, whereas other firstborn humans often produce normal cortisol levels in similar situations because they may have got used to their mothers' absences. Unless the possibility of a coincidence can be removed, the author cannot claim with certainty that birth order has an effect on an individual's levels of stimulation.

Another likely explanation is that the spikes in cortisol are related to monkeys' and humans' natural growth cycle, age, or gene. The study seems to have only focused on infants and pregnant mothers. Therefore, it could be that the increase in cortisol production is nothing more than a byproduct of the birthing process, which might account for the lack of the same cortisol levels in more experienced mothers. It could also be that because they are older, firstborn monkeys are better at recognizing potential danger, for example, when meeting a strange monkey, and therefore produce cortisol more readily. It could even be that in a potentially small sample, while siblings often have similar genes, those that are genetically programmed to release more cortisol happen to be born first. Similarly, the group of monkey mothers that are genetically more likely to produce more cortisol happens to be preparing to give birth to their first children. Without considering and ruling out these factors that could contribute to an increase in cortisol levels, the author cannot confidently claim that there is no theory for high cortisol levels other than the birth order explanation.

Still another possible explanation for the increase in cortisol is simply the diet of the monkeys or humans. It may be that firstborn children of either monkeys or humans are more physically mature and take food from their weaker siblings, a behavior that may help the former produce cortisol. It may also be that they are born in a situation where resources are plentiful to allow for an increase in production of cortisol, whereas their younger siblings are not. It may even be that the diet of the firstborn humans studied is high in added-sugar, saturated fat, and similar stuff that will probably lead to high cortisol levels, or that their mothers may have such diets during pregnancy. Perhaps if the researchers did another study in which they controlled for the nutrition level and types of food eaten by mothers and infants, they would see different results. Any of the scenarios, if true, would cast serious doubt on birth order as the only factor in high cortisol levels.

In conclusion, the assertion that being firstborn is a factor in increased stimulation is an interesting if not completely convincing theory. Mere coincidence, a natural growth cycle, conditioned response, and even diets could all be equally valid explanations. We would be able to evaluate the argument fully if the author analyzed more variables in the given study, such as a larger variety of stimuli, included a wider range of age groups, and controlled for nutrition consumed by mothers and infants throughout the birth and rearing process. If the author wishes to further claim that the same may be true in humans, then she must also provide similar observations in humans.

158. Litter and vandalism in Central Plaza blamed on skateboarders (Questions to Be Answered)

The author recommends that the city ban skateboarding in Central Plaza in order to recover lost business and reduce vandalism and litter that has sprung up recently. However, we need answers to some questions to determine the soundness of the recommendation.

The first question that the author must answer is whether the decline of business in Central Plaza is a result of increased skateboarding. The author mentions that the number of shoppers has been dropping while skateboarding has been rising significantly, but no other details are provided in this regard. It is possible that because Central Plaza is located in a small suburb where most people rely on a few companies to provide most of the jobs, a recent mass layoff and in turn reduced purchasing power could be to blame. It is also possible that online shopping and delivery has become cheaper and more convenient. It is even possible that some popular shops or eateries have left, or that factors other than the skateboarders' presence in Central Plaza have contributed to a considerable increase in crime rates in surrounding areas. Any of the scenarios, if true, would undermine the claim that the current drop in business in Central Plaza is attributable to skateboarders' behavior. Thus, the recommendation of prohibiting the skateboarders could be unfounded and would only leave Central Plaza with even fewer visitors.

The second question that the author should address is whether skateboarders have been the perpetrators of the vandalism and litter. The author assumes that the concurrence of the skateboarders' presence and the increase in vandalism and litter is evidence enough to lay the blame on the skateboarders. However, the exact nature of the vandalism and litter is not mentioned in the letter. Therefore, the author must first find evidence of fault on the part of the skateboarders for the vandalism and litter. Perhaps some security camera footage of the area could shed some light on this issue. It is likely that some hooligans or gangs have committed vandalism. It is also likely that the shop owners have caused the litter. In either scenario, the author's assumption that the skateboarders have caused vandalism and litter would be unwarranted and the recommendation risks delaying resolution of the problem and alienating the skateboarders, a group of potential shoppers. Thus, accusations against the skateboarders should be withheld until the author has more details of what has been damaged or left around and whether the skateboarders have indeed caused the said destruction and littering.

If it is discovered that skateboarders are to blame, there is, then, the question of whether prohibiting them would help the business recover and whether the prohibition is viable. The author must provide data of their effect on business decline. If they have played a minor or no role in the scenario, the assumption that banning them will restore the business to its former glory would be unfounded. Also, enforcing the prohibition of skateboarding in the area requires funding. There would need to be an increase in security, a step that requires funding from what is already described as a shopping center with a dearth of funds. It is entirely possible that spending extra money on more security to remove skateboarders from the area could cause a backlash from the community, or the skateboarders themselves, and any damage that may have been accidental could become far more vindictive. In this case, banning skateboarders would not be a viable strategy. Thus, before the author considers alternative measures such as attracting popular shops or eateries to the plaza, it is unfair to assume that the ban is feasible and sufficient to reverse the decline in business in Central Plaza.

In conclusion, before the city takes any extreme measures, it needs to investigate broader socio-economic issues in the area to have some insights into why there has been less business of late. It should also research who is damaging the property and leaving trash around. Finally, it must take a look at how forbidding skateboarding would be enforced and whether that would succeed.

159. Is Adams Realty a better real estate agency? (Assumptions)

The author claims that Adams Realty is a better real estate firm than Fitch Realty. To support the claim, the letter cites the relative size of the firms from both an employee and revenue perspective. It also mentions that Adams sold houses faster than Fitch. Before we determine the soundness of the argument, we need to scrutinize the assumptions that underlie it.

The author assumes that having a larger number of full-time realtors is somehow automatically better than being smaller, yet provides no evidence to substantiate this assumption. There is the possibility that having fewer realtors and the part-time schedule means Fitch is more effective than Adams, or that the part-time schedule that many Fitch workers follow is an incentive given for the purpose of motivating them, similar to how modern tech companies award from-home office hours. The two firms' different worker profiles underlie the claim that Adams is a better choice than Fitch. If the assumption about the profiles proves to be false, the author cannot corroborate the claim. If a larger number of full-time employees indicate less productivity per capita, the author's claim regarding Adams' superiority would be groundless. To better assess the argument, we need information about two firms' employees' comparative performance per capita, including part-time employees as well as full-time employees.

In addition, the author implies that simply because Adams earned more revenues last year, it is somehow a better choice for the homeowner. However, this is not necessarily the case. It is likely that Adams made more revenues because it provides service for an area where turnover in homeownership is quicker regardless of its efficacy. Also, Adams' performance last year could have been an aberration. It is possible that Adams only made more money than Fitch last year but has made less money than it in other years. Even if Adams garnered more revenues last year, it might have garnered less revenue per capita. Any of the scenarios, if true, would cast serious doubt on the author's claim that Adams is superior to Fitch. As to the fact that the average price of homes sold by Adams is higher than that of homes sold by Fitch, it could be that regardless of Adams' efficacy, the homes that Adams sold were worth more on average than the ones that Fitch sold, or that a few outliers of each firm distorted the average prices. Should this be the case, the assumption about the relative performance of both firms on the basis of total revenues and average sales prices would be unwarranted and lend little support to the argument, unless it can be shown that Adams' revenues last year were a result of its employees' outstanding performance, and the trend is representative of its performance in general.

Finally, the author suggests that a single case is sufficient evidence that Adams can sell houses faster than Fitch. However, the example last year may have been an anomaly and purely anecdotal. There could have been any number of reasons for the speed with which Adams was able to sell the author's home so fast. For example, it may have been a coincidence that someone else was looking for a matching piece of property to buy. It may also have been that it was being sold at a price lower than its market value, since the article does not mention exactly how much the author sold her property for. Even if Adams sold it fast, there is no guarantee that it sold it faster and at a better price than Fitch, since the author does not point out how fast and at what price Fitch could have sold the same house. Similarly, regarding the house that took Fitch over four months to sell ten years ago, the event could also have been an isolated one. A myriad of factors beyond Fitch's control, such as the deteriorating economic situation or the home's conditions, might explain the speed of Fitch's sale. Even if this is evidence of Fitch's inferior performance ten years ago, this does not necessarily mean that it has not improved. Without considering and accounting for these scenarios, the author cannot justifiably claim that Adams is better than Fitch because it sold one house fast last year.

In conclusion, many assumptions underlie the claim that as a real estate firm, Adams is a choice preferable to Fitch. Were we to take it at its word, we could easily be led to put our properties in the hands of a firm that is only successful at random. To evaluate the argument fully, we need to examine the assumptions to see whether they are warranted by the data relating to the time it takes the firms to sell a home and by their sales revenues per annum, among other things.

160. Reducing Balmer Island's moped accidents by learning from Seaville (Questions to Be Answered)

The author recommends that in order to decrease the number of moped accidents during the summer months by 50 percent on Balmer Island, it place a limit on the number of mopeds that companies can rent out per day during the summer season, specifically from 50 to 25. To justify the recommendation, the letter presents the neighboring island of Seaville as an example of having successfully implemented the policy, as it was able to reach the same reduction in moped accidents after taking the course of action. However, we must have answers to certain questions before we determine whether the same result would indeed occur if Balmer places its own caps.

We want to know whether the use of mopeds in Balmer during the summer season is responsible for the moped-pedestrian accidents and whether reducing the number of moped rentals will decrease the number of accidents. However, the author offers no information in this regard. The letter simply states that the population increases to a huge number on Balmer during the summer months and that there are accidents involving mopeds and pedestrians. Yet we do not know if other factors, such as malfunctioning traffic lights, unclear road signs, alcohol or drug abuse, lack of road maintenance and lack of convenient sidewalks, contribute to these accidents. If they do, the assumption would be unwarranted. Without ruling out these and other alternative possibilities, the author cannot confidently claim that decreasing the number of moped rentals at any given time will decrease the number of accidents. Nor do we know Balmer's original population. If we are speaking of an increase of only a few hundred people, the author cannot reliably conclude that moped accidents will rise considerably. Similarly, we just do not know what portion of the new people are moped operators or pedestrians. If few of them rent a moped, they may have little impact on the number of moped accidents. Also, merely enforcing limits on moped rentals may be ineffective. The author needs to assure us that other conditions in Balmer that serve to increase the accident rate will not change. For example, people may buy mopeds instead of renting them in response to the enforcement of moped rentals, or pedestrians may increase in large numbers. Either scenario might lead to a higher rate of moped accidents. Unless there is relevant evidence, it is unfair to assume that use of mopeds has contributed to moped-pedestrian accidents in Balmer and restricting the number of moped rentals will attain the desired reduction of accidents.

We also wonder whether success of a policy on moped rentals on Seaville is proof that such a policy will be effective on Balmer as well. However, the two places may be too different from each other to justify implementing the same policy. We do not know of many circumstances that might have played a role in the accidents on Seaville. For example, we do not have information on the weather and population of Seaville or what the moped rental limits were in that area last year. It is likely that Seaville had very fine weather and experienced no population increase. It could very well be the case that Seaville receives comparatively few visitors during summertime relative to their overall population, thus decreasing the number of potential accidents and easily meeting the statistical requirement of a 50 percent reduction. It is also likely that few people rented mopeds last year. It is even likely that Seaville enforced higher moped rental standards. For example, outlets might have been only allowed to rent newer mopeds to their patrons. Therefore, factors other than limits on the number of moped rentals might have contributed to its fifty percent decrease in moped accidents. Balmer, with its population possibly exploding during the summer months and possibly different causes of moped accidents, could find it difficult to replicate the results. Even if they have the same reasons for moped accidents and enforce similar measures, there is no guarantee that Balmer will be able to enforce them as effectively as Seaville has done. For example, people on Seaville may prefer to rent mopeds, whereas people on Balmer may prefer to own mopeds. Should this be the case, the prediction would prove unjustified. Unless there is evidence that the two islands are similar enough to warrant the implementation of the same policy, the author cannot reliably predict that one island's success in decreasing moped accidents will automatically carry over to the other.

Of course, we need the answer to whether alternative solutions exist aside from simply limiting the number of rentable mopeds. Even if Balmer enforces similar restrictions on moped rentals, there is no guarantee that the overall number of moped rentals will drop, because the companies could satisfy the demand by opening more rental shops instead of supplying more rental mopeds at each shop. In this case, the assumption that restricting the number of moped rentals is the only course of action proves gratuitous. It is likely that alternative solutions exist and can be as effective or even more effective. Driver safety awareness programs could be released before and during the summer season; certain lanes could be designated as moped lanes for the duration of the summer months. There is even the possibility of simply reducing the speed limit so that riders would be forced to slow down. Many other alternatives could be suggested, ones that would help reduce moped accidents and allow the moped rental companies to continue to do business and make profits during peak travel months. Should this be true, the argument would be weakened. Without accounting for alternative solutions, the author cannot reasonably claim that limiting the number of rental mopeds is the only viable policy.

In conclusion, we need more information about the example of Seaville to see if the moped rental cap would be as effective on Balmer. There is a possibility that other factors such as a difference in population and other extenuating circumstances have been responsible for the decrease in accidents on Seaville. It is also important to consider other means of reducing accidents, ones that would not negatively impact the moped businesses on Balmer that probably rely on summer tourism for most of their income. Without answers to relevant questions, we cannot fully assess the argument.

161. Disappearance of Canada's arctic deer (Specific Evidence)

The author concludes that because reports of decreasing populations of deer coincide with warming trends that have melted sea ice, the decline must be a result of being unable to follow their usual migration patterns across frozen parts of the sea. However, before we determine whether this cause of the deer's population crisis can be declared a definitive one, we need additional evidence.

One piece of evidence that we must have involves the decline in deer populations. The most obvious issue with the argument is the reports from local hunters about the Arctic deer population. The author mentions nothing about the number of reports or actual population statistics, which leads one to think that this evidence is merely anecdotal. It may be that the hunters report fewer deer simply because they do not find them when the deer are inactive or that only two or three hunters report having observed fewer deer. In this case, the reports may be unreliable, invalidating the claim about the connection between the decline in deer populations and their inability to migrate due to global warming. In order to see if there has been any decline, the author would need to supply the hunters' concrete headcounts of the deer with which to compare to previous years' populations. Population records that show a significant decrease would corroborate the claim that there is a problem with the arctic deer's numbers but do not necessarily mean that global warming is the root cause.

Another piece of evidence that should be available has to do with the possibility that the deer have simply relocated to another area. According to the article, global warming trends have led to the melting of sea ice; therefore, it can be reasonably assumed that perhaps there are larger areas that can now grow the plants on which the deer feed, since those places are no longer covered in ice. It could be that deer populations are not dropping in arctic regions but have moved from one area to another in the regions, a scenario that would weaken the argument. It could also be that since the habitat is able to provide all the food for the deer because of the warming trend, they do not need to migrate as usual to look for more food. It could even be that the areas have not been affected as much by global warming as other areas; therefore, the deer could still migrate as in the past. Any of the scenarios, if true, would made the conclusion implausible. It would be prudent for those monitoring the deer populations to do a wider survey of the region before they declare an official state of decline. Further investigations of the surrounding regions would also help to see whether other animals have been similarly affected. If the answer is affirmative, it may lend credence to the author's argument.

Even if there is indeed a drop in deer populations, we need evidence that it is the result of merely the deer's being unable to follow their usual migration patterns across frozen parts of the sea. However, this is not necessarily the case. One possibility is poaching. It is likely that there has been a surge in demand for deer meat that would almost definitely lead to poaching, so this may be something that needs looking into. If no evidence of poaching can be found, then there would be a stronger case for disrupted migration patterns. Another possibility is disease. Some endemic disease may be affecting the deer, causing their populations to decrease significantly. If the author could provide evidence that such factors do not contribute to the decline, the argument would be strengthened. Otherwise, the author cannot reliably conclude that the mere possibility that the deer are unable to follow their usual migration patterns across frozen parts of the sea as a result of global warming trends would account for the drop in their populations.

To conclude, taking only the anecdotal evidence of some hunters and the concurrent heating trend at face value is insufficient for explaining the decline of the Arctic deer population. For full assessment of the argument, there must be more research into the actual population statistics of the herds, along with canvassing of larger areas to see if relocation may account for the reduced number of sightings. There should also be further investigation of factors other than deer's inability to follow their usual migration patterns across frozen parts of the sea.

162. A new café for Monarch Books (Questions to Be Answered)

The author recommends that Monarch Books open a café in its store in order to attract more customers and compete with Regal Books that recently started a café. To justify the recommendation, the article claims that it could remove the children's book section to make space for the café, citing census data showing a considerable decline in the percentage of the people under the age of ten. However, before we determine whether Monarch should undertake such a renovation, we need answers to some questions.

The first question that must be addressed is whether opening a café in Monarch's store would help it entice more customers. The article mentions that Monarch has a large customer base and is well-known for its book selection. It is important for the board of directors to consider whether having a café would attract more customers than it already has. The article makes no mention of declining profits or a loss of customers, nor does it indicate whether Monarch's readers are interested in having a café in its store, so we must wonder whether spending the money to renovate its store would even be necessary. Should this plan fail, not only would the store lose money from the initial renovation, but it would then need to spend even more money to renovate once again to remove the café. More importantly, it risks losing a great number of customers because of the chaos and diminishing space for books. In this case, Monarch may not need a café in its store, rendering the recommendation unreasonable.

Another question that should be answered is whether Regal has benefited from its new café. The recommendation assumes that opening this café will help Monarch to compete with Regal, which already opened its own café. However, the article gives no evidence that opening a café has helped Regal at all. For all we know, it could have hurt its business by adding a huge maintenance cost to its budget. After all, a bookstore by itself is fairly easy to maintain; all one needs to do is to keep the building at a certain temperature and humidity, but a café has to be constantly cleaned, repaired, and resupplied. As a result, Regal may have been adversely affected by its own coffee shop. If this is true, there is no guarantee that Monarch will benefit from one, not to mention that launching a café will help it to ward off competition from Regal. A long-term analysis of the effects of Regal's café on its business is needed before Monarch passes judgement on the benefits of having one. If there is evidence that Regal has not profited from its café, the author cannot confidently claim that Monarch should open one in its own store.

A final question that needs to be considered is whether the census data is relevant. The article suggests making room for the café by getting rid of the children's book section, using national census data that shows a decline in the percentage of the population under the age of ten. However, as we know, census data accounts for past trends and cannot always be trusted to predict future scenarios. Monarch has been in business for over twenty years and is known for its wide selection of books, after all. If it hopes to stay in business for another twenty years, or even longer, it needs to plan for the real trend. If there is no decrease in the number of children younger than ten in the future, the store may lose much business by replacing its children's book section with a café because doing so may hurt its reputation as a store with a variety of books on every subject and with one section devoted to children's books. Even if there is a drop in the portion of the people below ten, there may not be a drop in the number of children below ten, because the total population could rise. Even assuming that there is an eventual decrease in the number of children under ten, there may be an increase in the number of children above ten. Granted that there is a decline in the number of all the children, there may be no decline in sales of children's books, because children may buy more books on average as a result of factors such as parents' desire to nurture their children's literacy skills through reading or programs that they participate in. Even if the national trend continues, there is no guarantee that it will be true for Monarch where the percentage of the population under age ten may not decrease locally and will remain so in the future. Any of the scenarios, if true, would cast serious doubt on the prediction that Monarch with a café in its store will attract more customers and become more competitive, rendering the recommendation unfounded.

In conclusion, the information in the argument needs further scrutiny before Monarch decides to spend a considerable amount of money to add a café to its store. It must consider whether its customer base or profits are under threat and whether the example of Regal is indeed a valid one. It must also take into account the long-term effects of removing its children's section if it is to maintain in the future its reputation for having a large selection of books.

163. Does Buckingham College need new dormitories? (Specific Evidence)

The author argues that Buckingham College should build new dormitories in order to meet the needs of its growing enrollment. To support the argument, the memo, citing the current growth trend, predicts a doubling of enrollment in the next 50 years and an increase in the average rent prices in the college's town. It also mentions the addition of new dormitories to make the school more attractive to potential students. However, these reasons alone are inadequate to support such a large venture. We need extra evidence before we determine the soundness of the argument.

To begin with, the author must provide evidence that Buckingham's enrollment will double over the next 50 years to make current dormitory space inadequate. The memo states that according to existing trends, the author expects the enrollment to increase one hundred percent over the next 50 years, but this projection is taken for granted. A myriad of factors may contribute to a decline in future student enrollment in Buckingham. For example, it is possible that college is considered worth the money now, because it is essential for a reasonable job, but many may question the utility of a college education over the next 50 years because it is too expensive. Even if people do not question the benefits of college education in general, they may doubt those of an education in Buckingham. It is also possible that many attend college now because federal loans are easily available, but fewer people may do so because it is harder to get federal loans. Even if the enrollment will increase over the next 50 years, there is no guarantee that it will double. Even assuming that it will increase to twofold the original size, this does not necessarily mean that existing dormitory space will fall short of the demand, because future students may choose not to live in the dormitory. Any of the scenarios, if true, would invalidate the claim that the enrollment will double in the future to make the dormitory space inadequate. If the college relies on the enrollment trend alone to make the decision to expand its on-campus housing, it risks making projections on the basis of a very limited amount of data.

Also, the author should offer evidence that students will find it hard to afford off-campus housing. The author points out that the average rent has increased recently, but this in no way means that it will continue to increase for 50 years. The college would do well to study housing bubble trends, which fluctuate wildly based on numerous socio-economic factors. It is doubtful that the rent would continuously increase for 50 years in any one area, as this unfairly assumes that there will be no factor that serves to decrease the off-campus rent. In fact, there could be new real-estate developments in the town during that period of time, reducing the average rent. If the rising trend of the rent does not persist, it is unjustifiable to assume that students will not be able to pay for off-campus housing, to say nothing of the possibility that the average apartment rent in the town may be very low at present and will be low for years to come relative to that for the dormitories. Even if off-campus housing will be more difficult to afford in the future, this does not necessarily mean that students will live in the dormitory. Some may choose to live with their parents if the college is not too far away from home. In that case, the dormitory space could still be adequate, rendering the recommendation of building new dormitories gratuitous.

Finally, the author needs to furnish evidence that nice new dormitories will be enough to make prospective students want to enroll. However, the author offers no evidence in this regard. Potential students choose to attend a college or university for different reasons. It is likely that some factors regarding higher education, for example, added features, will be popular at some points, but other factors will be popular at other points. In some years nice new dormitories may be attractive but still cannot persuade students to attend Buckingham. In other years, they may not be attractive at all. Should this be the case, there would be little justification for building impressive new dormitories simply on the basis of their potential to draw more applications to the college. Absent relevant evidence, the author cannot reasonably claim that nice new dormitories will be adequate to attract prospective students, and it is risky to rely on a tactic that may become useless as the attraction for potential students shifts to other considerations. In that event, the recommendation would be unreasonable.

To conclude, Buckingham must pay attention to the time frame for which it is projecting the benefit of new dormitories, for in 50 years, its projections of increased enrollment and higher average rents in the city may be far from correct. It must also consider whether dormitories fit into what college students desire. With adequate relevant evidence, we can better ascertain the soundness of the case for new dormitories.

164. Nature's Way looks to open a new branch in Plainsville (Assumptions)

The author claims that the new Nature's Way store in Plainsville will be successful because this town fits the targeted demographic of people with an interest in healthy living. To justify the claim, the article cites the local merchant sales of running shoes and exercise clothing, health club membership and attendance, and the fact that the Plainsville school system requires children to participate in a fitness program that encourages regular exercise. However, the argument is replete with assumptions and loopholes that we must scrutinize before we ascertain its validity.

First, the author assumes that the reports by merchants on the sales of exercise clothing and running shoes represent an overall mindset of the populace that will continue into the long-term future. However, the reports are not accompanied by any statistics or time-frames. It is possible that this recent sales trend is nothing more than a short-lived fad, or, depending on the size of the town, a trend that will end once products reach market saturation. The fact that sales of running shoes and exercise clothing are at all-time highs means little by itself. The sales may be miniscule to begin with and still insignificant compared with sales in other comparable cities. Moreover, all-time highs in these sales do not necessarily mean Plainsville residents live healthy lives –perhaps people often buy such merchandise to show off rather than use it. Even assuming that they lead healthy lives, the author has yet to establish the connection between living healthy lives and buying enough products of Nature's Way to make the new store profitable. If this turns out to be the case, then there is a high chance that the new Nature's Way store in Plainsville will not be profitable. If the assumption is warranted that this trend is indicative of a mindset of the populace and will persist, the residents in Plainsville may live healthy lives, making the argument more persuasive.

The author also implies that the health club's membership and class attendance is a sign that the entire town follows a healthy lifestyle. However, this could be an overestimation based on a small sample. Gyms and health centers usually cater to middle to higher-income earners, who may make up a smaller percentage of a population. Thus, it is entirely possible that the number of members in the health club represents only a small portion of Plainsville's total population, despite an increase in membership and some full classes. The market capacity could be negligible to begin with, so an all-time high in numbers could be an increase of a handful, hardly justifying the opening of a new store. The fact that the weight training and aerobics classes are full is not convincing, either, as it may simply be that the club is too small to accommodate many clients or does not have enough people to teach many classes. The fact that it almost closed for lack of business five years before could also be a cause for concern. If Plainsville does not have enough people of sufficient income levels to purchase Nature's Way products, the new store may not last long, let alone becoming very profitable.

Finally, the author suggests that because schoolchildren are required to participate in a fitness-for-life program, they will be potential customers in the future. However, compulsory participation does not necessarily mean genuine interest in health and may even provoke a reaction against health-conscious living, especially among teenagers. Besides, children may not hold onto every idea that we attempt to imprint on them when they are very young, and while some may well become Nature's Way customers in the future, there is also the possibility that none of them will. The program may not be successful at present, and even if it is effective now, there is no guarantee that it will be successful in the future. Even assuming that it will prosper in the future, the author cannot be certain that Plainsville's schoolchildren will become Nature's Way customers as a result. The author must establish the connection between stressing the benefits of regular exercise at an early age and living a healthy life later. If Plainsville schoolchildren do not grow up to lead healthy lives and buy Nature's Way products, the new store may not be affected much in the short term but needs to seek out a different target demographic in the long term, or risks going out of business, not to mention being very successful.

In sum, the assumptions that underlie the argument are based on data that is far too vague to be reliable. To better evaluate the argument, we must have more concrete market data to see whether the sales of health-related products are a short-lived fad and more detailed population statistics to decide whether the people of Plainsville can afford the store. We should also scrutinize the fitness-for-life program to determine whether it has had any real effect on contributing to the healthy lifestyles of children as they age. Only in this way can we fully assess the claim that a new store of Nature's Way in Plainsville will be very successful.

165. Child-rearing practices on the island of <u>Tertia</u> (Questions to Be Answered)

The author points out that Dr. Karp claims that Dr. Field was completely wrong in his observation-based conclusion that Tertian children were raised by their entire village. She also notes that some anthropologists recommend that the interview-centered method rather than the observation-centered approach be used to study child-rearing in the future. Dr. Karp's claim and the anthropologists' recommendation are based on the fact that in later interviews with the children conducted by Dr. Karp, he found that the children spent more time talking about their biological parents than about other village adults. To fully assess the recommendation and its argument, we need answers to some key questions.

The first question that must be answered is whether any significant changes have taken place since Dr. Field's research. His observations took place twenty years ago, enough time for an entire generation of young people to mature into adulthood. It is entirely possible that over the past twenty years, the island of Tertia has seen significant socio-economic changes. Perhaps children on Tertia were raised by a whole village twenty years ago, but they were raised by their biological parents because of outside influences when Dr. Karp conducted the interviews. Researchers should look into the recent history of Tertia to see if such influences have existed that may account for the apparent change in child-rearing practices. If yes, the claim that Dr. Field drew a wrong conclusion about child-rearing practices on Tertia would be weakened. Otherwise, there would be a stronger case for the claim. Without relevant information, the author cannot convince me of Dr. Karp's claims regarding Dr. Field's conclusion and the comparative merit of interviewing versus observation.

The next question that should be answered is whether Dr. Karp used the proper methodology to measure the Tertians. There is the possibility that Dr. Karp's method was not an accurate metric by which to measure the child-rearing habits of the Tertian people.

After all, he merely interviewed the children, who he claims talked mostly about their biological parents. He did not observe the children in their daily lives as Dr. Field's had done, so his conclusion is based only on what the children said. These interviews should be met with scrutiny, as we do not know what questions could have been asked. If the questions were mostly about who gave birth to them and whom they missed most, the majority of the children's answers would focus on their biological parents. In that case, Dr. Karp's claims regarding Dr. Field's conclusion and observational research and some anthropologists' claim regarding the interview-centered method would be rendered invalid. Even if Dr. Karp's use of interviews was superior to Dr. Field's use of observations, a single case does not necessarily mean that the interview-centered approach is generally better than the observation-centered approach at obtaining accurate information about child-rearing practices. Before the claims are established, the author needs to provide many similar studies comparing the merits of interviewing methodology with those of observational methodology.

A final question that needs to be answered is whether all the people in the group of islands that Dr. Karp studied are comparable to those on Tertia. Dr. Field's observational research was conducted only on the island of Tertia, whereas Dr. Karp's study took place throughout the group of islands which included the island of Tertia. This implies that all the people of these islands share the same culture, and Dr. Karp's study results dilute the data that specifically relates to Tertia. One could assume, for example, that all the children from the island of Tertia talked about most of the adults in their village. However, these responses may not be typical when all the children throughout the island chain are considered. This would mean that Dr. Field's conclusion that children on Tertia were reared by an entire village may have been sound, undermining Dr. Karp's claim to the contrary.

In sum, if we were to accept Dr. Karp's assertion that Dr. Field was wrong and that future child-rearing studies should use an interview-centered method, there must be a timeline of recent historical events on Tertia that may have contributed to a shift in child-rearing methods. There should also be careful attention to the specific questions asked during the interviews to avoid guided answers and to the demographic information of the island chain to see if the cultures are distinct from one another. Finally, there need to be many studies of benefits of interviewing relative to observation in terms of yielding accurate information before a claim can be made about superiority of each methodology. Only with answers to such questions can we determine the soundness of the recommendation.

166. Bridge Bay to resume its contract with Arko to restore visitor numbers to its local beach (Questions to Be Answered)

Citing the fact that Bridge Bay switched to Satellite Waste Corporation early last year and the number of visits to its local beach declined considerably, whereas Ocean Harbor has continued to use Arko Trash Collection and the number of visits to its beaches has reached all-time highs, the author recommends that Bridge Bay return to Arko for garbage collection service. While resuming its contract with Arko may lead to a return of beachgoers, Bridge Bay needs answers to several questions before taking such action, because the relationship between the events at this point seems to be merely correlative and must, therefore, be further examined.

We must know whether Arko is responsible for the record levels of attendance in Ocean Harbor. However, the author offers no data in this regard. The record number of visits requires clarification. If the original levels were high, an increase of record levels would be significant. Otherwise, it would be statistically insignificant. Even if the number of visits is considerable, this does not necessarily mean that it has resulted from Arko's service. It is possible that Ocean Harbor has spectacular views or popular shopping centers, whereas Bridge Bay has none. It is also possible that it charges no fee for visiting its beaches, whereas Bridge Bay charges a fee. It is even possible that it has been advertising its beaches more heavily than Bridge Bay. Any of the scenarios, if true, would cast serious doubt on the assumption about the connection between garbage collection and beach attendance and on the recommendation of using Arko rather than Satellite for garbage collection on the beach in Bridge Bay. Unless there is evidence that other factors are not involved, the author cannot fairly assume that Arko's superior garbage service alone has contributed to the high levels of attendance in Ocean Harbor.

Similarly, we should know whether Satellite has caused the significant drop in beach visits. However, the author provides no information in this respect. Just because Satellite began to provide garbage collection early last year does not necessarily mean that it has caused the beach visits in Bridge Bay to decline. The author mentions that complaints about garbage on the beach in Bridge Bay have risen this year. Yet the author does not give the number of complaints or the number of people who have complained. It could be one or two people complaining time and again. Nor does the author provide the number of complaints in other years, so there is no way to tell whether the increase is slight or dramatic. Despite complaints about garbage on the beach, this does not necessarily mean that they are about Satellite's garbage collection service; they could be about how the visitors have disposed of the garbage. In this case, it is unfair to assume that Satellite's service last year was responsible for the decrease in beach visits in Bridge Bay. Even assuming this company was behind the decrease, without the figures before last year, a fifty percent decrease may be statistically insignificant. The author also unfairly assumes that the result represents Satellite's performance in the future. However, it is possible that the result last year was an aberration, and the number of visitors will rise dramatically in the years to come. Should this be true, the recommendation of replacing Satellite with Arko would be gratuitous.

Finally, we need to know whether returning to Arko for garbage collection service would restore Bridge Bay's beach attendance to its former levels. However, there is no relevant information. The author provides no assurances that Arko's service has been superior to Bridge Bay's. Even if its service has been relatively good, there is no guarantee that it will continue to be so in the future. The author also assumes that all other factors affecting beach visits in Bridge Bay will remain unchanged after it resumes its contract with Arko. Yet the author fails to offer evidence to substantiate this assumption. It is entirely possible that while Arko's service will in fact increase the beach visits, some other factor beyond Arko's control, such as weather, tides, or even local preferences of travelers, will serve to decrease the visits. Without accounting for these and other factors that may serve to reduce the beach visits, the author cannot confidently claim that using Arko again for garbage collection service will help Bridge Bay's beaches return to its former levels of attendance.

It is understandable that Bridge Bay would wish to rectify its dwindling number of visitors quickly, because tourism and regular foot traffic are vital to the survival of beaches. Cleanliness is a deciding factor regarding the appeal of a beach. Thus, the focus placed on the quality of the trash collection services of Satellite and Arko is necessary. However, the author's proposed solution should be thoroughly investigated before any final decision is made.

167. Plexma to begin manufacturing and selling self-driving vehicles in Canbury (Questions to Be Answered)

Self-driving vehicles will likely one day be a ubiquitous part of everyday life in the future and Plexma's efforts to make this a reality are noble. However, the remarks made by Plexma's president should not be taken at face value. We must have answers to certain questions about them, particularly about results of Plexma's self-driving vehicle test in downtown Canbury before we determine whether the city council of Canbury should permit Plexma to start to manufacture and sell its self-driving vehicles in the city.

We wonder whether the respondents of the survey conducted by local media are representative of Canbury residents in general. The finding that 60 percent of the survey participants would buy a Plexma driverless vehicle sounds convincing, but if the surveyed population is tiny, it does not typify general population of the city. If the percentage of respondents is small, it is even less representative. They could be an aberration that consisted mostly of people who liked the Plexma self-driving vehicle. They could also have reported their plan to sound smart. Perhaps the survey asked them whether they preferred safe Plexma self-driving vehicles to unsafe vehicles, leading them to choose the Plexma driverless vehicle. If this should be the case, the sample would not represent Canbury residents in general. Unless there is evidence that the sample is representative, the author cannot fairly conclude that Canbury will have enough residents to warrant the recommendation that the city council should support manufacturing and marketing of Plexma driverless vehicles in the city.

We also want to know whether the author's report and survey are reliable. Successful testing of Plexma self-driving vehicles in downtown Canbury does not necessarily mean that the testing will succeed in other parts of the city. The result last summer may be an aberration when there were few people and vehicles downtown; five vehicles are a sample too small to represent this line of Plexma self-driving vehicles. Two months are too short to draw any conclusion about the vehicles' safety. It is likely that they will report many more accidents if the testing lasts longer. All such scenarios would cast serious doubt on the reliability of the report. Besides, the survey after testing may not be reliable, because we do not know how people have been surveyed, or how many have responded. It is likely that 90% of the respondents were just a small, biased group that tended to feel safe, whatever the situation. It is also likely that they reported feeling safe just because they did not know what was happening. Furthermore, the report that they felt safe downtown when the vehicles were operating downtown is different from the report that they feel confident in the vehicles' safety. Any of the scenarios, if true, would call into question the survey after testing. If the author's report and survey should be unreliable, the recommendation would be unconvincing.

Finally, we need to know whether there will be a great demand for the Plexma self-driving vehicle. The author needs to provide evidence that the survey respondents are representative. If the findings of the surveys do not apply to other residents in Canbury, they may not feel confident in the vehicles' safety. Even assuming that they are certain about the vehicles' safety, this does not necessarily mean that they will buy the vehicles. They may not be able to afford one in the future. They may also change their mind. Even if they buy the vehicles in the future, the number may not constitute a great demand. The phrase "steady demand" is vague and since we do not know Plexma's population, which may be small, the demand for the vehicles may not be significant enough to benefit Canbury's economy considerably. Should this be true, the recommendation would be unreasonable. Given the enormous costs of supporting Plexma in manufacturing and marketing its self-driving vehicles in Canbury, including the opportunity cost that may come with the course of action, the recommendation would be further unjustified.

There may come a time when Canbury will be host to self-driving vehicles and Plexma will likely be at the head of the industry. Indeed, the town may reap untold benefits in terms of jobs and safety when such vehicles make it to the road. Yet today is not that day. The president of Plexma makes many claims which raise a number of important questions to be considered before its vehicles can be manufactured and sold in Canbury.

168. Employees at Dexter Gorman Instruments to work 40 hours per week (Questions to Be Answered)

Improving efficiency and efficacy of the workforce is an integral part of the continued existence of any company. Thus, it is reasonable for Dexter Gorman Instruments to evaluate the accuracy of overtime workers as compared to those working a standard work week. Yet, the results of the internal study raise more questions than it attempts to answer, and these questions must be addressed before any mandates regarding employee worktime can be made.

The author must answer whether the overtime employees making many documented errors are representative of the company's overtime employees in general and whether their performance is inferior to that of the non-overtime employees. However, no information is provided about the number of employees of the overtime group making many documented errors. If most of the documented errors of the overtime employees were made by a few people, they could be an aberration that happened to work more hours and make more documented work errors. In this case, they do not typify the company's overtime employees in general. Even if they do, this does not necessarily mean that their performance is worse than that of the non-overtime employees. Perhaps the errors of the overtime group are much less serious than those of the other employees. Or perhaps the company's documented work errors are far outnumbered by its undocumented work errors and with both types of errors combined, the overtime group could have done much better than their fellow employees. Even if the overtime group contributed to considerably more work errors, it could be responsible for much fewer work errors per capita. Or perhaps the result last year was an aberration, and the trend may not last into the future. In such scenarios, the internal study would be unreliable, and the recommendation of working a standard work week would be gratuitous.

The author should also answer whether overtime work alone has contributed to more documented work errors. The author assumes that overtime work is responsible for more errors. However, there is no evidence to substantiate this. It is likely that the overtime employees were assigned tasks more difficult to accomplish and therefore made more errors. It is also likely that they were less educated or less experienced than the other employees. It is even likely that they documented every work error, whereas the non-overwork employees only documented the errors that they considered important or simply forgot to document many of their work errors. Perhaps as found on this year's survey about work habits, less time for assigned work means worse quality. Any of the scenarios, if true, would cast serious doubt on the assumption about the causal link between working overtime and more documented work errors and on the recommendation that all employees should finish their work during the regular 40-hour work week.

Finally, the author needs to answer whether the number of documented work errors is the only way to determine employees' work schedule. On the basis of the findings of a potentially unreliable and unrepresentative study, the author recommends a 40-hour work schedule rather than a longer one for all the employees of the company. This could lead to more documented work errors instead of reducing them. Those who need more hours have to rush and may make more errors. While the number of documented work errors is a measure of employees' performance, this does not necessarily mean that it is the only way to ascertain their work schedule. Other aspects of work performance, such as innovation, may be equally important. It is also possible that some employees have special medical conditions that require them to work slowly. It is even possible that new employees need time for training and practice before they can follow a shorter work schedule. Without ruling out such scenarios, the author cannot fairly assume that the number of documented work errors alone can help the company formulate its work schedule. In this case, the recommendation would be baseless.

Decreasing work errors is something that all companies should aspire to. Doing so adds to the credibility and value of a firm. However, without research into the validity of Dexter Gorman Instruments' internal study, disallowing overtime work based on the findings of the study would not be advisable. Therefore, until the questions surrounding the study have been answered, the suggested course of action must not be taken.

169. Is Motilac effective in preventing many serious gastrointestinal disorders? (Alternative explanations)

The author claims that the substance Motilac is an effective preventative supplement against gastrointestinal disorders. To support the claim, the article presents a comparative correlative example: the city of Greenhorne has experienced an increase in the consumption of Motilac supplements and a year with fewer gastrointestinal issues, whereas the neighboring town of Etolin a decrease in sales of them and a steady increase in its cases of gastrointestinal symptoms. While the examples may be compelling, there are explanations other than the consumption of motilac supplements for the respective decline and increase in gastrointestinal cases in Greenhorne and Etolin.

One alternative explanation is the diet. It is likely that the increase in consumption of motilac supplements among Greenhorne's residents has happened over the six years before last year and they began to eat food with more fiber and water and avoided excessive caffeine, leading to easier digestion and fewer incidences of serious gastrointestinal disorders. If this is the case, it indicates that healthy eating rather than consumption of motilac supplements is effective in preventing the severe gastrointestinal disorders. By contrast, while sales of motilac supplements in Etolin have been dropping, most of the drop has happened two years before and in the last two years, the sales began to level off and only experienced a negligible decrease. However, the residents started to eat food with less fiber and water and were addicted to caffeine, giving rise to more cases of constipation. Should this be true, it indicates that unhealthy eating rather than less consumption of motilac supplements was responsible for more cases of the gastrointestinal symptoms. In connection, Greenhorne's water treatment facilities may be better at preventing severe gastrointestinal disorders than Etolin's, resulting in the difference in the number of cases of the disorders.

Another likely explanation is exercise. It is possible that Greenhorne's residents exercised more regularly and made their exercises more intense last year than before. This may have contributed to better sleep or rest and increased the ability to cope with stress. It is also possible that last year they began to have a better knowledge of how to prevent gastrointestinal disorders by participating in exercise. It is even possible that the city has fewer elderly people who tend to do less exercise and are more vulnerable to the disorders. In such cases, the residents might be less likely to have serious gastrointestinal symptoms. On the contrary, it could be that in the past two years Etolin's residents had little exercise and their exercise was not intense if they exercised at all. It could also be that the city experienced an influx of elderly people who reported significantly more cases of the disorders. Thus, exercise could also account for the facts given in the argument.

Still another explanation is screening and diagnosis. Perhaps Greenhorne's residents were less health-conscious last year and had no gastrointestinal screenings, whereas they had had such screenings before. Or perhaps many residents did not go to the hospitals when they had serious gastrointestinal symptoms. They might even go to places other than the hospitals for diagnosis. For example, they might travel to nearby Etolin for medical service, a scenario that could also account for the rise in the number of cases in Etolin. Or perhaps at the same time, the hospitals felt less inclined to report incidences of serious gastrointestinal symptoms. All such scenarios could be reasons why Greenhorne's hospitals reported fewer cases of disorders. Conversely, Etolin's residents could have been more concerned with their health and had gastrointestinal screenings in the last two years, whereas they had had few such screenings two years before. Coincidentally, the hospitals were more willing to report severe gastrointestinal disorders. This indicates that the number of cases of serious gastrointestinal disorders could have been the result of screening and self-reporting rather than the actual number of cases. Unless there is evidence that consumption of motilac supplements alone contributed to the difference in the number of incidences of the gastrointestinal disorders, the author cannot fairly assume that screening and diagnosis did not play their part.

Although there may be a strong case for the consumption of Motilac as a preventative measure against gastrointestinal issues, other explanations for the examples of Greenhorne and Etolin must also be considered. Differences in the diet of Greenhorne and Etolin residents could have accounted for their differences in gastrointestinal health, so could the regularity of their exercise. Furthermore, the accuracy of self-reported gastrointestinal issues and frequency of screenings among the towns' residents could have contributed to the respective drop and rise of gastrointestinal cases. Only after looking into these potentialities can we be more certain of any true correlation.

170. Linford's art students to complete an internship with Skyway before graduation (Questions to Be Answered)

With much of college education focusing on theory instead of practical job skills, internships have become more important than ever in aiding new graduates in finding successful careers. Thus, there is much merit to the alumni's letter to Linford College's art department. Yet, we need answers to several questions regarding the recommendation of requiring all art students to intern at Skyway Designs before graduation before we determine its soundness.

The survey raises questions about the representativeness of the respondents. The author does not mention the number of people surveyed, nor the number of respondents. The people could be a small group of college graduates that happen to have interned with companies and found jobs after graduation. If few people responded, a ninety-percent response rate could be statistically insignificant. If this is the case, the group does not represent other college graduates. The fact that only forty percent of Linford's graduating art students had finished an internship last year may indicate that the survey's findings do not apply to them and internship may not be important for all of Linford's art students. It is likely that 60 percent of Linford's graduating arts classes did not complete an internship but could have all been employed or found their desired career paths. If art students go to graduate school instead of finding a job or need outstanding GPAs and art portfolios rather than working experience for good jobs, the claim that internship boosts one's chances of securing employment after graduation would be unfounded. Even if internship is essential for the college's art students, perhaps the situation last year was an aberration, and it was difficult to find internship opportunities. Without more information about the respondents' representativeness, the author cannot justifiably recommend requiring all art students of the college's art department to intern at Skyway Designs before graduation.

Even if there is evidence that internship is beneficial for securing employment after graduation, we also wonder whether Skyway Designs is the perfect company for Linford's students to intern with. While Skyway Designs provides internships in all its departments, this does not necessarily mean that everybody of art department of the college can find a relevant internship position, because the company focuses on design, whereas the art department also covers fields beyond design. It is also possible that the company only serves businesses in the city, so internship with it may not be very useful for those who want to work outside the city. It is even possible that while Skyway Designs has served the design needs of more than 80 percent of businesses in the city, it is not a reputable company in the industry, as the article does not indicate whether the businesses are satisfied with its work, or whether they will continue to use its service. Even if all students of art department are willing to participate in internship with Skyway Designs, there is no guarantee that the company is willing to or can accept them. It could be that the company has signed contracts with other schools in internship and cannot accommodate any more students. If this is the case, Skyway Designs may not be the ideal company for Linford students to complete internship before graduation.

Even assuming that Skyway Designs is a good fit for Linford's art students, we want to know whether it should be the only option. However, the author provides no data in this regard. If Skyway Designs is designated as the only option for students, they may not find work they are interested in. They may also fail to benefit from an internship in other ways. It is likely that Skyway Designs pays students nothing for their internship, whereas other companies pay a reasonable compensation. It is also likely that students may receive little professional guidance in the process, whereas they could receive a large amount of such guidance in other companies. It is even likely that the company's internship program has not been as highly rated by the students' potential employers as that of other companies. Any of the scenarios, if true, would cast serious doubt on the recommendation of Skyway Designs as the only option for Linford's art students seeking internship opportunities. To better evaluate the recommendation, we must know whether Skyway Designs will fully serve their needs related to internship.

Ultimately, an internship may be beneficial to the career prospects of college graduates. Such experience augments the theoretical knowledge students have learned in their courses. Nonetheless, to mandate an internship at a single company, as advised by Linford College's alumni, would be hasty and potentially detrimental to current students. To fully assess the recommendation and the argument, we must have answers to relevant questions.

171. The restrictions of <u>Maple County</u> on the development of existing farmland (Questions to Be Answered)

The council of Maple County predicts that, after introducing the proposed measure against the development of farmland in the county, its housing prices will rise considerably. To validate the prediction, the article cites two examples: Pine County that restricted the development of new residential housing has experienced a more than two-fold increase in housing prices, whereas Chestnut County that implemented a comparable policy has only seen a modest rise in the prices. Given that the former example may support the prediction, whereas the latter example may weaken it, we need answers to a few questions before we determine whether the council should implement the measure.

One question that must be answered involves the root cause of the increase in housing prices in Pine County. The author seems to assume that limiting the development of new residential housing in the county fifteen years ago has caused a spike in its housing prices. However, the author provides no evidence to substantiate the assumption. Therefore, we wonder what the true cause is. It is possible that restricting the development of new residential housing has nothing to do with the change in housing prices. Fifteen years have passed between the implementation of the measure in Pine County and the significant increase in housing prices; thus, there may have been other causes of this price change, such as inflation, or even gentrification. Similarly, the modest increase in housing prices in Chestnut County may be attributed to factors other than restrictions on the development of its farmland, such as a mass departure of population from the county. In these scenarios, merely changing the number of houses available by placing restrictions on the development of new residential housing or on the development of farmland is unlikely to cause the spike in housing prices. Therefore, the prediction of a considerable housing price increase in Maple County may be unjustified. Otherwise, we could reasonably anticipate a significant increase in housing prices there if the development of existing farmland were restricted. Regardless, knowing the true source of price changes will allow the council to make a more informed decision.

The next question that should be considered relates to the comparability between Pine County and Maple County. Even if the significant increase in housing prices in Pine County has resulted from the restrictions on the development of new residential housing, this does not necessarily mean that Maple County will experience a considerable rise in housing prices as a result of the measure against the development of its current farmland. Both counties need to be sufficiently alike in ways that might affect the impact of farmland development on housing prices to draw the same conclusion. However, they may be vastly different from each other. It could be that Pine County has largely relied on farmland for building houses and restrictions on development of new residential housing by limiting the development of farmland might have led to a significant increase in its housing prices, whereas Maple County does not rely heavily on farmland for housing development and therefore limiting its development of farmland may not have a similar impact. This could also account for the modest increase in housing prices in Chestnut County that has adopted a measure similar to Maple County's, because likewise, Chestnut County may not have depended heavily on farmland for housing development. In addition, perhaps while the restrictions on the development of new residential housing have increased housing prices in Pine County, factors that tend to decrease the prices have remained constant. The author must provide information about whether other factors affecting housing prices in Maple County will remain unchanged after it restricts the development of farmland. Yet the author fails to offer data in this regard. Perhaps the restriction will in fact serve to raise housing prices, whereas other factors, such as the overall economic downtown, or an exodus of population from the area, among other things, will serve to lower the prices. Given these and other differences between Pine County and Maple County, Pine County may not be comparable to Maple County. Without accounting for the differences, the author cannot confidently claim that the measure of limiting the development of current farmland will lead to a significant rise in housing prices in Maple County.

Another question that needs to be addressed is whether the examples given by the author are representative. Pine County could be an aberration. It is likely that the county has given generous subsidies to house buyers in the past two years, boosting the number of buyers and in turn raising the housing prices. It is also likely that the number of houses available for purchase has diminished because they have been damaged by bad weather or earthquakes. Such scenarios would cast serious doubt on the claim regarding the effectiveness of limiting the development of new residential housing in Pine County and on the prediction of a considerable rise in housing prices in Maple County after it imposes restrictions on the development of its existing farmland. Also, the example of either Pine County or Chestnut County alone, whether for or against the measure, is far too small a sample to make such broad assumptions about the possible effects of the prevention of farmland development. The council should consider studying other counties that have implemented similar measures to see if they have experienced similar or different effects, thus providing a better yardstick by which to measure the potential success or failure of its own proposed plan.

In sum, Maple County's decision to limit the availability of new housing by restricting the development of its current farmland is doubtless a significant one. Thus, the council should analyze real estate trends in its own county and similar ones over a reasonable period of time and consider the possible factors that could affect housing prices, aside from the measure itself.

172. Terminating student evaluation of professors at Omega University (Specific Evidence)

The author recommends that student evaluation of professors, a survey program, at Omega University be terminated to improve its students' employment opportunities. To justify the recommendation, the article claims that higher grades assigned by professors, occurring after the implementation of the evaluation procedure, have been suspected of being fraudulent by employers, allegedly hurting post-graduation employment rates of the students at Omega University in comparison to those from Alpha University. To fully assess the argument, we need additional evidence regarding why Omega professors have assigned higher grades, why Omega students are less employable than Alpha students, and why the evaluation procedure has to be discontinued.

There must be evidence regarding the connection between the professor-evaluation procedure at Omega and the increase in grade averages of its students. However, the author does not inform us how many students at Omega participated in its professor-evaluation procedure. The fewer the participants, the more unreliable the conclusion about the connection between student evaluation and professors' grade inflation. If the increase in grades has resulted from students who are more intelligent and more diligent, or from better instruction, there would be less justification for the proposal to end the survey program. If it is attributable to grade inflation by the professors, there would be more justification for the proposal. However, even in this case, termination of the survey program could be unwarranted, because it may have no connection to Omega students' post-graduation employment rates. In addition, the article does not provide any concrete evidence that the increase in grade averages is fraudulent; it merely says that potential employers believe this to be true. No employers in particular have been named, and those who refuse to employ Omega graduates based on this belief would be at risk of a defamation lawsuit without evidence, pending an investigation into any allegations of discrimination on account of baseless presumptions of inflated grades. In fact, given a span of fifteen years, a 30% increase in grade averages may not be grade inflation, because a few excellent grades could boost the averages by a great margin if the original averages were very low. In that event, the recommendation of ending student evaluation of professors at Omega would be unreasonable, undermining the argument.

There should also be evidence that Omega can emulate Alpha to boost its students' employment opportunities. However, there is no evidence that Alpha students' success at landing jobs results from its lack of grade inflation. Several factors other than lack of grade inflation could lead to their success at finding employment. For instance, Alpha could simply have better internship opportunities, or corporate recruitment programs. Even assuming that Alpha's students are more successful at securing employment because of no grade inflation, this does not necessarily mean that Omega's students will automatically do well for the same reason. If Omega's comparison to Alpha is to be a useful one, the two institutions should be sufficiently alike in ways that might affect the impact of grade inflation on graduates' job prospects. However, Omega may have inferior teaching quality or career services. It is also likely that Omega offers less marketable academic programs. It is even likely that Omega admits less academically competent students. Any of the scenarios, if true, would cast serious doubt on the assumption that Omega can boost its graduates' employment opportunities by emulating Alpha. Even if Omega can succeed in helping its students find jobs by taking the same course of action, there is no guarantee that the jobs found will be better. If this should be the case, then the author's recommendation would be severely weakened, as Omega would be implementing measures based on a false precedent.

Finally, there needs to be evidence that ending the survey program is viable and the only way to help Omega students find better jobs. Even if terminating the professor-evaluation procedure is able to eliminate grade inflation and in turn help Omega graduates find jobs, there is no guarantee that it is viable. There must be a cost-benefit analysis to reveal advantages to terminating the survey program relative to the disadvantages. Ending the program may help Omega students find jobs momentarily, but keeping the program may offer far greater benefits. For example, it could provide a key third-party metric to see how well their professors teach. If there is no such metric, the university could hardly know whether it has excellent professors, a primary factor that attracts potential students. Even if the procedure is viable, it need not be the only way. For example, raising its admission standards, hiring better teachers, and improving its career services, could all be viable alternatives. The program could even improve if the university implements it in a way that does not give rise to grade inflation. For example, students can evaluate their professors first but the professors are not allowed to see the evaluation until they have submitted their students' grades. Without ruling out these and other possibilities, the author cannot justifiably claim that terminating the survey program would be the only viable option for boosting Omega graduates' job opportunities.

In conclusion, ending the professor-evaluation procedure without establishing it as the cause of declining employment success rates of its graduates would ultimately harm Omega rather than help it. If the blame is to be placed squarely upon the procedure, there would need to be proof showing that the professors did indeed inflate the grades because of the procedure, that the superior rates of employment of Alpha students are not the result of other factors, and that ending the procedure is the only viable option.

173. Initiating road improvement in Prunty County to improve highway safety (Specific Evidence)

Citing the car accident issues faced by Prunty County that, in spite of a recent lowering of the speed limit, have continued to plague the county, the author recommends that it undertake a road improvement project similar to that of Butler County, which the article claims has led to a 25 percent reduction in accidents reported compared to five years ago. However, the evidence is not adequate to justify such a costly undertaking. To determine whether the argument is well-founded, we need extra evidence regarding the actual effect of Prunty lowering its speed limit, the role of roads in accidents, and comparability between Prunty and Butler.

We must have evidence that the lowered speed limit has not been effective in Prunty. Just because reducing the speed limit to 45 from 55 miles per hour has not resulted in a lower number of accidents in Prunty, the author assumes that it has not worked. However, this is not necessarily the case. The fact that the number of accidents has not decreased while a great number of drivers are still exceeding the speed limit is itself evidence that speeding may have given rise to the accidents and imposing a lower speed limit may have been efficacious. It is likely that without the lowered speed limit, there could have been more accidents. It is also likely that while the speed limit has worked, other factors, such as increasing numbers of teenager drivers in the county, have contributed to accidents at the same time. If the increase in accidents caused by other factors is equal to or even more than the decrease in accidents caused by the speed limit, it is possible that the overall number of accidents has not dropped. Unless there is evidence that the policy of lowering the speed limit has not been successful in Prunty, the author cannot fairly claim that it should follow the example of Butler.

Furthermore, we should have evidence that the roads are the issue. As mentioned in the article, highway patrol reports that many drivers have been ignoring the speed limit altogether, a fact that indicates that people's respect for safety, not the roads themselves, is the issue. This implies that improving the roads would have almost no effect, making the author's suggestion likely to lead to a significant waste of money. If speeding is to blame for the accidents in Prunty, then perhaps there should be higher fines or speed bumps set up to discourage fast driving. Even if factors other than speeding have been responsible for the current situation, they could be something other than the roads. Driving under the influence of narcotics, or wildlife encounters could be among the reasons, which would also render road improvements moot. If scenarios such as those are to blame, Prunty would probably be better served by having stricter punishments for the illegal driving or more public service announcements warning drivers of the local fauna.

Finally, we need evidence that Prunty and Butler are essentially the same in terms of the accident rate and causes. Using Butler as an example raises too many questions. We do not know the actual numbers of accidents in Butler that occurred five years before or today; therefore, a 25 percent reduction could be as low as one fewer accident, if just four had taken place previously. That is hardly significant enough to warrant the recommendation that Prunty emulate Butler's road-safety measures. It is also likely that a large number of accidents are not reported in Butler, distorting its true accident rate. It is even likely that its speed limit of 55 mph has been responsible for an increase in accidents whereas its decrease in accidents has largely come from roads that impose a speed limit lower than 55 mph. Also, we do not know the exact causes of Butler's accidents as compared to Prunty's. Butler's poor road conditions may have contributed to its accidents whereas Prunty's poor weather and less strict standards of obtaining a driver's license its accidents. If the causes are not the same, then there is no reason to believe that the solutions would be. Unless there is evidence that both counties are sufficiently alike in ways that might affect the impact of road-safety measures, the author cannot confidently recommend that Prunty follow Butler's example.

To conclude, Prunty must do its due diligence before it decides to greenlight a road improvement project. It should investigate the cause of accidents in its county to see if it is linked to the quality of the roads, and if perhaps the drivers themselves are to blame. The example of Butler would be far more convincing if more data on the number and kind of accidents over the past five years were given for scrutiny to see if there is any real connection to its own road improvement program. Without such evidence, we are not sure whether the recommended road improvement project will be justified.

174. Should businesses hire only people who need less than <u>six hours</u> of sleep per night? (Assumptions)

Relying on the finding that Mentian advertising firms whose executives reported requiring sleep of six hours or less each night achieved higher profit margins and faster growth, the author concludes that companies should only employ people who need less than six hours of sleep per night if they want to succeed. However, the argument is based on several assumptions about the reliability of the study results, the link between a company's supposed prosperity and its executives' amount of sleep, and the generalizability of the study results to employees of other positions and other industries. The assumptions, if wantonly generalized, could have negative consequences for a company. To fully assess the argument, we need to examine the assumptions.

The author assumes that the study results are statistically reliable. However, there is only one study, which, from a scientific perspective, is far from sufficient to support any claims about the efficacy of sleeping less. The executives studied may have had individual predispositions that allowed them to function better with less sleep, making them the exception rather than the rule. They may also have been old people who tended to sleep less. They may even have chosen to report the need for less sleep time for fear that needing more sleep time will be considered a sign of weakness. Another major issue with the study is the sample size and number of respondents. The sample of 300 participants seems impressive, but it could be tiny if the executives totaled 10, 000. We just do not know. If just a negligible number of them have responded, they might not be representative of the participants, let alone of all advertising executives. All such scenarios would render the assumption about the representativeness of the study unwarranted, undermining the argument for hiring only employees who need to sleep for fewer than six hours per night. Without more information about advertising executives' reasons for sleeping six hours or less, the author cannot confidently conclude that all advertising executives only need such an amount of sleep to contribute to their firms' success.

The author also implies that a correlation between events means a causation between them. However, there is no evidence that the higher profit margins and growth of the companies were a direct result of the amount of sleep their advertising executives got each night. For all we know, those companies may have had favorable market shares or products with quality superior to that of their competitors'. They may also have had more productive employees or better technologies. If this is true, the author has yet to establish the connection between the advertising executives' amount of sleep every night and their companies' success. Otherwise, the article's entire premise is invalid. Without extra information, it is impossible to know for sure, and therefore it is not fair to assume that the advertising executives who slept less are to thank for the beneficial results.

Building on the implication that the advertising executives' amount of sleep each night is responsible for their firms' prosperity, the author suggests that what is true for one position in one industry will also be true for other positions and other industries. However, the assumption is based on a study of advertising executives only and makes no mention of any other positions and other industries and their relationship to sleep. We have no information on the particular duties of advertising executives and factors unique to their work that are affected by sleep or the lack thereof. Such factors could be nonexistent in other positions and could lead to severe fatigue among workers that perform more physically demanding jobs. They could also be absent in other industries that require a different schedule and a different profile of employees. The assumption underlies the claim that all positions in all industries will benefit from employing people who only need to sleep for fewer than six hours. However, the scenarios noted above indicate that such an assumption is unsubstantiated, thereby rendering the claim invalid. Even if the connection between advertising executives' sleep times and their firms' higher profit margins and faster growth applies to other firms, it does not necessarily mean that other firms will prosper, because prosperity requires much more than just higher profit margins and faster growth, whose significance must be determined with further information. It could be that a company has higher profit margins and faster growth than other companies, but it is still not profitable itself, making it unsustainable, let alone prospering. In this case, the assumption about the generalizability of the study results to employees of other positions and other industries is unwarranted, undermining the argument.

In conclusion, the argument relies on a vague correlation that requires further analysis. If we are to take the study's results as a factor on which to base hiring practices, there need to be more studies that find similar results, as well as studies that take into account many factors, in order to rule out possible contributing factors aside from sleep times. It would also help if we knew more details about how sleep affects the performance in specific job fields beyond the executive level and in other industries. If the author can offer evidence that warrants the assumptions, the argument will be more compelling. Otherwise, the argument will collapse easily.

175. Should Happy Pancake House replace butter with margarine? (Alternative Explanations)

Relying on the fact that just about 2 percent of customers have made complaints and on reports that some customers asking for butter but receiving margarine instead have not complained, the author assumes that the replacement of butter with margarine in Happy Pancake House restaurants has had little effect on their customers. However, there could be other reasons for the low number of complaints resulting from the change.

First, it should be mentioned that simply because only two percent of customers have complained does not necessarily mean, as the memorandum suggests, that ninety-eight out of one-hundred people are happy with the change. It could be that only two percent care enough to complain directly to the company, whereas the others are unhappy, but do not wish to spend the time complaining about the change. This is a common phenomenon that occurs in restaurants, especially in a breakfast establishment, as such a minor change is usually not worth the time and energy needed to complain, since people have to go to work after they eat. It could also be that merely two percent of customers want to complain formally to the company and their complaints are properly recorded, whereas other customers complain informally or in ways that the company fails to notice and record, for example, on social networking sites. There is even the chance that only two percent have complained, but the majority of customers who would complain, instead of doing so, have chosen to take their business elsewhere. Such scenarios, other than high rate of customer satisfaction, could account for the low rate of customer complaints.

This unwillingness to say anything extends to the customers who seemingly cannot tell the difference between butter and margarine when given the latter. It is equally likely that they can tell the difference, but do not see it as something worth complaining about. After all, it is not the waiters' fault. Alternatively, perhaps customers can tell the difference between butter and margarine, but simply do not care, since they taste similar enough and add flavor to their food. It is also possible that people can tell the difference, but they do not mind unless they are very health-oriented and dislike artificial foodstuffs. Besides, the restaurant workers, including the waiters, may have provided excellent service. Specifically, the food may have been palatable, and the waiters may have responded to customers' needs in a timely manner, making most of the customers satisfied in every way except replacement of butter with margarine. In this way, customers can make the distinction between butter and margarine, but may be unwilling to complain. Any of the scenarios, if true, would rule out the high rate of satisfaction as the sole factor in the small number of complaints.

Finally, it may be that the small number of complaints has to do with the reliability of the statistics. The memorandum claims that the change has had little impact on the restaurants' customers but does not provide any data on whether there has been a change in the number of customers they get. There is the chance that customers who have complained account for only about 2 percent of all customers, because not many people have asked for either butter or margarine when ordering food, such as pancakes. On the contrary, many people have called for other toppings when ordering pancakes, or have ordered waffles, omelets, and other items instead of pancakes. In this case, even though those who have complained only make up a small portion of all customers, they may constitute a much greater percentage of those who have asked for butter. There is also the chance that the change has taken place too recently for the author to collect sufficient data to draw reliable conclusions about customer satisfaction. Besides, it is possible that waiters have misrepresented the number of complaints by accident. Most waiters work long shifts and are very tired by the time they get off work. It is, therefore, likely that they simply forget how many people have complained that day. It is also possible that waiters report a low number of complaints to the management to seem competent at providing service and avoid potential punishment. Without ruling out such scenarios, the author cannot reliably conclude that the high rate of satisfaction alone is responsible for the low number of complaints.

In sum, this memorandum does not consider the possibility that people may complain in ways that the company is unaware of or may simply want to avoid complaining because of the extra time it takes. It also fails to consider the idea that customers can tell the difference between butter and margarine. Finally, it does not rule out the possibility of unreliable statistics. Without addressing such explanations, the author cannot fairly claim that the replacement has had no overall effect on the company's customers. If Happy Pancake House wishes to be certain that this change has not significantly affected its business, it should check its recent profits and customer traffic compared to those of the past and do further surveys on customers' satisfaction with the change.

176. Changing WWAC radio station's music from rock to a news-and-talk format (Specific Evidence)

Reasoning that a recent decline in music sales is the result of a limited interest in music, the author recommends that WWAC radio station change to a talk news format from a rock-music format. However, this recommendation is not based on enough hard evidence to warrant such a change; thus, further investigation into the issue is called for.

To begin with, the author must provide evidence regarding whether the decline in local music sales is indicative of a limited interest in rock-and-roll music. However, the author provides no data in this regard. Decreased sales of recorded music do not necessarily mean people's interest in rock-and-roll music has also decreased. The decrease in sales could be negligible. Even if there is a drop in local sales of recorded music, there may not be a drop in sales of recorded rock music. Even assuming that there is a decrease in sales of recorded rock music, this does not necessarily indicate a limited interest in music or in rock music in particular. A myriad of other factors might explain this phenomenon. For example, the introduction of the internet may have harmed the sale of music everywhere due to illegal downloading and online music solutions. Therefore, it is highly possible that people are still very much interested in rock music, but simply do not wish to buy it in physical format. Even if listeners have been losing interest in rock-and-roll music, this does not necessarily mean that they prefer 24-hour news. If this should be the case, the assumption about the connection between music sales and people's interest in rock music would prove unjustified, and the argument that the radio station should change from rock-and-roll music to continuous news would collapse. The radio station would do well to conduct surveys to find out if people have lost interest in music or have simply found other ways of obtaining it. If it is found that people have lost interest in music and specifically in rock music, WWAC radio station would be better served by changing its format.

Next, the author should offer evidence that the change to a news talk format is the condition necessary for reversing a drop in the number of WWAC's listeners. Yet, the memorandum offers no details in this respect. Just because there is a drop in listener numbers does not necessarily mean there should be a change of the form of radio. The drop could be negligible and normal fluctuations. Also, just because the news talk form of radio has become more and more popular in the area does not necessarily mean it is the only viable option. It could be that while a news and talk format has become increasingly popular, listeners prefer the format of an existing competitor only. Perhaps there is a strategy better than changing to a news and talk format, for example, changing to a music format to the retirees' tastes. Or perhaps listeners have dropped in number because they dislike the music anchor or the time the music is broadcast; simply changing the anchor or the broadcasting time would accomplish the goal. Or perhaps WWAC has transmission problems; repairing the transmission would achieve the outcome. In such scenarios, the claim that a change to the new format may benefit WWAC radio station would be weakened. It would be far more convincing if there were some actual survey data to back up this claim. Without identifying what is responsible for the decline in listener numbers, the author cannot fairly assume that the news talk format is the only strategy for increasing the number of WWAC's listeners.

Finally, the author needs to furnish evidence regarding what the retirees' actual tastes are. There is mention of an increase in the population of retirees, but no specific mention of what their actual tastes are except the claim that they may not be interested in music. A decline in local sales of recorded music does not necessarily mean people have no interest in music. Even if some people have lost interest in music, this does not necessarily mean that the retirees have no interest in music. Considering that most retirees grew up during the rock-and -roll era, it is likely that they would be interested in rock music radio. Until there is a survey to find out, we cannot know for sure. Also, even if the retirees have no interest in rock music, there is no guarantee that they will be interested in the news and talk format of the radio. Perhaps they like other types of music or a mix of music and news. Moreover, there is no mention of the population of the retirees moving to WWAC's area. Even if they favor the talk news format over rock music, there is the chance that their numbers are too small to compensate for the drop in listeners. There is even the chance that population growth resulting from the outside retirees would stop completely. In these scenarios, the recommendation of switching to a news and talk format would be unreasonable.

In conclusion, this memorandum lacks evidence to support its recommendation, specifically survey data. It makes broad claims about the interests of listeners in WWAC's area without providing any proof. A series of listener surveys would help WWAC uncover more about why it has experienced a decline in the number of listeners and assist it in deciding whether to accept the suggestion of changing formats.

177. A television station to expand coverage of weather and local news (Assumptions)

The author argues that a television station should expand its coverage of weather and local news, reasoning that this course of action would prevent loss of advertising revenues and attract more viewers. To support the argument, the memorandum cites recent viewer complaints concerning the station's coverage of local news and weather, as well as the cancellation of advertising contracts during the late-night news program. However, the argument is replete with assumptions and loopholes that require further analysis before we determine its soundness.

The first assumption is that less coverage of weather and local news has caused the complaints. However, the complaints about the local news and weather are not explained at all. It is possible that the complaints were small in number, or that the complaints were made by one or two individuals who had been persistent in doing so rather than by many people. It is also possible that the trend over the past year was an aberration and viewers generally make few complaints about weather and local news. It is even possible that one of the hosts of the late-night show has said something offensive. Even if the complaints were great in number and viewers are not satisfied with the station's coverage of local news and weather, these complaints could have been made because of poor quality rather than a small quantity, for example, inaccurate weather forecasting. If this is true, the author's assumption about the connection between the coverage of weather and local news and the complaints cannot be substantiated, thereby rendering the argument for more coverage invalid. If the assumption proves warranted, the argument would be more convincing. Therefore, the television station should look into the details of the complaints before making any major changes.

Another assumption is that reduced coverage of local news and weather during the late-night news program has resulted in cancellation of advertising contracts. However, the author gives no reasons for the businesses withdrawing from the deals. It could be that the businesses have their own financial difficulties and have to reduce their costs by cancelling the advertising contracts, or that they find the advertising ineffective. It could also be that the station's marketing and sales team is unable to persuade the businesses to continue to sign contracts with the station. It could even be that the businesses have found other ways to advertise their products, for example, by using social websites. In these scenarios, cancellation of advertising contracts is attributable to factors other than less coverage of local news and weather. Any of the scenarios, if true, would cast serious doubt on the assumption about the link between cancellation of advertising contracts and less coverage of local news and weather, undermining the argument. Without knowledge of the root cause first, any change based on the link would be a waste of time and resources.

A final assumption is that the expansion of local news and weather coverage will have the desired result. However, no evidence is provided by the memorandum for the viability of expanding local news and weather coverage as a means to attract viewers and advertising partners. After all, there is no mention of any advertisers that specifically demand local news and weather coverage, nor is there any mention of a loss of viewers. Thus, changing the programming runs the risk of causing a loss of the viewers who may watch the late-night show for the national news. Even if the recommended strategy works for the late-night news program, there is no guarantee that it will work for all the news programs. By focusing on the expansion of local news and weather coverage, the author also overlooks the possibility that other ways will help the station attain the same goal. In the case of the businesses' financial difficulties, very little can be done except to look for new advertising partners. In the event of rude hosts, all that is needed is a replacement of the anchor or host. Without considering and ruling out these and other possibilities that might contribute to the failure of the recommendation, the author cannot convince me that more coverage of local news and weather will guarantee more viewers and stop loss of advertising revenues.

In sum, the television station makes a number of assumptions and uses them to justify a change in programming, one that may cause more harm than good. Before making the change, it should find out more about the recent complaints surrounding weather and local news coverage and about the specific reasons for the cancellation of their ad contracts with local businesses. It should also conduct surveys of viewers to see if they would favor the change over the current programming available.

178. KICK radio to include more call-in advice programs (Questions to Be Answered)

The author recommends that the radio station KICK include more call-in advice programs to gain a larger audience, citing the recent success that the radio station WCQP has had in Rockville with such programming as well as a nationwide survey that found many radio listeners being interested in call-in advice programs. However, we should have answers to a few questions before we determine whether KICK should adopt the recommendation.

The first question that must be answered is whether WCQP's recent success has resulted from its increased call-in advice programming. The supposed success began two years ago, and while WCQP did experience a subsequent growth in its share of listeners, there is no information given about what may have caused that increase. While it is likely that the surge in listeners is attributable to the change in programming, there is also the possibility that other factors have contributed as much or more. For example, in the past two years, WCQP may have invested more in promoting its brand, may have added other programs that attract potential audience, and may have recruited some new popular hosts. If it is discovered that WCQP's success was in fact not the result of its addition of call-in programming, then KICK may be wasting its money in mimicking WCQP, rendering the recommendation unreasonable.

Another question that should be considered is whether KICK will experience the same growth in listeners, or if any growth at all, by including more call-in advice programming. After all, WCQP is located in a different city, and while a nationwide survey hinted at a listener interest in such programming, it may give a false perception of the local market. Without a survey to find out more about the local area, there exists the possibility that local listeners have little or no interest in the kind of programming KICK wishes to include. Even if they have, there is also the possibility that KICK is too different from WCQP to warrant a similar course of action. It may have already had enough call-in advice programs and including more programs of this kind could adversely affect its other important programs, causing the radio to lose listeners who are interested in them and its share of the audience to decline in its listening area. On the contrary, WCQP might still have had space for more call-in advice programs two years ago. Even if KICK has space for more call-in advice programming, it may not have the required staff and funding. In these scenarios, the recommendation that KICK incorporate more call-in advice programs would prove unjustified.

A final question that warrants investigation is the potentiality of local competition in Medway. The article does not mention anything about other radio stations in KICK's area, and unless Medway is a very small town, there are likely to be other radio stations. Even if we accept that WCQP's success was directly related to call-in advice programming, and that the results of the national survey do represent the local population's interests, there still remains the chance that there is another radio station in the area that already provides that programming. If this should be true, then it could be a waste of money to try to compete with a station that already holds the market share of those listeners. In that event, the recommendation would be unreasonable. If no radio station currently offers similar call-in advice programming locally, the argument would be strengthened. To better evaluate the plan, we need more information about KICK's local competitors.

In conclusion, without further research into the definitive causes of WCQP's increase in listeners or more local surveys, the author cannot justifiably claim that KICK should make similar changes to its programming. Furthermore, the author needs to investigate the local radio market to make sure that it will not be trying to enter a market that is already dominated by another station.

179. Child-rearing practices on the island of Tertia (Specific Evidence)

The author claims that Dr. Field was completely wrong in his observation-based conclusion that Tertian children were raised by their entire village and that Dr. Karp's interview-centered method is more valid than the observation-centered approach for studying child-rearing in the future. To justify the claim, the article notes that in later interviews with the children conducted by Dr. Karp, he found that the children spent more time talking about their biological parents than about other village adults. To fully assess the argument, we need additional evidence.

The first piece of evidence needed is some information about whether any significant changes have taken place since Dr. Field's research. His observations took place twenty years ago, enough time for an entire generation of young people to mature into adulthood. It is entirely possible that over the past twenty years, the island of Tertia has seen significant socio-economic changes. Perhaps children on Tertia were raised by a whole village twenty years ago, but they were raised by their biological parents because of outside influences when Dr. Karp conducted the interviews. Researchers should look into the recent history of Tertia to see if such influences have existed that may account for the apparent change in child-rearing practices. If yes, the claim that Dr. Field drew a wrong conclusion about child-rearing practices of Tertian people would be weakened. Otherwise, there would be a stronger case for the claim. Without relevant information, the author cannot convince me of Dr. Karp's claims regarding Dr. Field's conclusion and the comparative merit of interviewing versus observation.

The next piece of evidence required involves the methodology Dr. Karp used to measure the Tertians. There is the possibility that Dr. Karp's method was not an accurate metric by which to measure the child-rearing habits of the Tertian people. After all, he merely interviewed the children, who he claims talked mostly about their biological parents. He did not observe the children in their daily lives as Dr. Field had done, so his conclusion is based only on what the children said. These interviews should be met with scrutiny, as we do not know what questions could have been asked. If the questions were mostly about who gave birth to them and whom they lived with, most of the children's answers would focus on their biological parents. In that case, Dr. Karp's claims regarding Dr. Field's conclusion and observational research and his own interviewing methodology would be rendered invalid. Even if Dr. Karp's use of interviews was superior to Dr. Field's use of observations, a single case does not necessarily mean that the interview-centered approach is generally better than the observation-centered approach at obtaining accurate information about child-rearing practices. Before the claims are established, the author needs to provide many similar studies comparing the merits of interviewing methodology with those of observational methodology.

A final piece of evidence necessary is data proving all the people in the group of islands that Dr. Karp studied are comparable to those on Tertia. Dr. Field's observational research was conducted only on the island of Tertia, whereas Dr. Karp's research took place throughout the group of islands which included the island of Tertia. This implies that all the people of these islands share the same culture, and Dr. Karp's study results also dilute the data that specifically relates to Tertia. One could assume, for example, that all the children from the island of Tertia talked about most of the adults in their village. However, these responses may not be typical when all the children throughout the island chain are considered. This would mean that Dr. Field's conclusion that children on Tertia were reared by an entire village may have been sound, undermining Dr. Karp's claim to the contrary.

In sum, if we were to accept Dr. Karp's assertion that Dr. Field was wrong and that future child-rearing studies should use an interview-centered method, there must be a timeline of recent historical events on Tertia that may have contributed to a shift in child-rearing methods. There should also be careful attention to the specific questions asked during the interviews to avoid guided answers and to the demographic information of the island chain to see if the cultures are distinct from one another. Finally, there need to be many studies of benefits of interviewing relative to observation in terms of yielding accurate information before a claim can be made about superiority of each methodology.

180. Adopting honor codes similar to Groveton's (Questions to Be Answered)

Relying on the fact that Groveton has experienced a decrease in the reported cases of cheating over a period of five years, as well as a recent survey which found that most students would be less inclined to cheat with an honor code in place, the author recommends that all colleges and universities adopt an honor code similar to that of Groveton college. However, before we determine whether any other college or university should take action, we need answers to certain questions.

First, the argument raises the question of whether the honor code has been successful. The system in which teachers monitored students found thirty cases of cheating, whereas in the newer student-reporting system, only twenty-one cases were reported in the first year, and then only fourteen five years later. This begs the question of whether there has been a reduction in the number of cases of cheating because the honor code was in place, or whether cheating has decreased for other reasons. For example, students often hesitate to report their classmates' cheating. They may simply have become more and more reluctant to report cheating each year since adoption of the honor code. They may also have been less adept at detecting their classmates' cheating than teachers and former students who had been more experienced. Potential cheaters may even have chosen not to cheat during the period regardless of the honor code. If one of the scenarios turns out to be true, we will need to reinvestigate Groveton's "success" before other universities adopt a similar honor code.

Secondly, the question arises of whether the survey is reliable, valid, and representative. The recent survey of Groveton's students found that most reported that they would not cheat with an honor code in place. However, since these answers were self-reported by the students, it is safe to assume that they would give answers on the survey that would benefit them the most. This raises the question of whether the honor code is reliable at all, since it obviously works in favor of dishonest students. Perhaps most students answered that the honor code would make them less likely to cheat because it made cheating easier, and therefore they hoped to keep it by falsely claiming that it would make them less inclined to cheat. This indicates that the participants of the survey may be an anomaly consisting mostly of people who hope to benefit from the honor code. Even if the respondents are representative of Groveton students, there is no guarantee that they will do as they have claimed in the survey. Besides, the researchers could have asked the irrelevant question of whether an honor code is better than none, instead of how it compares to the old system of teacher monitoring. In all such scenarios, the survey is neither valid nor representative, rendering the recommendation and its argument unreasonable.

Lastly, there is of course the question of the cultural differences among all universities and colleges that may affect the success rate of an honor code system. For example, Groveton could be a small school where the honor code is easily implemented and naturally efficacious, whereas at larger universities it would be hard to implement the code and even if implemented, the code would be less effective. Groveton students could be more likely to report cheating, or less likely to cheat with an honor code in place, than students in other universities and colleges. Even if it has worked in Groveton, this does not necessarily mean that it will work in other colleges and universities. All this is incumbent on the willingness of students to follow the honor code, and currently there is no accurate measure of this variable. Even if the code will be effective in other colleges and universities, there is the possibility that some universities and colleges may have had in place an honor code comparable to Groveton's, thereby making a new one redundant. If Groveton is typical in respects relevant to the incidence of cheating, it will be plausible for other universities and colleges to enforce a similar honor code. Otherwise, the recommended action would be indefensible.

In conclusion, the adoption of an honor code across all universities and colleges requires further analysis in the areas of its actual success rate, not only at Groveton, but at other institutions as well. Furthermore, surveys of student opinions of the system change should be disregarded as those who wish to cheat will skew the results, since they stand to benefit from an honor code system. Finally, there should be further testing of the honor code system nationally and internationally to see if institutional differences will affect the willingness of students to report on one another.

181. Wearing helmets may not actually be good for bicycle safety (Alternative Explanations)

Reasoning that the increase in helmet usage over a ten-year period by bicyclists has led to a two-hundred percent rise in bicycle-related accidents, the author concludes that the reason for the increase in the accidents is that bicyclists ride less safely as a result of an increased sense of security from wearing helmets. However, there could be other viable explanations for the phenomenon.

It could be that the respondents of the two studies are not representative of bicyclists nationwide. With reference to the studies, no clear details are given by the memo. One study only mentions the increase in the number of cyclists who wear helmets, which was self-reported, and the other study the 200 percent increase in bike accidents. The self-reported data may not be reliable, because the respondents may have reported wearing helmets simply to appear that they are responsible and safety-conscious. Besides, the increase in accidents is not combined with any other data, such as the actual number of bike related accidents before and now. It is possible that there were only a small number of accidents ten years prior, and thus a two-hundred percent increase would still be a relatively insignificant number. Even if the increase in the number of serious bicycle-related accidents is significant, there may be a decrease in non-serious bike accidents, causing a decrease in the total number of bike accidents. Even if there is a considerable rise in the overall number of bike accidents, the bicyclists could have worn no helmets. In such scenarios, there could be no increase in the number of people who wear helmets, invalidating the claim that more helmet usage by bicyclists over a decade has resulted in a dramatic rise in bike-related accidents. Therefore, the author must rule out wearing helmets as the only reason for more bicycle-related accidents.

It could also be that the results of the local survey do not apply to bicycle riders in general. The survey respondents could be an aberration that tends to cause more bicycle-related accidents. Given that they ride bicycles frequently, it is likely that they will have more bike accidents, regardless of whether they wear helmets. Similarly, there may be more bicyclists today than ten years ago. Considering that they ride on busy roads, it is also likely that they will be involved in more accidents. Even if they wear helmets, busy roads, such as intersections, may make it more difficult to avoid bike accidents. It is even likely that specific local conditions make the place surveyed more vulnerable to bike accidents. For example, it rains and snows more heavily there than in other places. Any of the scenarios, if true, would cast doubt on wearing helmets as the only factor contributing to more bike accidents.

Finally, it could be that other factors are responsible for more bicycle-related accidents. The riders may be more careless than their counterparts ten years ago. They may also ride longer distances or break laws and rules more often. For example, they may not use lights properly, may speed, and may make unsafe lane changes. Perhaps they wear protective gear other than helmets. All such scenarios could be the reasons for more bike accidents. Factors beyond riders' control could also be to blame. Reckless drivers, drunk drivers, or even inexperienced drivers of cars may be at fault. The increase in accidents may also be attributable to roads in bad condition. This indicates that aside from unrepresentative respondents of both studies and a survey, the riders themselves and circumstances beyond their control could also account for more bike accidents. Without more information about exactly what has happened in each case from post-accident interviews or traffic camera footage, it would be very illogical to simply link the cause to a feeling of safety that may not exist.

In conclusion, to ascertain the soundness of the argument, we must first have more study data to show that the two-hundred percent increase in accidents represents a significant number of accidents, and that an increased feeling of safety from wearing a helmet was the direct cause of the accidents. Otherwise, it would be unfair to claim that there are no alternative explanations for them.

182. Will Primo's new Elkie doll make it more profitable than Optima? (Questions to Be Answered)

The article claims that Primo Doll Manufacturing, Inc. will make more profits than its competitor Optima Doll Manufacturing this year. The president bases the claim on the results of two surveys of parents in which the parents complained of the speed at which their Elkie doll wore out. The president also assumes that using allegedly higher quality materials that Optima uses for its dolls will improve the Elkie doll's durability and thus increase sales. However, to fully assess the prediction and the argument, we need answers to some questions surrounding the reasons for the doll's wearing out quickly, Optima's materials, and comparative profitability of both companies.

One question which needs to be addressed is whether the respondents of the two surveys are representative of Elkie buyers in general. We do not know the sample sizes. While a 90-percent response rate is impressive, the number of respondents involved could be a tiny group whose children happen to use the Elkie most often, causing it to wear out fast with use. The children could also have allowed others to use the Elkie very often. Last year could even be an aberration when the children, for some reason, used it more often than in other years. On the contrary, most buyers' children might use it much less often. They might also use it more properly than the respondents' children, making it unlikely to become useless soon after the purchase. In these scenarios, the sample does not typify the general population whose children buy the Elkie. While an 80-percent response rate in the follow-up survey also appears compelling, the number involved may also be insignificant, rendering the sample unrepresentative of parents who buy the Elkie. Also, to bolster the argument, the author needs to clarify what the survey participants mean by stating that "they would recommend a more durable version of the doll to their friends." If this indicates that while they are considering making the recommendation to their friends, they will continue to buy the original Elkie, the survey would be invalid.

Even if it is granted that the two samples represent Elkie buyers in general, one might wonder why Primo should use Optima' materials. Perhaps while Optima is Primo's most successful competitor, because of the materials that it has been utilizing, it is not very popular. Or perhaps even though the materials used by Optima are superior in quality, they are not durable enough. Or perhaps they are durable, but they compromise the features of the new doll in some ways, making it less attractive. It is even possible that most buyers of the Elkie prefer the materials used in the original doll that are the main reason for their choice of the Elkie over dolls of other brands. Any of the scenarios, if true, would cast serious doubt on the move to use Optima's materials. To better evaluate the argument, we need more information about Optima's materials used by Primo to see if they are durable enough and blend well with the features of Primo's original Elkie Doll.

Another question that needs to be raised is whether Primo will be more profitable than Optima this year. The author assumes that parents can buy the new version of the Elkie Doll that does not wear out with use fast. However, the author provides no evidence to substantiate the assumption. It is possible that using Optima's materials makes the product more durable but much more expensive so that many parents cannot afford it. Even if parents can afford the product that does improve in durability, there is no guarantee that it will be profitable. Profit is a function of revenue minus costs. Given the costs of using Optima's higher quality materials and making other necessary changes for the new version of the Elkie Doll as well as other costs, it is highly likely that the new product will not be profitable. Even if the new product will make profits, there is no guarantee that Primo's profits will exceed those of Optima, because Primo's other products may incur great losses or barely make profits, offsetting its profits from selling the new doll. Should this be the case, the prediction of greater profitability for Primo compared with Optima this year would be unjustified. To determine whether the prediction is reasonable, we need more information about the costs of manufacturing and marketing the new product as well as the revenue and about Optima's potential profits this year.

In sum, there remain a number of questions which must be answered before we determine the validity of the president's claims. The sample of parents surveyed must be proven to be representative of the majority of Primo's customer base, Optima's materials must be found to be both durable enough and attractive enough to satisfy parents' complaints, and the proposed time frame of one year to improve profitability must be laid out clearly from a cost vs. revenue perspective. Once we have relevant information, we can better evaluate the President's claim.

CHAPTER 5

Argument Topics Ordered by Frequency

The argument topics of the official pool may be grouped according to whether they have the same claim or keywords. Each row of the following table contains high-frequency keywords of the pool and the topics that share the keywords but have different instructions. Therefore, you should always pay attention to the instruction specific to each topic and the slightly different wording when you analyze the topic before you begin to write. It will be unfortunate if you write on a topic different from the one you are assigned just because you fail to pay attention to the specific keywords or claim of the topic! It will also be unfortunate if you fail to follow the particular instruction and instead write a vague response that seems to suit a very general topic.

Many topics are used more than once in the pool. The topic remains the same or almost the same, but it becomes a different prompt with a different instruction. Such prompts are put together in the following table so that you can study them as a group that is likely to be tested very frequently because the group accounts for a number of the topics of the pool. It is important to note that the order of a topic in the official pool may change in the future, and a few topics may be added or substituted every one or two years. Therefore, you need to search the keywords given below to locate similar topics in the latest version of the pool and analyze them as a group.

	Topic	Order of Topic in the Pool
1	Increased demand for heating oil (and investment in Consolidated)	37, 118, 119, 122, 126, 127
2	Shortening work shifts to reduce the number of on-the-job accidents at Quiot/Butler/Alta	10, 77, 78, 79, 139
3	Should Happy Pancake House replace butter with margarine?	28, 103, 104, 106, 175
4	Cutting funding for the Grandview Symphony	38, 112, 114, 116, 134
5	Building a jazz club in Monroe	3, 73, 75, 136
6	Restricting showerhead water flow in Sunnyside Towers	13, 29, 101, 102
7	Wearing helmets may not actually be good for bicycle safety	19, 96, 98, 181
8	Using UltraClean in our hospital system	39, 94, 95, 97
9	Does Buzzoff provide better pest control services than Fly-Away?	52, 87, 89, 90
10	Should Acme require all of its employees to take the Easy Read Course?	86, 99, 100, 133
11	Adopting honor codes similar to Groveton's	92, 93, 111, 180
12	Child-rearing practices on the island of Tertia	1, 165, 179
13	Reducing headaches using salicylates	2, 4, 6
14	Monitoring employees' internet use	12, 35, 67
15	Using fish oil supplements (or supplements derived from beneficia) to prevent colds and reduce absenteeism by emulating East Meria	14, 135, 138
16	Will Sartorian's new alpaca overcoat sell well?	16, 68, 69
17	Reducing operating hours at Movies Galore to cut expenses	24, 84, 85

18	More healthful lifestyles in Forsythe/Benton	30, 117, 123
19	Dura-Sock, Inc. to discontinue its Endure manufacturing process	33, 34, 55
20	Reducing in-store imported cheese inventory	42, 80, 81
21	Is Zeta a superior/Alpha construction company?	45, 46, 88
22	Health Naturally (or Nature's Way) to build a new store in Plainsville	61, 63, 164
23	Is living in small towns like Leeville healthier than living in big cities like Masonton?	65, 74, 76
24	A new café for Monarch Books	71, 72, 162
25	Mandatory driver's education course at Centerville High School for students	105, 107, 109
26	Should high school teachers assign homework less frequently as Marlee teachers do?	108, 110, 113
27	Should Grove College remain all-female?	120, 121, 128
28	Reducing Balmer Island moped accidents by learning from Torseau/Seaville	131, 144, 160
29	Building a new bicycle lane on Blue Highway	5, 7
30	Will a new seafood restaurant in Bay City be successful?	17, 145
31	Humana University wants to expand online degree programs	23, 26
32	Disappearance of large mammal species on the Kaliko Islands	31, 137
33	Building a new golf course and resort hotel in Hopewell/Brindleburg	51, 141
34	Study of reading preferences of Waymarsh citizens called into question	58, 60
35	Should the company XYZ use Delany rather than Walsh for laid-off employee assistance?	59, 62

36	Changing WWAC radio station's music from rock to a news and talk format	66, 176
37	KNOW radio station to shift to a 24-hour news format	82, 83
38	Should businesses hire only people who need less than six hours of sleep per night?	91, 174
39	Should Bargain Brand Cereals start selling other low-priced foods?	124, 125
40	Should Top Dog stores advertise in Exotic Pets Monthly?	129, 130
41	Should high-intensity lighting be installed in Amburg?	132, 143
42	Litter and vandalism in Central Plaza blamed on skateboarders	146, 158
43	Do teens eating the most family meals have better behaviors?	149, 151

CHAPTER 6

Argument Topics Grouped by Logical Fallacies or Themes

Grouping argument topics by logical fallacies or themes may help you better understand how to spot logical fallacies and ways of addressing them. Each group consists of a logical fallacy or theme, the approach to addressing either, and specific topics of the official pool that have the fallacy or theme. You may follow the approach, try to spot as many fallacies as possible in each topic given below (For the official pool of argument topics, please find them at **https://www.ets.org/gre/revised_general/prepare/analytical_writing/argument/pool),** and then compare your list of fallacies to those that each corresponding sample essay of Chapter 4 discusses. You may even spot one that the sample essay does not include. This is acceptable as long as you have spotted most of the fallacies that the sample essay has discussed.

CAUSE AND EFFECT

When critiquing the topics in this group, you need to discuss more than one reason for the result.

2/4/6. Reducing headaches using salicylates

18. Consuming dairy products to prevent osteoporosis

21. The available space in West Egg's landfill may last much longer than expected

27. Using lavender to help with chronic insomnia

32. Sales of Whirlwind video games to increase dramatically

54. Promofoods denies a potential health risk caused by its canned tuna

57. Causes of Xanadu National Park's amphibian population decline

64. Predators responsible for decline of gazelle population from the Western Palean Wildlife Preserve

65/76. Is living in small towns like Leeville healthier than living in big cities like Masonton?

77. Shortening work shifts to reduce the number of on-the-job accidents

89. Does Buzzoff provide better pest control services than Fly-Away?

92. Adopting honor codes similar to Groveton's

95. Using UltraClean in our hospital system

137. Disappearance of large mammal species on the Kaliko Islands

147. Stimulating economy of Dillton

151. Do teens eating the most family meals have better behaviors?

152. Declining donations to educational institutions

153. Rising Relannian dairy prices

154. Uses of Dodecan pemchints

155. Link between health and stair usage

157. Study of rhesus monkeys and humans finds link between birth order and stimulation

161. Disappearance of Canada's arctic deer

169. Is motilac effective in preventing many serious gastrointestinal disorders?

175. Should Happy Pancake House replace butter with margarine?

181. Wearing helmets may not actually be good for bicycle safety

ANALOGY (AN EXAMPLE TO FOLLOW)

When critiquing the topics in this group, you need to discuss differences between two places or companies.

5/7. Building a new bicycle lane on Blue Highway

10/77/78/79. Shortening work shifts to reduce the number of on-the-job accidents at Quiot/Butler/Alta

15. Revitalizing Transopolis through industrialization of a residential area

41. Drop in popularity of Stanley Park

43. Making big changes to save the Rialto Movie Theater

47. Reducing traffic in Waymarsh by learning from Garville

51/141. Building a new golf course and resort hotel in Hopewell/Brindleburg

70. The Classical Shakespeare Theatre to attract more audience members by learning from Avon

71/72/162. A new café for Monarch Books

129/130. Should Top Dog stores advertise in Exotic Pets Monthly?

131/144/160. Reducing Balmer Island moped accidents by learning from Torseau/Seaville

132/143. Should high-intensity lighting be installed in Amburg?

171. The restrictions of Maple County on the development of existing farmland

173. Initiating road improvement in Prunty County to improve highway safety

ANALOGY (EXPANSION OF A POLICY TO OTHER PARTS OF THE GROUP)

When critiquing the topics in this group, you need to discuss differences between one part of a group and the other parts.

13/29/101/102. Restricting showerhead water flow in Sunnyside Towers

28/103/104/106. Should Happy Pancake House replace butter with margarine?

39/94/97. Using UltraClean in our hospital system

42/80/81. Reducing in-store imported cheese inventory

92/93/111/180. Adopting honor codes similar to Groveton's

CHOICE BETWEEN TWO

When critiquing the topics in this group, you need to discuss the reasons for the differences between two places or companies.

9. Does Parson City care more about good education than Blue City?

45/46/88. Is Zeta/Alpha a superior construction company?

52/87/90. Does Buzzoff provide better pest control services than Fly-Away?

59/62. Should the company XYZ use Delany rather than Walsh for laid-off employee assistance?

142. Should Appian Roadways be hired to construct access roads for shopping malls?

159. Is Adams Realty a better real estate agency?

166. Bridge Bay to resume its contract with Arko to restore visitor numbers to its local beach

POLICY AS A SOLUTION TO A PROBLEM

When critiquing the topics in this group, you need to discuss whether the policy is necessary and/or sufficient as a solution to a problem.

12/35/67. Monitoring employees' internet use

14/135/138. Using fish oil supplements (or supplements derived from beneficia) to prevent colds and reduce absenteeism by emulating East Meria

19/96/98. Wearing helmets may not actually be good for bicycle safety

20. Beach sand erosion on the island of Tria

33/34/55. Dura-Sock, Inc. to discontinue its Endure manufacturing process

36. Increasing the size of the family rooms and kitchens in new homes built by Bower

38/112/114/116/134. Cutting funding for the Grandview Symphony

40. Should Parkville discontinue organized children's athletics?

44. Partnership between Sherwood Hospital and Sherwood Animal Shelter

49. Milk prices in Batavia to be regulated by the government

66/176. Changing WWAC radio station's music from rock to a news-and-talk format

82/83. KNOW radio station to shift to a 24-hour news format

105/107/109. Mandatory driver's education course at Centerville High School for students

120/121/128. Should Grove College remain all-female?

124/125. Should Bargain Brand Cereals start selling other low-priced foods?

131/144/160. Reducing Balmer Island moped accidents by learning from Torseau/Seaville

140. Should non-residents be allowed on the Committee for a Better Oak City?

146/158. Litter and vandalism in Central Plaza blamed on skateboarders

168. Employees at Dexter Gorman Instruments to work 40 hours per week

170. Linford's art students to complete an internship with Skyway before graduation

172. Terminating student evaluation of professors at Omega University

177. A television station to expand coverage of weather and local news

178. KICK radio to include more call-in advice programs

INVESTMENT PLAN

When critiquing the topics in this group, you need to discuss the costs of a plan as well as its revenue to determine the likelihood of its profitability.

3/73/75/136. Building a jazz club in Monroe

8. Cutting Calatrava's funds budgeted for education and sports facilities

11. Is construction of new generating plants unnecessary?

16/68/69. Will Sartorian's new alpaca overcoat sell well?

17/145. Will a new seafood restaurant in Bay City be successful?

23/26. Humana University wants to expand online degree programs

37/122/126/127. Increased demand for heating oil (and investment in Consolidated)

42/80/81. Reducing in-store imported cheese inventory

50. Should investors own stock in Old Dairy?

61/63/164. Health Naturally (or Nature's Way) to build a new store in Plainsville

86/99/100/133. Should Acme require all of its employees to take the Easy Read Course?

148. Building a Hobco Hobby Shop in Grilldon

163. Does Buckingham College need new dormitories?

167. Plexma to begin manufacturing and selling self-driving vehicles in Canbury

Made in the USA
Coppell, TX
05 April 2023